John Calvin, the Church, and the Eucharist

John Calvin, the Church, and the Eucharist

KILIAN McDONNELL, OSB

PRINCETON UNIVERSITY PRESS

PRINCETON, NEW JERSEY

1967

Publication of this book has been aided
by the Whitney Darrow Publication Reserve Fund
of Princeton University Press

Imprimatur No. 97/1964
Trier, 15 ✠ Decembris 1964
Vicarius Generalis Paulus

Printed in the United States of America
by Princeton University Press, Princeton, New Jersey

To Mr. and Mrs. Patrick Butler and family:
Patrick, Jr., Peter, and Kate Butler Peterson

Preface

THE ACADEMIC DEBTS incurred in the process of research are difficult to acknowledge much less to pay. Every researcher will admit that some academic persons, though consulted infrequently, or only once, had a considerable influence on the outcome of the research. It was, for instance, a casual remark of Father Gregory Baum which was decisive in my choice of John Calvin as my general field of interest, and it would be a matter of surprise to me were he to remember either the remark or to whom it was directed. My gratitude to Professor Wilhelm Breuning of the theological faculty at Trier, Germany, who was my *Doktor-Vater* and who with unfailing generosity and kindness advised me on my academic thesis of which the present book is a revision and expansion. For help of various kinds at different stages of my research I wish to mention Professor Balthasar Fischer, Professor Wilhelm Bartz, Professor Erwin Iserloh, and Abbot Laurentius Klein of Trier; Professor Ernst Walter Zeeden and Professor Francis Xaver Arnold of Tübingen; Professor Eduard Stakemeier and Doctor Albert Brandenburg of Paderborn; Professor Paul Jacobs of Münster; Professor Heinrich Bornkamm of Heidelberg; Professor T. F. Torrance of Edinburgh; Professor John M. Barkley of Belfast; Max Thurian, Sub-Prior of Taizé. Special mention, in justice, must be made of Professor Hans Küng who, during my stay at Tübingen, repeatedly gave of his time, criticizing methodology and content. Most especially am I indebted to him for firing my enthusiasm for a topic which had, at times, gone cold. No one who has engaged in research over a long period of time will doubt what an important contribution that is.

Through the generosity of Mr. and Mrs. Patrick Butler, Mr. Patrick Butler, Jr., Mr. Peter Butler and Kate Butler Peterson of the Butler Family Foundation, St. Paul, Minnesota, I received two grants underwriting my studies in Protestant theology abroad. Without financial aid my research would not have been possible. The Butler Family Foundation was among the first in the United States to subsidize ecumenical projects of this nature. It is with deep gratitude that I dedicate the present volume to the members of the Butler family.

I also wish to express appreciation to my superior, Abbot Baldwin Dworschak, for extending the four and a half years leave of absence to pursue doctoral studies.

Dedicated typists are a rarity in any land and I was therefore many times blessed with the competence of Frau Riedel of Münster, Germany, who, though unacquainted with English, turned out a letter-perfect first draft.

K.M.

St. John's Abbey
Collegeville, Minnesota
March 16, 1966

Contents

John Calvin, the Church, and the Eucharist

ABBREVIATIONS

CR—*Corpus Reformatorum*
   Joannis Calvini Opera quae supersunt omnia.
   Huldreich Zwinglis Sämtliche Werke.
   Philippi Melanchthonis opera quae supersunt omnia.

Denz.—*Enchiridion Symbolorum, Definitionum et Declarationum de rebus fidei et morum.* 33rd edn.

Inst.—*Institutes of the Christian Religion.*

OOT—*Opera Omnia Sancti Thomae.*

OS—*Johannis Calvini Opera Selecta.*

PL—*Patrologia Latina* (Migne).

RGG—*Die Religion in Geschichte und Gegenwart,* 2nd edn.

RGG—*Die Religion in Geschichte und Gegenwart,* 3rd edn.

SS—*Huldreich Zwinglis Werke,* eds. Schuler and Schulthess.

WA—*Weimarer kritische Gesamtausgabe.*

Introduction

IN THE PAST, as a careful look at the Bibliography for this study will indicate, Calvin's eucharistic doctrine was studied almost exclusively against the background of the Lutheran and Zwinglian controversies. Such an approach is methodologically justified since the greater number of his eucharistic writings deal with these controversies. However his initial eucharistic position and his initial polemics are more specifically anti-Roman than anti-Lutheran. Calvin never set aside his initial anti-Roman polemics. Indeed, into each succeeding edition of the *Institutes* he worked more anti-Roman polemics. It is universally acknowledged among Calvin researchers that there is little development in his eucharistic doctrine. Therefore one cannot understand Calvin's eucharistic doctrine, even in its definitive form, if one confines oneself to the anti-Lutheran and anti-Zwinglian writings, even if these writings, taken quantitatively, far exceed those of his anti-Roman polemics. It goes without saying that neither can the controversies with the Lutherans and the Zwinglians be neglected in any appraisal of Calvin's eucharistic doctrine.

The 1559 edition of the *Institutes* gives the definitive form of Calvin's doctrine. This book limits itself to Calvin's doctrine as found in this edition. His other works are cited to throw light on the doctrine as found in the 1559 edition, the last before his death in 1564: earlier editions of the *Institutes*, his commentaries, sermons, church orders, letters, and the numerous *opuscula*.

When studying the theological pre-history of Calvin's eucharistic doctrine it seems best not to isolate the eucharistic witnesses from the broader movements which, in part, gave character to his theological structure. For this reason attention is given in Chapter I to some of the broader currents of pre-Reformation thought: the Scotist tradition and revival (including Thomas Bradwardine, Gregory of Rimini, and John Major), the nominalism of William of Occam, the mystical tradition, *devotio moderna*, humanism, and the Platonic

3

renewal. In Chapter II those whose doctrine is more immediately related to Calvin's eucharistic thought are examined: Augustine, the medieval disputants, and the eucharistic doctrine of Calvin's contemporaries—Luther, Bucer, Zwingli, and Melanchthon.

It is not possible in such a study to limit oneself to the books one knows Calvin read—and here our knowledge is meager indeed. It is even more hazardous to limit oneself merely to the authors that Calvin cites. For instance, Erasmus, it is generally agreed, greatly influenced Calvin, yet he is not cited once in the *Institutes*. When Calvin underwent his conversion experience in 1533, the eucharistic controversy among the reformers was already one of the scandals of Reformation Europe. These problems, which caused so much dissension and ill-feeling among the reformers, would quite naturally be the frequent topic of conversation among the university students. Their knowledge of the various positions would come from disputations, formal and informal, and from the general academic interest in the eucharistic conversations and confessions such as Martin Bucer was always promoting. Such events would be of interest to a student attending the university during the 1520's and the 1530's. Even if it were not possible to obtain their books, the student would be well acquainted with the eucharistic doctrine of Luther, Bucer, Zwingli, and Melanchthon.

The purpose in sketching the broader currents such as the Scotist revival and nominalism is not, in every instance, to indicate a direct relationship, much less a dependence, but to indicate the intellectual and theological atmosphere in which Calvin grew up and worked. Nor is it suggested that each author whose eucharistic doctrine is examined had a direct influence on Calvin. These theologians do form the eucharistic context of Calvin's theological development.

Calvin does not develop his doctrine in an isolated chapter devoted to the Eucharist. Rather his eucharistic doctrine is developed in the fourth book of the *Institutes*, which is the book in which he elaborates his ecclesiology. Since Calvin develops his eucharistic doctrine ecclesiologically, the whole of this book reflects the ecclesiological framework of his doctrine. The objections Calvin raises to Roman eucharistic doctrine are not, therefore, confined to narrow eucharistic doctrine. The objections are also ecclesiological objections. For this reason Chapter III of the book is an exposition of Calvin's objections to Roman doctrine and practice. Roman eucharistic practices must be studied because Calvin frequently, though not always, proceeds from an existential situation. These objections are studied in their broad ecclesiological context. Therefore such topics as ritualism, ritual Pelagianism, liturgical clericalism, and structural churchmanship are developed.

In Chapters IV and V an attempt is made to uncover those particular eucharistic concerns and preoccupations to which Calvin gave emphasis in his reactions against Romanism and the Roman eucharistic doctrine. Calvin's systematics is not deductive but rather the play of shifting centralities, the erection of ellipsoidal tension and union between theological polarities. Two centralities important for his eucharistic doctrine are given special consideration: the transcendent God in Chapter IV and union with Christ in Chapter V. In order to clarify the relationship between the shifting centralities and the eucharistic doctrine these two chapters are introduced by a section on Calvin's dialectical methodology.

In Chapters VI and VII Calvin's eucharistic doctrine is developed against the background of his anti-Roman polemics and of his broader eucharistic preoccupations treated in Chapters III, IV, and V. Two of the shifting centralities within Calvin's systematics are normative here, Christology and Pneumatology. Therefore Chapter VI is an exposition of Calvin's eucharistic doctrine seen Christologically, and Chapter VII is his doctrine seen pneumatologically.

Chapter VIII attempts to show the ecumenical relevancy of Calvin's objections to Catholic eucharistic doctrine. No attempt is made to give an exhaustive presentation but rather to indicate the direction such open questions can take.

Chapter IX contains a short conclusion and a critique of Calvin's doctrine, an evaluation, positive and negative, of Calvin's eucharistic doctrine against the background of the historical circumstances in which he developed it.

The terms Roman and anti-Roman are used instead of Catholic and anti-Catholic because Calvin considered himself Catholic though not Roman. The footnotes, both as to number and length, have been considerably reduced from the original thesis. Copies of the work with full documentation can be found in the following libraries: the Theological Faculty, Trier, Germany; Chateau Bossey, Celigny (near Geneva), Switzerland; Alcuin Library, St. John's Abbey, Collegeville, Minnesota.

I. The Intellectual Pre-History:
The Ecclesiological and Eucharistic Flight
from Secondary Causality

The Theological Imperatives of Voluntarism

DUNS SCOTUS: THE PURE WILL UNDETERMINED BY EXTERNALS

THERE can be little doubt that Calvin, the French Reformation theologian who was born in Noyon, Picardy in 1509, had studied and knew the scholastics, early and late. He quotes St. Anselm, Peter the Lombard, and Thomas Aquinas. He had been exposed to the theology of Thomas Bradwardine and Gregory of Rimini. As Louis Goumaz has shown, Calvin's scholastic background left unmistakable traces in his vocabulary.[1] And perhaps his love of polemic is not unrelated to his training in scholastic disputation. His studies at the Montaigu in Paris would of necessity mean that he was exposed in some depth to the thought of Duns Scotus. When Calvin entered the College of the Montaigu it was in the midst of a movement to restore the neo-Scotistic theology. Erasmus is a testy and vocal witness to the dominance of Scotism in Paris at the time when Calvin was a young man. Karl Reuter notes the distaste with which Erasmus wrote of the necessity of mastering Scotus in order to attain a baccalaureate and he heaped the *odium philosophicum* upon the Scot for the spectacle he had created in the schools, as though all that was knowable poured forth from the Scot's horn of plenty.[2] It was under the tutelage of another Scot, John Major, who came to the College of the Montaigu in 1525, that Calvin became immersed in anti-Pelagian and Scotistic theology as well as in a renewed Au-

[1] Cf. *La doctrine du salut d'après les commentaires de Jean Calvin sur le nouveau testament*, Nyon, 1917, 92f. Cf. also Karl Reuter, *Das Grundverständnis der Theologie Calvins*, Neukirchen, 1963, 47.

[2] Cf. Reuter, *op.cit.*, 20.

gustinianism. It was, in fact, John Major who published the Parisian works of Duns Scotus for the first time. From early in 1528 until 1531 Calvin studied under Major.

A great deal has been written on Calvin's indebtedness to Duns Scotus, some asserting it, others denying it.[3] Otto Ritschl was the first to conclude that Calvin's doctrine of double predestination implies the *potentia absoluta* of the nominalists, with Seeberg and Walker concurring. Doumergue and Lecerf, citing what seems to be Calvin's clear wish to disassociate himself from the Scotistic position, reject the hypothesis of Calvin's dependence on Duns Scotus. In this passage Calvin declares: "We do not approve of the dream of the papist theologians touching the absolute power of God; for their ramblings about it are profane, and as such must be held by us in detestation. Nor do we imagine a God without any law, seeing that he is a law to himself."[4] At the present stage of discussion it seems that in spite of this rather strong passage that Calvin is indeed indebted to Duns Scotus. What Calvin complains about in the passage cited refers to the arbitrary speculations and exaggerations of some of the late medieval philosophers of the nominalist school, or refers to his contempt for vain speculation which multiplies distinctions, a case in point being the distinction between the absolute power and the ordered power of God, which Scotus took over from Alexander of Hales.[5]

The discussion of the whole question is somewhat obscured by false ideas as to what Duns Scotus really taught. It is now generally recognized that Duns Scotus did not intend to postulate a God who was nothing more than a bloodless will, a systematic fickleness. The God of Scotus is limited by the principle of contradiction, what he has previously de-

---

[3] François Wendel has described this controversy. Cf. *Calvin, The Origins and Development of His Religious Thought*, New York, 1963, 127-129.

[4] *Inst.*, III, 23, 2. *Institutes of the Christian Religion*, ed. John T. McNeill, tr. Ford Lewis Battles. Vol. xx and xxi of LCC. Copyright © 1960, W. L. Jenkins. The Westminster Press. Used by permission.

[5] Cf. Wendel, *op.cit.*, 129.

creed, and the goodness which is his very nature.[6] This is something quite other than a God who is contrary almost by definition, willing fitfully and truculently, without regard for a continuing order of things. But in reading the following quotation from the *Institutes* one hears unmistakable overtones of Scotus: "The will of God is so much the supreme and sovereign rule of justice that whatever he wills must be held to be just insofar as he wills it. So that when one asks, 'Why did God do this?' that is asking for something greater and higher than the will of God, which there cannot be."[7] Calvin wishes merely to say, as did Scotus, that the will of God is not determined by nor subject to any causality external to himself. Scotus will admit that the will of God is determined by his love—a determination which will be subsequently denied by William of Occam. Gabriel Biel, with whose doctrine Calvin became familiar through John Major, summed it up quite simply: "The divine essence is the divine will."[8] In addition to the influence of Scotus, Calvin's legal training would have made him familiar with the principle of Roman law: *Princeps legibus solutus est*. Calvin would quite naturally apply this juridic norm to him who is the Prince of princes, the King of kings.[9] This is what Calvin seems to be saying when in his *Commentary on Exodus* he says that God is "independent of all law in this sense, that he is his own law and is the norm of all things."[10] Even more clearly he states that "it is not permissible for any mortal to attack or find fault with the least of the commandments of God, not only because his government is above all laws, but because his will is the most perfect norm of all the laws."[11]

[6] Cf. W. Betzendörfer, "Duns Scotus," RGG[3]. Cf. also Reinhold Seeberg, *Die Theologie des Joh. Duns Scotus*, Leipzig, 1900, 163f.

[7] *Inst.*, III, 23, 2.

[8] Cited from Reuter, *op.cit.*, 142.

[9] Cf. Jean Boisset, *Sagesse et sainteté dans la pensée de Jean Calvin*, Paris, 1959, 222.

[10] CR 24:49.

[11] *ibid.*, 24:131. The voluntarism Calvin asserts in his doctrine of God he denies in his doctrine of man. Cf. T. F. Torrance, *Calvin's Doctrine of Man*, London, 1949, 65.

In the pursuit of the knowledge of God, Calvin turns to the knowledge of self. There is in this self-knowledge the remnant of that "intuitive knowledge" found in Duns Scotus and developed by Occam, a knowledge which is individual, empirical, immediate. Calvin develops his theology of the ruptured relationship between God and man in terms of a personalism and voluntarism which stands in the Scotistic tradition, a tradition which Calvin received, in part, through Gregory of Rimini and John Major. These two theologians and Calvin look upon sin in voluntaristic, personalistic terms. For Scotus sin is the ultimate assertion of self, the apotheosis of self. Gregory of Rimini and John Major together with Calvin consider the essential character of sin in its voluntaristic opposition to God and his law.[12]

There seem to be traces of Scotus also in Calvin's Christology. Duns Scotus had said that the passion of Christ was not, in and by itself, of any particular value. The passion received its value by being accepted by the divine will. Because it was accepted by the divine will and was ordered to the work of redemption, the passion had value.[13] It is difficult not to think of Duns Scotus when one reads in the *Institutes* II, 17, 1: "In discussing Christ's merit, we do not consider the beginning of merit to be in him, but we go back to God's ordinance, the first cause. For God solely of his own good pleasure appointed him Mediator to obtain salvation for us. . . . Apart from God's good pleasure Christ could not merit anything." Calvin, it should be noted, is not denying that Christ really merits. There are those, says Calvin in the same passage, who "cannot bear to hear the word 'merit,' for they think that it obscures God's grace." Further, there is a Nestorian overtone to Scotus' doctrine of the two natures in Christ. Scotus stresses that the subsistence of the humanity of Christ in the Logos as the carrier is not to be defined as unity but as union. Aquinas had stressed the instrumental function of the human nature with regard to the divine, but Scotus, con-

[12] Cf. Reuter, *op.cit.*, 27.
[13] Cf. Wendel, *op.cit.*, 129.

10

cerned as he is to safeguard the real humanity of Christ, maintains that the human nature has a certain independence from the Logos.[14] It would be unfair to label Scotus a Nestorian. For him, as for Calvin, it is not a heresy, but a manner of looking at things, a theological disposition.

Scotus had seen in the infinity of God the most characteristic mark of his divine nature. Calvin took over this emphasis from John Major who in 1506 and again in 1530 had published his *propositum de infinito*. Under the influence of Major, Calvin came to measure God and his attributes in terms of infinity.[15] To this degree he is a Scotist. In addition, infinity is the most prominent metaphysical property of God, that quality which most clearly distinguishes the divine nature. When one thinks of Calvin's doctrine of God one tends to think of Calvin's passion for transcendence. However an examination of Calvin's system will reveal that the concept of transcendence plays a smaller role in his theology of God than his concept of infinity.[16]

There is also in Duns Scotus a eucharistic concern dear to Calvin: to maintain the integrity of the bread. Duns Scotus, among other scholastics, made some desperate attempts to reintroduce the substance of bread into the sacrament without doing violence to the doctrine of transubstantiation. Scotus teaches a *transubstantiatio adductiva* instead of the *transubstantiatio productiva* of St. Thomas. The *adductiva* doctrine assumes that the substance of the body of Christ is added to the substance of the bread. There might also be another eucharistic influence. François Wendel suggests that "it would not be altogether arbitrary, after all, to look for possible points of contact between the Scotist theory of the concomitancy of the action of the Holy Spirit and of the reception of the eucharistic elements, and Calvin's enlargements upon the

[14] Cf. Heiko A. Oberman, *The Harvest of Medieval Theology*, Cambridge, 1963, 253, 254.

[15] Budé's interest in the concept of infinity was another influence to which Calvin was open. Cf. Josef Bohatec, *Budé und Calvin*, Graz, 1950, 306-325.

[16] Cf. Reuter, *op.cit.*, 136.

same subject—provided, of course, one left out of account that notion of a divine covenant with the Church which Duns Scotus introduced here."[17]

Besides inheriting his voluntarism from Scotus, Calvin inherited his personalism. Scotus saw God in his role as ruler and lord, but only as a personal ruler and a personal lord. And there was, therefore, only possible a personal obedience for man. For Scotus, God alone was a person in the proper sense; man was a person only in the improper sense. But to both the person of God and the person of man he attributed two characteristics: existence and "this-ness." Calvin was introduced to the personalism of Scotus through John Major.[18] It was especially in relation to Scotus' personalism that Calvin's theology took on a bipolarity. This dialectical structure, which was inherited from Scotus on one level, was inherited from Bernard on another level. From Scotus (and Plato) Calvin inherited the dialectical structure of his philosophical presuppositions and formulations; from Bernard the bipolarity of his theology of piety.[19]

THOMAS BRADWARDINE: THE DIVINE PARTICIPATION AND THE MORE IMMEDIATE CAUSE

Two medieval theologians to whose theology Calvin was exposed during his stay in Paris are Thomas Bradwardine (c. 1290-1349) and Gregory of Rimini (c. 1300-1358). Bradwardine was a teacher at Merton College, Oxford and procurator of the University of Oxford. Duns Scotus, who had taught at Oxford from 1297-1301, was still the dominating intellectual influence at Oxford during Bradwardine's studies there. The two universities of Oxford and Paris had many intellectual contacts and it is not surprising that as early as 1360 the Sorbonne possessed at least two hand-written exemplars of Bradwardine's work *De causa Dei contra Pelagianos*. This book was to be found in all the libraries of Europe. In the sixteenth century there were in the Sorbonne a number

[17] Wendel, *op.cit.*, 129.   [18] Cf. Reuter, *op.cit.*, 22.
[19] Cf. *ibid.*, 9.

12

of hand-written exemplars. Calvin came to know Bradwardine through John Major, and it would have been easy for Calvin to read Bradwardine's work against the Pelagians either in Paris or in some other place. Evidence of Bradwardine's influence can also be found in Germany where he was the object of study by Flacius Illyricus. In recent years the influence of Bradwardine on Calvin, not necessarily direct, has been briefly noted by Pannenberg and Laun, but has been developed in depth by Karl Reuter, to whom these pages are heavily indebted.[20]

The concept of providence, which Christianity had taken over from Cicero, had had a long tradition by Calvin's time. Augustine had borrowed the concept from Cicero in order to combat a rigid fatalism and determinism. This is presupposed in Calvin whose doctrine in its essential lines, claims Reuter, is indebted to Bradwardine.[21] Bradwardine had arrived at a clear understanding of God as an only cause through his study of St. Paul, the Old Testament, Augustine, and the whole anti-Pelagian movement. Calvin is in essential agreement with this conception. God's will is primary but it is not arbitrary and without principle.[22] Both as regards motive and nature, the will acts out of love. The motive of any act of God is love; and the will, when it moves, gives expression to the nature of God, which is goodness.

Essential to Bradwardine's system is the principle of divine participation. He made God the most immediate cause of all that man does; this deprives man of all autonomy. Man's dependence on God is dependence in the most radical sense. On him he depends for his being, his acting, and his worth. Bradwardine's system is built on the denial of human worth. Man possesses no positive qualities or powers which are

[20] Cf. J. F. Laun, "Thomas Bradwardine," RGG.[2] Cf. also Reuter, op.cit., 158, 272n.

[21] Cf. ibid., 158.

[22] Reuter is certainly wrong when he says that for Bradwardine the will of God is without presuppositions. Cf. Gordon Leff, Bradwardine and the Pelagians, Cambridge, 1957, 42, 43; Cf. also Oberman, Archbishop Thomas Bradwardine, A Fourteenth Century Augustinian, Utrecht, 1958, 60.

properly his. Man and the world are, in fact, an extension of God's will; no part of the universe can act but by divine decree. It is Bradwardine's avowed purpose to assert God's dominion to the exclusion of all other powers, all other kinds of determinism. In Bradwardine's system it is not possible to describe anything created as entirely the immediate cause of its own actions; in every case, God will be more immediately the cause than any creature. Bradwardine was concerned with emphasizing the chasm between God and man, as is Calvin, but in effect Bradwardine closes it. The principle of divine participation leads dangerously near to pantheism, since God is made to participate in the most immediate way in every movement of a created order.

Foreknowledge of God's creatures in Bradwardine is through the will, and through the will God participates in every action of his creatures. His doctrine of grace must be seen in this context, that is, it is determined by the principle of divine participation. Grace becomes completely gratuitous and is necessary for any good act. Merit or good works have no part in gaining grace, but, on the contrary, are the result of grace. Finally, every disposition to good in a creature is the result of a previous grace.[23] Here one anticipates Luther's and Calvin's rejection of all merit. Further, when prescience corresponds with predestination and God is the most immediate cause of every act, then the concept of merit becomes dubious legal tender in relation to grace. Merit depends solely on the will of God and is not distinct from grace and therefore it is not negotiable.

Bradwardine's principle of divine participation creates a dilemma in his doctrine on sin. Everything that God knows about his creatures he also wills, and therefore, God cannot be limited to merely conserving what he wills. The doctrine of the permissive will of God is a subterfuge and Bradwardine will have no part of it. "When God permits He also acts."[24] God, it seems, is involved in a rather immediate way

---

[23] Cf. Leff, *op.cit.*, 66.   [24] *ibid.*, 58.

in every act of sin in Bradwardine's system, a position Calvin adopts in the *Institutes III*, 23, 8. But this cannot be. How can the highest good be the cause of evil? The dilemma, then, is this: either concede that God causes sin, or that man has a measure of independence. Bradwardine, in fact, evades a solution to the problem of sin but his theological system is so permeated by the principle of divine participation that to grant man a measure of independence is excluded. His methodology here resembles Calvin's, namely, the dialectical tension between opposing centralities, each speaking its absolute, each unyielding. Calvin, too, left the problem unresolved.

Like Calvin, Bradwardine was not interested in purely philosophical and metaphysical problems. Problems of being and speculative problems on the essences did not concern him. Nor was he greatly interested in discussing the possible alternatives to a given ordinance. He was writing against a fourteenth-century skepticism which had cast doubt upon all reality, God included. Faith alone had a voice for Bradwardine. This is not to be equated with Calvin's dismissal of all save the voice of the elect, but the movement is in that direction.[25] When logic and skepticism challenged faith, Bradwardine turned to Scripture. If it was said that God's existence was either a mere possibility or probability but unproven, Bradwardine invoked personal experience. As shall be seen Calvin will also use experience to justify his eucharistic doctrine. When faced with problems of logic in a eucharistic context Calvin will simply say "I experience rather than understand it."[26] Bradwardine's theology will have further relevance for Calvin's eucharistic doctrine. Like Duns Scotus, the Scotists, and the Occamists, both Bradwardine and Calvin insist that God is not dependent on causes of second rank. God uses them but he will not be tied to them. Neither Bradwardine nor Calvin give secondary causes an important role in their theology.

[25] Cf. *ibid.*, 263, 264.
[26] *Inst.*, IV, 17, 32.

GREGORY OF RIMINI: GOD ACTS AS HE WILLS

Gregory of Rimini had studied at Paris for six years, then had returned to Italy to teach at Bologna, Padua, and Perugia before returning to Paris for the second time in 1341. In 1345 Pope Clement VI attempted to obtain a chair at the University of Paris for Gregory, a request which was heard with sympathy. During the period from 1341 until 1351 Gregory commented on the *Sentences* at the University of Paris. His major work was his *Commentary on the Sentences*. There have been various efforts to label him either as an Occamist, or an anti-Pelagian, or finally, with more unanimity, as an Augustinian.[27]

Gregory of Rimini, together with William of Occam, can see no gain in subjecting the first principles of theology to a rational demonstration. Gregory denies that the truths that God exists and that he is of infinite perfection are truths which admit of a rational proof. These truths are accepted as commonly held assumptions and from these assumptions Gregory proceeds to show their implications for God and his creatures.

In his doctrine on sin, Gregory proves himself a great upholder of orthodoxy and a true follower of St. Augustine. In contrast to Bradwardine, with his principle of divine participation, Gregory bases his position on two main tenets: he makes a distinction between God's different kinds of willing and he holds the negative nature of sin, which is lacking in essence. Unlike Thomas Bradwardine, Gregory is not forced by his system to implicate God in an immediate way in every sinful act. Sin is attributed to God only so far as it inheres in a being but not insofar as it is specifically sin. God is not the cause of sin but of sinful men and only in this partial sense is he a cause of sin.[28] Calvin was to come into contact with Gregory's doctrine of sin through the person of John Major.

[27] Cf. Leff, *Gregory of Rimini*, New York, 1961, 1.
[28] Cf. *ibid.*, 214-216.

In common with Occam and others of his contemporaries Gregory did not consider the habit (*habitus*) of grace as inherently necessary, and this by reason of the absolute power of God. The conceptual tools common to his contemporaries are also Gregory's tools and therefore he fully accepts the idea of absolute power. But he does not see in it, as Leff points out, an instrument to be used indiscriminately.[29] He is concerned, rather, to limit an unthinking extension, right, left and center, of so formidable a tool. God is limited by his own nature and by the law of contradiction; he cannot sin, be unjust, or do that which is logically contradictory. However, by reason of God's absolute power he can dispense with the habit and move the will directly. As can be seen, divine aid is not dispensed with, it merely takes on another more direct form. God's will is the supreme arbiter: God can act in man's regard even when man has no habit, and a habit is efficacious only if he wills it. The *habitus* is not inherently necessary but divine aid is. When man has the habit he still needs God's general and special graces to accomplish good.

Gregory's importance for Calvin studies, in addition to certain affinities in the doctrine of sin and grace (pointed out by Karl Reuter), is to be found especially in his doctrine of double predestination.[30] One finds here a kind of terrible and terrifying transcendence which safeguards the absolute freedom of God's will as regards man's final destiny. God's will is the sole cause of either election or reprobation. The decision is free and unconditional, and has no other motivation than his willing it. There is no connection between divine love and divine election as it is found in Duns Scotus' formulation. In Gregory's tautological terms, God acts as he wills.[31] In the most literal sense God is the cause both of glory and reprobation, and Gregory is seemingly as careful to exclude any role of man in his reprobation as he is to exclude him any role in his election. Man's disability as regards both election and reprobation is due entirely to God.

[29] Cf. *ibid.*, 98, 99.   [30] Cf. Reuter, *op.cit.*, 173.
[31] Cf. Leff, *Gregory of Rimini*, 198, 199.

There is no attempt on Gregory's part to mitigate God's refusal to save all men, and to this degree he departs from the traditional teaching. His doctrine of double predestination is without any palliative; an implacable construct which looks upon predestination almost exclusively in its cause. The effects of predestination are interesting only insofar as they illuminate a divine will which is its own *raison d'être*.

Since he represents a voluntarist tradition in grace and predestination, Gregory is interesting for Calvin's general sacramental background. The importance of the will and of God's direct sanctifying action will raise problems in developing a truly incarnational sacramental doctrine. Calvin is perhaps indebted to both Bradwardine and Gregory of Rimini for his strong anti-Pelagian tendencies, which, as shall be seen, is not unimportant for his sacramental doctrine.

Gregory of Rimini's importance for Calvin is underlined when it is remembered that John Major, the most important teacher at the Montaigu during Calvin's years there, was an ardent student of Gregory's writings. Major was an upholder of the traditional Catholic faith and, like Béda, he taught against Wyclif, Huss, and Luther.

WILLIAM OF OCCAM: THE GOD WHO IS NO MAN'S DEBTOR

A warning should be given at the outset about the study of William of Occam (c. 1300-c. 1350). It should be remembered that Occam, like Bonaventure, represents more than a philosophical tradition. William of Occam is also part of a mystical tradition, and he taught as he did partly because of his intense devotional life. He should not be studied apart from the broader framework of the mystical movement of the Middle Ages.

When Calvin came to Paris to pursue his university studies it was the nominalistic theory of knowledge and logic of William of Occam together with the conclusions which the Scotistic scholastics drew from that philosophy, which dominated university life. In 1473 nominalism was under censure and forbidden, but was again allowed in 1481, and after this latter date it reigned supreme at Paris. Calvin had an immediate contact with nominalism through John Major, whose theory of knowledge and logic was simply that of Occam.

Calvin had learned from the nominalists how to doubt the metaphysical powers of reason. This is one of the reasons why Calvin has so little time for speculation. In justification he quotes Holy Scripture's reserve in speaking about the essence of God.[32] This nominalist position was given further support by the school reform Calvin undertook in Geneva, where scholasticism was excluded from the curriculum and philology was preferred to philosophy. Calvin would go further than the nominalists for he was unhappy with even the formal use of reason.[33] To this degree Calvin represents a de-philosophizing of theology.

Calvin belongs to the voluntarist tradition but he rejects the nominalist teaching on the absolute power of God. Yet he is not entirely free of its influence. Rather than isolate the will and sing hymns to its absolute freedom, he gives much attention to the relationship between the divine freedom and a divine rule, order, justice, and judgment. And in opposition to any fickle God, Calvin conceives the will of God as ordered, right, just, and most just. From John Major, who had taught the doctrine of Gabriel Biel at Paris, Calvin could have heard Biel's dictum: "What God wills, he wills in the most ordered manner because his will is the first rule of fairness and justice."[34]

Occam was accused in Reformation times of Pelagianism. In 1517 Luther already took exception to Occam's Pelagian teachings. According to Luther, Occam stood at the summit of Pelagianism because he taught that the Holy Spirit and the grace of God are not necessary to do good works, to ful-

[32] Cf. CR 2:152, 155.

[33] Cf. H. A. Enno van Gelder, *The Two Reformations in the 16th Century*, The Hague, 1964, 270, 2n.

[34] *Inventorium seu repertorium generale*, II, dist. 20, Tübingen, 1501.

fill the commandments, and to love God. The point is interesting because Occam is both a confirmed Pelagian and a dedicated anti-Pelagian. As a Pelagian he teaches that man can, with his own natural powers, love God above all things although such love is not meritorious. He can make acts of faith and hope which are distinguished from the same acts made by the man possessing the habit of grace only, at best, by reason of greater intensity. Essentially such acts are the same; what sets them apart is the greater intensity with which a man acts when he has the habit of grace. The more an act is under the dominance of man's freedom and will the more meritorious it is. He also suggests that man can prepare himself for grace.[35] This is undoubtedly Pelagianism and Luther's accusations are justified. On the other hand, Occam has a strong anti-Pelagian strain. God is completely free to accept or reject man whether or not he has the habit of grace. In this manner God is in debt to no man whatever his condition. Insofar as Occam wishes to exclude all of man's claim on God, to abolish the habit's right to fulfillment and glory, he is an anti-Pelagian. Luther himself calls him "my dear master,"[36] and stands in closest relation to him in the doctrine of the *acceptatio divina*, God freely accepting man; man without established rights over against God by reason of a habit. It is difficult to know to whom Calvin is indebted for his doctrine of justification. Reuter suggests that the doctrine of *acceptatio divina,* found in both Occam and Gregory of Rimini, was taken over by Calvin from Gregory through the teaching of John Major.[37]

Because Occam denied the real distinction between substance and quantity and therefore denied that there was a quantitative presence of Christ as distinct from his substantial presence, he reinforced a eucharistic spiritualist tradition. Later his teaching was identified with that of Wyclif

[35] Cf. Erwin Iserloh, *Gnade und Eucharistie in der philosophischen Theologie des Wilhelm von Ockham*, Wiesbaden, 1956, 116, 129.

[36] WA 30/2:300.

[37] Cf. Reuter, *op.cit.*, 150. For Occam's influence on Luther cf. Iserloh, *op.cit.*, 116, 132.

and Huss. This was a development which was little to Wyclif's liking and he went out of his way to show that his teaching was drawn not from Occam but from Scripture and tradition.[38] Biel, on the other hand, used Occam's teaching to avoid a hypermaterialistic interpretation of the real presence.[39] Undoubtedly there is a decided spiritual element in Occam's teaching on the sacrament. For instance, he defines a sacrament as: *significare efficaciter effectum dei gratuitum*.[40] According to Occam, it is quite possible for God to use something purely spiritual as a sacramental sign. No such sacraments, that is purely spiritual signs, are to be found in the present economy, but they remain within the realm of the possible, and must therefore be taken into account in any definition. A further spiritualization is seen in his teaching that the eucharistic forms or species do not make any contribution to the presence of Christ in a given place, that the presence of Christ can remain even when the species are destroyed. Such a stand hardly represents a very incarnational sacramentalism. In the matter of transubstantiation he explicitly spoke his obedience to the teaching authority of the Church, but he nevertheless set forth the opinion that a type of consubstantiation was better accommodated to the demands of reason and easier to justify.

In broad terms it is difficult to assess the extent of Occam's influence on Calvin. But this much can be said: he was not left untouched by nominalism. The fickle, tyrannous God is rejected, but in the manner in which Calvin handles proofs one finds a certain nominalistic atomism. Reuter suggests that Calvin himself was not aware of the Scotistic-nominalistic influences which helped form his doctrine.[41] Certainly the Occamist theory of knowledge helped Calvin build his doctrine of revelation, Calvin filling with scriptural theology the void Occam's distrust of reason had created. This was not peculiar

[38] Cf. Iserloh, *op.cit.*, 252.

[39] Oberman, *The Harvest of Medieval Thought*, 279.

[40] *Supra Quatuor Libros Sententiarum*, IV, q. 1B. *Opera Plurima*, Lyon, 1494—1496, vol. 4. (Republished London, 1962).

[41] Cf. *op.cit.*, 154.

to Calvin since Bradwardine and others had done likewise. It would be hazardous to claim any direct connection between Occam's eucharistic doctrine and that of Calvin. Occam undoubtedly prepared the way by his voluntaristic non-incarnational sacramentalism. The large place he gave to the sovereignty of God and to primary causality, and the consequent small place given to secondary causality will find an echo in Calvin. This is in accord with the nominalistic tendency to separate names from things, faith from reason, will from grace, primary from secondary causes, justification from infused charity, glory from the habit of grace. Calvin will manifest such a tendency when he explains the eucharistic communion with Christ. The believer is put into contact with Christ and the sacramental elements in a simultaneous but separate fashion.[42] Here is the nominalistic proclivity for separation. In both Occam and Calvin the sacraments will be seen more and more as signs of God's favor, as seals of a covenant, and less as true, efficacious instruments of grace. As shall be seen, Calvin will retain the concept of instrumentality but in a weakened form. There should be no simplistic concentration on a weakened instrumentality, so as to forget the dialectical form of Calvin's theology and thus to neglect the other pole of the dialectical ellipse with its unyielding absolute.

The Pre-Reformation Search for the Earthly and the Heavenly

THE MYSTICAL TRADITION: "I BELIEVE THAT I MAY EXPERIENCE"

Occam may have given Calvin and Luther the tools of their reform trade, but the reformation made no distinction between the despised scholastics and Occam when it came to making judgments upon systems of thought dominated by nonbiblical, and, as far as the reformers were concerned, nonreligious categories. It was a matter of more than just cate-

[42] Cf. Alexandre Ganoczy, *Calvin, théologien de l'église et du ministère*, Paris, 1964, 240.

gories, more than just structure. Neither structure nor content were sufficiently religious. Such theologies could not feed the soul, whatever they offered to the mind. The Church itself, as seen in the Avignon papacy, was involved more and more in external administration, given to the task of perpetuating its own structure as though that were the reason for its existence. Since piety could be found only with difficulty in theology and in the Church, it sought its sources within—more precisely, in experience.

Though, of course, not influenced by the ecclesiastical externalism of later times, St. Augustine's theology of grace had in large part been a theology of experience. An actualist in his doctrine of grace, he, in 417, was saying that the divine indwelling is always related to some knowledge or experience. The indwelling is not actualized until the believer can actually know him by a conscious act. Baptized infants have the Spirit but they do not yet know him.[43] Bernard of Clairvaux, who made a large contribution to the intellectual history of the last three hundred years of the Middle Ages and to the reformation itself, stands in the same experiential tradition. For Bernard "the important word is no longer *quaeritur*, but *desideratur*; no longer *sciendum* but *experiendum*." Bernard would not say *credo ut intelligam* but *credo ut experiar*.[44] Integral to the knowledge of the Trinity is a certain experience of divine sonship. This must be said without implying that Bernard's (or Augustine's) only concern was for experience. Both Bernard and Augustine represent a large element in the mystical tradition of the later Middle Ages.

There is another school of mysticism—St. Victor in Paris—which was more philosophical in its forms. Hugo (d. 1141) and Richard (d. 1173), both contemporaries of St. Bernard, were members of the monastery of St. Victor. Besides theology they were interested in philosophy and attempted to

[43] Cf. C. Moeller and G. Philips, *The Theology of Grace and the Ecumenical Movement*, London, 1961, 12.

[44] Cf. Jean Leclercq, *The Love of Learning and the Desire for God*, New York, 1961, 7, 263.

bring together sacred studies and mystical attitudes. This fusion of theology and mysticism reappears in the greatest scholastics of the thirteenth and fourteenth centuries and it exercised an influence on Luther and Calvin. The Franciscan movement, too, was concerned with personal experience, the direct relation between the human soul and Christ, and also with evangelism of a more personal kind. No longer is Christ either the solemn Lord of the sculptured doorways of Romanesque and early Gothic churches, nor the eternal Logos of the theologians. He is the Son of Mary, the Man acquainted with infirmity, the crucified Christ.[45]

The monastery of Helfta in Thuringia was a virtual nest of mystics: Mechthild of Magdeburg (d. 1283), Mechthild of Hockeborn (d. 1299), and Gertrude the Great (d. 1302). Mechthild of Magdeburg was visited with a mystical experience she called the *jubilus*. She described it as a state, not without its emotional element, in which she could bear witness to her burning love for God "in a voice too beautiful to be human, but not in meaningful words."[46] This direct communion and unity of the soul with God was, by 1250, called the "new art." It was usually sought within the framework of the church, and was not infrequently experienced during a liturgical rite, such as the mass or the office in choir. But since it was essentially an individual experience, it tended to divorce itself from common liturgical worship and from the sacramental life of the church. There was no rejection of the priest nor of his role, nor of the sacraments, but they had ceased to be important; all were enveloped in a mystical haze.[47] Adelheid Langmann, a nun, summed it all up when she rather truculently prayed: "If you have any love for me at all, then come to me yourself, instead of just sending messengers."[48] Master Eckhart, the German fourteenth-century mystic,

[45] Cf. Frederich B. Artz, *The Mind of the Middle Ages*, New York, 1962, 427.
[46] Michael Seidlmayer, *Currents of Medieval Thought*, Oxford, 1960, 151.
[47] Cf. *ibid.*, 153.
[48] Cited from Seidlmayer, *op.cit.*, 151.

represents the highest expression of the more speculative approach. Its speculative nature should not be misunderstood. Eckhart fully intended that it should inspire and form the practical life of the community. It was, however, based on neo-Platonic ideas and, his own protestations to the contrary notwithstanding, is not without a strong element of pantheism. For this German mystic, God and soul were everything; for the material world, he had little understanding. This spiritual element is coupled with a theology of sanctification in which the birth of God in the soul of man is of supreme importance. There is no denial of the traditional explanation of the birth of Christ, the Mediator, but this is of minor importance when compared to the rebirth in the soul. God acts directly, without agency. One finds here in Eckhart the same flight from secondary causality which one finds in Duns Scotus, Bradwardine, and Occam. Eckhart did not reject the sacraments but he implied that they are not decisive and that ultimately they are not necessary.

DEVOTIO MODERNA: THE SUBJECTIVE EVANGELICAL SIMPLICITY

It may be argued that *devotio moderna* is not distinct from the medieval mystical movement. Since, however, contemporaries gave it a distinct name, it would seem that they themselves considered it to be distinctive. Its adherents had none of the mystical compulsion to storm heaven and to lay hold of the Absolute so that the finite and the Infinite were one. They were not characterized by a mystical intensity so much as by an evangelical earnestness, not by an eagerness to speak unspeakable words but rather by an aggressive simplicity, slightly anti-intellectual. They represented a deeply eucharistic piety, a consciousness of man's sinfulness, a pursuit, in more modest forms, of religious experience. This personal, individualistic pursuit was realized dogmatically within the church, but psychologically outside of it. *Devotio moderna*, being personal and subjective, tended to make people more self-reliant and independent in an ethical situation. The individual person was also more independent of the priesthood in its function as guide and ruler. In fact, the direct influence of the priest had been considerably weakened. It was, in summary, a turning away from the objective-universal toward the peripheral-individual,[49] and, in its way, a flight from secondary causality.

Calvin came into contact with *devotio moderna* through the Brethren of the Common Life. John Standonck (1450-1504) had been born in Malines in Belgium and raised by the Brethren of the Common Life. After being a student at the college of Montaigu he became its rector in 1483. The rather strict discipline of the Montaigu, such as Calvin experienced, was administered according to a mitigated form of the statutes Standonck had written for the college.[50] In writing the statutes Standonck was influenced by his own many years with the Brethren, no fewer than eight, perhaps as many as ten or twelve, and also influenced by his relationship to Gerhard Groote, John van Ruysbroek, and Thomas à Kempis. Noël Béda, trained by Standonck and his confidant, was Standonck's immediate successor as rector of the Montaigu. John Major was also a follower of Standonck and the teacher who influenced Calvin most during his years at the college. Major became rector in 1525, the year after Calvin arrived.

As a student Calvin would have copied out excerpts from the devotional literature of the Brethren of the Common Life which he found on the shelves: the writings of Gerson, von Ailli, Groote, and, above all, St. Bernard. It is clear from Calvin's theological and devotional vocabulary that he was exposed to the *Imitation of Christ*. From it he learned to place the greatest weight on the inner condition or state of man. There are overtones of the *Imitation* in Calvin's doctrine of wisdom, which are found in the very first sentence of the *Institutes* published after 1539. The influence of *devotio moderna* gave a further impetus to that de-philosophizing of

---

[49] Cf. Joseph Lortz, *Die Reformation in Deutschland*, vol. 1, *Voraussetzungen, Aufbruch, Erste Entscheidung*, 3rd edn., Freiburg, 1949, 121.

[50] Cf. Albert Hyma, *The Christian Renaissance, a History of the "Devotio Moderna,"* New York, 1924, 236-250.

theology already found in the Scotistic, nominalistic, philosophical tradition. Both the devotional and philosophical traditions induced Calvin to think of theology in terms of a pious knowledge and a pious conduct; pious here to be taken in its most virile sense. Reuter suggests that there is scarcely a theme in the piety of the *Imitation* which is not exploited by Calvin in his own theology; and Breen finds these themes in the first edition of the *Institutes*.[51] They shared in common a consciousness of sin, a moral imperative, an anti-intellectual note coupled with a zeal for education, a devotional vocabulary, the love of simplicity, frugality, and service.

A word must be said about St. Bernard. Roland Mousnier has shown how Luther is indebted to St. Bernard,[52] and a similar project could easily be undertaken in regard to Calvin. Among the influences on Calvin were certainly Augustine, Duns Scotus, Gregory of Rimini, Thomas Bradwardine; to this list, by no means complete, must be added St. Bernard. Calvin does more than take over en masse from Bernard typical biblical and theological formulations, a distinctive piety, and, in part, a vocabulary; these are carefully reworked so that they are truly Calvin's. For these elements, however, as well as for the broad bipolar character of his theology of piety, Calvin must, in part, thank St. Bernard. Undoubtedly Calvin came to know Bernard early through the many books of excerpts which had been made of Bernard's works. Another contact would have been through Martin Bucer whose book, *Über das Reich Christi*, shows that he was conversant with Bernard as well as with Augustine.

ERASMUS AND THE HUMANISTS: THE HEAVENLY PHILOSOPHY
WHICH WAS NOT QUITE CHRISTIAN

Erasmus will serve as a link between *devotio moderna* and another medieval movement which had its impact upon

[51] Cf. Reuter, *op.cit.*, 137; Quirinus Breen, *John Calvin: A Study in French Humanism*, Grand Rapids, 1931, 21.

[52] Cf. Roland Mousnier, "Saint Bernard and Martin Luther," *The American Benedictine Review*, vol. 14 (1963), 448-462.

Calvin: humanism. Erasmus gave a scientific form to the *devotio moderna,* which was, in effect, a "philosophy of Christ" or a "Christian philosophy." This form of the *devotio moderna* greatly influenced Calvin. He himself spoke of a "Christian or heavenly philosophy."[53] From Erasmus and from the mystics Calvin took the concept of wisdom, which for him was not just self-knowledge, but the bipolarity of the knowledge of God and of man.[54] Like Erasmus he was vastly impatient with vain speculation, and with a presumptuous search into the essence of God.

The condemnation of the works of Erasmus in 1526 by the Sorbonne, the only body to whose opinion Luther had deferred (1519-1521), would most certainly have awakened the interest of the seventeen-year-old John Calvin. The Royal College which Calvin was attending in 1531 was also censured. The first of the condemned propositions was: "The Holy Scripture cannot be well understood without the Greek and Hebrew and the other (biblical) languages."[55] This proposition was labeled *temeraria et scandalosa.* Two teachers of the College were ordered to appear before the Parlement on charges of heresy. This hostile attitude toward a movement promoting the study of the languages in which the Bible was written must have appeared unpardonably obscurantist to the eager young student. Calvin had considered himself a humanist, though his humanistic book was unsuccessful. His commentary on Seneca's *De Clementia,* published in 1532, went practically unnoticed by the humanist world, but it has its own importance for the development of Calvin's theology of God. The young author had applied the interpretation of the imperial idea to the concept of the sovereignty of God.

There was, of course, more to humanism than the study of the ancient languages and authors. In general the literary humanists were appreciative of life for its own sake and they saw life in highly individualistic terms. The individual was

---

[53] CR 2:625. Cf. also *ibid.,* 8:17; *ibid.,* 2:506.
[54] Cf. Reuter, *op.cit.,* 11.
[55] A. Lefranc, *Histoire du Collège de France,* Paris, 1893, 122.

something unique, unrepeatable. Petrarch had proclaimed the tenets of a professional individualism with vatic declamations about self-fulfillment and vows to be true to himself. All the experiences they sought in books, learning, nature, love, friendship, and even religion had as their center the ego. The norm by which a thing was judged was its contribution to the service or enhancement of the ego. The humanists took on arduous tasks and aimed at high achievement but the dedicated humanist looked upon himself as his own great masterpiece. In common with the other prereformation movements, the Scotistic and nominalistic philosophy, the mystical and pietistic trends, humanism represented a turning away from the general, objective outlook to an individual and subjective outlook. Though some of the humanists were clerics, humanism as a movement was anything but clerical. Rather it was the intellectual ascent of the secular middle class, a class which had been uneasy and uncertain in its attitude toward the cleric. Expression was found for its uneasiness in diatribes against monks and clerics. There was, however, among the humanists a deep appreciation for the *vita privata*. Originally modeled on the life of the monks and hermits, it gradually lost its religious orientation. The *vita privata* became the retirement of the gentleman scholar. Erasmus had held up the *vita privata* as the life ideally suited to the man who cherishes freedom; and, it should be remembered, Erasmus was something of a refugee from monastic life. Calvin, had he been left to follow his own course, would have chosen some form of this *vita privata*, though it would have taken on a less humanistic and more apostolic character.[56]

Together with the mystical and pietistic movements the humanist movement, in both its literary and biblical adherents, fed on contempt for the scholastics, although the humanists were not successful in wholly escaping scholasticism. They thought the scholastics' Latinity lacked form and

[56] Cf. CR 31:23-25.

style, and was sterile and pompous; in a word, the scholastics were barbarians.

Calvin was trained in the humanist tradition and he never lost the humanist's love of style, of the philosophers and the ancients, and of philology. Into the 1539 edition of the *Institutes* Calvin introduced a section on secular studies as God's gifts. Even after he wrote the *Treatise on Scandals* in 1550 attacking the literary humanists and the atheistic humanists, the section remained in the *Institutes*. In the last edition this section extends from II, 1, 12 to II, 2, 17. The clearest expression, indeed the classic expression, of Calvin's enduring humanism is found in the *Institutes*, II, 2, 15:

> If we regard the Spirit of God as the sole foundation of truth, we shall neither reject the truth itself, nor despise it wherever it shall appear, unless we wish to dishonor the Spirit of God. For by holding the gifts of the Spirit in slight esteem, we contemn and reproach the Spirit himself. What then? Shall we deny that truth shone upon the ancient jurists who established civic order and discipline with such great equity? Shall we say that the philosophers were blind in their fine observation and artful description of nature? Shall we say that those men were devoid of understanding who conceived the art of disputation and taught us to speak reasonably? . . . No, we cannot read the writings of the ancients on these subjects without great admiration.

Calvin would attack the humanists as he did in the *Treatise on Scandals*, but he would not repent of his essential approbation of the goals of humanism. The difference between Calvin and the literary humanists was one of orientation. The humanists' self-centeredness, their individualistic absolutism, their confident and self-assured glorification of human dignity, their noisy self-sufficiency, their exaltation of the genius and power of man, their easy accommodation to the joys of the world, and their refusal to bow down in humility and repentance—all of this separated Calvin from the literary and atheistic humanists.

Calvin sees earthly life as a transitory stage in a journey toward eternal life;[57] the humanists, though they would agree with Plato that the soul can develop completely only after its liberation from the body, accepted the world and life as a realm of true human activity with ends which were valid in themselves. For Calvin, virtue is submission to and service of God, while the literary humanists practiced virtue because it was the means of realizing the fullness of human dignity. The literary and atheistic humanists felt a responsibility to themselves and to the community, but in a real sense Calvin thinks of responsibility as something which is owed directly and immediately only to God. Briefly, Calvin's attitude toward the literary humanists was dictated by their inability to be truly Christian.[58] The Christian veneer given to scholarly decorum and a basic decency was not enough, in Calvin's mind, to make a Christian. Their religious concern was so muted by their self-ennobling hedonism and their polished aphorisms that the scandal of the faith was not taken seriously. "They change half Christianity into a philosophy, or at least they do not take matters (that is, religion) seriously. . . . In addition, a section of them have Platonic ideas in their heads and thus excuse most of the foolish superstitions known to the papacy as being matters from which it is not

[57] This does not mean that Calvin will be negligent of the world. Quite the opposite. Sure of the one to whom he is responsible, and sure of his calling and election, he gives himself to molding society according to the will of God with an efficiency which will bring down upon himself both praise and blame. Cf. Ernst Troeltsch, *The Social Teaching of the Christian Churches*, New York, 1931, vol. 2, 588, 589.

[58] H. A. Enno van Gelder has Calvin undergoing a conversion as a result of which he turns his back on humanistic studies. "He shared, until 1533, the general admiration for the Classical writers, as appears from his edition of Seneca's *De Clementia*. Then something similar happened to him as had befallen Luther when he was studying Erasmus's works: Calvin realized that by the penetration of the philosophy of the Ancient writers important values in faith threatened to be lost, values in faith which for Calvin, just as much as for Luther and the Catholics, constituted the heart of Christian religion: the strictly transcendental concept of God, the supernatural salvation from sin and death . . ." *op.cit.*, 268. This is surely to misread Calvin. He did not reject humanism but rather the humanists who were not truly Christian.

possible to escape. This band consists almost entirely of men of letters. I would prefer that all human knowledge were exterminated from the world rather than it should be the cause of cooling the enthusiasm of Christians in this way and causing them to turn away from God."[59] Though his judgment upon the literary humanists is harsh, one cannot find in Calvin's thought a radical condemnation of all humanism.[60] If he rejects the postures of grandeur and sufficiency proper to the humanists, he still values the humanists' love of quiet, of learning, of languages, and of primary sources.

The combination of Calvin's humanist training, the high regard he had for its many merits, and his harsh judgment upon the literary humanists has relevance for Calvin's eucharistic doctrine. One of the accusations leveled against him, especially by Westphal, was that he was a rationalist, a judgment to be repeated down the centuries. Whatever one thinks of Calvin's eucharistic doctrine, it cannot be rejected because it is rationalistic. There are arguments which Calvin will hold in common with rationalists, but his stand against the literary humanists shows that his intellectual posture is essentially religious. It is true, his logic can be unmerciful. However, the depth of his religious convictions, the authenticity of his eucharistic piety, and his dogmatic and biblical presuppositions make it clear that Calvin's motivation and thought are essentially religious and biblical. Further, were Calvin inclined to rationalism, he might well have chosen Aristotle over Plato, while in fact he vastly preferred Plato.

PLATONISM: PARTICIPATION AND THE DIALECTIC

Jean Boisset has shown that Plato's influence on Calvin cannot be accounted for simply by recalling the large role Augustine and the fathers play in his theological thinking.[61] There was in addition the rather decided Platonic atmosphere

---

[59] CR 6:600.

[60] Cf. Boisset, op.cit., 321. Cf. also van Gelder, op.cit., 267-273.

[61] This section on Plato's influence is, for the most part, indebted to Boisset, op.cit., 221-314.

of the sixteenth century, and there was a tendency to identify humanism with anti-Aristotelian invective in the first half of the fifteenth century as shown in the work of Laurentio Valla. In 1504 a minority of theologians in the Sorbonne had been won over to the new ideas and methods: Giles of Delft, Josse Chlichtove, Louis Ber, Martial Mazurier. In *Pantagruel*, which Rabelais published in 1533, he speaks of the enthusiasm with which Plato was studied at this time.[62] The Royal College, which Calvin attended in 1531, was not a center of Platonic thought. It was known, however, to be interested in the new orientation and to have set itself against the Aristotelianism of the Sorbonne, a fact which no doubt contributed to the condemnation of the Royal College by the Sorbonne in 1530. Among the other influences, Platonic in character, must be numbered Lefèvre d'Etaples and Guillaume Budé (both of whom were students of Plato as well as Aristotle), Briconnet, Vatable, Gerard Roussel, Guillaume Farel, and Marguerite of Navarre and her court.

Plato's influence on Calvin cannot be limited merely to an atmosphere vaguely Platonic. He was also directly influenced by Plato, and this influence increased as the years passed.[63] Because Calvin's acceptance of Plato was more guarded than was St. Augustine's, Calvin was not under the necessity of repenting of his enthusiasm, as was Augustine. The Calvin who does not hesitate to judge the fathers and councils in the name of Scripture will also not hesitate to judge Plato.

Since Platonism is more a spirit than a system, it was a spirit and, in part, a methodology which Calvin took over. The dialectical quality of Calvin's theology, as we shall see later, was partly due to the Platonic dialectic. Were one to name the Platonic themes found in Calvin, one would mention the following: the prison of the body and the immortality of the soul, the mistrust of the world, the tranquility in

---

[62] Cf. text established and commented on by Jean Plattard, Paris, 1929, 42, 43.

[63] Cf. Boisset, *op.cit.*, 225-227, 294.

the face of death, the two worlds, contemplation, the return to a lost state of purity, the structure of the terrestrial city, eschatology, and, finally, a rather extended series of images and points of view—shadow and light, sun and obscurity, purity and impurity of heart, true and false wisdom, the necessity of interiority, God as appeasing the inquietudes of man. Further, Calvin is sympathetic with Plato's intuitionism and with its personalist overtones of emotion, experience, discovery, and taste. From Plato he borrows a terminology and to some extent a structure, but not doctrine or content. Calvin, to give an example, never openly refers to Plato in order to characterize the way in which man is related to God. Though he will make use of the notion of the two worlds, the notion of analogy and of participation, especially in his ecclesiology and sacramental theology, it is worthy of note that this application of a Platonic idea to revelation is never indicated by Calvin. In a word, Calvin "does not refer to Plato in order to apply Platonism to the Gospel."[64]

Calvin's use of the theme of the two worlds is so extensive that it amounts to a borrowing of a structure. Sensible things, says Plato, are the images of the intelligible reality, and they are what they are through their participation in that intelligible reality. Any authenticity a creature has is due to the reflected image which the creator willed to the creature. "But, Parmenides, the best I can make of the matter is this: that these forms are as it were patterns fixed in the nature of things; the other things are made in their image and likeness; and this participation they come to have in the forms is nothing but their being made in their image."[65] There are unmistakable accents of this teaching in Calvin: "His (God's) essence is incomprehensible; hence, his divineness far escapes all human perception. But upon his individual works he has engraved unmistakable marks of his glory. . . ."[66] Calvin

[64] *ibid.*, 308.

[65] *Parmenides*, 132c. Francis M. Cornford, *Plato and Parmenides*, London, 1950, 93.

[66] *Inst.*, I, 5, 1. Cf. also *ibid.*, 5, 3.

transposes Plato's doctrine of the sensible world as the image of the intelligible into creation as the image of the Creator.

In ecclesiological terms this will mean that the church is essentially spiritual, a reality which exists in the eternal decrees of predestination. God alone has knowledge of his true church because the true church has its foundation in the secret election; the visible church is a church only with respect to men, and it is possible for the church to exist without a visible appearance.[67] The visible church has ultimate reality only insofar as it participates in the church as found in the eternal decrees.

Calvin did work out his ecclesiology in terms of Christ's mystical body. He had said: *Haec est ecclesia catholica, corpus Christi mysticum.*[68] But it must be noted, for instance, that Calvin's point of departure for the doctrine of the mystical body is not the Incarnation but the eternal election and predestination.[69] This would seem to give support to the theory that Calvin's ecclesiology has been influenced by Platonic structures.

Plato's concept of participation is to be seen with even greater clarity in Calvin's doctrine of the sacraments. The sacraments are outward signs of that invisible good will which God has toward us. They give invisible truths to man under a visible sign.[70] The sacrament constitutes and expresses a proportion or an analogy between the "thing" and its sign, and, finally, the sacraments make us participators in Jesus Christ.[71] To the objection that since the sacraments consist of physical things "they cannot suffice or be adequate to seal God's promises, which are spiritual and eternal," Calvin answers: "Indeed, the believer, when he sees the sacraments with his own eyes, does not halt at the physical sight of them, but by those steps (which I have indicated by analogy) rises up in devout contemplation to those lofty mysteries which lie

---

[67] Cf. *ibid.*, IV, 1, 2. Cf. also *ibid.*, 1, 7 and the Prefatory Address to King Francis I.

[68] CR 1:77.   [69] Cf. Ganoczy, *op.cit.*, 420.   [70] Cf. CR 7:14.

[71] Cf. *ibid.*, 9:181. Cf. also *ibid.*, 9:184.

hidden in the sacraments."[72] Plato would recognize in these words the doctrine of a true disciple.

How this Platonic background affects Calvin's formulation of the sacrament of baptism is not a matter of concern here. In his eucharistic doctrine Calvin gives a great deal of attention to the Platonic concept of participation. *Participatio* or its cognate appears four times in the very short *Confessio Fidei de Eucharistia* of 1537, while *communicatio* or its cognate is used five times, and the framework of the *Confession* is that of the two worlds. The Lord's Supper is seen as a sign of communication of and participation in Jesus Christ. It is that corporal, earthly, visible sign of communion with the spiritual, heavenly, intelligible reality. The material signs of bread and wine do not lose their corporal, earthly reality when they exercise their significative function. Even in so holy a function they remain bound to the transitory world. More than that, it is only on condition that they remain bread and wine that they are able to signify the spiritual, heavenly reality. He who would destroy the materiality of the bread in its significative function would destroy the communion and participation of which it is a sign. As shall be seen, this is one of the reasons why Calvin will reject transubstantiation; it denies the permanent substance of bread and, therefore, denies its function of signifying the spiritual reality.

It is, on the other hand, necessary to go beyond the wine and beyond the bread because they are signs and not the reality.[73] He who remains with the sign will never penetrate to the spiritual (intelligible) reality. The Platonic background makes it possible for one to see the unity of Calvin's thought in regard to the church and the sacraments. The ecclesiological and sacramental doctrine of Calvin is basically antithetical. The church is invisible and she is visible; to the degree the earthly, sensible church participates in the eternal and intelligible, she has reality and validity. The Eucharist is the presence of Christ, and the Eucharist is not the presence of Christ; to the degree that the earthly sensible signifies the heavenly intelligible, the sacrament has reality and validity. And given this Platonic background with its union with Christ and its participation in the secret mysteries of God, one is not surprised to find Calvin talking of the "mystery surpassing human search."[74] He urges his readers to seek the reality which cannot be expressed. "I urge my readers not to confine their mental interest within these too narrow limits, but to strive to rise much higher than I can lead them."[75] How reminiscent these passages in Calvin are of that Platonic invitation to contemplation of the divine and the ineffable.

The Scotistic and Occamist philosophies, together with the mystical movement and the *devotio moderna* piety, are important for the general background to Calvin's eucharistic doctrine. They represent a disquietude at the heart of the Christian conscience in the presence of too much ecclesiastical incarnationalism, a doctrine of grace which is, perhaps, too efficient and too precise, namely the habit of grace seen as a thing, an object, and as an inalienable claim to glory to the extent that God becomes man's debtor. They also represent, in the minds of some, a sacramentalism too given to imperialistic claims and to formulations which seem to imprison God ("sacraments contain grace"). They form part of a series of religious movements which, beginning in the twelfth century, seem to be saying "Give us less church and more Christ."[76] They manifest themselves in a flight from secondary causality and, as seen in Thomas Bradwardine, Gregory of Rimini, and William of Occam, in a reassertion of the sovereignty of God as the only cause. They are, in their way, an attempt to give divinity back to God, to restore a measure of transcendence. Also, in their way, they are a move to dis-incarnate a church, a doctrine of grace, and a sacramental system which had, it was thought, come to too

---

[74] *ibid.*, 9:81.   [75] *Inst.*, IV, 17, 7.

[76] Yves Congar, *La tradition et les traditions, essai historique*, Paris, 1960, 183.

comfortable terms with the world and with Aristotelian realism.

In view of this dis-incarnational concern it was possibly due to the deep eucharistic piety of *devotio moderna* that Calvin retained as much eucharistic realism as he did. One of the four books in the *Imitation of Christ* is devoted to eucharistic piety and this would help explain the importance of the Eucharist for Calvin's piety.

The move away from the objective, which is represented each in its way by nominalism, mysticism, and *devotio moderna*, is important for the framework within which Calvin worked out his theology. If this movement must be seen as a turning away from what can be called a raging objectivism, it must not be used to dismiss either Calvin or the reformation as mere subjectivism. This would be the cheapest burlesque of what Calvin and the reformers stood for. Rather it is an effort to restore personalism to its proper role and to issue a call to inwardness and interiority.

Calvin's attitude toward humanism and Platonism is also representative of a turning toward inwardness and a rejection of what appeared to be, and sometimes was, Aristotelian rationalism. The Christian philosophy of the humanist failed to move Calvin because it was not sufficiently Christian, because it was too comfortable, too proud, and too individualistic. Calvin shows himself a humanist of some distinction who cannot abide the rationalism of even a baptized philosophy. The Platonic dialectic he will use to break up the Aristotelian structures and to reinforce the dialectic in revelation. As a Platonist he will pursue interiority and will direct with almost implacable zeal all to the eternal intelligible reality. In terms of participation and the dialectic, he will render the church and the sacraments less incarnational, concerned less with the earthly image and more with the heavenly reality. The ecclesiological and sacramental implications of Aristotelian causality will be replaced with a dialectic which is not without its realism. Calvin's realism is, however, tied less firmly to incarnational forms, structures, and elements. It is a realism which rests upon image, participation, and the *opposita*. And, most importantly, causality has been restored to God. Neither the church nor the sacraments are causes of grace in the traditional sense. The flight from secondary causality is seen as a return to transcendence.

These are some, although by no means all, of the influences which helped form Calvin's general theological background. Nothing, for example, has been said of Calvin's hermeneutics nor of the pre-reformation hermeneutical tradition. Care must be taken not to attribute both the form and content of Calvin's doctrine to a kind of unconscious theological determinism while neglecting his conscious biblical motivations. In other words, Calvin is essentially a biblical theologian and this should never be forgotten.

II. The Imperatives of the Ascension in Earthly Image and Heavenly Reality

The Creation of a Spiritualist-Realist Vocabulary

AUGUSTINE: PERSONALISM AND OBJECTIVISM AS TENTATIVE ANSWERS TO THE ASCENSION

AFTER THE WORKS of Beckmann and Smits there can hardly be any doubt as to the extent of St. Augustine's influence on Calvin.[1] No father is quoted so frequently in the sections of the *Institutes* treating of the sacraments as is Augustine. Though he did show a preference for Chrysostom's more literal exegesis over Augustine's more allegorical exegesis, he considered St. Augustine the greatest dogmatician of the ancient church.[2] Wendel has found 341 citations of Augustine in the last edition of the *Institutes*; in his commentaries on the New Testament Goumaz has found 85; the acts of the *Congrès national augustinien* mention 1,400 in the entire writings of Calvin while Roux thinks that the number of citations in all of Calvin is at least 3,000.[3] Calvin's defense of his own doctrine against Westphal, the Romans, and the Zwinglians was conceived as a defense of Augustine. Never for a moment did he think that his own doctrine was anything else but the doctrine of Augustine. Whether Calvin did, in fact, interpret Augustine correctly is a matter of secondary concern here.

Smits has shown the extent of Calvin's eucharistic borrowings from Augustine in the various editions of the *Institutes*.[4] Calvin's dominant theological concern as he wrote

[1] Cf. Joachim Beckmann, *Vom Sakrament bei Calvin*, Tübingen, 1926; Luchesius Smits, *Saint Augustin dans l'oeuvre de Jean Calvin*, Assen (Holland), 2 vols., 1957.

[2] Cf. CR 4:215; *ibid.*, 9:834-837.

[3] Jean Boisset has collected these figures. Cf. *Sagesse et sainteté dans la pensée de Jean Calvin*, Paris, 1959, 221, 222.

[4] Cf. *op.cit.*, 30-36, 43-47, 59-64, 82-84, 104-110.

the first edition of the *Institutes* was sacramental doctrine. And here his borrowings from Augustine are extensive. He borrows Augustine's definition of a sacrament as a *verbum visibile*, his teaching on sacramental efficacy, and the unity of the two testaments. Calvin identifies the Anabaptists with the Donatists of Augustine's time and uses Augustine's arguments against them in the question of baptism. He repeats Augustine's teaching on Christ's physical body having its *locus* in heaven. For both of them the fruit of the Eucharist is above all mutual charity. Calvin quotes a letter of Augustine in favor of receiving communion under both species. Allusions are made to Augustine when Calvin explains why the Roman teaching on the mass as a sacrifice is unacceptable. All in all Augustine is quoted 39 times in the section on the sacraments in this first edition of the *Institutes*.

In the 1539 edition Calvin adds only four new references to Augustine, but in the 1543 edition Calvin re-examines Augustine's doctrine with regard to the reception of the sacrament by the unworthy, the differences between the sacraments of the two testaments, the frequency of the celebration of the Eucharist, the use of the term "sacrifice," and, finally, the Roman theory that there are seven sacraments. Citing Augustine, Calvin insists that the church has always clearly distinguished between the visible sign of the Supper and its signification. Another noteworthy addition is that of Augustine's words "Men cannot be welded together in any name of religion, whether true or false, unless they are bound in some partnership of signs or visible sacraments."[5]

Smits calls the 1559 edition, "*Institutes* of the Supper and predestination."[6] Into this last edition Calvin worked the arguments he had developed against Joachim Westphal. Three previous times Calvin had answered the attacks of Westphal with small eucharistic tracts. In response to yet another attack, based on a *florilegium* of texts from Augustine, Calvin wrote a fourth tract which he, obviously in some desperation, en-

[5] PL 42:355.   [6] Smits, *op.cit.*, 109.

titled *Ultima Admonitio* . . . This tract is a little commentary on Augustine's eucharistic doctrine as interpreted by Calvin. It contains, according to Smits, 336 points of contact with Augustine's doctrine, with 62 of the references given by Calvin himself.[7] His special concern is to give a more symbolic interpretation to the words of institution than Westphal and to assert that the unworthy do not receive the body of Christ. Finally, a point of supreme importance for Calvin, the body of Christ is absent from the earth since Christ has ascended into heaven. All of these are buttressed with references to Augustine.

Calvin believes himself supported by the authority of Augustine on three aspects of general sacramental doctrine: the constitutive importance of Word and faith for the sacrament, the peculiar relationship of the reality and sign in their unity and distinction, and, finally, the sacramental way of speaking, namely, metonymy or the use of the name of one thing for that of another associated with or suggested by it.[8]

Both have similar Christological presuppositions and concerns, namely to reject any monophysitic tendency,[9] though, strictly speaking, Augustine's rejection of the ubiquity of Christ is not specifically eucharistic, as it is with Calvin, but more properly Christological.[10] Proceeding from this common ground, Calvin draws conclusions which he feels are in complete agreement with Augustine's position: there is no local presence, no substantial presence, and no carnal presence. Though Augustine holds that there is only a corporal presence of Christ at the right hand of the Father, he concedes that it is possible for the Son of man to be at the same time both in heaven and on earth. He also holds, despite his rejection of monophysitism, that during his earthly life Christ was also

---

[7] Cf. *ibid.*, 90.

[8] Cf. CR 1:103; *Inst.*, IV, 17, 1; CR 9:155. Cf. also Beckmann, *op.cit.*, 8.

[9] Cf. Beckmann, *op.cit.*, 115.

[10] Cf. Karl Adam, *Die Eucharistielehre des hl. Augustin*, Paderborn, 1908, 103, 115, 120.

in heaven, not just as the Son of God, but also as the Son of man.[11] Christ's presence is effected through the power of the Spirit.

The church, in Augustine's thought, is itself eucharistic insofar as the community has life and union with Christ by means of the Eucharist. This is not the church in its external, empirical form, but rather that mystical reality, the church of the predestined. Calvin defines the church in predestinarian terms and from this definition he proceeds to erect his sacramental presuppositions: election and faith. When it comes to Calvin's doctrine of the continual eating of faith of which the eucharistic eating is a given moment, he invokes Augustine.[12] Together with Augustine, Calvin can say that the eating is nothing else than faith, but he avoids the Zwinglian position by insisting that faith does not displace the eating. When there is a real eating it is none other than an eating of faith.

Both Augustine and St. Leo the Great held that the corporal presence, that is a sensible, local presence here on earth, came to an end with the Ascension. As shall be seen, the Ascension was to play a large role in the eucharistic doctrine of the whole succeeding Augustinian tradition.[13] From the very first the Ascension was a major factor in Calvin's doctrine of the Lord's Supper. In the 1536 edition Calvin already uses the word *ascensio* or its cognates nine times in the section devoted to the Eucharist. This is even more explicit in the *Last Admonition* of 1557. In keeping with this tradition, Calvin develops his doctrine of *sursum corda*, that is, to seek Christ at the right hand of the Father not in the earthly elements. The Ascension, in fact, is one of the decisive factors in the development of Calvin's doctrine that the presence is noncorporal but real.

[11] Cf. PL 44:144; *ibid.*, 38:1341; *ibid.*, 35:1617.

[12] Cf. CR 9:163.

[13] Cf. Henri de Lubac, *Corpus Mysticum, l'eucharistie et l'église au moyen âge*, Paris, 1949, 177. Cf. PL 35:1617, 1763; *ibid.*, 38:1246, 1247.

Because Augustine had written against the ubiquity doctrine of the Monophysites and the exaggerated physical conceptions of the presence of Christ common among the Manicheans, he would be careful to avoid any bold eucharistic realism.[14] He opposes the symbolic to a too material way of conceiving the sacrament. He uses expressions indicating that Christ is not always present in the Eucharist. Christ is present in one of three ways: *praesentia pulchritudinis et divinitatis* by which he is always with the Father; *praesentia corporis* by which he is at the right hand of the Father; *praesentia vero fidei* by which he is in all Christians.[15] "He betrays no knowledge of a fourth sacramental presence."[16] Therefore it would be very difficult to assert that Augustine held anything like the scholastic doctrine of transubstantiation; rather the supposition is that the consecrated bread retains its nature as bread. For these reasons Calvin will invoke the authority of Augustine for the strict localization of the body of Christ in heaven, and the rejection of a direct relation of the symbol to the flesh and blood of Christ. This will make it easier for Calvin to reject the doctrine of Westphal that unworthy men receive the true body of Christ. Augustine is called to witness that the body of Christ infallibly sanctifies.[17] Since the unworthy are the unbelieving, says Calvin, and these cannot be sanctified, what they in fact receive are the naked elements. Here too Augustine's whole dimension of election and faith is turned against Westphal.[18] In one eucharistic area Calvin takes issue with Augustine; he rejects the practice of giving the Lord's Supper to infants. Calvin corrects Cyprian and Augustine by appealing to Paul.[19]

The question can be asked: Did Calvin notice a shift in Augustine's eucharistic teaching after he entered the lists against the Pelagians? A new objectivism then appears to-

---

[14] Adam, *op.cit.*, 119. Cf. also PL 33:835; *ibid.*, 42:211, 369.

[15] PL 35:1763.   [16] Adam, *op.cit.*, 118.   [17] Cf. CR 9:165, 166.

[18] In the matter of the unworthy receiving the body of Christ, Calvin seems to have read Augustine wrong. Cf. Josef Rupert Geiselmann, *Die Eucharistielehre der Vorscholastik*, Paderborn, 1926, 37.

[19] Cf. *Inst.*, IV, 16, 30.

44

gether with the disappearance of the former accent upon the personal element.[20] No one can attain salvation outside of baptism and the participation in the table of the Lord.[21] There is no life in God outside or apart from the Eucharist.[22] The norm for the last judgment of baptized infants is the reception of the Eucharist, and this without consideration of any personal faith, be it that of the child or of the godfather.[23] "The personal factor is completely excluded."[24] Augustine's earlier tendency to avoid any identification of the material, visible appearance of Christ, that is the historical Christ, with the Eucharist now gives way to a fuller appreciation of the flesh as the source of life, and, consequently, to a fuller appreciation of the true presence of Christ in the sacrament. The strong symbolic character of the Eucharist disappears; the way is prepared for the identification of the historical Christ with the eucharistic Christ, and ultimately, for transubstantiation. Augustine in his anti-Pelagian period approaches the teachings of Ambrose and Gregory of Nyssa. Typically Augustine does not draw the final consequences of his position. It was not his way to work out a complete theology on topics not at the moment under debate. Besides being incomplete there is a pervasive lack of clarity, a fact noted also by Protestant authors.[25] It is not at all clear, for instance, why, even after the shift to a more objective doctrine, he would speak of a general presence of Christ which is the same in faith, baptism, and the Eucharist.[26] Calvin would take this lead and spell it out in his doctrine: there is no specific eucharistic gift, no objective bond between sign and signified.

It should be noted that the historical situations in which Calvin and Augustine wrote were very different. For Calvin, the problem of the Lord's Supper was one of the two great theological disputes of his life, the other being that of predestination. However reluctantly, Calvin was forced to treat

[20] Cf. Geiselmann, *op.cit.*, 37.   [21] Cf. PL 44:128.
[22] Cf. *ibid.*, 38:944.   [23] Cf. *ibid.*, 33:984.   [24] Adam, *op.cit.*, 159.
[25] Cf. Hermann Sasse, *This Is My Body*, Minneapolis, 1959, 30.
[26] Cf. PL 35:1763.

at length the doctrine of the presence of Christ. For Augustine this was never a theological problem in the sense of a great dispute. The problem simply did not arise because never denied.[27] For this reason great care should be taken before transferring the state of the question in the fourth and fifth centuries, with its tentative, incomplete answers, to the state of the question in the sixteenth century.

ISIDORE OF SEVILLE: PNEUMATOLOGY AND THE MEDIATION OF AUGUSTINIANISM

Isidore of Seville (c.560-636), who stands in the Augustinian tradition, casts his doctrine in a dialectical form. Isidore will be important as the link with the whole subsequent eucharistic tradition. His Augustinian definition of a sacrament will be taken up almost word for word by Rabanus Maurus, Ratramnus, and Paschasius Radbertus, the last name accommodating it to his own realistic understanding of the sacrament. Though Isidore represents a eucharistic metabolic realism, this realism is expressed in spiritualistic, dynamic categories. He understands the Eucharist as the presence of the body and blood of Christ through the transformation of the elements. Just as through the consecration of the waters of baptism the elements (water) become the objective carriers of sacramental grace, so through the consecration of the bread and wine the sacramental elements become carriers of the body and blood of Christ. The elements become sacrament through the consecration.[28] There is a change in the elements here, but not in the metaphysical sense understood by the later scholastics. The metaphysical problem was posed first by the writings of Berengarius.[29] Following Augustine the presence of the real body of Christ is ascribed to the power of the Holy Spirit.[30] In fact, the role of the Holy Spirit is two-

[27] Cf. Beckmann, *op.cit.*, 120; Adam, *op.cit.*, 111.

[28] Cf. Geiselmann, *Die Abendmahlslehre an der Wende der christlichen Spätantike zum Frühmittelalter*, Munich, 1933, 242, 250.

[29] Cf. Hans Jorissen, *Die Entfaltung der Transsubstantiationslehre bis zum Beginn der Hochscholastik*, Münster, 1965, 4.

[30] Cf. PL 82:255.

fold: to make the body of Christ present, and to bind himself, that is the Holy Spirit, to the body of Christ in order to mediate the power of the sacrament to those who receive it. Isidore had received from the Greek theologians the teaching on the role of the Holy Spirit as effecting the presence of the real body of Christ. Through Isidore the concept made its way into the stream of medieval eucharistic doctrine, remaining vital until the middle of the eleventh century. It was assured a certain permanence by being taken over into the eucharistic theology of Peter Lombard (c. 1100-1160).[31] Humbert of Silva Candida (d. 1061) brought in a strong Christological element, explaining the sacramental body from the standpoint of the hypostatic union. For him the sacramental body is alone and exclusively the body joined in hypostatic union with the Logos, and is therefore simply the body of Christ. Instead of speaking of the body of Christ being present by means of the Holy Spirit, Humbert ascribed it to the whole Trinity. This approach will modify the strong pneumatological explanation and will prepare for that double Christological-pneumatological framework in which Calvin will set his eucharistic doctrine.

PASCHASIUS RADBERTUS: THE MARRIAGE OF THE SPIRITUALIST AND METABOLIC TRADITIONS

Paschasius Radbertus (c. 785-c. 860) stands in the Augustinian tradition yet represents a strong sacramental realism. He represents a marriage of Augustine's theology of the Eucharist with the eucharistic practice of the church which was dominated by the eucharistic thinking of Ambrose.[32] He asserts that the earthly elements are transformed so that the Eucharist is the sacramental body of him who was born of the Virgin, was crucified, died, and was raised from the dead. Here then is an undoubted identification between the historical Christ and the sacramental Christ. ". . . and since he willed

[31] Cf. Geiselmann, *Abendmahlslehre*, 236, 250.
[32] Cf. Bernard Lohse, *Epochen der Dogmengeschichte*, Stuttgart, 1963, 143.

to remain, though under the figure of bread and wine, we must believe that after the consecration these are nothing else at all but the flesh and blood of Christ. . . . And, that I may speak more marvelously, (this flesh) is in no way at all distinct [*non alia plane*] from that which was born of Mary and suffered on the cross and rose from the tomb. . ."[33]

He retains the Platonic dialectics of *figura* and *veritas*, and is much influenced by the doctrine of the Ascension: the body of Christ remains in heaven. What is received is something that is not locally circumscribed, yet the reality received is more than the power or *virtus carnis*; it is the very body and blood. In Radbertus, as in Calvin, the concepts of *spirituale* and *vere* are not mutually exclusive. "But if we truly study the question, it [the Eucharist] is rightly called both figure and truth: that which is perceived externally is figure or image of the truth; the truth itself is all that is rightly understood or believed of this mystery. . . . And in this way, as a result, [the Eucharist], is revealed as nothing else but the truth and sacrament of his flesh."[34] This realism is not to be confused with a crass Capernaitic conception of the body, a conception he expressly attacks. However bold his realism, it is not conceived in metaphysical terms.[35] Nor is it the doctrine of transubstantiation. Radbertus' philosophical tools are too primitive for such sophistication, but all the elements present in transubstantiation are to be found in Radbertus. For his realism Radbertus is indebted to Isidore, mediated through the writings of the Venerable Bede. Also following Isidore, Radbertus speaks of a divine power which effects both the real presence and the sanctification of the believer who receives the bread.[36] However much Paschasius Radbertus represents sacramental realism, he maintains that the Eucharist is not food for the unworthy. *Non nisi electorum est.*[37] The true believers receive the flesh of Christ spiritually and the un-

---

[33] PL 120:1269.   [34] *ibid.*, 120:1278f.

[35] Cf. Geiselmann, *Eucharistielehre*, 168. Cf. also Geiselmann, *Abendmahlslehre*, 231.

[36] Cf. PL 120:1275.   [37] *ibid.*, 120:1336.

worthy receive only a morsel of bread. Though one finds here an uncompromising realism together with a spiritualist vocabulary, there is a reluctance to grant that aggressive objectivism which insists that both believer and unbeliever receive the body of Christ. Worthy of note is Radbertus' voluntarist emphasis in the first chapter of his treatise on the Eucharist on the all-powerful will of God as the ground of all natural events and God's arbitrary will as the ultimate cause. "By the will of God the nature of all things is constituted."[38] Because the will of God is the cause of all things, including all existing natures, there is no event which is against nature.[39] And the problem of the one body given to many on many occasions is solved in terms of the will of God. Using this point of departure, a eucharistic realism is not too difficult. One need not fear eucharistic problems raised by a realistic conception if the will of God is there to solve them all. Radbertus' methodology is the very antithesis of the later Aristotelian dialectic.

RABANUS MAURUS: THE EUCHARISTIC CHRIST IS NOT THE HISTORICAL CHRIST

Like Paschasius Radbertus, Rabanus Maurus (776 or 784-856) is dependent on the eucharistic teaching of Isidore of Seville. Almost word for word he takes over Isidore's definition of a sacrament and his ideas on how the eucharist is brought about. Yet under the influence of the Augustinian distinction between *sacramentum* and *virtus sacramenti* (which is the *res sacramenti*), Rabanus stressed the dynamic, spiritualistic side of the Eucharist. For instance he rejects Radbertus' contention that the flesh of Christ in the Eucharist is identical with that of the historical Christ. Though the doctrine of transformation of the elements is not rejected entirely, this transformation is interpreted more in a sacramental manner that is noncorporal, mystical. One does not find Isidore's dynamic and spiritualistic teaching balanced with an

[38] *ibid.*, 120:1267.
[39] Cf. Geiselmann, *Eucharistielehre*, 169.

outspoken realism. He did take from Isidore the teaching on the elements being sanctified by the Holy Spirit.[40] This teaching Rabanus combines with the mystical body doctrine of St. Paul as developed by Augustine. Here also is to be found a more Christological explanation of the sanctifying power of the Eucharist. Through the visible bread and wine an invisible effect is attained. The invisible effect in man is brought about not by the body of Christ but by the divine Logos. The effect itself, according to Rabanus, is the incorporation of the recipient into the mystical body of Christ. Such an ecclesiological accent when seen together with Isidore's concept of the church gives one a clue to the dynamic, spiritualistic tendencies of the eucharistic teaching of the early Middle Ages. Isidore shares the old patristic idea of the ecclesiological nature of a sacrament. The concept of the sacrament is to be found in the nature of the church, in which the Holy Spirit works. The individual sacraments are only the work of the Holy Spirit concretizing the nature of the church.[41] A broad ecclesiological concept of the structure of the Eucharist as seen in Rabanus Maurus and Isidore would encourage a more dynamic, spiritualistic sacramental theology.

RATRAMNUS: THE PLATONIC DIALECTIC BETWEEN THE REAL PRESENCE AND THE HISTORICAL CHRIST

The continuity of the eucharistic tradition is assured through Isidore and Augustine's influence upon Ratramnus (d. 868). So high is the esteem in which Ratramnus holds Isidore that he is quite simply the *doctor catholicus*.[42] Ratramnus borrows Isidore's Augustinian definition of a sacrament and further builds his sacramental structure on categories taken from Augustine, principally the concept of *similitudo*. Ratramnus sets himself over against the metabolism of Radbertus' Ambrosian tradition. Geiselmann holds that in this antimetabolic sense he denies that the Eucharist is *veritas*.[43]

---

[40] Cf. PL 105:240.   [41] Cf. Geiselmann, *Abendmahlslehre*, 245, 246.
[42] PL 121:145.
[43] Cf. *Eucharistielehre*, 217. Cf. also PL 121:130.

Veritas is here that which is literally true rather than what is mediated by a sign. He therefore sets aside the physical-real change in the elements and represents a virtualist position. Historically he represents the point at which the ametabolic conceptions of the Augustinian tradition becomes antimetabolic, and in this way prepares the road for Berengarius, who will carry the antimetabolic critique further with the help of the Aristotelian terminology of substance and accidents.[44]

This is the position of Geiselmann to which J. H. Fahey and C. Gliozzo take exception, defending the orthodoxy of Ratramnus in regard to eucharistic realism and eucharistic consecration.[45] Fahey's contribution to the discussion, and it is a substantial one, is the elucidation of the Platonic philosophical presuppositions to Ratramnus' teaching. In his chapter "The Philosophical Origin of Ratramnus' Doctrine," he shows that in Augustine the concept of *sacramentum* already stood for the earthly form while the *res* corresponded to the Platonic intelligible idea or reality.[46] Ratramnus presupposes the Platonic concept of participation, namely that sensible things are the image of the intelligible reality and they are what they are through their participation in that intelligible reality. Using this framework, Ratramnus presents Christ as present in the Eucharist according to the Platonic mode of an idea. In this way he can hold both the real presence and still deny the identity of the eucharistic body of Christ with the historical body of Christ. As is immediately evident Ratramnus' doctrine and framework are very similar to that of Calvin.

Here too one finds the Christological accent; it is the Word

[44] Cf. Geiselmann, *Eucharistielehre*, 217.

[45] Cf. J. H. Fahey, *The Eucharistic Teaching of Ratramn of Corbie*, Mundelein, 1951; C. Gliozzo, *La dottrina della conversione eucaristica in Pascasio Radberto e Ratramno Monaci di Corbia*, Messina, 1945. Geiselmann has a summary of the controversy over Ratramnus' teaching up to 1926. Cf. *Eucharistielehre*, 176-181. The further history up to 1964 can be found in Jorissen, *op.cit.*, 4, 5.

[46] Cf. Fahey, *op.cit.*, 130-162.

of God who effects the sanctifying action of the Eucharist. In Ratramnus one finds Isidore's doctrine of the Holy Spirit and also the broad ecclesiological context. The Eucharist is not the historical body of Christ, but rather the mystery of the body and, it should be noted, the mystery of the church. In Ratramnus one finds a good example of the concomitant use of both a spiritualist and a realist vocabulary. Though he will insist that body be understood *spiritualiter* yet one finds in him the realistic liturgical formulas in which are to be found such realistic expressions as *converti, commutari, confici*.[47] However, the elements are not changed: "How can this be called the body of Christ which, it is known, does not change?"[48] The elements remain bread and wine though they image the body and blood, and thus they are present. "What appears exteriorly is not the reality but the image of the reality; what the mind grasps and understands is the truth of the thing."[49] Thus the consecrated elements offer something to our faith, that which cannot be seen, the heavenly intelligible reality. "Faith does not receive what the eye sees but what it believes, because this is a spiritual food and a spiritual drink, spiritually feeding the soul and giving the life of eternal satiety."[50] The food that is offered, then, is the food of faith, and he who does not have faith cannot receive it. This is not to be interpreted to mean that the presence is merely a subjective or a figurative presence, a fact even Harnack notes.[51] What he is intent upon is to assert the absolute necessity of faith. If there are realities which only the senses can apprehend, there are also realities which only faith can grasp; he who has no faith would not recognize the faith reality and therefore he cannot receive it.[52]

With justification, Emile Doumergue notes the similarity between Calvin's doctrine and that of Ratramnus.[53] Here is

[47] PL 121:131, 139, 140, 147.

[48] *ibid.*, 121:152.   [49] *ibid.*, 121:160.   [50] *ibid.*, 121:170.

[51] Cf. Adolph Harnack, *History of Dogma*, London, 1898, vol. 4, 320.

[52] Cf. PL 121:132, 147.

[53] Cf. *Jean Calvin*, vol. 5, *La Pensée ecclésiastique et la pensée politique de Calvin*, Lausanne, 1917, 364-367.

a Calvinist before Calvin. Though there is no direct evidence that Ratramnus influenced Calvin, it is quite possible that Calvin had read Ratramnus. For centuries the work of Ratramnus was lost only to be rediscovered in 1526 by Hiobus Gast, a Lutheran opponent of John Oecolampadius. The reformation party at once saw its importance and it was printed and reprinted: in 1532 at Cologne, and in 1541, 1557, and 1608 at Geneva. In 1550 it was translated into French and published at Basel, and Ridley translated it into English in 1549.

Not to be lost sight of at this period, that is, up to the time of Berengarius, is the lack of any ecclesiastical censures or condemnations. The church was in peaceful possession of its eucharistic faith and was quite content to let the theologians discuss. Though the theologians inclined either to the objective-realist or to the subjective-symbolist school, they did, in fact, employ a common vocabulary. In this vocabulary were both strong realistic expressions and strong symbolic expressions. This problem will be treated at length in Chapter VIII.

BERENGARIUS: THE GRAMMARIAN INTRODUCES METAPHYSICS

The situation changed radically when Berengarius (c. 999-1088) came on the scene. He seems to have been much offended by the realism of Paschasius Radbertus whom he understood to teach that the individual hosts after the consecration became pieces of Christ's bloody body. To the argument that he was a rationalist, bent on denying the mystery of the Eucharist, he replied that it was his opponents who effectively excluded all mystery by asserting that all takes place *sensualiter*. Berengarius and the whole medieval (and, in part, the reformation) tradition can trace their eucharistic problem chiefly to Augustine's theology of the Ascension.[54] If the body of Christ has ascended, gone from his earthly place to a heavenly place, this must be taken into account in any eucharistic elaboration, and for the philosophical realist it is

[54] Cf. de Lubac, *op.cit.*, 164.

not a difficulty to be lightly dismissed. Given the fact of the Ascension and the weight of Augustine's elaboration upon it, how, wondered Berengarius, could one assert that there was a change in the elements so that the body of Christ was present on the altar? That bread could be body and that the body of Christ could be in some manner "doubled" so that it was present in heaven and on earth was, in his mind, contrary to reason. Berengarius denied the possibility of material change in the elements and, also for eschatological reasons, denied that the body of Christ could be brought down from heaven upon the altar in a carnal way. That would be to anticipate the *eschata*, a manner of reasoning to be met also in Calvin. To wage his war Berengarius introduced for the first time the concepts of *materia, forma, subjectum* and *id, quod in subjecto est (accidens)*. These concepts however do not yet have the meaning they will have in the later scholastics. However, the problem of change in the elements is now posed in metaphysical terms for the first time.[55]

Berengarius' doctrine is not at all clear but he seems to have based his position on his belief in universal ideas. The body of Christ which exists only in heaven is effective for humanity through its sacramental image or type. The presence of Christ is not precisely virtual nor figurative, though Berengarius uses expressions which sometimes give this impression, but rather Christ is present ideally. For Berengarius, furthermore, the Eucharist is a faith reality and only the believer can receive it. After the consecration, the bread and wine become the body and blood to faith and true understanding.

Ecclesiastical history, which seldom judges heretics overgenerously, does not deal lightly with Berengarius and has made him out to be the dark angel of the eucharistic tradition. Hounded, cited, summoned, forced to sign an extremely dubious if not erroneous declaration of faith in the Eucharist, he should not be accused beyond his guilt. Not even his most competent and least generous opponent, Guit-

[55] Cf. Jorissen, *op.cit.*, 6, 7.

mond of Aversa, thought that he was a pure symbolist.[56] On the other hand, he did not teach either the doctrine of Ratramnus, nor of the fathers. He was an Augustinian who used the common theological vocabulary, even that used by his adversaries, but his larger framework was different. He approached theological language somewhat in the manner of a linguistic analyst and was, in fact, "a fanatical speculative grammarian, anxious to push the conclusions of his subject as far as possible and to apply them to the clarifying of dogma."[57] No man should judge his intentions—and here let a Lanfranc beware. However, judging from his theology, and more specifically from his theological formulations, he appears to be more the logician than the theologian. He believed, for instance, that Plato and the other philosophers were able to know that there is a Trinity and he himself attempted to prove the doctrine of the Trinity by reason. This trust of reason goes beyond anything Calvin would attribute to it, though Calvin too invokes reason in his polemic against both the Lutherans and the Romans.

JOHN WYCLIF: CHRISTOLOGICAL REALISM OPPOSED TO EUCHARISTIC REALISM

Much against his own will John Wyclif (c. 1329-1384) has been associated with Berengarius. They do have points of contact, but in actual fact Wyclif considered Berengarius a heretic.[58] Wyclif often cites Guitmond of Aversa, Berengarius' dedicated opponent, to show his own orthodoxy by the extent of his agreement with Guitmond. Berengarius' methodology does differ considerably from Wyclif's, the former being a nominalist before nominalism and the latter being a rather violent opponent of nominalism, having attacked both Duns Scotus and William of Occam.[59] Less the grammarian and

[56] Cf. de Lubac, *op.cit.*, 164. Cf. also PL 149:1430; *ibid.*, 150:237; Geiselmann, *Eucharistielehre*, 344.

[57] R. W. Southern, *The Making of the Middle Ages*, New Haven, 1953, 198.

[58] Cf. Herbert B. Workman, *John Wyclif*, Oxford, 1926, vol. 2, 37, 1n.

[59] Cf. *ibid.*, 37.

more the philosopher, his attack upon transubstantiation is philosophically inspired. Later reformers would take abuses as their point of departure, but Wyclif's objections are essentially metaphysical. What disturbs Wyclif are the prevailing theories based on the annihilation of the bread, a position which the more cautious Thomas Aquinas had rejected.[60] The theory of annihilation offends the realist in Wyclif because it postulates phantoms and unrealities. In one of his later sermons he complains: "For many years I sought to learn of the friars what the real essence of the consecrated host might be. They at length had the boldness to maintain that the host is nothing," or as he formulates the problem elsewhere, "a bundle of accidents in which Christ is."[61] Anticipating Calvin, Wyclif denounces such a view because it reduces Christ in the sacrament to a phantom. What disturbs Wyclif is not the mystery, but this particular explanation of the mystery; whatever his attempt is, it is not an attempt to do away with mystery. Wyclif, too, is an Augustinian, and for him too Augustine's emphasis upon the Ascension and the *locus* of Christ's body in heaven raises real problems. Briefly, it is the problematic of a Christological realism being opposed to a sacramental realism, a dilemma to be found also in Calvin.

Wyclif's problem is not the primary fact, real presence, but the secondary explanation, transubstantiation. Not even when he is asserting that Christ is present in the Eucharist as a king is present in every part of his kingdom does he intend to deny real presence. He will go a good deal further and affirm that his position was that of the confession Berengarius signed in 1059.[62] He would have been content to say that Christ is present sacramentally and hoped that he would not be pushed to be more precise. When pushed he will say that

[60] Cf. *Summa Theologica*, III, 75, 3.

[61] Cited from Workman, *op.cit.*, 33.

[62] John Wyclif, *On the Eucharist*, in *The Library of Christian Classics*, vol. 14, *Advocates of Reform*, ed. Matthew Spinka, Philadelphia, 1953, 67, 68. Cf. also *ibid.*, 29.

the presence is figurative, although not simply a figure, but that it has a special efficacy and reality of its own. No unbeliever can receive the effectual sign, a view he reads into all of the fathers, including John of Damascus. In the course of controversy he moved from position to position, ending up with a kind of consubstantiation. His arguments here are Christological: the Eucharist is a renewal of the miracle of the Incarnation with its two substances in one person.

Wyclif is concerned with what to him appears to be eucharistic materialism. He anticipates the horror Calvin had of worshiping earthly elements. Since the consecrated host is "not the Lord's body, but an efficacious sign thereof," to bow down in worship before it or to parade with it in procession would be idolatry.[63] He is disturbed by the contention that "a hog, a dog, or a mouse can eat our Lord."[64] With Calvin he shares a distrust of an uncompromising objectivism. Though he has not a systematized or consistent eucharistic system, he is, like Calvin, more taken up with the spiritual meaning than the physical facts. While not denying all sacramental objectivism, he looks to the interior, to spiritual acceptance of Christ, to union with Christ, to find the meaning of the Eucharist. He shows a reformation reluctance to put God at man's disposal. "Nothing can be more awful than that any priest can daily make or consecrate the body of the Lord. . . . For our God is not a God newly made."[65] He repeatedly warns that the bread after consecration remains bread and "is not really the body of Christ but the efficacious sign thereof," and makes a point of not mistaking the sign for the thing signified.[66] His view of the Eucharist is much less clerical, though he himself was a priest; he believes that under certain circumstances the Eucharist might be consecrated even by a layman.

One important question of concern to both Calvin and Luther, not yet posed by the early medieval theologians, is communion under both species for the layman. This became known as a Hussite doctrine even though it had been first formally defended by Jacob of Mies at the University of

---

[63] *ibid.*, 64.   [64] *ibid.*, 61.   [65] *ibid.*, 65.   [66] *ibid.*, 70.

Prague in 1414, a year before Huss' death. John Huss (c. 1369-1415) had been attracted to the writings of Wyclif—his political doctrine and his ecclesiology, especially its predestinarian framework. Huss translated Wyclif's *Trialogus* and was known as a propagator of Wyclif's ideas. It was not surprising that the demand for the chalice should be taken up by his followers even though Huss himself never pressed the issue. Communion in both kinds was conceded to the laity by the Prague Compacts of 1433, an action of which Rome later repented and Pius II formally canceled the "privilege" in 1462. However, the laity were not so easily to be deprived of their due and the practice was maintained until the Bohemian Diet of 1567.

This sketch of Augustine's eucharistic doctrine and that of the early medieval theologians is not meant to be exhaustive. Its purpose is to show a large measure of dependence on Augustinian doctrine, and, in reference to the early medieval theologians, to show that almost all of Calvin's eucharistic concerns were part of the earlier eucharistic tradition. Calvin's doctrine as found in these early writers is, in brief:

Augustine: definition of a sacrament; constitutive importance of Word and faith for the sacrament; unity and distinction of sign and signified; the sacramental way of speaking (metonymy); unity of the two testaments; role of Ascension; communion under both species; no specific eucharistic gift; communion of believers only; role of the Holy Spirit; election and faith as sacramental presuppositions; and the general dialectical character taken over in part from Augustine's neo-Platonic background.

Isidore of Seville: eucharistic realism expressed in spiritualistic dynamic categories; role of the Holy Spirit; and the ecclesiological context of the sacrament.

Humbert of Silva Candida: the introduction of a strong Christological point of departure for eucharistic theologizing, which modifies the pneumatological explanation, thus establishing two related frameworks.

Paschasius Radbertus: the two vocabularies; the voluntarist accent on the will of God; only the elect receive the body of Christ; and no aggressive objectivism but still objectivism.

Rabanus Maurus: rejection of strict identity between the historical and the sacramental Christ.

Ratramnus: the Platonic presuppositions of the sacramental structure; the earthly element as a sign or image of the heavenly intelligible reality; the combination of the presence of the body of Christ and the denial of the identity between the eucharistic body and the historical body; and a realistic terminology combined with a spiritualistic tendency.

Berengarius: fear of sacramental materialism; eschatological reasons for rejecting material change in the elements; and a concern for eucharistic logic.

John Wyclif: vigorous rejection of any annihilation theories; Christological realism opposed to sacramental realism; reluctance to define the mode of Christ's presence; horror of idolatry (worshiping the earthly elements); finality of the Eucharist found in union with Christ; greater concern for spiritual meaning than for the physical facts; and refusal to put God at man's disposal.

Followers of Huss: eucharistic communion under both species.

Care must be taken not to claim too much since obviously Calvin's historical situation is not that of, for instance, either Augustine or of Ratramnus. What can be claimed is that Calvin is not an innovator and that he can find some support in the earlier theologians. Whether he read and interpreted his sources correctly in every case is not of concern here.

The Reformation Concord and Discord

MARTIN LUTHER: THE MEDIEVAL TRADITION MODIFIED

Scholars have not been in agreement on the extent of Calvin's dependence on Luther. Beckmann says categorically that Calvin is not dependent on any of the reformers for his eucharistic doctrine.[67] Wilhelm Niesel chides Beckmann for a methodology which is not entirely "clean," with presuppositions which cannot be substantiated, and, finally, with an ax to grind. Just as categorically he asserts that Calvin "took his point of departure from Luther."[68] Since the research of Luchesius Smits it cannot be doubted that even in the first edition of the *Institutes* the influence of Augustine is very strong. On the other hand Luther was the talk of Europe and the hero of many a university student. Perhaps the polemic such teachers as John Major and Noël Béda directed against Luther was sufficient to arouse the interest of the students, always ready to uphold what their teachers condemn. The first professor that Calvin heard speak favorably of Luther was probably Melchior Volmar, a professor of law, who taught courses on Luther at Orleans and Bourges. During the whole course of his student life, Calvin had a number of fellow students who were "Lutheran," and in the early days after his conversion, Calvin was considered by Lutherans to be one of them.[69]

It is not clear just which of Luther's works Calvin had read when he wrote his first edition of the *Institutes*. Excerpts from Luther's prayer book appeared in a French translation at Basel in 1522, and in 1529 Louis de Berquin translated some of Luther's writings into French. Also translated at this time by a certain Simon du Bois were the writings of Luther on the Lord's Prayer, on the Creed, and on the Ten Commandments. Martin Bucer translated into Latin some of Luther's sermons which appeared in three volumes from 1525 to 1527. It can be asserted with some probability that Calvin used the following works of Luther in composing the first edition of the *Institutes*: the *Prayerbook, Small Cate-*

[67] Cf. Beckmann, *op.cit.*, 4.

[68] Wilhelm Niesel, *Calvins Lehre vom Abendmahl*, 2nd edn., Munich, 1935, 32.

[69] Cf. Ernst Bizer, *Studien zur Geschichte des Abendmahlsstreits im 16. Jahrhundert*, Gütersloh, 1940, 244, 245. Cf. also Reuter, *op.cit.*, 59, 60, 68, 70.

chism, On the Freedom of the Christian Man, On the Babylonian Captivity of the Church, the sermon *On the Blessed Sacrament of the True Body of Christ,* and the sermon *On the Body and Blood of Christ Against the Fanatics.* To this could possibly be added Luther's letter to Herwagen (1527) and Bucer's Latin translation of Luther's sermons.[70] Whether these few works are sufficient to grasp Luther's eucharistic thought in all its depth can be doubted. There is, to give an example, Bullinger's reproach in October 1554 that Calvin has never read Luther's works in the original German, and his suggestion that perhaps the man who has read so little of Luther should not be too vocal in his defense.[71] Ritschl, Pauch, and Lang have noted that the 1536 edition is modeled on Luther's *Small Catechism.*[72] This is not a matter of surprise since Calvin's objective was similar to Luther's, namely, to systematize the rudiments of the faith for the evangelical Christians. Niesel seems to doubt the importance of the *Small Catechism* and points rather to the doctrinal similarities between the first edition of the *Institutes* and *The Babylonian Captivity.*[73] Calvin seems to have borrowed the concept of the sacrament as a testament or covenant, the Eucharist as praise and thanksgiving, the ideas on the sacrament as promise, and his faith presuppositions from *The Babylonian Captivity.*[74] His concern for union with Christ and the union of Christians with one another could have been taken from the sermon *On the Blessed Sacrament of the True Body of Christ,* which Luther preached in 1519.[75] There is a section of Luther's

[70] Cf. Niesel, *op.cit.,* 24. Cf. also *ibid.,* 13n.

[71] Cf. CR 15:274.

[72] Cf. Otto Ritschl, *Dogmengeschichte des Protestantismus,* vol. 3, *Die reformierte theologie des 16. und 17. Jahrhunderts in ihrer Entstehung und Entwicklung,* Göttingen, 1926, 160, 161; Wilhelm Pauck, "Calvin's Institutes of the Christian Religion," *Church History,* vol. 15 (1960), 19; August Lang, "The Sources of Calvin's Institutes of 1536," *The Evangelical Quarterly,* vol. 8 (1936), 134, 135.

[73] Cf. Niesel, *op.cit.,* 23, 24.

[74] Compare OS I:136, 137 with WA 6:513-515; OS I:137, 138 with WA 6:517. Cf. also Niesel, *op.cit.,* 23, 7n.

[75] Compare OS I:137 with WA 2:743-745; OS I:145 with WA 2:748.

sermon *On Confession and the Sacrament*, 1524, included in both the book of sermons Bucer translated and in the *Prayer-book*, which gives the same answer as did Calvin on the question of the worthiness of communicants.[76]

There are some general theological areas where Calvin's system seems to be related to Luther's: the doctrines of justification and of penance. But when it comes to the doctrine of predestination and the concept of God, Calvin noticeably diverges from Luther. Calvin, from the very first, manifested an independent spirit. He would have nothing to do with Luther's teaching on consubstantiation, the presence of the glorified body, and the identification of the elements with the body and blood. In the 1536 edition Calvin's early polemic against Luther was strong enough to exasperate the German reformer.[77] Touched, however, by Luther's generous judgment on their differences, Calvin attempted to placate him by stating in his preface to the *Commentary on Romans*, that the essential polemic of the *Institutes* was directed against the Roman Catholics rather than against Luther.[78] This was only a temporary truce; the pamphlets of Joachim Westphal exacerbated the situation with the result that the major portion of Calvin's eucharistic polemic, seen quantitatively, was directed against the Lutherans. Paul Wernle, not always a reliable interpreter of Calvin, holds that anti-Lutheran polemic as expressed in the 1559 edition belongs to pathology rather than to faith and thought.[79] Strong though Calvin's convictions were in this area, as indeed in every theological question, he still kept the very highest regard for Luther and pleaded with the followers of Zwingli, Bullinger, and Oecolampadius, not always successfully, to bear with Luther's intemperate manner, a bit of advice he himself found no mean task to keep. If Calvin disagreed more fundamentally with Zwinglians, he fought more vigorously against

[76] Cf. Niesel, *op.cit.*, 24, 10n.

[77] Cf. CR 10:432.   [78] Cf. *ibid.*, 9:844.

[79] Cf. *Der evangelische Glaube nach den Hauptschriften den Reformatoren*, vol. 3, *Calvin*, Tübingen, 1919, 114.

the Lutherans; Lutherans were more of a problem for him than was Luther.

Luther's Christological suppositions to eucharistic doctrine were quite different from Calvin's. Like Calvin he rejects both Nestorius and Eutyches, and he proceeds from the unity of the natures in the person of Christ. He could not abide the thought that the whole Christ did not save us. It was unbearable that only one nature of Christ should suffer and die and not the whole Christ. To assert otherwise would be to deny the unity of the person of Christ.[80] The most characteristic mark of Luther's Christology is the *genus majestaticum* which asserts that the human nature of Christ shares in the properties of the divine nature, such as omnipotence, omnipresence. This is to assert that there is no *locus* where one finds a separation between the divine and human natures; everywhere and in every place Christ is present as the man who, because of the unity of the person, is the creator and the sustainer of the world. Whether such a Christology is only a crutch or is integral to Luther's whole eucharistic stance is disputed.[81] More than Luther's acceptance of the theory of consubstantiation—a word he himself never uses[82]—it was the eucharistic implications of this Christology which so profoundly disturbed Calvin. To pinpoint this divergence further it should be noted that an essential characteristic of Luther's eucharistic doctrine is the radical manner in which Christ is bound up with the elements, yet not limited by the elements. In this matter Luther was quite conscious that he was one with the Roman Catholics.[83] When Luther says that Christ is in, under, and with the bread, this is not to be understood as a spatial relationship, but rather a not too clear description of the identity between the elements and the sacrificial body of Christ.

The somewhat physical relationship Luther established be-

[80] Cf. WA 26:321.

[81] Cf. Albrecht Peters, *Realpräsenz, Luthers Zeugnis von Christi Gegenwart im Abendmahl*, Berlin, 1960, 168.

[82] Cf. *ibid.*, 98.   [83] Cf. WA 54:145.

tween Christ and the elements made Calvin suspect that Luther held some kind of crass local presence; and for Calvin all local presence was indeed crass. Local presence, says Luther, is not a mathematical reality; it is a definitive way of being present without being local. Luther will not equate, as does Calvin, a real, corporal presence with local presence. The body has one place, that is heaven; and though it is present in the sacrament it is not there as in a place. "Let not the reality of the body be denied here simply because it is believed that it [the body] is present in various places; rather what exists in one place in heaven is at the same time in the sacrament, not [as] in a place, although it is seen and touched. It is present, however, truly, really, invisibly, and in a manner incomprehensible to us."[84] As is evident, local presence here is not an enclosed space; Christ remains free and unbound.

The words of consecration have a double meaning in their eucharistic framework: insofar as they are directed to the gathered community they are proclamation, and insofar as they are directed to the elements they are consecratory.[85] To direct words of proclamation to the elements is, in Calvin's thinking, preaching to bread. He will not bind the Word to the bread. But for both Calvin and Luther it is the Word which comes to the element and thus constitutes the sacrament. Ultimately man contributes nothing; the creative Word of Christ does all.[86]

The problem of the communion of the unworthy is closely related to the problem of the elements. To Calvin's thesis that Christ gives himself only to his elect, and the elect alone are worthy, Luther answers that God forgives all who come to him and is therefore present to all; believer and unbeliever receive the gift but only the believer derives benefit from it. Luther's point of departure is the transcendent God who is neither bound nor determined by man's worthiness or unworthiness. The Eucharist is not founded upon our faith nor upon our holiness; rather its foundation is fidelity to Christ's

[84] *ibid.*, 8:297.
[85] Cf. Jürgen Diestelmann, *Konsekration*, Berlin, 1960, 42.
[86] Cf. WA 38:242.

own word.[87] This frees man from concentrating upon his own mean self and turns his eyes to God's decree and institution.[88] The greatest difference between the Lutheran and the Calvinist tradition, according to Ernst Kinder, is the Lutheran affirmation and the Calvinist denial that the unworthy receive the body of Christ.[89] Without a doubt Luther stands much closer to the medieval sacramental objectivism than does Calvin.

While Calvin rejects the oral eating in the physical sense and gives his attention to that "continual eating" in faith, Luther combines the two. In his earlier writings it was the *manducatio cordalis* which was given so much attention, but slowly he developed a theology of the *manducatio oralis*. The *manducatio oralis* is directed to the *manducatio cordalis* and both feed on the same food. Beyond this there is a mutual coinhesion between the oral eating and the eating of the heart. "God brings it about that the mouth eats bodily for the heart and the heart spiritually for the mouth and both are satiated by the one and same food. . ."[90]

A further difference can be seen in the very clear distinction Luther makes between consecrated elements and unconsecrated elements.[91] Wolferinus, a Lutheran pastor, had said that there was no difference between unused consecrated bread and ordinary bread because no sacrament exists outside of the sacramental action. Proceeding on this premise Wolferinus, to the great scandal of Luther, placed the consecrated breads not consumed back in the box with the unconsecrated breads, and poured the unconsumed consecrated wine back into a bottle of unconsecrated wine. Luther himself did not have a complete theological answer to the problem and, in fact, wanted to avoid facing it precisely for that reason. However, he was clearly unhappy with Wolferinus' solution. He wrote a letter of warning to Wolferinus telling

[87] Cf. *ibid.*, 26:288; *ibid.*, 26:490-492.   [88] Cf. Peters, *op.cit.*, 100.
[89] Cf. "Die lutherische Kirche," *Und Ihr Netz Zerriz*, ed. Helmut Lamparter, Stuttgart, 1957, 254.
[90] WA 23:191.   [91] Cf. *ibid.*, 6:377.

him that evidently he did not realize how dangerous the problem was and suggested that his solution reflected a Zwinglian concept of the Eucharist. As a solution to the problem he suggested that Wolferinus simply avoid it by consuming all of the unused breads, following the practice in Wittenberg.[92] To remove all doubts Luther interpreted Melanchthon's dictum that there is no sacrament outside of the sacramental action to mean the whole of the sacramental action, not just the moment of reception: "We define the time or the sacramental action as beginning with the inception of the Our Father and lasting until all have received, the chalice emptied, the particles consumed, the people dismissed, and [the minister] has left the altar."[93] It should be noted that in Luther's *Deutsche Messe* and in the orders of Bugenhagen, the "Our Father" stands before the words of consecration.

Luther looks upon the whole sacramental action as consecratory and therefore Christ is present from the beginning of the "Our Father" to the dismissal of the people. In addition Luther extended the real presence of the Eucharist to those occasions when the Eucharist was carried to a sick man, further evidence that for him presence was not identical with reception. In one instance Luther burned a host which was not consumed by a man who was near death.[94] It is reported that he took even more drastic measures when he spilt consecrated wine on the floor or upon his clothes.[95] He could not abide eucharistic processions, but he thought the Eucharist should be adored when it was elevated during the mass. "When Christ is truly present in the bread why should this food not be handled with the highest reverence and worshiped?"[96] "If I saw the Holy Spirit descending from heaven in the form of a dove I would want to fall on my knees, raise my hands, and say, 'Holy Spirit, be gracious to me.' Should I do otherwise when I see the sacrament where Christ is present?"[97] The suppression of the elevation in 1542,

[92] Cf. *ibid.*, 10:336 *Briefwechsel*. Cf. also *ibid.*, 10:341, 9n. *Briefwechsel*.
[93] *ibid.*, 10:348 *Briefwechsel*.   [94] Cf. *ibid.*, 30/2:624.
[95] Cf. Peters, *op.cit.*, 92.   [96] WA 5:308 *Tischreden*.
[97] *ibid.*, 9:420, 7n. *Briefwechsel*.

which Bugenhagen effected in his absence, was by no means pleasing to him, and he threatened to reintroduce it. This aspect of Luther's eucharistic doctrine is foreign to Calvin, indeed, repugnant.

There is a tendency to say that Luther's eucharistic teaching is a relapse into Roman doctrine or that he has not yet freed himself from medieval categories.[98] Though he remained firm in his convictions, he indicates that he too had had his eucharistic temptations.[99] He was "imprisoned" by the words and could not teach otherwise.[100] It was not a question of the first hesitations of a young reformer, from which he later freed himself. In the matter of the consecration and the elements his later teaching does not differ from his early teaching.[101]

The broader framework of Luther's eucharistic doctrine is found in his teaching on the Holy Spirit. Proceeding from the concept of a sacrament as a promise, Luther holds that it is the Holy Spirit which unites the promise and the sign. No other power but that of the Holy Spirit causes Christ to become present in the Word and makes that Word the Gospel which enflames the heart with faith. The Holy Spirit is likewise the power by which the promise and the sign are made one and placed in relationship to Christ. Through the Spirit the living unity of promise and sign received by faith becomes the sacrament.[102] There is no other way in which God comes to man than through the Holy Spirit. This is as true of the Eucharist as of any of the ways in which God comes to man. "For as soon as Christ says: 'This is my body,' it is his body through the Word and power of the Holy Spirit."[103] As the body of Christ comes from the womb of Mary through the power of the Holy Spirit, so that Spirit per-

[98] Cf. Ernst Sommerlath, "Das Abendmahl bei Luther," *Vom Sakrament des Altars*, ed. Hermann Sasse, Leipzig, 1941, 102.

[99] Cf. WA 18:143.

[100] Cf. *ibid.*, 15:394. Cf. also Heinrich Bornkamm, *Martin Bucers Bedeutung für die europäische Reformationsgeschichte*, Gütersloh, 1952, 10.

[101] Cf. Diestelmann, *op.cit.*, 39.

[102] Cf. Regin Prenter, *Spiritus Creator*, Philadelphia, 1953, 160, 161.

[103] WA 19:491.

meates and dominates the body in its changing earthly condition, sanctifying all, even "eyes, mouth, hands, feet, and all the members, indeed, the clothes and the whole life."[104] Through the power of the Holy Spirit the body was freed from its shroud, lifted up to the right hand of the Father, is present everywhere, and is present in the sacrament. Just as at the first creation it is the *Spiritus Creator* who works, so also it is the *Spiritus Creator* who effects the presence of the body and blood of Christ under the species of wine and bread.

Albrecht Peters is quite right in saying that this highly developed Pneumatology passed Calvin's notice, or he thought it a doctrine mutilated to serve Lutheran purposes.[105] A foundation for this suspicion can be seen in Luther's teaching on the condescension of God which he uses to weaken what would be Calvin's doctrine on *sursum corda*. God condescends to give himself in this earthly sign so that we do not need to seek him out in all creatures, nor do we need to be raised up to heaven to find him. He is not to be found in Compostella or Rome, not in visions and voices, but here "in your city or village, before your door."[106] This incarnational emphasis upon the earthly presence of Christ takes away, so thought Calvin and the Swiss, the tension between the heavenly and the earthly. Bluntly put, this is the *Deus corporeus* which scandalizes the world;[107] Luther is quite aware that such a God scandalizes the Swiss and he makes no attempt to use a conciliating euphemism. Through the power of the Holy Spirit the *Deus corporeus* can be found upon the eucharistic table; man has no need to raise his heart and mind to heaven when God can be found here below with such earthy particularity.

In spite of this, Luther accepts, and accepts without embarrassment, the Augustinian tradition of Christ at the right hand of the Father. "That Christ is at the right hand of God is well

104 *ibid.*, 37:59.
105 Cf. Peters, *op.cit.*, 46. Cf. also *Inst.*, IV, 17, 31; *ibid.*, 17, 33.
106 WA 30/2:605.
107 Cf. *ibid.*, 1:467 *Tischreden*.

known. The right hand of the Father, however, is at every extremity [*an allen Enden*] . . . and is certainly also in the bread and wine on the table."[108] To be at the right hand of the Father is a geographic and cosmographic expression, but it is not a place to which Christ is tied.[109] Even given this distinction, all of this will be too much for Calvin. The eucharistic body in Luther's doctrine is too much of a "givenness" in the sense of an object. As shall be seen, Calvin by no means wishes to exclude all sacramental objectivism, but the *Deus corporeus* is clearly further than he will care to go. And, in an eschatological view dear to Calvin, the eucharistic doctrine of Luther robs man of his hope of resurrection; it anticipates the *eschata* and therefore destroys the hope of resurrection. The *opposita* dear to Calvin are rendered less tense, less demanding by reason of Luther's radical sacramental incarnationalism. To a degree, Luther was forced to adopt a position characterized by the *Deus corporeus* because of his long and bitter disagreement with the Swiss theologians. Before he was pushed into such a radical incarnationalism he showed himself a true son of Augustine in a passage which would certainly have given Calvin comfort had he read it: "It is more needful that you discern the spiritual than that you discern the natural body of Christ, and faith in the spiritual is more needful than faith in the natural. For the natural without the spiritual profits us nothing in the sacrament. . ."[110] However even the early Luther conceived of the "natural" and the "spiritual" as belonging together, and "sign" was not what it meant for Hoen or Zwingli. On a later occasion he distinguishes between a philosophical sign, which denotes something that is absent, from a theological sign, which denotes something present.[111]

The eucharistic order which Calvin used is articulate in a not very muted way about man's sinfulness.[112] Here is a point

108 *ibid.*, 23:143.   109 Cf. *ibid.*, 23:133.
110 *ibid.*, 2:751. Cf. also Sasse, *This Is My Body*, 113.
111 Cf. WA 4:666 *Tischreden.*
112 Cf. William D. Maxwell, *The Liturgical Portions of the Genevan Service Book*, Edinburgh, 1931, 17-52, 121-143.

of contact with Luther. The Eucharist is a testament or a promise made by which Christ assigns his inheritance to his heirs. The testament is a gift, and the precise character of this gift in the Eucharist is the forgiveness of sins. Luther's interest is not in the eucharistic representation of the cross as a saving event, but a eucharistic representation of the passion of Christ as the forgiveness of sins won on the cross. The eucharistic gift is necessarily bound up with the forgiveness of sins. The body is given for the forgiveness of sins, an emphasis which begins to be quite marked about 1520.[113] The emphasis on the forgiveness of sins is strong enough in Luther to make Brilioth wonder if he had not made it into a doublet of the sacrament of penance.[114] As strong as the forgiveness of sins is in Luther's doctrine on the Lord's Supper, it does not constitute the central determination. Quite the contrary, Luther considered the reduction of the real presence to its relationship to forgiveness of sins as the decisive mistake of the antinomian groups.[115] Forgiveness of sins, and therefore the Eucharist, can have only one purpose: union with Christ. This will be one of the major themes in Calvin's eucharistic doctrine, and like Luther he will conceive of union with Christ, in the first instance, quite apart from and independent of the Eucharist. For both of them the faith dimension is paramount and the eucharistic moment is a particularization of a union with Christ in faith through the Holy Spirit. What is said of the eucharistic union with Christ can be said of the union with Christ in faith. At every moment, not only at the eucharistic moment, Christ is our bread and our drink. The manner of the eucharistic particularization will be explained differently by Luther and Calvin, and the faith relationship will be exegeted differently. For Calvin eating is an effect of faith; for Luther it is, in a radical sense, a fulfillment of faith.

---

[113] Cf. Peters, *op.cit.*, 64.

[114] Cf. Yngve Brilioth, *Eucharistic Faith and Practice: Evangelical and Catholic*, London, 1961, 102.

[115] Cf. WA 50:599.

Both Luther and Calvin move from union with Christ in faith to the eucharistic union with Christ, and from there to communion-fellowship. Here both are indebted to the Pauline and Augustinian traditions. Communion-fellowship was also part of the humanistic tradition as manifested by Colet and Erasmus.[116] We become one cake (*Kuchen*) with Christ so that we can become one cake with one another, and are therefore truly brothers.[117] The bitter fight with the Swiss threw Luther momentarily off balance; he stressed the physical aspect in relation to the individual so much that the sacrament of the community-fellowship was almost forgotten. However, Luther made his own peculiar contribution to the reformation rediscovery of communion-fellowship; for him as for the other reformers it became a vital element of eucharistic experience and the basis of both social and liturgical reform.[118]

A break with the medieval heritage is clearly made when Luther speaks about the proper gift of the Lord's Supper, a point in which Calvin stands in essential agreement. For instance, Luther never says that the presence of Christ in the Eucharist is something special; nor does he attempt to give the Eucharist a special dignity. The gift of Christ in the Eucharist is the same gift given in baptism and in the preaching of the Word: the whole person in his divine and human totality, the whole living Christ.[119] Baptism and the Word also bind us to the Logos become man so that we are one body and one life with him. If one says that the proper gift of the Eucharist is the union with Christ by means of the bodily eating of the elements, one must also say that the proper gift of baptism is the union with Christ by the pouring of the water according to Christ's command. The proper gifts are the same, and therefore there are no proper gifts.

[116] Cf. D. Stone, *A History of the Eucharist*, London, 1909, vol. 2, 3.

[117] Cf. WA 2:743-745; *ibid.*, 4:701; *ibid.*, 7:695.

[118] Cf. Brilioth, *op.cit.*, 97.

[119] Cf. Paul Wilhelm, *Die Christologie Luthers im Abendmahlsstreit*, Königsberg, 1929, 138. Cf. also WA 20:541.

Albrecht Peters could find no declaration in Luther's writings that the Lord is present in the Eucharist alone in a manner altogether special.[120] If one must speak of a gift proper to the Eucharist it is the forgiveness of sins given into our hands, mouth, ears, eyes, as well as into our hearts. The whole man participates in the sacrificial body of Christ.[121] In speaking of the gift of the Eucharist, Luther does not stress the identity of the Lord's body with the elements. The identity is declared but left without special emphasis.

Neither Calvin nor Luther are greatly interested in the theoretical question about concomitance, but both are extremely unhappy with the conclusions which the Romans draw from the concomitance doctrine. The Romans use concomitance to subvert the command of Christ "Take and eat. . . . Take and drink." Luther has much less trouble with concomitance than Calvin. When the Bishop of Meissen rejected Luther's demand for communion under both kinds by appealing to the doctrine that the whole Christ is under either species, Luther did not hesitate to agree with the premise and to deny the conclusion. "Who has ever doubted that the whole Christ is under either species?"[122] Luther objected also to the speculative nature of the question, an objection he shared with Calvin. He believes that Christ is given whole and entire under the species of bread and whole and entire under the species of wine. Christ does not give himself in stages, nor does he give himself twice in giving himself under the form of bread and wine. Even in a truncated sacrament, namely communion under one species, the whole Christ is given. The Romans who give only the consecrated bread to the laity fulfill only a half of Christ's command. Later Luther felt forced to take a more negative attitude toward concomitance, but only because a mutilated sacramental practice, communion under only one kind, sought to justify itself by the doctrine.[123]

[120] Cf. Peters, *op.cit.*, 137.
[121] Cf. WA 30/3:560, 561. Cf. also *ibid.*, 26:471.
[122] *ibid.*, 6:139. Cf. also *ibid.*, 6:151.   [123] Cf. *ibid.*, 26:495.

Luther's stand on the problem of communion under both species underwent considerable development. He begins by holding that though it is not right to withhold the cup, the practice does not invalidate the sacrament.[124] It is, however, his wish that the cup be restored to the laity. The Bohemians, with whom one would suspect he had deep sympathies, have sinned no less than Rome because they demand that every time one receives the sacrament it must be under both species. "I disapprove of the Bohemians for not having followed the major part of the church or obeyed authority by being content with one species."[125] In August 1520, Luther was still saying that "neither practice is wrong."[126] And he is opposed to abolishing by law the practice of receiving under only one species. In 1522 he still opposes making the gift of the Gospel an ordinance of the law. Here, as in so many other areas, he demands not legal uniformity, but evangelical freedom: "I see how Satan intends to make both species a common rule, just as the Pope has made one species his rule. . . . We need, therefore, to remain in the middle of the road and to pray that God may help and keep us there."[127] By 1523 he had arrived at the position that those who had received careful instructions and still refused to take communion under both species should be encouraged to altogether abstain from the sacrament, a practice which became a rule for the Lutheran Church.[128] However, Luther conceded as late as 1528 in the *Instruction for Visitors* (actually written by Melanchthon but approved by Luther) that those who in conscience did not feel they could accept the cup, could take communion under the species of bread alone. After the appearance of the *Augsburg Confession* in 1530, Luther took a firm position against any exception to the practice of receiving communion under both species. Melanchthon was still willing to admit such a possibility in special cases, as had the *Instruction for Visitors*. Luther was now beyond any concessions and he gave classic expression to his mature position in the Smalkaldic Articles:

[124] Cf. *ibid*., 2:742. [125] *ibid*., 6:79. [126] *ibid*., 6:456.
[127] *ibid*., 10/2:24. [128] Cf. Sasse, *This Is My Body*, 96.

"Although it may perhaps be true that there is as much under one as under both, yet the one form is not the entire ordinance and institution established and commanded by Christ. And we especially condemn and in God's name execrate those who not only omit both forms, but also tyrannically prohibit, condemn and blaspheme them as heresy, and so exalt themselves against and above Christ, our Lord and God."[129] It was this mature judgment of Luther which Calvin took into his teaching. At no time was Calvin of the mind that reception of one species was sufficient, though he had no great quarrel with concomitance as such.

Ernst Bizer correctly notes that for Luther the Eucharist was not an appendix of the worship service; nor was the controversy with the Swiss a matter of secondary importance.[130] What concerned the reformation of worship could hardly be of only secondary importance. If one seeks to understand the vehemence with which he rejected Zwingli's teaching, as he understood it, one must look to that diminished eucharistic function and the want of sufficient appreciation of eucharistic life and worship in Zwingli's system, which is not to say that he had no appreciation. For Luther it was one of the central questions of Christianity. He is appalled—the word is not too strong—because he felt that Zwingli was depriving the tempted of the comfort they need.[131] This strong pastoral care for the tempted, the weak, and the spiritually sick is to be found again in Calvin. For Calvin too, the Eucharist is the food of the needy, the tempted. Though Calvin will speak of the Eucharist as an appendix to the Gospel, this must be understood against the background of sacramental imperialism. He would hardly have expended so much effort on a matter which lacked centrality.

[129] III, 6. *Die Bekenntnisschriften der evangelisch-lutherischen Kirche*, 5th edn., Göttingen, 1963, 451.
[130] Cf. Bizer, *op.cit.*, 18.
[131] Cf. WA 23:620.

MARTIN BUCER: UNION WITH CHRIST AND
THE ECCLESIOLOGICAL CONTEXT

Martin Bucer attempted to mediate between warring parties and he had a mediator's fate: a species of ecumenical crucifixion. If he was not fully appreciated it was in part due to a faulty methodology, a failure to understand the complexity of the situation and a certain theological naïveté about the meaning and importance of words. In his defense it should be said that his broad formulations were in large part due to his desire to use scriptural language and not to go beyond it. In a letter to Calvin he wrote: "It displeases me greatly that they and others avoid [using] the words of the Lord and the Holy Spirit."[132] Further, his ecumenical zeal should not be attributed to political motivations, ecclesiastical or otherwise, but rather to his desire to see the element of truth in the other man's position. His own theological position was dictated not only by dogmatic considerations but also by a deep religious feeling.[133] Though Bucer did construct an ecclesiology he never developed a true theological system. He was impatient of speculative problems not immediately related to the demands of the moment and concerned with the direct relation of dogma to action that is a godlike life, and, above all, with the bond that held all Christians together, the *communio sanctorum*.[134]

There is a marked eucharistic development in Bucer: up to the end of the first half of 1524 his outlook was Lutheran, during the second half of 1524 he passed through a period of hesitation and doubt, from 1525 to 1528 he was under the dominant influence of Zwingli, and from 1528 to 1536 he leveled off into what can be called Buceranism, which is

[132] CR 13:351. Cf. also Hastings Eells, *Martin Bucer*, New Haven, 1931, 97.

[133] Cf. Lang, *Der Evangelienkommentar Martin Butzers und die Grundzüge seiner Theologie*, Leipzig, 1900.

[134] Cf. Pauck, "Calvin and Butzer," *The Journal of Religion*, vol. 9 (1929), 254.

favorable to Luther without really being Lutheran.[135] The impetus to his eucharistic investigations came about through Carlstadt, then a *persona non grata* with Luther. In October 1524 Carlstadt visited Strassburg, though he did not visit Bucer's home or Bucer himself. Unsettled by Carlstadt's teaching and inclining to agree with Carlstadt's symbolist interpretations, he was further influenced by the visit of Hinne Rode who brought the famous letter or small treatise of the Dutchman, Cornelisz Hoen. This visit of Rode, who spoke to him about the symbolist doctrine of the Dutch pre-reformer, Wessel Gansfort (1420-1489), seems to have been decisive.[136] In the next month Bucer received a dogmatic letter from Zwingli and he became Zwinglian. Even though his logic now becomes Zwinglian, his mystique is still Lutheran. He cannot be content with an abstract notion of man's relationship to God; the relationship must be one of personal union with Christ.[137] Even during this period of Zwinglian dominance he attributed a greater value to the celebration of the Supper than a mere memorial service. The corporal presence in a physical sense is rejected and the Eucharist is no longer seen as a means of grace in any traditional sense. What is most significant for our purposes is that Bucer's most important commentaries were written during this Zwinglian period: his *Apology* (1526), the *Commentary on the Gospels* (1527), which was actually on Matthew, Mark, and Luke, with Matthew getting almost all of the attention, and his *Commentary on St. John's Gospel* (1528).

In February of 1528 Bucer read Luther's *Statement of Faith about the Last Supper of Christ* and he realized that he had not understood Luther correctly. As he now read Luther, the German reformer did not teach a belief in the physical presence of Christ in the Supper which was the same as the

[135] Cf. Frédéric Bresch, *Strasbourg et la querelle sacramentaire au rapports de Bucer a ce propos avec Luther, Zwingli et Calvin*, Montauban, 1902, 48, 49.

[136] Cf. Gustav Anrich, *Martin Bucer*, Strasbourg, 1914, 47.

[137] Cf. Bresch, *op.cit.*, 59-61.

Romans' doctrine. Luther had not expressed himself correctly before but now it was clear, thought Bucer, that Luther's "sacramental union" was in reality what the Zwinglians had been trying to say.[138] In the second edition of his *Commentary on the Gospels* (1530), Bucer attempts to defend the contents of the *Marburg Articles* (1529), essentially a Lutheran document. On the other hand he defends the position of the Swiss and argues against Luther's refusal to call them brothers. Finally, and this is important, he is eager to show that at Marburg he gave consent to nothing which he had not earlier taught.[139] In spite of the signature which he appended to the *Concord of Wittenberg* (1536), another Lutheran document, Bucer cannot be considered a Lutheran. In his *Commentary on Romans* (1536) and the third edition of the *Commentary on the Gospels* (1536), his references to the Eucharist (he does not treat of it explicitly *in extenso*) are simpler, clearer, and much more sympathetic to Luther than the views expressed in his previous commentaries; he does not, however, become a Lutheran.

Martin Bucer was an exasperating friend to his contemporaries, to Luther, Zwingli, and Calvin. His eucharistic fluctuations earned him a bad name and in the end there was a tendency to place little trust in him. He himself asserted that his ideas had not changed. However if the ideas had not changed, his expression of them and the policies he based on them did. What was unchanged was his contention that the elements were symbols with the addition of some form of divine presence. To understand what Bucer is saying about this truth, attention must be paid to the period of which one is speaking.

The extent of Bucer's influence on Calvin is a matter of disagreement among scholars. August Lang sees a real dependence of Calvin on Bucer, an opinion in which Gustav Anrich and Hermann Sasse concur.[140] Jacques Courvoisier,

---

[138] Cf. Eells, *op.cit.*, 87.

[139] Cf. Lang, *Evangelienkommentar*, 63-67.

[140] Cf. Lang, *Evangelienkommentar*, *passim*. Cf. also Lang, "Sources,"

while calling attention to Calvin's more forceful personality, to the greater vigor, clarity, and precision of his writings, yet warns that justice must be done to Bucer.[141] What Calvin owes to Bucer is great enough to say that neither his ecclesiology nor his doctrinal forms would have been the same without Bucer. On the other hand Boisset warns against exaggerating the influence of Bucer on Calvin, Peter Barth asserts that Calvin is not essentially dependent on Bucer, and Joachim Beckmann declares that Calvin is dependent on none of the reformers.[142] Hastings Eells, whose fine biography of Bucer suffers from too little attention given to the theological content of Bucer's development, admits the similarity of their ideas but doubts that the dependence has been proven.[143] François Wendel warns against ascribing too much influence to Bucer but concedes that it was considerable.[144]

Calvin himself gives reason for some confusion because his own feelings toward Bucer are somewhat ambivalent. In October of 1541 Calvin writes to Bucer: "If in anything I do not respond to your hopes, you know that I am under your power. Warn, chastise, do all that a father may do for his son."[145] In his preface to his own *Commentary on Romans* (1540), he praises Bucer and takes him for his model, though differing on some points. He defends Bucer against Bullinger's impatience: "I love and honor him so much that as often as it seems best I advise him freely."[146] In his preface to his own *Commentary on a Harmony of the Gospels* (1555), he again praises Bucer and takes him for a model.[147] On the

---

Evangelical Quarterly, vol. 8, 137-141; Anrich, *op.cit.*, 143; Sasse, *This Is My Body*, 321, 322.

[141] *La notion d'église chez Bucer dans son développement historique*, Paris, 1933, 147.

[142] Cf. Boisset, *op.cit.*, 234; Barth, "Fünfundzwanzig Jahre Calvinforschung, 1909-1934," *Theologische Rundschau*, Tübingen, 1934, 172; Beckmann, *op.cit.*, 4.

[143] Cf. Eells, *op.cit.*, 236, 237.

[144] Cf. *Calvin: The Origins and Development of His Religious Thought*, New York, 1963, 137-144.

[145] CR 11:299.   [146] *ibid.*, 12:729.   [147] Cf. *ibid.*, 45:4.

other hand he was offended by Bucer's diplomatic and generous interpretation of all sides of an argument: "If you want a Christ, who is acceptable to all, you must not fabricate a new gospel for that purpose. . . . Does one truly praise God [*Deum vere sanctificare*] by granting so much to man that his truth no longer rules us?"[148] Bucer's easy ecumenism at the Colloquy of Regensburg (1541) brought down upon his head almost universal reproach. Luther said that he had lost all his confidence in him, that he would never trust him again, and Melanchthon felt likewise. Calvin took exception to Bucer's overconfidence in his own integrity [*securior est quam utile*] and his casual dismissal of the opinion of the other theologians not as ecumenically minded as himself.[149]

However, considering the length of his stay in Strassburg (1538-1541) it would be surprising if Bucer did not influence him. While at Strassburg Calvin wrote his famous *Letter to Cardinal Sadolet* (1539), and in the same year the second edition of the *Institutes*, which was such a thorough re-working of the 1536 edition that it was in fact a new work, his *Commentary on Romans* (1540), and the *Small Treatise on the Holy Supper* (1541).

The work of Lang and Niesel would indicate that Calvin used Bucer's *Apology* (1526) and *Commentary on the Gospels* as he wrote the first edition of the *Institutes*, and this specifically with regard to the Eucharist.[150] Lang also sees a relation between Bucer's *Commentary on Romans* and Calvin's 1539 edition of the *Institutes*.[151] Calvin seems to have used Bucer's *Commentary on Romans* for his own commentary on that work.[152] In his introduction to the *Commentary on the Psalms* (written in 1555 but published in 1557), Calvin acknowledges that his own book would have been of little use

---

[148] *ibid.*, 10B:142.   [149] Cf. *ibid.*, 11:217.

[150] Lang, *Evangelienkommentar*, 47 asserts Calvin used the *Commentary on the Gospels*. Cf. *ibid.*, 435 where selections of Bucer's *Commentary on the Gospels* are to be found. Niesel points to the similarity between these selections and OS I:138. Cf. Niesel, *op.cit.*, 30.

[151] "Sources," *Evangelical Quarterly*, vol. 8, 140, 141.

[152] Cf. Eells, *op.cit.*, 234.

had he not read carefully what Bucer had already written.[153] And most explicitly he expresses his indebtedness to Bucer in the introduction to his *Commentary on the Harmony of the Gospels* (1555). "Chiefly I have wished to follow Bucer, a man of sacred memory, that excellent doctor of the church of God; who above all others, in my judgment, has done much in this field."[154] Courvoisier has shown that Calvin's *Catechism* of 1542 follows that edited by Bucer in 1534 almost literally; Calvin had obviously used Bucer's catechism while he was in Strassburg and knew its formulas by heart.[155]

Calvin researchers have indicated a number of theological areas in which Bucer's influence is evident. As early as 1897, Scheibe noted the identity of Calvin's and Bucer's teaching on predestination, a contention upheld by Lang.[156] Other related areas are: the doctrine of sanctification, the manner of approaching the Scriptures, the theology of mediation, the concept of faith, the ethical motivation, the ecclesiological structure, the independence of the church in the spiritual sphere, the polemic against the Roman Church, the religious concept of the state, the relationship of the sacraments of the two testaments, the teaching on baptism, the eucharistic order or rite, and the rejection of the liturgical year.[157] In contrast to the Lutheran ecclesiology both Bucer and Calvin gave a large role to discipline. Though the myths have cast Calvin in the role of the great disciplinarian of the reformation, Bucer, in actual fact, gave an emphasis to discipline which went beyond anything Calvin, not an easy man to

[153] Cf. CR 31:14.   [154] *ibid.*, 49:vii.

[155] Noted in H. Strohl, "Bucer et Calvin," *Bulletin du Protestantisme Français*, vol. 87 (1938), 356. Courvoisier's research itself was not accessible to me.

[156] Cf. *Calvins Prädestinationslehre*, Halle, 1897, 17, 69; Lang, *Evangelienkommentar*, 365, 366.

[157] Cf. Pauck, "Calvin and Butzer," *The Journal of Religion*, vol. 9, 237, 238; Lang, *Evangelienkommentar*, 260, 365, 366; Anrich, *op.cit.*, 143; Sasse, *This Is My Body*, 302; J. M. Usteri, "Calvins Sakraments—und Tauflehre," *Studien und Kritiken*, Gotha, 1884, 417-456; Eells, *op.cit.*, 234, 235; Smits, *op.cit.*, 62; G. J. van de Poll, *Martin Bucer's Liturgical Ideas*, Assen (Holland), 1954, 20.

please in this matter, held. "The word 'discipline' was constantly upon his lips until it became an obsession."[158]

That Bucer in reality decisively influenced Calvin in all these areas can be doubted; frequently the assertion of influence or relationship is made without presenting any evidence. Much of what is to be found in Bucer is also to be found in Augustine, Thomas Bradwardine, Gregory of Rimini, and Luther. It does not seem unlikely that, for instance, the doctrine of election was taken from Augustine through Bucer. What Bucer's relationship was with Bradwardine and Gregory of Rimini has not, to my knowledge, been the subject of research. There is no sign of either in Bucer's register of books of April 1518, which is not very significant as there are no books of Augustine to be found there, and Bucer himself says that he sold some of his books.[159] Further, it is very dubious methodology to base a hypothesis on the absence of books from the library of a poor student, especially a poor student in the early sixteenth century.

Since Bucer was himself so involved in the eucharistic controversies, his doctrine, as has been noted, bears the marks of his decisions, indecisions, and revisions. It goes beyond the purpose of this general background to trace Bucer's development from his Lutheran, to his Zwinglian, to his Bucerian positions. Rather, indications will be given of those permanent concerns important for his relationship to Calvin.

Bucer's problem is in large part the Augustinian emphasis upon the Ascension, a problem shared by Zwingli, Oecolampadius, and Calvin.[160] Given such a preoccupation, Bucer

[158] Eells, *op.cit.*, 386. Cf. also Lang, *Evangelienkommentar*, 312.

[159] Cf. "Bucers Bücherverzeichnis," *Martin Bucers Deutsche Schriften*, ed. Robert Stupperich, Gütersloh, 1960, vol. 1, 281-284.

[160] Cf. Martinus Bucerus, "Altera Confessio Martini Buceri De S. Eucharistia in Anglia ab eo scripta et postea in Germania N N transmissa, 1550," *Nova et Vetera Qvatvor Evcharistia scripta svmmi et acvtissimi Theologi Doctoris Martini Buceri Argentoratus*, ed. Joannes Sturmius Vetus, Argentorati (Strassburg), 1561, 29a, 29b. As is noted this treatise was written in 1550, a year before Bucer's death.

will develop a theology which gives great importance to local presence of Christ in heaven, the raising up of our spirit to Christ at the right hand of the Father, and the heavenly Lord giving the heavenly gift, though remaining in heaven.[161] Bucer's fears are the same as Calvin's: he moves away from any sacramental divinization. He wants to make the sacraments depend on the Holy Spirit alone. For this reason he will be shy of emphasis on the outward sign, and will direct the attention rather to that which is interior, the body of Christ. "The word and fact and power must not be referred to the ministers nor to the externals [of the sacrament] but to Christ. . . ."[162] It is the spirit which receives the true body and blood of Christ. Bucer further fears that to make the sacraments means of grace in the Roman or even in the Lutheran sense would mean that man is not wholly dependent on the Holy Spirit. To give such a decisive role to the sacraments would leave the way open for sacramental imperialism. It would also bind God to the sacraments and to his church, which would be to fall back into Romanism. A sacramental doctrine founded on such fears can be detected as late as his *Commentary on Romans* of 1536. It should be noted that Bucer feared an imperialism of the Word no less than sacramental imperialism. If the sacraments were not means of grace, neither was the Word.[163] In his later development Bucer came to esteem more positively the sacraments as means. Later he also gives greater attention to the objective gift which he places in a positive relationship with the external sign, a development also found in Calvin. Bucer was not so much afraid of giving the sacraments a large role in the life of the church as he was of binding God [and man's inner life] to baptism and the Lord's Supper. What was decisive was not to be found in the

[161] Cf. Lang, *Evangelienkommentar*, 241, 286; Anrich, *op.cit.*, 54.

[162] Bucerus, "Brevis et Simplicissima Explicatio D. Martini Buceri De vero usu S. Eucharistia, 1542," *Nova et Vetera*, 15a.

[163] Cf. Lang, *Evangelienkommentar*, 244, 248, 249, 253, 268; Cf. also Bresch, *op.cit.*, 65.

sacramental moment but in eternal election. Election and predestination are the determinants of Bucer's sacramental theology,[164] a role they also play in Calvin's.

Bucer shows the same reluctance as Calvin to speak of how the body of Christ is present and received.[165] What is rendered present and given is not just the divinity, but also the humanity. In this regard Bucer brings to the fore the teaching on the "givenness" of the *totus Christus* but not the *totum Christi*, which was to be taken up by Melanchthon, Calvin, and the Heidelberg Cathechism.[166] He believes in a real presence which is real indeed, but only for those with faith. The presence is not effected in virtue of the words of institution spoken over the elements but in virtue of the faith which is determined by the words of institution. The body of Christ is truly present and given but the bread remains bread. One attributes to the body of Christ what is true of the symbol because of the sacramental union. It should be remembered that at no time, even during his Zwinglian days, did he think of the sacraments as empty signs. He warns that it is not enough to say that the sacrament stirs up our faith by thinking of the benefits, and in this way to raise up our spirit to Christ. This surely takes place, but it is not sufficient to explain the eucharistic moment.

The problem of the communion of unbelievers plagued Bucer as it was to plague Calvin. Since this was the ultimate test of sacramental objectivity it was the ultimate test that the differences between the warring parties were not just verbal differences, as Bucer, in the face of almost universal opposition from all sides, was wont to say. Bucer was forced to admit to Luther that the communion of unbelievers was, in sober fact, the chief problem and the *tessera* of concord or discord. For years Bucer rejected the communion of unbelievers, but at the Wittenberg Concord (1536) he con-

[164] Cf. Lang, *Evangelienkommentar*, 250.
[165] Cf. Wendel, *L'église de Strasbourg*, Paris, 1942, 148.
[166] Cf. Bizer, *op.cit.*, 23.

ceded that the unworthy receive the body of Christ because Scripture speaks of unworthy eating. But Bucer even then insisted upon a distinction. The wicked were to be divided into two classes: the unworthy and the unbelievers. The unworthy were those who give intellectual assent to the tenets of the faith but receive the sacrament carelessly and without thanksgiving; the unbelievers were those totally without faith. Though Calvin will not take up this distinction, he will give a similar formulation to what is given and what is received. Bucer says that Christ offered [*exhibet*] his grace to all but gives it only to the worthy;[167] Calvin will say that what is objectively offered to the unworthy cannot be received because he lacks faith.

Bucer, too, has a eucharistic doctrine of the Holy Spirit, which however has a different character from Calvin's. For Calvin the Holy Spirit effects the presence of the body of Christ, though that body remains at a distance in heaven. Bucer's doctrine is not directed so much to the body of Christ as to the heart of the believer. The reception of either the word of Christ or the body of Christ presupposes the possession of the Holy Spirit. The Holy Spirit creates faith in the heart of man and the Eucharist is a witness to that faith.[168]

What chiefly characterizes Bucer's doctrine of the Lord's Supper is its ecclesiastical quality. The Eucharist is the church's memorial meal, the church's thanksgiving and confession. The community stands in the eucharistic foreground. There is to be no Eucharist unless the whole worshiping community, or "at least the greater part [*nisi Ecclesia vel tota, vel maxima ex parte collecta*], the unworthy and the irreligious being removed . . . may receive the communion of Christ. . . ."[169] Bucer also gives expression to this ecclesial character of his eucharistic doctrine when he in-

[167] Cf. Lang, *Evangelienkommentar*, 264.

[168] Cf. Bizer, *op.cit.*, 23.

[169] *De Regno Christi*, I, 7. *Martini Buceri Opera Latina*, ed. François Wendel, Gütersloh, 1955, vol. 15, 69. Cf. also Courvoisier, *Une traduction Française de commentaire de Bucer sur l'évangile selon Saint Matthieu*, Paris, 1933, 37.

sists that communion given to the sick should not take place privately but others should celebrate the Eucharist together with the sick so that there is a true eucharistic community. The ecclesial character of the Eucharist was not to be lost sight of in administering to the needs of the sick.[170] Calvin was to take over Bucer's ecclesial preoccupation in regard to the sick too.

For Bucer, and, as shall be seen, for Calvin, this ecclesiological concern has little to do with structural churchmanship or with ritual exhibitionism. Quite the contrary, it is a move away from externality (though Bucer has a highly developed ecclesiology) toward interiority. In a word, it has to do with that ecclesiological inwardness founded in union with Christ. In the four small eucharistic tracts of Bucer, edited by John Sturm, each begins the discussion of the Lord's Supper in terms of union with Christ.[171] "The use and legitimate reception of this sacrament is defined as the Κοινωνίαν of the body and blood of Christ."[172] ". . . All our salvation consists in this: Christ lives in us."[173] Union with Christ is one of the centralities of Bucer's thought—and here Calvin will be a faithful disciple.

ULRICH ZWINGLI: THE PROFANE LOGIC
AND THE AGGRESSIVE TRANSCENDENTALISM

A study of the sources, as shall be seen, will bear out Niesel's contention that Calvin "had no positive relationship to Zwingli."[174] Care should be taken not to push this contention too far. Though Calvin was unhappy with the solutions Zwingli came to, and much preferred Luther to him, there is little doubt that Zwingli's theological motivations and his presuppositions and fears have much in common with Calvin's.

[170] Cf. Wendel, *L'église de Strasbourg*, 215.
[171] Cf. *Nova et Vetera*, 2b, 9b, 16a, 26b, 27a.
[172] "Altera Confessio," *ibid.*, 26b.
[173] Courvoisier, *Une traduction Française du Commentaire de Bucer*, 37.
[174] Cf. Niesel, *op.cit.*, 33.

Even before Calvin fled France, and therefore before he wrote the first edition of the *Institutes*, he had rejected Zwingli's eucharistic position as *falsa et perniciosa* in a letter to Andrew Zébédée, who "perfidiously" made public this judgment, made in a private letter, bringing down upon Calvin's head the wrath of the other Swiss theologians.[175] What offended Calvin was the profane character of his sacramental doctrine. He admitted that he had not read all of Zwingli's works and was quite aware that Zwingli may have corrected his doctrine later in his life, which indeed, to a degree, did occur.[176] Because of the account of Zwingli's teaching given by Luther and because of Luther's harsh judgment upon it, Calvin was, for a time, dissuaded from reading Zwingli.[177] Walter Köhler maintains that Luther spoke his condemnation upon Zwingli before he had read anything Zwingli had written.[178] It is evident from the first edition of the *Institutes* that Calvin had read Zwingli's *Commentarius de vera et falsa religione* of 1525.[179] Calvin could not abide Zwingli's teaching, as mediated by Luther, that the sacraments were only bare and empty figures.

Zwingli's early eucharistic doctrine is marked by spiritualizing tendencies. His mature eucharistic doctrine dates from his acceptance of Carlstadt's teaching (whom he had, however, refused to see during his visit to Zurich), and dates chiefly from the reception of the "letter" of Cornelisz Hoen. By the end of 1524, therefore, Zwingli is no longer satisfied with spiritualizing the Roman doctrine, but frankly sets forth a significative interpretation.

In eucharistic doctrine Zwingli represents a spiritualist theology which is only an expression of a whole spiritualist way of looking at things. His Nestorian Christology goes beyond any Nestorian tendency found in Calvin. The union between the divinity and the humanity is not a real union.

---

175 CR 103:346. Cf. also *ibid.*, 15:572, 573.
176 Cf. *ibid.*, 11:438.   177 Cf. *ibid.*, 9:51.
178 Cf. *Huldrych Zwingli*, Stuttgart, 2nd edn., 1952, 178.
179 Cf. OS I:137.

There is an absurdity in even positing the question. How can the infinite be really united to the finite? Here one sees clearly an uncompromising transcendentalism which will dwarf Calvin's passion for God as the "entirely Other." The humanity of Christ is not an object of faith nor an object of our trust; it too is only a creature. Therefore the humanity of Christ cannot be adored; only the godhead can be rightly adored.[180] The humanity of Christ is radically incapable of being an object of faith because faith can only be directed to that which is invisible. When one thinks of that which is necessary for religious existence, one can abstract from all that is external, including the humanity of Christ.[181] Zwingli hardly ever mentions the union of the two natures without immediately noting the sharp distinction between the two. And this attitude he carries over into all that has to do with the divine and the human. This is not to say that Zwingli rejects the humanity of Christ; the humanity receives its full due in his Christology. To distinguish sharply between doctrines is not necessarily to think less of one than the other.

It would be difficult to fit the communication of idioms into such a Christology and into the religious posture behind such a Christology, and logically Zwingli relegates it to a manner of speaking of the two natures. Zwingli has more problems with the communication of idioms than Calvin has, but both share the Christological axiom: *finitum non est capax infiniti.*[182]

Zwingli, unlike Calvin, did not develop his Christology specifically as a tool for his eucharistic polemic. But when applied to eucharistic thinking it would have far-reaching consequences, and one sees immediately that what nourishes the soul is not the body of Christ, but the divinity of Christ. The divinity is not in need of a material instrument or channel to mediate the divine presence and therefore the elements

[180] Cf. Maurice Schwabl, *Etude comparative des doctrines de Melanchthon, Zwingle*(sic) *et Calvin*, Strasbourg, 1859, 68.
[181] Cf. Eduard Zeller, *Das theologische Systems Zwinglis*, Tübingen, 1853, 96.
[182] Cf. *ibid.*, 95.

can never have an essential or substantial connection with sanctification.[183]

The accusation "rationalist" was leveled with a certain open-handed liberality in the sixteenth century; the humanists were frequently so accused and both Zwingli and Calvin were targets. There is a certain justification for the accusation in the case of Zwingli, as can be seen from his Christological stance. Paul Wernle, for instance, has said that Zwingli is really not a theologian, but essentially a philosopher.[184] That is clearly saying too much. It is true that reason moves to the foreground in his theology. Reason, says Zwingli, need not be transformed by faith in order to speak a truth, nor does Scripture imprison it so that it is without a certain independence. When Zwingli speaks of reason involved in a strictly theological process, he is speaking of the reason of faith, which is something quite other than the reason of flesh.[185] Though Zwingli took over philosophical concepts from the pagan philosophers, especially Cicero and Seneca, he did not take over their whole philosophy. His eucharistic teaching, for instance, is not determined by carnal reason but by the teaching and the word of Christ.[186] One notices that the emphasis upon reason which was not great in the beginning takes on greater importance later in his theological development. Yet the accusation that Zwingli is a thoroughgoing rationalist cannot be harmonized with the essential religious quality of his theological thought.[187] To give an example, Zwingli's accent upon satisfaction and the equation he postulates between satisfaction and the Gospel do not seem to be proper baggage for an implacable ra-

[183] Cf. Cyril C. Richardson, *Zwingli and Cranmer on the Eucharist*, Evanston, 1949, 16.

[184] Cf. *Der evangelische Glaube*, vol. 2, *Zwingli*, Tübingen, 1919, 304.

[185] Cf. CR 5:618; SS 3:517; CR 5:502.

[186] Cf. CR 5:787; *ibid.*, 5:665, 918. Cf. also Gottfried W. Locher, *Die Theologie Huldrych Zwingli im Lichte seiner Christologie*, Zürich, 1952, vol. 1, 25, 20n.

[187] Cf. Abel Burckhardt, *Das Geistproblem bei Huldrych Zwingli*, Leipzig, 1932, 4.

tionalist. The importance of his faith in the glorified Christ and in the Holy Spirit, with regard to his eucharistic doctrine, are not manifestations of rationalism. Zwingli has suffered unjustly by the false opposition postulated between Luther's biblicism and Zwingli's humanism. It was Zwingli who attempted to quote from the Greek New Testament at Marburg, only to be told by the biblical Luther to quote either the German or the Latin text. The prominence given to reason and logic must be judged in its reformation context. Seen from Luther's point of view, Zwingli is no better than the faithless scholastics. Here Luther touches on something essential to the understanding of Zwingli. Though he is not just a renegade scholastic, he does stand in the scholastic tradition and much of his seemingly humanistic posture is in fact the remnants of his scholastic past, for example, his doctrine on God and his teaching on providence. He is a reformation incarnation of the scholastic belief that reason and faith can be harmonized. "The truth is from God alone."[188] His philosophical structures are still supportive, ancillary, though at times restive; his philosophical methodology is not without dogmatic presuppositions and is not, in the radical sense, free. Reason possesses truth only insofar as it is in harmony with faith.[189] It must therefore be admitted that the humanist, rationalist picture of Zwingli has been largely overdrawn and that he is much more of a biblical theologian than was thought.

One could go further and say that Zwingli represents a desperate and aggressive supernaturalism. Paradoxically the reason for this unimpeachable spiritualism and the rejection of the creaturely is a quite unhumanistic distrust of the earthly to give certitude.[190] Only the divine can touch the soul spiritually and give certitude, a touch which is effected in faith. Here can be seen the concern for certitude in fiducial faith: "Faith is a true and constant thing [*res*] given to man by the triune God [literally *a numine*, which

[188] CR 3:142.   [189] Cf. Locher, *op.cit.*, 45, 46.
[190] Cf. *ibid.*, 162, 163.

is trinitarian in Zwingli] in which he alone rightly hopes, by which he certainly and firmly believes the invisible God."[191] Faith in Zwingli is not to be identified with a psychological category, though the faith has psychological effects. In Zwingli's definition it is a being [*res*], brought into existence by the Holy Spirit which stands over against mere knowledge, opinion, or imagination.[192] Not the effect of man's thought-world, not created by temporal initiatives, not originating either in the exterior word or in the sacraments, faith is the divine gift given by the divine Spirit, and for Zwingli it is decisive. Whether he approaches a problem from a dogmatic point of view or from a strictly exegetical point of view, his point of departure is always the faith, hardly the accredited procedure of a pure rationalist.

The lordly role of faith makes it difficult for Zwingli to evolve a positive understanding of the sacrament and, in fact, it did not have a great religious meaning for him. If one has faith, he has all; if one does not have faith, the sacrament is of no avail. This is Niesel's formulation and it has a true Zwinglian ring.[193] There cannot be two ways of salvation, one sacramental and the other by faith. Faith is all and it is normative. In 1523 Zwingli wrote to his master and friend, Thomas Wyteenbach: "Think of it this way; you eat the Eucharist there where faith is."[194] Quite simply the food is faith. The Eucharist does create a certain historic faith: faith in the birth and passion of Christ. But this is not the faith that comes from God and returns to God. Because given from above faith can never be given by exterior acts or elements; were one to attribute any worth to an external sign instead of to faith which alone sanctifies, then one would have returned to a justification based on works and all the perils of good-works theology.[195] Christ is present in faith and only for the faith. Christ does not come to us in the sacrament but we bring him into the sacrament by

---

[191] SS 4:121.   [192] Cf. CR 3:760.   [193] Cf. Niesel, *op.cit.*, 33, 34.
[194] CR 8:85.   [195] Cf. SS 3:460, 469.

faith.[196] This makes it evident that the subject of the eucharistic act is not Christ but the believer, or, more precisely, the worshiping community.[197] Union with God, for Calvin, is always a matter of the Spirit, as is union with Christ in the worshiping community. This he holds in common with Zwingli, but he will not use this position as a belligerent denial of every relationship between the Holy Spirit and the bread. Here Zwingli and Calvin part company.

The unmitigated supernaturalism of Zwingli's concept of faith both as a declaration and a methodology, is basic to his spiritualism. There are Platonic and Stoic presuppositions here: the Nestorian fear of uniting the divine and the human; humanity cannot be the object of faith; the uselessness of the flesh; the external sign can effect nothing in the spiritual soul; the opposition on the one hand, between the real eating of Christ in some way physically present and bound up with the elements, and on the other hand, the spiritual eating; the radical inability of the elements to be bearers of spiritual power (a view he mitigated later); the exhortation not to stop at the flesh but to go on to the spirit; and the enormity of making the spiritual redemption dependent on the carnal sacraments. This is all of a piece in Zwingli and is not to be attributed merely to the truculence of one whose views of the Lord's Supper had been called into question. In eucharistic terms this will mean a sharp distinction between the sign and the thing, a preoccupation he shares with Calvin. The sign is not and cannot be the thing; the bread cannot be the body. There is more than a sharp distinction here; there is a cleavage, a contradiction between the spirit and the body. Though there is danger of equating Zwingli's doctrine with the Marburg Colloquy (1529), his declaration there that "spirit and flesh contradict each other" is an expression of an authentic Zwinglian élan.[198] What is corporeal is harmful, as is the body of Christ insofar as it

---

[196] Cf. Bizer, *op.cit.*, 13.
[197] Cf. Locher, "Zwingli," RGG³.
[198] SS 4:176.

distracts from the divinity and draws attention to itself.[199] Indeed even if the body became substantially present this would have no religious value as the flesh cannot feed the faith; only the Spirit is capable of so spiritual an office.[200] Therefore the "essential and substantial eating," common to both the Lutheran and the Roman doctrine, "is wrong by the whole width of heaven."[201] Two reservations must be made. The flesh of Christ does profit, profits beyond measure, but because it is slain not because it is eaten.[202] Then, too, Zwingli would not want to deny that in faith the whole Christ, also his corporality, is present to the soul.[203] What concerns Zwingli here is not the denial that the body is present in faith. Rather he denies that its undoubted presence renders it profitable. This is why the whole eucharistic dispute is such an exasperating waste of energy: "The flesh profits nothing; why therefore dispute about the flesh?"[204]

Zwingli's polemic against Luther was based on the tropology of biblical language ("I am the vine" was a favorite text) and on the Ascension of Christ's body. Sasse suggests that he learned this Augustinian argument from Carlstadt, but, as has been seen, it has a large place in the eucharistic tradition of the spiritualist interpreters and is also a presupposition to Thomas Aquinas' eucharistic realism.[205] Zwingli sees the choice between the realism of the body in heaven and the sacramental realism and chooses the former. He tends to confuse the means of grace with the sacramental red flag of the reformation, *opus operatum*, and he confuses the real corporal presence of Christ in the Eucharist with a crass physical presence.[206]

Calvin and Zwingli shared many of their sacramental fears. Zwingli too voiced objections to a type of sacramental mechanism and to rendering the sacrament a thing. "None but the Holy Spirit gives faith, which is confidence [*fiducia*]

---

[199] Cf. Burckhardt, *op.cit.*, 55.   [200] Cf. CR 3:340, 341.
[201] *ibid.*, 3:341.   [202] Cf. *ibid.*, 3:782.   [203] Cf. *ibid.*, 3:341.
[204] SS 2/2:86.   [205] Cf. Sasse, *op.cit.*, 126.
[206] Cf. Bresch, *op.cit.*, 85.

in God and no external thing gives it."[207] Both feared dominance of the sign over the signified, the external over the internal. Zwingli moved with decision and dispatch away from the external toward interiority and inwardness to a point where one wonders what is left of the incarnational dimension of Christianity. Together with Calvin he was determined not to bind the Creator to the creaturely. Not only are God and the Spirit not bound to the sacraments but also faith is not bound. "Faith rests alone in God; faith can use corporal things but it can never be bound to them."[208] He also feared sacramental imperialism, that sacramental power-thrust which simply takes over the whole of man's relationship to God. Finally, both feared the sacramental self-confidence and self-possession by which the sacrament is rendered a total reality in itself, sanctified and sanctifying through its own power, freeing the consciences of sin by its own *fiat*.[209] "He who has a strong faith in God can in no way be strengthened in this faith except by something of which this faith is born: this is the Spirit of God who is the goodness and the light and the strength of conscience."[210]

Beyond Zwingli's relationship to Calvin in these questions, they have a common interest in the communion-fellowship character of the Lord's Supper. "They who here eat and drink are one body, one bread; that is, all those who come together to proclaim Christ's death and eat the symbolical bread, declare themselves to be Christ's body, that is, members of his Church; and as this Church holds one faith and eats one symbolical bread, so it is one bread and one body."[211] The communion-fellowship is essentially joyous in character as it is a Eucharist, a thanksgiving, a common rejoicing, the common confession by those who announce the death of the Lord.[212]

It is extremely difficult to be fair to Zwingli. Some claim

---

[207] SS 4:55.   [208] *ibid.*, 4:10.
[209] Cf. Köhler, *op.cit.*, 177; Raoul Gaudard, *La doctrine de la sainte cène d'après Zwingle*, Paris, 1890, 70.
[210] CR 5:625.   [211] *ibid.*, 3:802.   [212] *ibid.*, 3:349.

that a grave injustice has been done to him in saying that he did not believe in the real presence.[213] At Marburg, as a matter of fact, he was ready to admit that Christ is present spiritually, a formulation Luther rejected as too weak. However his thought is so polemic in character in this area, both anti-Lutheran and anti-Roman, that one gets the impression, not necessarily the correct one, that what he is rejecting is of more importance than what he is affirming. Ultimately the problem is whether or not Zwingli's crude, improbable transcendentalism leaves any room for a true sacramental encounter. The presuppositions found in his larger framework make one wonder if history has really been unfair. Do these not, in fact, invalidate any meaningful sense of real presence? Does he not confuse the actual presence of Christ in the worshiping community—a concept the Romans are only now recovering, though it has a rich patristic tradition—with the real presence of Christ in the Eucharist? The one cannot be merely substituted for the other. A pure rationalist he is not; rather a supernaturalist in the nominalist tradition who has created a void only reason and logic can fill.

The Eucharist does not play as central a role in Zwingli's religious thought as it does in Luther's or Calvin's. Given his premises this cannot be a matter of surprise. But it is quite another matter to say that he thought the Lord's Supper unimportant. This he never said. Here Zwingli must be judged within the framework of his whole religious thought and not within the framework of a Lutheran or Calvinistic system. Nor should his words at Marburg be isolated as though this was all he had to say. Further, researchers have learned not to identify Luther with Lutheranism and Calvin with Calvinism. Might they not extend the same courtesy to Zwingli?

Whether Calvin ever read extensively in Zwingli is highly doubtful.[214] Calvin, prejudiced by Luther's distorted views,

---

[213] Cf. Alexander Barclay, *The Protestant Doctrine of the Lord's Supper*, Glasgow, 1927, 42; Richardson, *op.cit.*, 16.

[214] Karl Holl's contention that Calvin later read more extensively in

clearly saw the weakness of the man but failed to perceive his essential supernaturalism and his transcendentalism. It was the profane logic which Zwingli exercised in the void he created (or inherited) between the heavenly and the earthly which Calvin, himself not a stranger to linear logic, found inadequate as a complete methodology. Had Calvin read more of Zwingli he would undoubtedly have seen that the profane logic sprang from premises which are essentially religious. These same premises, paradoxically, made it almost impossible for Zwingli to attribute sufficient religious importance to the Eucharist. Though they shared many eucharistic motives, fears, and presuppositions, though there are superficial similarities, their eucharistic doctrines are vastly different.

PHILIP MELANCHTHON:
THE VOLUNTARY PRESENCE AND THE PACT

August Lang has shown that Calvin knew and borrowed from Philip Melanchthon's *Loci communes*.[215] Also known to him was Melanchthon's *Confessio Augustana*.[216] How early Melanchthon's literary and theological influence is to be found is hazardous to guess. According to a sixteenth-century chronicler, Florimond de Raemond, Lefevre d'Etaples suggested to Calvin, then a refugee, that he regulate his doctrinal position according to Melanchthon's teaching.[217]

Zwingli is not convincing. Cf. "Johannes Calvin," *Gesammelte Aufsätze zur Kirchengeschichte*, vol. 3, *Der Westen*, 1928, 255, 1n. Calvin himself says in 1542 that he had not read all of Zwingli and admits that Zwingli might have made retractations and corrections at the end of his life. "Neque enim omnia legi et fortassis sub finem vitae retractavit ac correxit . . ." CR 11:438. Calvin seems to be making a charitable judgment simply because he has not read sufficiently to say anything but "perhaps." Nothing in Calvin's later writings presents a strong case for a more extensive knowledge of Zwingli's thought.

[215] Cf. "Sources," *Evangelical Quarterly*, vol. 8, 133, 134. Cf. also Lang, "Melanchthon und Calvin," *Reformation und Gegenwart, Gesammelte Aufsätze*, Detmold, 1918, 91.

[216] Cf. Niesel, *op.cit.*, 33, 47n.

[217] Cf. *La naissance, progrez, et décadence de l'hérésie de ce siècle*, Paris, 1605, vol. 8, 922. Doumergue and others have some reservations about

This was in 1534 and would place the influence early. In 1543 Calvin dedicated his work against Albert Pighius to Melanchthon, and in 1546 he wrote the preface to the French edition of the *Loci*, praised and recommended it, even though Melanchthon's categories and his teaching on free will differ from his own, and even though the French translation might supplant his own work. The two became personally acquainted when they met for various colloquies: at Frankfurt in 1539, at Worms in 1540, and at Ratisbon in 1541. Both August Lang and Philip Schaff have chronicled the history of their friendship.[218]

There was much to bind these two kindred souls together but there were also large differences in temperament and theology. Calvin found it necessary to reproach Melanchthon in 1545 for cowering before Luther: "We all of us acknowledge that we are much indebted to him. But in the church we always must be on our guard lest we pay too great a deference to men."[219] All of which is easy enough to say when one is not living with a prophet. When, after the defeat of the Protestants in the Smalkaldic War, Melanchthon was forced to accept the Leipzig Interim (which, from a Protestant point of view, was more endurable than the Augsburg Interim), with its demands of conformity to the Roman ritual, Calvin wrote again: "This is the sum of your defence: that, provided purity of doctrine be retained, externals should not be pertinaciously contended for. . . . But you extend the distinction of non-essentials too far. . . . You ought not to have made such large concessions to the papists."[220]

Paradoxically, the two men differ in that of which both are accused: rationalism. Calvin is accused of rationalism be-

---

Raemond's reliability as to dates cited but not as to the facts themselves. Doumergue suggests that he must be judged by the norms of the 16th century chroniclers. Cf. *Jean Calvin*, vol. 1, *La jeunesse de Calvin*, Lausanne, 1899, 524-526.

[218] Cf. Lang, "Melanchthon und Calvin," *Reformation und Gegenwart*, 88-135; Schaff, *History of the Christian Church*, vol. 8, *Modern Christianity*, New York, 1892, 385-398.

[219] CR 12:99.   [220] *ibid.*, 13:594.

cause of his implacable logic and because of what appears to be a denial of the eucharistic mystery. Melanchthon's rationalism is of a different stamp and is founded on the analogy between the human soul [*mens*] and God. The image of God, given in creation, lost at the fall, is restored through the Gospel. The authority of scriptures as the source of revelation is founded on its antiquity and miracles. God's existence and will can be known and proven by reason. All of these dogmatic statements manifest a neat harmony between the order of reason and the supernatural order. For Calvin this would be to tailor the divine to fit the human. He had reservations about Melanchthon's high regard for reason as giving entrance to revelation.[221]

Melanchthon had by far a greater philosophical interest than did Calvin. It was Luther who persuaded the young humanist to give up his project of publishing Aristotle and to turn his talents to theology. To mark his conversion from philosophy to theology he edited Aristophanes' *Clouds*, a biting satire on philosophy. In the preface to the 1521 *Loci*, Melanchthon took the occasion to publicly disavow philosophy and to criticize those who give themselves to its study. But the conversion, if indeed ever complete, was short-lived. By 1523 he is already grumbling that his talents are better suited to philosophy than to theology and he proceeded with his work of editing Aristotle's *Nicomachean Ethics*, which appeared in 1527.[222] After the appearance of the 1521 *Loci*, his formulations took on greater philosophical content and he gave greater place to the dogmatic tradition of the fathers and the creeds. Reuter suggests that Calvin reacted against this "philosophized theology" of Melanchthon, which was an intellectualization of the reformation's evangelical categories.[223] As evidence of this Reuter cites the use of the word *sapientia* in the opening sentence of the

[221] Cf. Karl Reuter, *Das Grundverstandnis der Theologie Calvin*, Neukirchen, 1963, 75.

[222] Cf. Jaroslav Pelikan, *From Luther to Kierkegaard*, 2nd edn., St. Louis, 1963, 29-31.

[223] Cf. Reuter, 9, 10, 15.

1539 *Institutes* and subsequent editions in place of the word *doctrina* in the 1536 edition.[224] This influence is not unlikely but Reuter offers no documentation. What does seem certain is that Calvin took over the concept of wisdom from Budé, Erasmus, and the mystics.[225] There does not seem to be much doubt that what Calvin abominated in the scholastics was their proclivity for philosophical structures and formulations; he would therefore not unnaturally find a similar preoccupation unseemly in a reformer. In a word, Calvin's so-called rationalism has very little in common with Melanchthon's.

Because of Calvin's own eucharistic problems with Luther, it is worth examining Melanchthon's relationship to his Wittenberg friend and master. Though he had always given emphasis to the eucharistic celebration rather than to the elements, and though he had never shared Luther's doctrine of the ubiquity of the body of Christ, he never openly broke with Luther.[226] He himself fully expected that Luther would take the initiative by exposing their differences publicly which he never did. Decisive for their eucharistic differences was the *Dialogus* of Oecolampadius, a refutation of Melanchthon's own *Sententiae*, a collection of patristic texts Melanchthon had made to give the weight of history to Luther's view at Marburg. Oecolampadius' work, printed in the summer of 1530, was also a collection of patristic texts, but in support of the Swiss view; Oecolampadius simply out-quoted Melanchthon and convinced him that a less realistic view of the real presence had large patristic support.

Seeberg sums up the difference between Luther and Melanchthon in the phrase: "the body in the bread and the

[224] Cf. *ibid.*, 9.

[225] Josef Bohatec, *Budé und Calvin*, Graz, 1950, 241-245.

[226] Cf. Sasse, *This Is My Body*, 313. For a theological evaluation of Melanchthon's relationship to Luther cf. Wilhelm H. Neuser, *Luther und Melanchthon—Einheit im Gegensatz*, heft 91, *Theologische Existenz Heute*, Munich, 1961.

body with the bread."[227] Melanchthon had always believed in the real presence but he became more and more unhappy with the binding up of the body with bread. He defined real presence in terms of the use of the sacrament, there being no presence outside the use of the sacrament. Melanchthon himself explains his stand: "God is not bound to the bread and wine outside of the use for which the Lord established the Supper. It is facetious to suppose that the words of consecration draw the body of Christ into the bread in such a manner that he is forced to remain there always, as wine poured into a jug remains there. The sacraments are rather conditioned by their administration. When the elements are eaten, Christ is at that moment present and effective. The sacramental presence is voluntary, not a geometrical or magical imprisonment so that Christ is forced to remain in the bread. . . . Therefore one should avoid all those questions as to whether a mouse, when chewing on a consecrated bread, receives the body of Christ. Also to be avoided is the custom of parading around with the bread in a monstrance. Therefore what is left of the bread and wine after communion, namely, that which is not consumed by those whose intention it is to receive the Lord's Supper (these remaining elements), are not the sacrament because the whole action is the sacrament. But because of the ignorant and out of reverence, I advise that the last communicant, either one or more, consume what is left in the chalice. In this way through ending the use of the sacrament, the sacrament itself comes to an end. Christ is not to be adored under the form of bread. The bread remains together with the body of Christ in the sacrament."[228]

What is important for Melanchthon is not the bread and the wine but the rite, not the substance of bread but the

---

[227] *Lehrbuch der Dogmengeschichte*, vol. 4/2, *Die Fortbildung der reformatorischen Lehre und die Gegenreformatorische Lehre*, 5th edn., Darmstadt, 1953, 449.
[228] CR 7:876.

event. There is a strong element of the *propter hominem* theology here which Melanchthon opposes to the *propter sacramentum* theology. Here again Melanchthon manifests the strong anthropological interest[229] in rite and theology, possibly as a reaction to the raging objectivism of much of Roman liturgical practice and sacramental doctrine, some of which was held over in Lutheranism. For Melanchthon what is important is not the matter which is administered but the will which is manifested. The sacraments are quite simply a sign of God's will in our regard. Instead of the Lutheran distinction between substance and use, Melanchthon sets up a distinction between rite and use. Over against bodily presence he places willed presence: "God the Son lives and reigns and wishes (*vult*) to be present to the sacrament intended for this purpose and to join us to himself as members."[230] The real presence, then, is not a specification of the metaphysical omnipresence of the body of Christ but the special effect of Christ's personal will. "The presence is voluntary."[231] "Christ as a free agent is present to the action which he instituted. After the action he does not wish [*non vult*] to be enclosed in the bread, he does not wish to be bound there."[232] This formulation is an expression of the Scotist sacramental theology: the sacraments are effective because of the pact God has made. Melanchthon's formula is: "effective because of the pact."[233]

His insistence that the consecrated bread be not adored betrays his concern to move away from a view of the sacrament which is concerned with the matter of the sacrament. This is seen with greater clarity in his vigorous rejection of transubstantiation. Luther was no lover of transubstantiation, but he was willing to tolerate it among his followers, and said so to the Venetians when they posed the problem. This was clearly further than Melanchthon cared to go. For him

---

[229] Cf. Neuser, *Der Ansatz der Theologie der Philipp Melanchthons*, Neukirchen, 1957, 107.

[230] CR 15:1112.   [231] *ibid.*, 4:264.   [232] *ibid.*, 5:208.

[233] *ibid.*, 2:315.

transubstantiation was the epitome of all that was erroneous in Roman teaching, indeed the decisive error.[234]

Melanchthon will also use a substantialist terminology, saying, for instance, that Christ is "not only present efficaciously but also substantially."[235] By this he does not mean a corporal union of bread and body, but rather uses substance to stand for the essence of the sacrament, that is, God, by reason of the pact, joining one to Christ. Gollwitzer declares that Melanchthon's concept of substance in the eucharistic context is essentially the same as Calvin's.[236] There are points of contact. Calvin does use substance to mean the essence of the sacrament, but Calvin's dialectic must be kept in mind and the *opposita* he is careful to preserve. Melanchthon's concept of substance is considerably more voluntaristic than Calvin's.

Melanchthon shared with Calvin the opinion that Zwingli's view of the sacrament was profane.[237] At no time did he believe in a naked spiritual presence, though some of his disciples later adopted a position tending to the Zwinglian interpretation. Melanchthon, on the contrary, was convinced that Zwingli was wrong when he said that Christ's body could only be in one place, that is in heaven. In the mode proper to a body it remained in heaven, but "in that manner which is proper to a sacrament, that is not locally," it is in the sacrament.[238] At times Melanchthon used terminology which was Zwinglian. In 1535 Melanchthon wrote to Brenz: "I affirm the true presence of Christ in the Supper," and then immediately afterwards he added in Greek, as was his wont when he was writing something offensive to Luther's ears, περὶ τύπου καὶ τροπικῶς, or of a type or trope.[239] Given the historical context this can only mean presence in a much weaker sense than Luther would have found acceptable. Well might Melanchthon have written the offend-

[234] Cf. Helmut Gollwitzer, *Coena Domini*, Munich, 1939, 80.
[235] CR 21:863.   [236] Cf. Gollwitzer, *op.cit.*, 92.
[237] Cf. CR 1:1067, 1075, 1077.   [238] *ibid.*, 2:224.
[239] *ibid.*, 2:824.

ing passage in Greek, and subsequent history can hardly be reproached for pinning a Zwinglian label on Melanchthon's eucharistic teaching, though he was not in reality a Zwinglian.[240]

It would be difficult to attribute much influence to Melanchthon in the area of Calvin's eucharistic doctrine. The *Confessio Augustana* and the *Loci* offer little in the way of eucharistic doctrine which could be seen as a source or influence. In the *Loci* of 1521 the Lord's Supper stands in the shadow of penance, and this no matter whether one approaches the subject from a systematic or from a practical point of view. In fact, Melanchthon's theological thought is so dominated by the concept of penance that it seems to be an answer to the question "How can a man receive forgiveness for his sins?" The central concept of Melanchthon's early theology is not grace but penance, which he used as a synonym for justification.[241] Calvin's consciousness of sin need not be attributed to Melanchthon as it is the common heritage of the anti-Pelagians (Augustine, Bradwardine, Gregory of Rimini), of the *devotio moderna* and the mystics and, of course, is to be found in Luther. Lang notes the similarity between the treatment of penance in the first edition of the *Institutes* and the *Loci,* but there does not seem to be any borrowing for specific eucharistic purposes.[242] Calvin had sent some articles to Melanchthon on the real presence, possibly as early as 1538, and therefore before their first personal meeting at Frankfurt, to which Melanchthon

[240] Cf. Lang, "Melanchthon und Calvin," *Reformation und Gegenwart*, 91.

[241] Cf. Neuser, *Der Ansatz der Theologie der Philipp Melanchthons*, 107, 108, 112, 113.

[242] Cf. "Sources," *Evangelical Quarterly*, vol. 8, 136. It should be noted that Luther never clearly rejected penance as a sacrament. As Laurentius Klein has shown, the later Luther is not at all clear and one cannot cite him either for or against the sacramental character of penance. Melanchthon's *Apologia* still numbers penance among the sacraments. The confessional documents taken as a whole are not uniform, some expressly rejecting penance as a sacrament, others not. Greater uniformity in rejecting penance as a sacrament is found in the period of Orthodoxy. Cf. *Evangelisch-Lutherische Beichte*, Paderborn, 1961, 54-57, 81, 84, 97, 98.

gave assent. Melanchthon made the famous changes in the text of the *Confessio Augustana* in 1540, which were not taken seriously at the time, even by Luther, but which admitted a Bucerian and Calvinistic interpretation. The *Invariata* of 1530 reads: "Our churches teach that the body and blood of Christ are truly present and are distributed to those who eat in the Supper of the Lord. They disapprove of those who teach otherwise."[243] The *Variata* of 1540 reads: "Concerning the Supper of the Lord they [that is, the churches] teach that with the bread and wine, the body and blood of Christ are offered to those who eat in the Lord's Supper."[244] The significant change is the word *cum* or "with" which can have an orthodox Lutheran meaning as found in the Wittenberg Concord. It can, on the other hand, be understood as "at the same time as," which would leave the door open for a non-Lutheran interpretation. Calvin, who was present at Worms, understood the formula in terms of his own theology and signed the *Variata*. Also worthy of note is the omission of the phrase, "they disapprove of those who teach otherwise."

Melanchthon's meaning is clearly seen in Chapter 5 of the *Variata* text which discusses the ministry of the church: "When we hear the Gospel and meditate on it or receive the sacraments and find consolation by faith, the Holy Spirit is at the same time [*simul*] effective. . ."[245] The *Invariata* text had unambiguously spoken of the sacraments as instruments. The introduction of the *simul* in the *Variata*, though not excluding instrumentality, would seem to be a deliberate move away from the sacraments as means of grace in the sense Luther understood. It is hardly to be wondered

[243] Chapter 10. *Bekenntnisschriften*, 64. The text given is a translation of the Latin text. The translation of the German text of the *Invariata* reads: "It is taught among us that the true body and blood of Christ are really present in the Supper of our Lord under the form of bread and wine and are there distributed and received. The contrary doctrine is therefore rejected." *The Book of Concord*, Philadelphia, 1959, 34.

[244] Cf. Sasse, *This Is My Body*, 317, 33n.

[245] Chapter 10. *Bekenntnisschriften*, 59.

then that Calvin who could not bring himself to agree with Luther's eucharistic doctrine could write to Melanchthon in June 1545: "I do not cease to offer my chief thanks to God, who has brought us to that agreement in opinion upon the whole of that question [of the real presence]; for although there is a slight difference in certain particulars, we are very well agreed upon the general question itself."[246]

During the years when the Lutheran Westphal efficiently turned out tract after tract against Calvin, and Calvin wearily impaled each upon his aggressive logic and invocations to Augustine, Melanchthon held his peace. This silence when his friend was under siege brought a coolness to their relationship, and in 1557 Calvin wrote complaining that he had not had any answer to his letters for the past three years.[247]

Melanchthon's importance for Calvin's eucharistic doctrine is not to be found in any demonstrable influence exercised upon him. It seems more likely that the influence was quite the other way. Rather he is important as showing the theological motivation behind a contemporary eucharistic position less realistic than Luther's and closer to Calvin's. For German Calvinism, however, Melanchthon has a place of historical importance. His students and followers (Curäus, Ursinus, Cruciger, Pezel, and Peucer, who was Melanchthon's son-in-law) absolutized the rational elements in his doctrine and became crypto-Calvinists.

[246] CR 12:100.   [247] Cf. *ibid.*, 16:556.

III. Calvin Accuses Rome

Calvin Faces Romanism

IN 1552 CALVIN was asked by a French congregation in London whether or not it was lawful to pray for the pope. To the dilemma Calvin gave this answer: "I know that we must make a due distinction between the individual and the abominable and accursed seat [of the beast]. But I do think that those who pray specially for him who bears the mark of reprobation, have surely much time to spare. I lay down laws for no man, but it is a matter of concern that the sobriety of our prayers should express the reverence we feel for the name of God."[1] To be, already this side of death, so surely marked with the sign of enmity as to make mention of the pope in prayer a matter of unseeming want of theological propriety and because of reverence for the name of God, this is surely a mark of an ultimate and inexorable enmity between the pope and his God. And this is true although the distinction between the person and the office is granted.

Calvin did not deny, however, that "the churches under his [the pope's] tyranny remain churches."[2] He makes the distinction between the right and the wrong state of the church, and admits that even in the wrong state of the church God preserves a remnant of his people, so that also in the Roman church there are many learned and virtuous men.[3] "To sum up, I call them churches to the extent that the Lord wonderfully preserves in them a remnant of his people, however woefully dispersed and scattered, and to the

[1] CR 14:365. Albert Haas suggests that Calvin was forced to take up a position with regard to Rome more often than Luther. Cf. "Calvin und Rom," *Reformierte Kirchenzeitung*, vol. 100 (1959), 33. Calvin, like others of his age, demanded a tolerance which he would not grant to others. Cf. E. W. Zeeden, "Calvin," *Lexikon für Theologie und Kirche*, 2nd edn., Freiburg, 1958.

[2] *Inst.*, IV, 2, 12.

[3] Cf. *ibid.* Cf. also A. Mitchell Hunter, *The Teaching of Calvin*, Glasgow, 1920, 157; Geddes MacGregor, *Corpus Christi*, London, 1959, 51.

extent that some marks of the church remain."[4] What he does deny to the Roman Church is the title of "the church." "I say that every one of their congregations and their whole body lack the lawful form of the church . . . required in the communion not only of the sacraments (which are the signs of profession) but also especially of doctrine."[5] Calvin held that one could not separate oneself from a church which was merely corrupt but which preserves the true ministry of the word and sacraments. To depart from such a church was to depart from Christ. "Departure from the church is renunciation of God and Christ."[6] "We are certain that, while we remain within the bosom of the church, the truth will always abide with us."[7] But since doctrine is the soul of the church, take away purity of doctrine and you destroy the church. And this is the sin and scandal of Rome. "If the foundation of the church is the teaching of the prophets and apostles, which bids believers entrust their salvation to Christ alone—then take away that teaching, and how will the building continue to stand? Again, if the true church is the pillar and foundation of truth, it is certain that no church can exist where lying and falsehood have gained way."[8] The mother of all churches must at least retain that purity of doctrine she is supposed to communicate to others. "How shall Rome be the mother of the churches who no more deserves to be esteemed a church than Babylon? The soul of a church is purity of doctrine. Since it is surer than certainty itself that this purity has been altogether banished from Rome, it follows that in that city there remains nothing but a dead body."[9]

Calvin's polemic with regard to the Roman Church was undoubtedly one of the most important and essential aspects of his apostolate.[10] And though he had a rather extended

[4] *Inst.*, IV, 2, 12.   [5] *ibid.*

[6] *Inst.*, IV, 1, 10. Cf. also John T. McNeil, "The Church in Sixteenth Century Reformed Theology," *The Journal of Religion*, vol. 22 (1942), 260.
    [7] *Inst.*, IV, 1, 3.   [8] *Inst.*, IV, 2, 1.   [9] CR 15:333.

[10] Cf. G. C. Berkouwer, "Calvin and Rome," *John Calvin Contemporary Prophet*, ed. Jacob T. Hoogstra, Grand Rapids, 1959, 185.

series of doctrinal difficulties with Luther and with Melanchthon—with Lutherans more than with Luther—one of the determining factors of his relationship with Luther and Melanchthon was the common front they presented against the Roman church.[11] His turning away from Rome greatly influenced his theology, though not in the sense that Luther's conversion influenced his theology.[12] From his conversion experience came not theological content for his theology but a dedication to the sovereignty of God,[13] a dedication which was sometimes fierce and fearful, always articulate, and, given the materials by which we can judge, unimpeachable in its sincerity.

Though Calvin wrote more against Lutheran eucharistic doctrine than he did against the Roman eucharistic doctrine, it should be remembered that Calvin's primary stance is against transubstantiation.[14] His antitransubstantiation polemics are given theological preference to his anti-Lutheran teaching. In this matter the sheer quantity of Calvin's anti-Lutheran writings can be deceptive. From the beginning his object is to destroy the illusions of Rome. The first edition of the *Institutes* of 1536 is determined in its general character by its anti-Roman polemic.[15] And with each new edition he worked in new material, so that by the time of the last edition (1559) he devoted a whole chapter to the sacrifice of the mass. His stand against the Roman church is of undoubted importance, but his eucharistic doctrine and his

[11] Cf. Andrea Wiedeburg, "Calvins Verhalten zu Luther, Melanchthon und dem Luthertum," typewritten thesis, University of Tübingen, 1961, 317. Cf. also Ernst Troeltsch, *The Social Teaching of the Christian Churches*, London, vol. 2, 1931, 579.

[12] Cf. Otto Ritschl, *Dogmengeschichte des Protestantismus*, vol. 3, *Die reformierte theologie des 16. und 17. Jahrhunderts in ihrer Entstehung und Entwicklung*, Göttingen, 1926, 157.

[13] Cf. Yves Congar, "Calvin," *Catholicisme*, Paris, 1949.

[14] This is also true of the confessional documents of the Calvinist tradition. Cf. Paul Jacobs, "Die Gegenwart Christi im Abendmahl nach reformiertem Verständnis und das römisch-katholisch Gegenbild," *Gegenwart Christi*, ed. Fritz Viering, Göttingen, 1959, 23.

[15] Cf. Gerhard Kretz, "Calvins Auseinandersetzung mit der katholischen Kirche," typewritten thesis, University of Tübingen, 1962, 10.

whole methodology are not just creatures of a reformer's occupational temptation: building a theology against someone. Nor are his anti-Lutheran and anti-Zwinglian writings the whole explanation of the ultimate form of his eucharistic doctrine. However great a role his polemic writings played, Calvin is more concerned to build a biblical theology and a eucharistic doctrine in which mystical union with Christ through faith, and fellowship with Christ through faith, is normative.[16] In this attempt he was not always successful, and this can be seen in the areas of biblical eucharistic doctrine which he left undeveloped,[17] from the somewhat over-developed theology of certain controversial aspects of eucharistic doctrine, and, in part, from his methodology. His exegesis tended to be in the service of his polemics rather than of his systematics.

Calvin's polemic is essentially pastoral in tone. He had studied his Aquinas and also the other Roman authors, John Cochlaeus, John Eck, Erasmus, Pope Eugenius IV, John Fisher, Gratian, and Kaspar Schatzgeyer, and he had kept abreast of what was happening at Trent. He had also studied conciliar history and was a competent patristic scholar. He frequently attacked Rome on a doctrinal level—it had lost its soul, doctrinal purity—but his polemics as a whole proceed from an existential situation.[18] Though he says that one cannot leave a church because of the many abuses within it, but only when it has abandoned purity of doctrine, his

[16] W. Kolfhaus is quite right in stressing the role which union with Christ plays in Calvin's eucharistic theology, but quite wrong in dismissing as influences both Calvin's polemic against the Romans and the postulated separation of the Creator and creature. Cf. *Christusgemeinschaft bei Johannes Calvin*, Neukirchen, 1939, 123, 124. Cf. also Paul Sprenger, *Das Rätsel um die Bekehrung Calvins*, Neukirchen, 1960, 93.

[17] Cf. Jean Cadier, *La doctrine Calviniste de la sainte cène*, Montpellier, 1951, 83.

[18] What Wim Boelens notes with regard to the adoration of the Eucharist is valid for Calvin's eucharistic polemic in general, namely that both Luther and Calvin had a common point of departure: what is most important is not Roman doctrine but Roman practice. Cf. "Die Arnoldshainer Thesen," typewritten thesis, University of Würzburg, 1963, 259. Cf. also Alfred Quervain, *Calvin, Sein Lehren und Kämpfen*, Berlin, 1926, 11.

point of departure is predominantly historical. It was the Roman religious experience which was defective and corrupt. Its defect was to be found in a divinization of the church and sacraments. The ecclesiological interpretation of Christology, as will be seen, failed to keep the Christological dialectic of the unmixed and undivided. The Roman ecclesiological interpretation of Christology placed large emphasis on union, so that identity between Christ and church issued in divinization of the church. Instead of an experience of God, Rome offered an experience of the church. Calvin, like many reformation figures, thought that there was too much church and too little Christ. To this extent he belongs to the ecclesiological tradition which fled from secondary causality.

Exaggerated Importance of the Sacraments

SACRAMENTAL DIVINIZATION

In Calvin's mind there was an image of the Roman Church which he thought corresponded to the prevailing Roman ecclesiology not so much as it was taught but as it was historically realized. In this conception the church possessed an exaggerated supernatural character. This church not only spoke the truth but created it, and laid claim, as without pretension, to the absolute and immediate authority which belonged to Christ. Enduring but ineffectual, she walked among men in the trappings of her lordship, dispensing small blessings and pieties, living in regal contempt of penitence, expecting to be served, binding others but herself unbound, finding her pleasures in ceremonial pronouncements and ritual busyness. Under pain of anathema she demanded submission to all that she said, or was about to say.[19] She was not content to invoke the Holy Spirit but conferred him. Such a church did more than represent Christ; she displaced divinity.

---

[19] Cf. *Inst.*, III, 2, 3. Cf. also Peter Brunner, *Vom Glauben bei Calvin*, Tübingen, 1925, 120.

To this tendency to divinize, Calvin opposed the teaching that there is only one Master of the church, Christ. "[Christ] alone should be Master of the church."[20] "He alone should rule and reign in the church as well as have authority or preeminence in it."[21] It is not the church which is the origin and giver of faith, but God alone. Since the "perpetuity of the Church is found in the person of Christ," to neglect Christ is to destroy the church.[22] If the church is essentially the body of Christ, then she ceases to be the church the moment she forgets Christ or attempts to displace him. And it is vain to claim that the pope is the head of the church on earth. There is no validity to the assertion that the nature of the church demands a head. This is valid for the local church, but not for the universal church. "It has Christ as its sole head," and this headship is not transferrable.[23]

In the strictly sacramental order the Romans, says Calvin, under the name of the church and in its authority, have carried forward this process of divinization. This process has been carried over from the ecclesiological to the sacramental order. Those men set aside for sacramental sacrifice have usurped the office of Christ. And they think to offer that sacrifice which the God-Man alone can offer. "We also deny that they are priests in the sense that they by such oblation intercede before God for the people and, having appeased God, obtain atonement for sins. For Christ is the sole Pontiff and Priest of the New Testament, to whom all priesthoods have been transferred, and in whom they have been closed and terminated."[24] There is no need for any other priest since both Christ and his priesthood are immortal. And these men, by laying claim to a sacrificing priesthood, claim what belongs to Christ. "By this substitution they not only deprive Christ of his honor and snatch from him the prerogative of that eternal priesthood, but try to cast him down from the right hand of the Father, where he cannot sit immortal without at the same time remaining eternal priest."[25] By

[20] CR 29:628. [21] *Inst.*, IV, 3, 1. [22] CR 48:194.
[23] *Inst.*, IV, 6, 9. [24] *ibid.*, IV, 18, 14. [25] *ibid.*, IV, 18, 2.

all these claims of offices which belong to the Eternal Priest, "an unbearable blasphemy and dishonor is inflicted upon Christ."[26]

Not only have men usurped divine powers, but they have attributed these powers to weak and senseless creatures. "There are those who attach to the sacraments some sort of secret powers with which one nowhere reads that God has endowed them," and thus the simple people are "taught to seek God's gifts where they cannot be found."[27] The sacraments are given such importance that "the cause of justification and the power of the Holy Spirit are enclosed in the elements, just as in vessels or vehicles."[28] God does "not resign the grace of his Spirit to the sacraments,"[29] neither does he hand over "his office to outward symbols."[30] In such a theory the divine realities given in the sacrament are made into objects, things, impersonal items which are manipulated with mechanical precision at will. Those who embrace this theory "think that a hidden power is joined and fastened to the sacraments by which they of themselves confer the graces of the Holy Spirit upon us, as wine is given in a cup."[31]

There are those who would "attribute everything to the power of water," and would assert "that our cleansing and salvation are accomplished by water, or that water contains in itself the power to cleanse, regenerate, and renew," and that "here is the cause of salvation."[32] They dare call the oil used in confirmation "the oil of salvation."[33] "Who taught them to seek salvation in oil?"[34] As will be seen, the specifically eucharistic aspect of divinization finds more characteristic expression in Calvin's treatment of idolatry.

SACRAMENTAL IMPERIALISM

In the liturgical life of Roman Catholicism of his day Calvin saw what he thought to be a sacramental imperialism, a sanctuary will-to-power, which made ever greater and

[26] *ibid.*	[27] *ibid.*, IV, 14, 14.	[28] *ibid.*, IV, 14, 17.
[29] CR 25:54.	[30] *Inst.*, IV, 14, 17.	[31] *ibid.*
[32] *ibid.*, IV, 15, 2.	[33] *ibid.*, IV, 19, 7.	[34] *ibid.*

ever more exclusive claims on the spiritual life of the people.[35] It was difficult for a man to meet his God and speak with him apart from the ceremonial sacramentalism, the ritual processions, and the sanctuary externality of the official church. The liturgical splendor to which the layman contributed only the obedient passivity of awe, and the juridic ritualism, from which one dare not depart one jot or tittle, had rendered the believers' contact with God too "churchy." The seven sacraments encompassed the whole life of man from the violence of birth to the violence of death, hallowing each stage of both his natural and spiritual life so that without them his life was unhallowed and his salvation uncertain, as though justification consisted in sprinkling with water, anointing with oil, or the words of absolution. Not only was there no salvation outside the church, there was no salvation within the church for those who withdrew from the organizational busyness of the sanctuary. Not only was there no salvation outside the church; there was no salvation outside the sacraments. So Calvin read the pastoral practice of the Roman Church of his times.

No justification but sacramental justification

This imperious demand of loyalty to the sacraments, as though they were not the instruments of justification but justification itself, led Calvin to accuse the Romans of sacramental imperialism. "Any man is deceived who thinks anything more is conferred upon him through the sacraments than what is offered by God's Word and received by him in true faith. From this something else follows: assurance of salvation does not depend upon participation in the sacraments, as if justification consisted in it."[36] Not only did

---

[35] Cf. *ibid.*, IV, 14, 14. Doumergue comments on how this sacramental will-to-power was given expression in the place assigned to the sacraments at the Council of Trent. Instead of treating them at the end, as Calvin does in the *Institutes*, the Council treated them immediately after having spoken of the sources of doctrine and before taking up original sin, justification, etc. Cf. *Jean Calvin, les hommes et les choses de son temps*, vol. 5, *La pensée ecclésiastique et la pensée politique de Calvin*, Lausanne, 1917, 321.

[36] *Inst.*, IV, 14, 14.

sacramental imperialism detract from Christ, in whom alone justification is to be found, but also from the other means of justification: "We know that justification is lodged in Christ alone, and that it is communicated to us no less by the preaching of the gospel than by the seal of the sacrament, and without the latter can stand unimpaired."[37] The gospel is not beholden to the sacraments as though without them something essential would be wanting. What was intolerable was that the Romans made the sacraments the causes of righteousness and salvation, while they were merely parts. At least on the pastoral level the sacraments were placed as the single cause of salvation, and this over against Christ who was himself the only cause of salvation: "I say that Christ is the matter or (if you prefer) the substance of all the sacraments; for in him they have all their firmness, and they do not promise anything apart from him. The less tolerable, then, is the error of Peter Lombard, who learnedly makes them the causes of righteousness and salvation, of which they are but parts. Accordingly, bidding farewell to all causes which man's ingenuity fashions for itself, we ought to hold to this single cause."[38]

In the view Calvin attributes to the Romans, the sacraments exercise their dominance as, under God, self-sufficient entities, as completed and static realities which already contain within them the dynamics of sanctification and justification. And this in a way that grace is tied to the sacraments in a mechanistic fashion: "We must again beware that we do not tie the grace of God to the sacraments; for the external administration of baptism profits nothing, save only that it pleases God that it shall."[39] It is shameless nonsense to affirm that by repeating an action proper to the divine power in Christ they effect what Christ effected. Christ said to the apostles, "Receive the Holy Spirit," and Christ, because of his divine nature, conferred the Holy Spirit. They imitate the action of Christ and think they possess the same right and power to confer the Spirit: "Indeed, they are so

[37] *ibid.*   [38] *ibid.*, IV, 14, 16.   [39] CR 48:497.

shameless as to dare affirm that they confer the Holy Spirit."[40] The Christological presupposition of such an ecclesiology is the identity between Christ and the church. Christ sends the Spirit; the church sends the Spirit.

There is no such sacramental order in which "graces are bound and enclosed in the sacrament so as to be conferred upon us by its power, but only because the Lord by this token attests his will toward us, namely that he is pleased to lavish all these things upon us."[41] There is in the sacraments no "secret force or other perpetually seated in them by which they are able to promote or confirm faith by themselves."[42] Calvin directs his remarks on the role of the Holy Spirit specifically against the Romans: "But the sacraments properly fulfill their office only when the Spirit, that inward teacher, comes to them, by whose power alone hearts are penetrated and affections moved."[43] There is no sacrament or sacraments which have efficacy or which are worthy of honor apart from that interior master. And how can the Holy Spirit remain master when he is supposedly enclosed in all sorts of trash? "Their rite of consecration corresponds very well to this office (of subdeacon): that the subdeacon receives from the bishop paten and cup, from the archdeacon cruet with water, the manual, and trash of this sort. They require us to confess that the Holy Spirit is enclosed within these trifles."[44]

Sacraments independent of the phenomenology of faith

The sacraments are not causes in their own right, and for this reason Calvin distinguishes between the sign, which man dispenses, and the grace, which God dispenses.[45] Though God does not institute vain signs, he does not so tie his grace to material creatures as to deprive himself of his

[40] *Inst.*, IV, 19, 29.   [41] *ibid.*, IV, 15, 14. Cf. also CR 12:483.
[42] *Inst.*, IV, 14, 9.   [43] *ibid.*   [44] *ibid.*, IV, 19, 33.
[45] Cf. *ibid.*, IV, 14, 11. In this passage Calvin is speaking specifically of preaching in relation to the sacraments. What he says here of preaching is also valid for his sacramental theology.

freedom.[46] Nor do the sacraments have that autonomous lordship over grace so that they dispense it even apart from the context of faith. Calvin's concern here, as so often, is pastoral as well as theological. The pastoral experience had shown that a pastoral practice divorced from the personalism of faith and given over to some objective dispenser of grace would fix the attention on something less than God himself and would lead to superstitious practices. Nor did the insistence that the sacraments conferred grace only when no impediment was placed through mortal sin, save the teaching from being diabolical. Quite the contrary. This only confirmed the suspicion that what the Romans were teaching was mechanistic and divorced from the phenomenology of faith: "The schools of the Sophists have taught with remarkable agreement that the sacraments of the new law (those now used in the Christian church) justify and confer grace, provided we do not set up a barrier of mortal sin. How deadly and pestilential this notion is cannot be expressed—and the more so because for many centuries it has been a current claim in a good part of the world, to the great loss of the church. Of a certainty it is diabolical. For in promising a righteousness apart from faith, it hurls souls headlong to destruction. Secondly, because it draws the cause of righteousness from the sacraments, it binds men's pitiable minds (of themselves more than enough inclined to earth) in this superstition, so that they repose in the appearance of a physical thing rather than in God himself."[47] The mechanics of a sacramentalism separated from faith is no substitute for a true sacramental experience of God.

The loss here suffered is not just that of an unenlightened pastoral practice at the level of the local church, a pastoral practice based on a sacramental imperialism, but goes deeper and farther, infecting the whole church both in its faith and its pastoral efforts. And for those who need proof of this,

[46] Cf. John Adam Möhler, *Symbolism*, 2nd edn., London, 1847, vol. 1, 308, 309. Cf. also Doumergue, *op.cit.*, 322.
[47] *Inst.*, IV, 14, 14.

behold the state of the church: "Would that we had not had so much experience of these two things—so far are they from needing an extended proof! But what is a sacrament received apart from faith but the most certain ruin of the church?"[48]

A sacramental theology conceived in such ambitious terms cannot help but erect the sacraments into independent causes and independent ends in themselves, quite apart from the whole faith experience. The piety derived from this sacramental theology will place its confidence in the instruments rather than in him whose instruments they are: "It is our duty to put no confidence in other creatures which have been destined for our use by God's generosity and beneficence, and through whose ministry he lavishes the gifts of his bounty upon us; nor to admire and proclaim them as the causes of our good. In the same way, neither ought our confidence to inhere in the sacraments, nor the glory of God be transferred to them."[49]

The sanctuary will-to-power seen in the general sacramental theology of Roman Catholicism, as interpreted by Calvin, is even more in evidence in the Eucharist, more specifically, in the mass. The mass dominates Roman life, but it also dominates Christ's death on the cross. Though Calvin is aware that Romans believe the mass to be an application of the merits of Christ's Passion, he accuses the Romans of requiring daily applications by means of the sacrifice of the mass "in order to make the death of Christ efficacious."[50] He felt that the compulsive concern of the Romans for the sacraments as the means of salvation, especially as seen in their doctrine of transubstantiation, ended in the sign dominating the reality, and ultimately in the sign obscuring the reality.[51] Transubstantiation objectivized God and made him palpable and man could dispose of him at will, so that the whole faith experience—God's sovereignty and man's utter subjection—had no meaning.

[48] ibid.   [49] ibid., IV, 14, 12.   [50] CR 55:128.
[51] Cf. Cadier, op.cit., 28.

As the center of liturgical life the mass dominated Roman Catholicism in its organizational structure, in its cultural expressions, and was the consuming concern of the church in both its public and private devotional life. "They have steered the whole vessel of their salvation into this one deadly whirlpool."[52] For many the mass is simply identified with the faith: "I know . . . how numerous persons believe that in the one word 'mass' they embrace the whole sum of faith."[53] How central and how all-pervasive is the whole eucharistic experience in the Roman Church can be seen from the ferocity with which the Romans defend the mass. "Surely, Satan never prepared a stronger engine to besiege and capture Christ's Kingdom. This is the Helen for whom the enemies of truth do battle with so much rage, fury, and cruelty—a Helen indeed, with whom they so defile themselves in spiritual fornication, the most abominable of all."[54]

Because the mass has this unchallenged and unchallengeable imperium over Roman Catholic life and because this imperium is untouched by the whole faith experience, Calvin accuses it of corrupting the devotional life and, in its economic implications, being the cause of grave abuses: "Offered in a golden cup, it has so inebriated all kings and peoples of the earth, from highest to lowest, and has so stricken them with drowsiness and dizziness, that more stupid than brute beasts, they have steered the whole vessel of their salvation into this one deadly whirlpool. . . . Here I do not even touch with my little finger those gross abuses which they might offer as an excuse for the profanation of the purity of their sacred mass: the base traffickings they practice; the unclean profits they make by their massings; the unrestrained greed with which they satisfy their covetousness."[55] No matter how the mass is considered, either as the "whole vessel of salvation," or as the "sum of the faith," or as the imperious center of Roman piety and pastoral practice, Calvin asserts that the "Mass, taken in its highest purity,

[52] *Inst.*, IV, 18, 18.   [53] *ibid.*, IV, 18, 1.   [54] *ibid.*, IV, 18, 18.
[55] *ibid.*

. . . swarms with every sort of impiety, blasphemy, idolatry, and sacrilege, from root to top."[56]

Exaggerated Sacramental Realism

SACRAMENTAL IMPERSONALISM

Theological impersonalism

The imperial will-to-power by which the sacraments in general and the Eucharist in particular attempt to bring all grace and all truth and all salvation under their domination becomes, when brought to a fine point in the doctrine of transubstantiation, sacramental impersonalism. In theology Calvin feared an impersonal systematization of abstract truths. "We are called to a knowledge of God: not that knowledge which, content with empty speculation, merely flits in the brain, but that which will be sound and fruitful if we duly perceive it, and if it takes root in the heart."[57] A theology which stood apart, which divided and subdivided, distinguished, and conceded, but was basically disengaged and uninvolved, could not bring man to the true knowledge of God. Nor could that bold and frigid speculation about the essence of God. Only that theology in which awe and wonder prepared the heart to see God where he could be seen, in his works, brings man to a true knowledge of God. True knowledge of God is itself personal because persons, God and man, are involved; it is experience because the involvement is not just intellectual apprehension of an abstraction, but because the involvement has to do with an event—God in his works. True knowledge of God demands, indeed presupposes, commitment; it renders God near, indeed communicates him: "We know the most perfect way of seeking God, and the most suitable order, is not for us to attempt with bold curiosity to penetrate to the investigation of his essence, which we ought more to adore than meticulously to search out, but for us to contemplate him in his works

[56] *ibid.*   [57] *Inst.*, I, 5, 9.

whereby he renders himself near and familiar to us, and in some manner communicates himself. . . . It is also fitting, therefore, for us to pursue this particular search for God, which may so hold our mental powers suspended in wonderment as at the same time to stir us deeply."[58]

A theology which is given over to an extreme form of speculation and abstraction, in which problems are invented to test the intellectual acumen of the theologians rather than to bring man to the true knowledge of God, in which propositions are used as springboards for the display of scholastic virtuosity, will readily succumb to the temptation to treat of the sacraments as things, as objects, and to conceive of sacramental activity in impersonal mechanistic terms: this act is done in order to produce that result; the priest says these words and bread becomes body.

Eucharistic empiricism

Prescinding from the justice of such a conception of scholastic theology, Calvin reacted against Roman theology so conceived, and he saw full justification for his position in the doctrine of transubstantiation. He saw transubstantiation as the real enemy, more so than the sacrifice of the mass, and he took a stronger position against transubstantiation than did Luther,[59] though it is interesting to note that he considered the Roman doctrine of transubstantiation "more tolerable or at least more modest" than the Lutheran doctrine with its presupposition of ubiquity.[60] Calvin, misled in part by that most unfortunate, not to say erroneous, first (1059) confession of faith in the Eucharist drawn up by Cardi-

---

[58] *ibid.* Cf. also Pierre Marcel, "The Humility of the Prophet," *John Calvin, Contemporary Prophet*, ed. Jacob T. Hoogstra, Grand Rapids, 1959, 28; Wilhelm Pauck, "Calvin's Institutes of the Christian Religion," *Church History*, vol. 15 (1940), 24.

[59] Cf. Jacobs, "Die Gegenwart Christi im Abendmahl," *Gegenwart Christi*, 23. Cf. also Hermann Sasse, *This Is My Body*, Minneapolis, 1957, 87. Yngve Brilioth, *Eucharistic Faith and Practice: Evangelical and Catholic*, London, 1930, 164.

[60] *Inst.*, IV, 17, 30.

nal Humbert for Berengarius' signing, understood the Catholic doctrine in a crude empirical sense rather than in the metaphysical sense.[61] For this reason Calvin labeled transubstantiation, quite simply, "that monster."[62] He considered the crudity of their doctrine equaled by the crudity of their methodology, for the Romans were "syllable-snatchers" as seen in their exaggerated literal interpretation of the words of institution.[63]

Transubstantiation, with its attendant local presence, and, in Calvin's mind, with its carnal presence, was a naturalization of God: "Bread came to be taken for God."[64] Physical, local presence was the reduction of Christ to a "givenness" of a thing, and this in the crudest terms: "They could never have been so foully deluded by Satan's tricks unless they had already been bewitched by this error, that Christ's body, enclosed in bread, is transmitted by the mouth of the body into the stomach."[65] "We must not dream of such a presence of Christ in the sacrament as the craftsmen of the Roman court have fashioned—as if the body of Christ, by a local presence, were put there to be touched by the hands, to be chewed by the teeth, and to be swallowed by the mouth."[66] When the words of consecration are thought of as an impersonal formula directed not to persons but to a thing, this should cause no surprise: "the cause of such crude imagination was that among them consecration was virtually equivalent to magic incantation. But this principle was hidden from them, that the bread is a sacrament only to those persons to whom the word is directed."[67]

Transubstantiation objectivizes the divine person, and this

---

[61] Cf. PL 150:140, 411.   [62] *Inst.*, IV, 17, 14.   [63] *ibid.*, IV, 17, 23.

[64] *ibid.*, IV, 17, 13. Calvin recognizes that Roman Catholics reject the idea of Christ being contained in the Eucharist in any circumscriptive or bodily fashion. However his interpretation of Catholic thought is still dominated by the crudest elements to be found in the Catholic tradition but not to be identified with that tradition. He also recognizes the presence of schools of theology which stand in the Roman tradition. Cf. *ibid.*, IV, 17, 12; *ibid.*, IV, 17, 13. Some of the schoolmen are saner than others. Cf. *ibid.*, IV, 18, 1.

[65] *ibid.*, IV, 17, 15.   [66] *ibid.*, IV, 17, 12.   [67] *ibid.*, IV, 17, 15.

is to Calvin quite literally blasphemy, because God is always a subject and never an object: "It is an intolerable blasphemy to declare literally of an ephemeral and corruptible element that it is Christ."[68] Roman Catholics have such an object fixation that they cannot think of presence in any other terms than of physical presence, and with this physical presence they are quite content: "Provided they have a physical presence of him, which they have fabricated apart from God's words, they think that they have presence enough."[69] What Calvin judged to be a false biblical realism lay beneath this object fixation and he considered it a surrogate for that personal act of God in the eucharistic moment.[70] What he sought in the Eucharist was a living experience of Christ's death: "For we do not eat Christ duly and unto salvation unless he is crucified, when in living experience we grasp the efficacy of his death."[71] This personalism, found in the self-giving of Christ, is reduced to something which can be manipulated when "the substance of bread is turned into Christ,"[72] when "unclean and profane men . . . whenever they like and for whatever abuse they please, fashion the body of Christ."[73] "They ... subject the worship of God to their fictions. How do we sin, if today we cannot bear what Paul has taught to be unbearable—that the lawful order of divine worship is reduced to men's decision? Especially, when they command men to worship according to the elements of this world, which Paul testifies to be against Christ."[74]

To seek Christ in a thing is to pursue an illusion. Personalism is of the essence of the Gospel and without it there is no true faith and no true fellowship with Christ. Those who objectify Christ in the Eucharist, hiding him under the species of bread, making fellowship with Christ a scholastic effect which can be produced at will, regulated, legislated,

---

[68] *ibid.*, IV, 17, 20. Cf. also Sprenger, *op.cit.*, 96.

[69] *Inst.*, IV, 17, 13.

[70] Cf. Peter Barth, "Calvins Stellung im Abendmahlsstreit," *Die Christliche Welt*, vol. 43 (1929), 928. Cf. also Doumergue, *op.cit.*, 15.

[71] *Inst.*, IV, 17, 4.   [72] *ibid.*, IV, 17, 13.   [73] *ibid.*, IV, 18, 8.

[74] *ibid.*, IV, 10, 9.

and rubricized, cannot be said to be concerned with the true faith: "It boils down to this: that Christ is to be sought in what they call 'species of bread.' . . . But whatever words they introduce to disguise it, this is the purpose of them all: through consecration, what was previously bread is made Christ, so that thereupon Christ lies hidden under the appearance of bread. . . . One can see in what great superstition not only the common folk but also the leaders themselves have been held for some centuries, and today are held in papists' churches. They are little concerned about true faith by which alone we attain fellowship with Christ and cleave to him."[75] The union with Christ through fellowship with him is a personal union, and this union cannot be attained by means of a thing. It is deeply personal and cannot be objectivized in a piece of bread. No species of abstract, impersonal reductionism can be the person to person moment when Christ meets man, and feeds him on his body and blood, and becomes one with him.

SACRAMENTAL IDOLATRY

There are few theological attitudes in Calvin's theology stronger than "God is himself the sole and proper witness to himself."[76] No created thing can ultimately contain the glory of God, and no creature can, in any adequate way, witness to God. To witness to God adequately is to be God. The desire of man to bring God near to him, and in some shadowed form to capture and contain the glory of God, not merely to domesticate God, but by means of this shadowed form of glory to attempt to witness to God with a semblance of propriety and adequacy, this desire is delusive, and, in its deepest meaning, idolatrous. God rejects as a sin against his glory all attempts on the part of a church to divinize itself and its sacraments in order that it may in this way give back the glory to God. Whatever excuses one may find for simple people who are misled, the temptation strikes at

[75] *ibid.*, IV, 17, 13.   [76] *ibid.*, I, 11, 1.

the root of man's relationship to God, and for this reason the temptation has about it the breath of malice, that cunning peculiar to the diabolical, which perverts the highest aspirations and clothes them in the shining armor of light, only to find it is not really light, but the bright phantoms of the blind. The temptation is as enduring as is man's awareness of God, and is not a temptation peculiar to primitive peoples. It has always been with the church, and what was true of the Old Testament idols is true of the New Testament idols: "God's glory is corrupted by an impious falsehood whenever any form is attached to him."[77]

Adequate witness as idolatry

It was Calvin's conviction that it was to this temptation that the medieval church had succumbed.[78] She was idolatrous not only in her use of statues, but in the proud assertion that she stood over against God, not as against an enemy, but as the self-divinized structure which bore God an adequate and proper witness. The highest expression of this presumption—or perhaps the lowest—was transubstantiation where, through the objectivization of the divine person, through the depersonalizing of the $\dot{\upsilon}\pi\dot{o}\sigma\tau\alpha\sigma\iota\varsigma$, through the localizing of the transcendent, an adequate witness to God could be given. And this witness is at man's good pleasure: "Unclean and profane men may, whenever they like and for whatever abuse they please, fashion the body of Christ."[79] God could be manipulated, taken by the hands and borne through the streets: "They consecrate the host, as they call it, to carry it about in procession, to display it in solemn spectacle that it may be seen, worshiped and called upon."[80] In a narrower theological context, this is idolatrous because it gives to bread what belongs to God. "What then? Shall

[77] ibid., I, 11, 1.

[78] "No sooner do we open the Institution Chrétienne than we are struck with Calvin's conviction that the fundamental error to be countered in medieval religion is idolatry." Louis Bouyer, The Spirit and Forms of Protestantism, Westminster, 1956, 60.

[79] Inst., IV, 18, 8.   [80] ibid., 17, 37.

we deny that this is superstitious worship when men prostrate themselves before bread to worship Christ there. . . . What is idolatry if not this: to worship the gifts in place of the Giver himself?"[81] "Now, let them go and deny that it is idolatry when they display bread in their masses to be worshiped in place of Christ."[82]

Calvin recognizes that the Roman practice is based on the doctrine of concomitance. Calvin does not think in terms of a speculative theology, but in terms of the biblical command, "This is my body. . . . This is my blood. . . . Take and eat." For this reason he has difficulties accepting concomitance: "What sane and sober man can convince himself that Christ's body is Christ?"[83] Further, the arguments for concomitance are based on an indeterminate. How can one take an indeterminate as a premise and arrive at a certainty? "Indeed, they think that they neatly prove this [concomitance] with their syllogisms. But since Christ speaks separately of his body and his blood, without describing the mode of his presence, how will they incontrovertibly prove what they wish by a thing that is indeterminate?"[84]

The lines of the solution are to be found in the clarity with which Christ sets before us bread as food and wine as drink: "The Lord shows us bread and says that it is his body: he shows the cup and calls it his blood."[85] If Christ had thought of himself as whole and entire under each form, he would have said so without ambiguity: "Obviously, if he had meant to signify his whole self, he could have said, 'It is I',—as he is accustomed to speak in the Scriptures—but not, 'This is my body; this is my blood.' "[86] Christ's intentions in giving himself under two forms are clear: "To teach us that he suffices for drink no less than for food."[87] From this Calvin draws the conclusion that he who receives communion only in one kind, receives "only one half the nourishment in him."[88] Calvin, it should be noted, does not say that he who re-

81 *ibid.*, 17, 36. 82 *ibid.*, 18, 8. 83 *ibid.*, 17, 35.
84 *ibid.* 85 *ibid.*, 17, 47. 86 *ibid.* 87 *ibid.*
88 *ibid.*

ceives only in one kind, receives only a half of Christ, but, something which is quite different, that such a communicant receives only a half a nourishment. Calvin does not categorically reject concomitance.

Calvin's problem here is not essentially in the theological order but in the existential order; he objects not so much to the Catholic teaching on concomitance in the abstract— though he is always a bit unhappy with speculation—as to the derivative pastoral practice in the concrete. He has no intention of basing a pastoral practice, exposition of and processions with the bread, on what he considers the uncertainties of a dubious speculation in the face of Christ's clear command to eat his body and to drink his blood. "Therefore bidding farewell to their quibbles, we must hold fast to the benefit that, with a double pledge we receive from the ordinance of Christ."[89]

Scriptural norm transgressed

Calvin asks the question, "What is their pretext for the boast that they worship Christ in that bread, when they have no promise of such a thing?"[90] This for Calvin is a valid question, because for him "there is no sacrament of God except where a ceremony is shown joined to a promise, or rather, except where a promise is seen in a ceremony."[91] Where there is no promise there can be no sacrament. Now, the eucharistic promise is found in the words of institution: "This is my body, take and eat. This is my blood which shall be shed for you. Take, all of you, and drink." The promise finds fulfillment only when the command to take and eat is fulfilled. What is the promise attached to the adoration of the host? There is none. And men cannot institute such a sacrament since they cannot give such a promise: "Since sacraments imply a promise of God, they ought to be instituted, not by angels, not by men, but by God alone, to whom alone it belongs to give the promise."[92] Nor can

[89] *ibid.*   [90] *ibid.*, 17, 37.   [91] *ibid.*, 19, 33.
[92] *ibid.*, 19, 27.

one say that the adoration of the Eucharist is just a valid extension of what Christ has given us. There can be no other use of the sacrament than that which Christ has explicitly commanded and for which there is a corresponding promise: "The promises of the Lord extend only to the uses which he has authorized."[93]

It is, then, clearly a matter of idolatry "when men prostrate themselves before bread to worship Christ there."[94] When Roman Catholics answer that it is not to the bread, which is no longer bread, nor to the whiteness or species, which remain, that the worship is rendered, but to Christ, Calvin answers: "If this were done in the Supper [Calvin contrasts the adoration given in the Supper with that given during benediction or that given during a procession] I would say that the only lawful adoration is that which does not rest in the sign, but is directed to Christ seated in heaven."[95] But this is not the case with the Romans. They pay "divine honors to the sign."[96]

The evil of this idolatrous practice is to be found not only in the giving of divine honors to a material thing, but also in halting that movement of adoration, of which the Eucharist is the occasion, by which men raise their hearts to God. When the adoration is halted at the outward sign, men raise their eyes to heaven. This is doubtless what the Council of Nicaea meant to forestall, says Calvin, when it forbade us "to fix our humble attention upon the symbols set before us."[97] And it was also to avoid any concentration on the external signs that "it was established of old that before the consecration the people should be told in a loud voice to lift up their hearts."[98] That also in this eucharistic moment our hearts should be raised above the earthly symbols is shown by the scripture, which, with conscious care, tells us of the Ascension of Christ "by which he withdrew the presence of his body from our sight and company, to shake from us all carnal thinking of him."[39] "But also whenever it re-

[93] OS I:526.   [94] *Inst.*, IV, 17, 36.   [95] *ibid.*, 17, 37.
[96] *ibid.*   [97] *ibid.*, 17, 36.   [98] *ibid.*   [99] *ibid.*

calls him, bids our minds be raised up, and seek him in heaven, seated at the right hand of the Father."[100]

The Ascension is the surety that Christ is to be sought only in heaven, that the *sursum corda* is the biblical norm of adoration, a norm which is personal and actual, in which God remains subject and is not objectivized. The *sursum corda* is the rule of prayer, eucharistic or otherwise. "According to this rule, we ought rather to have adored him spiritually in heavenly glory than to have devised some dangerous kind of adoration, replete with a carnal and crass conception of God."[101] To set aside this rule and to seek God in the sign is to set aside the norm of scripture. It is to act without either a commandment or a promise. "We have not been commanded to adore, but to take and to eat."[102] When we act without either a commandment or a promise "this holy sacrament is made a hateful idol."[103] This idol is repudiated by God with the same aversion with which he rejects other idols, and the idolatry is no less crass because it is supported by the sophistication of scholastic speculation: "Without exception he [God] repudiates all likenesses, pictures, and other signs by which the superstitious have thought he will be near them."[104] To depersonalize God, to objectify him, to domesticate him, to cast him in a form or species, to place him at man's good pleasure, even if this is done with the intention of giving adoration to God, is essentially diabolical because it goes beyond and against the Word of God, because it forgets what God is and what man is, because it forgets that "God himself is the sole and proper witness to himself."[105]

Ceremonial Exhibitionism

RITUALISM

The church which divinizes itself and its sacraments, which makes absolute claims for the sacramental order, which reduces the "personality" of the Eucharist to the im-

---

[100] *ibid.* [101] *ibid.* [102] OS I:522.
[103] *ibid.*, I, 11, 1. [104] *Inst.*, IV, 17, 36. [105] *ibid.*, I, 11, 1.

personality of a thing which can be summoned at will, housed and unhoused in the tabernacle, and carried about in solemn procession, will, not surprisingly, easily give in to the temptation of ceremonial exhibitionism. It is a short and logical step from sacramental impersonalism to ritual impersonalism, from sacramental mechanism to ritual mechanism. The church which forgets to renew its life by the daily experience of the Word will soon forget to live by the Word and will seek its justification in the techniques of logic and in the virtuosity of scholastic speculation. The externality of a highly structured abstract theology which has lost its biblical roots will not feel uneasy with the externality of ceremonial exhibitionism. And the divinization of the church will give to this great mass of sanctuary etiquette—some legislated, some the product of unthinking imitation of Christ, some the product of custom, some the product of abuse, some taken over from the courtly manners of the secular princes—a kind of eternal validity.[106] And to this posturing there is no end. Though created from below it must be received and observed as though given from above. The church becomes the place where the rubrician's dream and command are the law of salvation and the preacher of the Word is unheard, and, not infrequently, unknown. The sacraments are not that "living experience" in which "we grasp the efficacy of [Christ's] death,"[107] but rather this incomprehensible rite, performed in an unknown tongue, which must be gone through with wooden fidelity, from which some heavenly effect is automatically received.[108]

106 Cf. *ibid.*, IV, 10, 8; *ibid.*, 17, 43–IV, 17, 46. It is certainly to mistake Calvin's intentions to think that he wanted to worship in a bare whitewashed room. Cf. Eduard Stricker, "Calvins liturgische Bedeutung," *Monatsschrift für Gottesdienst und kirchliche Kunst*, vol. 14 (1909), 219, 220.

107 *Inst.*, IV, 17, 4.

108 Cf. *ibid.*, 14, 4; *ibid.*, III, 20, 33. The want of personalism in sacramental theology was seen as a complement to the lack of personalism and inwardness in ecclesiology. Doumergue comments on Bellarmine's ecclesiology as representative of that against which Calvin fought. Cf. Doumergue, *op.cit.*, 14 Cf. also Willem Nijenjuis, "Die Aufgabe der Reformierten Kirchen in der ökumenischen Bewegung," *Calvin—Studien 1959*, ed. Jürgen Moltmann, Neukirchen, 1960, 68.

Triumphant theatricalism

Calvin is not against all ceremony, but rather he takes a position against attaching too much importance to a given rite. He chides John Knox for being unbending on a matter of ritual, unbending even to the point of disturbing a refugee congregation with Anglican ritualistic leanings.[109] For Calvin this is clearly going too far and he will have none of it, and says so.

When ceremony becomes pomp, Calvin is up in arms. He takes it as a matter of principle that "wherever there is great ostentation in ceremonies, sincerity of heart is rare indeed."[110] Long public prayers, repetitive and garrulous, accompanied with triumphant parading and chancel prancing can only be the prayer of a hypocrite who speaks much but does not reflect that he is speaking to God: "For Christ does not forbid us to persist in prayers, long, often, or with much feeling, but requires that we should not be confident in our ability to wrest something from God by beating upon his ears with a garrulous flow of talk, as if he could be persuaded as men are. For we know that hypocrites, because they do not reflect that they have to do with God, make the same pompous show in prayers as they would in a triumph."[111] There is much of the purely theatrical in this pomp, as though to impress the simple with techniques borrowed from the stage: "How much better it would be to omit from baptism all theatrical pomp, which dazzles the eyes of the simple and deadens their minds; whenever anyone is to be baptized, to present him to the assembly of believers and, with the whole church looking on as witness and praying over him, offer him to God."[112] The Romans also surround the ordination of priests and deacons with noisy grandeur; but then all this is a mere mask to hide the emptiness of these supposed sacraments: "They disguise their action [ordina-

[109] *The Works of John Knox*, ed. David Lang, Edinburgh, 1895, vol. 4, 51, 52.
[110] *Inst.*, I, 2, 2.   [111] *ibid.*, III, 20, 29.   [112] *ibid.*, IV, 15, 19.

tion of priests and deacons] with such pomp so that by the very show it may hold the veneration of simple folk. But among the same, what value can these masks have when nothing solid or true underlies them?"[113] Then there is the sham examination of candidates for ordination in the rite itself. "It is the same sort of concoction when they are led to the altar for ordination, and someone asks three times, in a language they cannot understand, whether they are worthy of that honor. Someone answers (who has never seen them, but that nothing should be lacking to the form, has his part in the play), 'They are worthy.' "[114]

Their ceremonial of ordination, they claim, is based on the example of Christ: "We are following—they say—the Lord's example. . . . They leave nothing which they do not preposterously counterfeit: I do not say like actors whose gestures have some art and meaning, but like apes, which imitate everything wantonly and without any discrimination."[115] The miracles of Christ are not proper matter for imitation, nor those acts peculiar to the divine nature such as Christ's breathing upon the apostles saying, "Receive the Holy Spirit." "Indeed they are so shameless as to dare affirm that they confer the Holy Spirit."[116]

Only God can make a rite

Calvin's norm for what is proper in the liturgy is scripture, and no human authority has the right to deviate from this norm. "There is . . . nothing safer than for us to lay aside all the presumption of human understanding and to cleave solely to what Scripture teaches. And surely, if we ponder that the Supper is of the Lord and not of men, there is no reason why we should allow ourselves to be moved even a hairsbreadth from it by any human authority or time-hallowed prescription."[117] A ceremony is not to be received simply because it is sanctified with age. Speaking of the ceremonies surrounding baptism, Calvin writes: "Though I

[113] *ibid.*, 5, 5. [114] *ibid.* [115] *ibid.*, 19, 29.
[116] *ibid.* [117] *ibid.*, 18, 12.

130

am aware how ancient the origin of this alien hodge-podge is, I still have the right, together with all pious men, to reject whatever men have dared to add to Christ's institution. . . . Spittle and such trumpery were openly brought in with unbridled license to the dishonor of baptism. By these experiences let us learn that there is nothing holier or better or safer than to be content with the authority of Christ alone."[118] Though he does not condemn all ceremonies instituted by the church—as an ideal he proposes the "least possible admixture of human invention"[119]—he tends to think of the institution of ceremonies along with the institution of sacraments. Since the Supper is of the Lord and not of men, men cannot institute additional ceremonies. Men cannot institute new ceremonies for the same reason that they cannot institute new sacraments. But this is precisely what the Romans have done. They have usurped a right which belongs to God and they have exercised this right in such a way that their rubrical fancies become binding in conscience. "The whole case rests upon this: if God is the sole lawgiver, men are not permitted to usurp this honor. . . . [They make rubrical decisions] that pretend to relate to the true worship of God, and that consciences are bound to keep, as if their observance were compulsory."[120] The sacraments have lost their scriptural purity by statutes and other elaborate embellishments because they are surrounded by ceremonies of human invention. "When I consider the proper end for which churches are erected, it appears to me more unbecoming their sacredness than I can tell to admit any other images than those living symbols which the Lord has consecrated by his own Word: I mean Baptism and the Lord's Supper, with the other ceremonies. By these our eyes ought to be more steadily fixed, and more vividly impressed, than to require the aid of any images which the wit of man may devise."[121]

In the Roman concern for ritual there is no concern for

[118] *ibid.*, 15, 19.   [119] *ibid.*, 19, 20.   [120] *ibid.*, 10, 8.
[121] *ibid.*, I, 11, 13.

the Word of God, either as justification for the ceremony, or as the normal context of a sacramental act: "We see how much the sacraments, as even today they are performed, have degenerated from their pristine purity. Everywhere there is too much of processions, ceremonies, and mimes; yet at the same time there is no consideration or mention of God's Word, without which even the sacraments themselves are not sacraments. Indeed, the very ceremonies established by God cannot lift their head in such a great crowd, but lie as if crushed down. . . . The Supper is completely buried since it has been turned into the mass, except that it is seen once a year, although in a mangled, halved, and mutilated form."[122] "Now, to get rid of this great pile of ceremonies [of the mass]" is how Calvin prefaces the description of his own eucharistic rite.[123] It is not that man has no need for ritual, but rather that God has foreseen the need for an external rite in ritual acts and spoken words, and by means of the sacraments and preaching he has fulfilled this need. If the church fulfills her function in preaching the Word of God faithfully, and if the sacraments are frequently set before the people, all the ritual needs of man are fulfilled. It is presumption to think that God has insufficiently provided for us in this matter. Why, then, this "muttering and gesticulating like sorcerers" on the part of the priests?[124]

RITUAL PELAGIANISM

Calvin's contempt for the liturgical externalism of Roman Catholicism, especially as experienced in the mass liturgy, goes deeper than this desire for personalism in eucharistic doctrine and in eucharistic liturgy. Surely theological personalism was a major concern in his systematics, as it was of all the reformation leaders. But to see in Calvin's rejection of liturgical externalism, and in his rejection of an even more moderate ritualism, only a desire for personalism in cult, for cultic norms less formalistic, less theatrical, less given to rubrical legalism, less pretentious of divinity, less

[122] *ibid.*, IV, 18, 20.   [123] *ibid.*, 17, 43.   [124] OS I:524.

imperialistic, would be to acknowledge undoubted truths, but to miss the point.[125] Nor was his highly vocalized contempt for the splendors of Gothic liturgy merely an attempt to return to a more interior, more penitential, more didactic form of worship, though it was all of these things. Further, it was not even his undoubted desire to return to the simple clarity of worship as found in the New Testament communities: spare, direct, clearly and simply structured— though it was also this. And, finally, it was, least of all, a desire to replace worship by sacrament with worship by the Word, though he shared with the other reformers the concern to restore the preaching of the Word to a more central role in the life of the church, and more specifically to give it a cultic role which it had once possessed but had lost.[126]

Calvin was impatient of liturgy not because he failed to recognize man's need for the symbolic and the act in sign, but because he saw in what he considered ceremonial exhibitionism the theological cousin of Pelagianism. Why all this muttering and incantation and posturing and offering of sacrifice if Christ has redeemed us? Are we attempting to redeem ourselves with these mimes? And why so much importance, even to a species of divinization, attached not only to the sacraments but also to the ritual of the sacraments? If all this ritualism and externalism, which is either produced by legislation or approved by legislation, is theologically valid, then Pelagianism could be respectable. If liturgy

[125] Cf. *Inst.*, IV, 15, 19.

[126] George Johnson is most certainly in error when he asserts that it was the intention of the Calvinistic forefathers "to re-establish *worship by preaching*." "Calvinism and Worship," *Evangelical Quarterly*, vol. 4 (1932), 381. William D. Maxwell would also reject this interpretation of Calvin (and Calvinism): "To imagine that Calvin wished to replace sacramental worship by a preaching service is completely to misunderstand his mind and work and to ignore all that he taught and did. His aim was twofold: to restore the eucharist in its primitive simplicity and true proportions—celebration and communion—as the central weekly service, and, within this service, to give the Holy Scriptures their authoritative place. The Lord's Supper, in all its completeness, was the norm he wished to establish." *An Outline of Christian Worship*, London, 1936, 112. Cf. also Wilhelm Niesel, *The Theology of Calvin*, Philadelphia, 1956, 215.

can be legislated, so can salvation. According to the theological presuppositions of Roman ritualism, Christ did not give us redemption but the power to redeem ourselves. Principally for this reason Calvin opposed the liturgical life of reformation Catholicism. He saw it as ritual Pelagianism.

Ritual Pelagianism as the medieval ethos

Ritual Pelagianism was not an isolated phenomenon, but rather the pervading ethos of medieval Christianity. Nor was it just the simple-minded who stood in awe of these sanctuary theatricals, but even those who made some claim to learning and worldly wisdom. "Today not only the untutored crowd but any man who is greatly puffed up with worldly wisdom is marvelously captivated by ceremonial pomp. Indeed, hypocrites and lightheaded women think that nothing more beautiful or better can be imagined."[127] It is not enough that "these traditions have been heaped one upon another and increased to such a number as to be unbearable to the Christian church,"[128] but the Romans make preposterous claims for them, maintaining that they contain the Christian mysteries. "I am speaking of those ceremonies under which the Romanist masters would have it that great mysteries exist."[129] The claims of Rome go beyond the insistence that in these ceremonies the mysteries of the faith are dramatized in some external and harmless way. Rather the ceremonies contain the mysteries of Christ in some definitive, self-contained manner. The mysteries of Christ are, in some way, bound up with the ceremonies so that the ceremonies confer salvation: "The ceremonies are sacrifices by which God is duly appeased, sins are cleansed, and righteousness and salvation obtained. . ."[130] Those who seek a salvation in ritual, seek in vain because God is offended by such presumption. Even in the Old Testament God would not allow either additions to, or abridgments of, the cultic laws given through Moses. Now that the "clearer doctrine"

[127] *Inst.*, IV, 10, 12.   [128] *ibid.*, 10, 13.   [129] *ibid.*, 10, 12.
[130] *ibid.*, 10, 15.

has been given through the prophets and through Christ we have even less excuse and are more strictly forbidden "to add anything to the law, prophets, psalms, and gospel."[131] "The Lord, who long ago declared that nothing so much offended him as being worshiped by humanly devised rites, has not become untrue to himself," now permitting man to follow his whims in worship.[132] "This is the reason for those wonderful words of the prophets which ought continually to resound in our ears: 'I did not speak to your fathers, in the day I brought them out of Egypt, words concerning burnt offerings and sacrifices. . . .' Does the Lord delight in burnt offerings and sacrifices and not rather that his voice be obeyed?"[133]

Calvin denies that "such works . . . derive their value from their own worth and merit," and it is pernicious to give "so much honor to works rashly devised at the will of men," and to believe that they are "meritorious for eternal life."[134] What can be said of the theological integrity or the pastoral sincerity of men who, "while commending the observance of God's commandments only coldly and perfunctorily . . . nonetheless zealously and busily urge an exact obedience of their own, as if these contained in themselves the whole force of piety?"[135] Calvin is not unaware that weak minds need external helps, that the symbolic life is a necessity, but, this notwithstanding, he objects "that this is not the way to take care of the weak—to overwhelm them with great heaps of ceremonies."[136] Much less is it pardonable that Rome permits the simple people to seek in these unending ceremonies a salvation which cannot be found there. "Our adversaries can therefore in no way excuse the fact that they let poor folk seek in those outward trifles a righteousness which they may offer to God, and which will uphold them before the tribunal of heaven."[137]

The Catholic experience of God is defective because it is peripheral. What is secondary—or tertiary—and marginal,

---

[131] *ibid.*, 10, 17.   [132] *ibid.*   [133] *ibid.*   [134] *ibid.*, 10, 15.
[135] *ibid.*, 10, 10.   [136] *ibid.*, 10, 14.   [137] *ibid.*, 10, 15.

what is commanded by men, has moved to the center. And that which is truly central, what is commanded by God, the preaching of the Word and the right celebration of the sacraments, is forgotten. In its simplest form Calvin's efforts are directed toward giving centrality to what is central. To purge the medieval ethos of its basic Pelagianism will need more than a minor shift of emphasis. How deep the Pelagianism goes can be seen in the eucharistic theology and practice.

Eucharistic self-redemption

What is true in general of the ceremonies which men have devised, is true also of the sacrifice of the mass, which too is a product of man's presumption.[138] The presumption is essentially Pelagian. It is "nothing else than to boast that we have been redeemed by Christ on condition that we redeem ourselves."[139] The mass contains "a new redemption" and "a new forgiveness," so that we have no need of Christ's death on the cross, indeed, do not even advert to his death: "For who can think himself redeemed by Christ's death, when he has seen new redemption in the mass? Who can trust that his sins are forgiven, when he has seen a new forgiveness? And it is no way out to say that we obtain forgiveness of sins in the mass solely because it has already been purchased by Christ's death. This amounts to nothing else than to boast that we have been redeemed by Christ on condition that we redeem ourselves."[140] There is no doubt as to what the priest who offers up the sacrifice of the mass and the people who participate intend: either "to merit God's favor," or to offer an "expiatory victim, by which they reconcile God to themselves."[141] "What now remains of Christ's Passion except that it is an example of redemption by which we learn that we are our own redeemers?"[142] The expiatory victim, who was offered once for all on the cross, is repeatedly offered in the mass by the priest so that "by repeating

[138] Cf. *ibid.*, 18, 19. [139] *ibid.*, 18, 6. [140] *ibid.*
[141] *ibid.*, 18, 1. [142] *ibid.*, 18, 6.

the oblation he obtains pardon for sins, appeases God, and acquires righteousness. But what else is done by performing masses except that by the merit of a new oblation we are made partakers in Christ's Passion?"[143] The attempt to repeat the oblation is nothing else than the attempt to make a "new and wholly different testament."[144] The testament demands the death of the testator and after his death nothing new can be added to the testament if it is to remain valid. By his death Christ has confirmed that testament by which he promised us "forgiveness of our sins and everlasting righteousness."[145] Those who dare to change or add to this testament which Christ has left us "deny his death and hold it of no importance."[146] "What is the mass but a new wholly different testament? Why so? Do not individual masses promise new forgiveness of sins, and new acquiring of righteousness, so that there are now as many testaments as there are masses?"[147]

The difference between the mass and the true sacrament of the Eucharist is the difference "between giving and receiving."[148] "The Supper itself is a gift of God, which ought to have been received with thanksgiving."[149] But this was not enough for the Romans. "The sacrifice of the mass is represented as paying a price to God, which he should receive by way of satisfaction."[150] So instead of receiving the Eucharist with thanksgiving, man has attempted to give something to God by means of which "he makes God, in this business, his debtor."[151] This is, indeed, "a strange inversion when a mortal man, who is commanded to take the body of Christ, claims the office of offering it; and thus a priest, who has been appointed by himself, sacrifices to God his own Son."[152] The priests not only attempt to offer the body of Christ, but they exercise a dominance over the body, "as if the Supper had been turned over to them."[153] One hears echoes here of the nominalist desire, as found in

---

[143] *ibid.*, 18, 14.   [144] *ibid.*, 18, 5.   [145] *ibid.*   [146] *ibid.*
[147] *ibid.*   [148] *ibid.*, 18, 7.   [149] *ibid.*   [150] *ibid.*   [151] *ibid.*
[152] CR 45:705, 706.   [153] Cf. *Inst.*, IV, 18, 7.

Thomas Bradwardine, Gregory of Rimini, and William of Occam, to free God from man's claims. Calvin too wishes to put man at God's disposal rather than God at man's.

Ethical derivatives

Because the priests have appropriated the Eucharist and have it at their disposal in the sacrifice of the mass and therefore have always at hand a new forgiveness and a new redemption, Roman Catholics have an excuse to give themselves to uninhibited knavery. They do not hesitate to trouble "widows with unjust dealings, to rob orphans, to afflict the poor, to seize the goods of others for oneself by devious tricks, to grasp after anyone's possession by perjuries and frauds, to oppress anyone with violence and tyrannous fear."[154] How is it that they dare to live such sinful lives, sinning with impunity and without regret? "If we only examine it, no cause encourages them more than this—the belief that they will satisfy God by the mass-sacrifice as a price that is paid, or at least that this is an easy way to settle with him."[155] Because they see in the sacrifice of the mass a new redemption, a price paid to God for their misdeeds, they have no shame. Nor does death hold any terrors for them. Rather they live and sin in comfort, assured that they have provided for their escape from the fires of purgatory by the bequest of a large sum of money which will be used to buy masses. After their death a great many masses will be read for the repose of their souls, indeed, the mass foundation which they erected before their death will assure them of a memorial mass yearly in perpetuity on the anniversary day of their death. Since the mass is the promise of forgiveness and the price of eternal life, they are assured the quiet conscience needed to plunder one's neighbor at ease and to give oneself to debauchery with dignity: "And what is the purpose today of yearly memorials and the greater number of masses, except that those who throughout life were the cruelest tyrants, or the most rapacious robbers, or men who

[154] *ibid.*, 18, 15.   [155] *ibid.*

stooped to every infamy, should, as if redeemed at this price, escape the fire of purgatory?"[156] The Romans have, however, observed a certain propriety in the selling of their masses; they sell their masses for the same number of coins as Judas sold his master. "They have kept a similarity in number. Judas sold him for thirty pieces of silver; these persons, according to the French reckoning, sell him for thirty pieces of copper; Judas, once; these, as often as they find a buyer."[157]

Whatever the Roman position, and Calvin acknowledges that Romans are not satisfied with his presentation of their teaching,[158] of these things we are sure: "We know that Christ's death and life are not at all in their [priests'] hands,"[159] and that Christ has "given us a table at which to feast, not an altar upon which to offer a victim; he has not consecrated priests to offer sacrifices, but ministers to distribute the sacred banquet."[160] The theological attitude proper to the Supper is not that of giving, but of receiving, not that of sacrificing, but of eating, not that of paying a debt, but that of receiving a gift—in a word, not of redeeming, but of receiving redemption. The Eucharist must not be made an excuse for casual sinning, nor for exploitation of one's neighbor. Rather, as shall be seen, it should inculcate a strong sense of social obligation.

Pastoral Ecclesiasticism

LITURGICAL CLERICALISM

Romanism, as Calvin experienced its ecclesiology on the pastoral level and as he interpreted it, was a clerical reality. An ecclesiology which is given to an exaggerated supernaturalism will also be given to various kinds of selectivity, a selectivity to the point of placing a part of the Christian community over against the other. Within the church there is the elite to whom the most sacred tasks are entrusted, and

156 *ibid.*   157 *ibid.*, 18, 14.   158 Cf. *ibid.*, 18, 5.
159 *ibid.*   160 *ibid.*, 18, 12.

this in some exclusive sense. The clerical elect, who are supposed to perform their liturgical role within the community, become separated from the community, and both the clerical group and their cultic tasks become highly structured, self-contained, self-perpetuating, having their justification in themselves, unrelated to the worshiping community of God's people. The clerical elect appropriate to themselves the title and function of God's people. Just as the church becomes identified with the clerical elite, so the worshiping activity of the church becomes identified with clerical worship. The clerical initiate, having appropriated both Word and sacrament, feeds his soul with ritual splendor and liturgical mystery within the sanctuary while the faithful noncleric, fed on neither the Word of Christ nor the body of Christ, stands in reverent passivity, beholding from beyond the sanctuary grill the glory of the real Israel at worship. Because he must have the strong food of Christ's Word and Christ's body and has not received it—the cleric is too busy incensing the altar—he turns to the peripheral, to relics and pilgrimages and indulgences. And the cleric liturgizes further, content to speak to his God in Latin and to his people not at all.

Cultic appropriation

Calvin could think of nothing more opposed to the theological understanding of the Eucharist than for it to be appropriated by the clergy and for the clergy to liturgize as though "the Supper had been turned over to them."[161] If the Eucharist was not the worship of the community, worshiping as community, participating as community, it was nothing. A liturgy which was without at least the type of cultic dialogue involved in instruction and preaching, could have no real validity. Not only in the abstract, in a given theological synthesis, is the Word inseparable from the sacrament, but also on the pastoral level. "The right administering of the sacrament cannot stand apart from the Word."[162]

[161] *ibid.*, 18, 7.   [162] *ibid.*, 17, 39.

Without the preached Word there is no sacrament, "therefore nothing more preposterous could happen in the Supper than for it to be turned into a silent action, as has happened under the pope's tyranny."[163] Instead of finding the meaning of the sacrament in the "visible word," that is the coming together of doctrine and sign, they have sought it rather in the intention of the priest alone. "They wanted to have the whole force of the consecration depend upon the intention of the priest, as if it did not matter at all to the people, to whom the mystery ought most of all to have been explained."[164] Since the Eucharist is an act of the assembled community and not just of one person, it is "a monstrous profanation of the mysteries" to make all depend on the intention of the priest instead of on the living Word given in the preaching which is to accompany each sacrament.[165] Both Word and sacrament are "because of the people"— *propter hominem*—but the Romans have "thought it enough if the priest mumbled the formula of consecration while the people looked on bewildered and without comprehension."[166] The clericalization of the eucharistic act is more than an accident of history; whatever the historical development, the intention is now clear: "Indeed, they deliberately saw to it that . . . nothing of doctrine should penetrate to the people; for they spoke everything in Latin in the presence of the unlearned [of the congregation]."[167]

In Calvin's mind this is to misunderstand the role of the Word or the promises which must accompany each sacrament. The promises, which in the case of the Eucharist are the words of institution, are to be spoken to the people, not to an inert piece of bread, "not to the elements themselves but to those who receive them."[168] And because they have lost sight of the essential function of the promises or the words of institution, the Romans have fallen into superstitions. "Afterward superstition came to the point that they believed consecration duly performed only in a hoarse whis-

[163] *ibid.*   [164] *ibid.*, 17, 39. Cf. also CR 45:823.
[165] *Inst.*, IV, 14, 4.   [166] *ibid.*   [167] *ibid.*   [168] *ibid.*, 17, 39.

per which few could hear," namely the clerical initiate gathered around the altar.[169]

Eucharistic spoliation: the private mass

In two areas especially Calvin sees the clericalization of the Eucharist: the private masses and communion under only one kind. In his mind even a public mass can be a private mass, if there is no communion of the people: "I call it a private mass (that no man may be mistaken) wherever there is no participation in the Lord's Supper among believers, even though a large multitude of men may otherwise be present."[170] The private mass cannot be harmonized with true eucharistic doctrine and it is more than just an abuse of something incidental to either eucharistic doctrine or eucharistic practice. "I say that private masses are diametrically opposed to Christ's institution, and are for that reason an impious profaning of the sacred Supper."[171]

The first error was that "there ought to be priests to perform sacrifice on the people's behalf."[172] And because the priests were thought to be performing the sacrifice on behalf of the people they soon acted as though "the Supper had been turned over to them."[173] Having appropriated the Supper for themselves, the Supper "ceased to be communicated to the believers' church according to the Lord's commandment," that is, the people were no longer given communion at each mass.[174] From this abuse followed the abuse of the private mass. Each priest, as though busy about some private devotion, reads his mass in some corner of the church, celebrating silently and receiving communion alone. Since there are "innumerable masses in every corner of the churches," and since the laity come to see but not to participate in or

---

[169] ibid., 14, 4. Cf. also ibid., 17, 39.

[170] ibid., 18, 7. It must be kept in mind that much of Calvin's polemic against Roman eucharistic practice is directed against the private mass in which there was no communion of the faithful. Cf. P. Vanbergen, "Le renouveau liturgique dans les églises issues de la réforme," Les Questions Liturgique et Paroissiales, vol. 41 (1960), 251.

[171] Inst., IV, 18, 8.   [172] ibid., 18, 7.   [173] ibid.   [174] ibid.

communicate, the people walk hither and thither about the church, from altar to altar visiting the various far corners in which a priest is reading his mass.[175]

The multiplication of many masses in various parts of the church, which "drag the people hither and thither," is in opposition to that unity of which the Eucharist is a symbol.[176] "Since he has only one body, of which he makes us all partakers, it is necessary that all of us also be made one body by such participation. The bread shown in the sacrament represents this unity."[177] The private mass represents a divisive force, pulling the people to various parts of the church "when they should have come together in one assembly to recognize the mystery of their own unity."[178] Under these conditions one can hardly speak of "that community established by the Lord," that oneness of the people of God as they stand before their Lord.[179] Quite the contrary, the private mass represents "an excommunication" of the people by the priest.[180] "The petty sacrificer, about to devour his victim by himself, separates himself from all believing folk."[181] That unity of which the Eucharist is a symbol is destroyed by the sacrifice of the mass, and the Eucharist becomes a cause of fragmentation in the worshiping community: "The Supper was to have been distributed in the public assembly of the church to teach us of the communion by which we all cleave together in Christ Jesus. The sacrifice of the mass dissolves and tears apart this community."[182]

The clerical cup

Because the Eucharist conceived in such exclusive hieratic terms is essentially clerical, communion under both kinds too will be looked upon as a privilege of "a few shaven and anointed men."[183] It is precisely because the mass is a sacrifice, and sacrifice is a priestly affair, that the layman has been denied the cup. The argument goes along scriptural lines.

[175] *ibid.*, 18, 8. [176] *ibid.* [177] *ibid.*, 17, 38. [178] *ibid.*, 18, 8.
[179] *ibid.*, 18, 7. [180] *ibid.* [181] *ibid.* [182] *ibid.*
[183] *ibid.*, 17, 47.

"Only the apostles, whom he [Christ] had already chosen and enrolled in the order of 'sacrificers,' were admitted by Christ to participate in this Supper."[184] In other words, Christ gave both body and blood to the apostles because the apostles were priests and therefore sacrificers. This, for Calvin, is a curious argument since "for the first thousand years after the apostles, all, without exception, partook of both symbols. Did the ancient church not know whom Christ had admitted as guests to his Supper?"[185]

The command of Christ is abundantly clear. "For what has the Lord bidden us? Is it not to take and divide among us?"[186] "Now among them, there is but one who eats the whole; and even at Easter, he gives but a part of it to the people."[187] "When therefore, one person receives it without sharing, what similarity is there" to what Christ commanded when he said "Take and eat. . . . Take and drink!"[188] The Catholics answer "that one man . . . does it in the name of the whole church."[189] But when "a person privately seizes for himself what ought to have been done only among many," this is surely to mock the command.[190] Beyond this "they pretend perils that could occur if this sacred cup were commonly offered to all."[191]

There is not a little of clerical arrogance in the assumption that profane persons—Calvin wonders how anyone who belongs to God's inheritance can be profane—should not be allowed to receive the cup. "The symbol of the blood, which, denied to lay and profane persons (these are titles they apply to God's inheritance), was given as a special property to a few shaven and anointed men. The edict of the eternal God is that all should drink; man dares supersede and abrogate it by a new and opposing law decreeing that not all should drink."[192] And in this way the clergy have "either stolen or snatched half the Supper from the greater part of God's people."[193]

---

[184] *ibid.*, 17, 42.   [185] *ibid.*   [186] *ibid.*, 18, 8.
[187] CR 13:22.   [188] *Inst.*, IV, 18, 8.   [189] *ibid.*   [190] *ibid.*
[191] *ibid.*, 17, 47.   [192] *ibid.*   [193] *ibid.*, 17, 47.

Their position is maintained in direct opposition to the practice of the first thousand years of the church's life and in opposition to condemnations and prohibitions of the fathers, indeed, of the popes themselves. Calvin quotes Chrysostom: "Not as in the Old Law the priest ate part, the people part; but one body and one cup are offered to all. Those things which pertain to the Eucharist are all common to priest and people."[194] And Gelasius uses even stronger language. Either the people are to receive both symbols or none: "We have found that some, receiving only the portion of the sacred body, refrain from the cup. Doubtless, since they seem to be bound by some sort of superstition, they are either to receive the sacraments entire or to be entirely barred from them."[195] That both the consecrated bread and the consecrated wine were to be received, as can be seen from the legislation and writings of the fathers of the first thousand years, "was considered not merely a custom but an inviolable law."[196] "This custom did not fall into disuse while one drop of integrity remained in the church."[197] It was more than a pastoral practice for the early church for they did "not doubt that it was a sacrilege to separate what had been joined by the Lord."[198] Yet the Roman Catholics "dare cloak such abominations with the name of church and defend them on that pretext."[199]

What is at stake here is not tradition nor the authority of the pope, but the Eucharist itself. "This mystery cannot be divided without great sacrilege."[200] To commit this sacrilege is not to abuse the sacrament but to destroy it. "Because Christ's and Paul's words are clear enough ('Take and eat. . . . Take and drink'), we . . . conclude that wherever there is not this breaking of bread for the communion of believers, it is not the Lord's Supper, but a false and preposterous imitation of it."[201]

The communion of believers was not a rare event in the early church. "There is not the least doubt that the sacred

---

[194] ibid., 17, 48 quoting Chrysostom. Cf. PL 61:527.
[195] ibid., 187:1756.   [196] Inst., IV, 17, 49.   [197] ibid.   [198] ib:d.
[199] ibid., 17, 50.   [200] ibid., 17, 49.   [201] ibid., 18, 8.

Supper was in that era of Zepherinus set before the believers every time they met; and there is no doubt that a majority of them took communion."[202] But the practice among the Roman Catholics is quite something else. "It has come about that almost all, when they have taken communion once, as though they have beautifully done their duty for the rest of the year, go about unconcerned. . . . Plainly this custom which enjoins us to take communion once a year is a veritable invention of the devil."[203]

Liturgical clericalism, then, is a ritualized form of excommunication by means of which the community of believers is excluded from active participation in the eucharistic liturgy. Both rite and chalice are clerical things. The Eucharist is atomized according to the number and devotion of the priests celebrating their own private masses. To atomize the Eucharist is to atomize the church. One cannot have a eucharistic problem of such magnitude without a corresponding ecclesiological problem. On the ecclesiological level the atomizing was a reduction of the church to structure.

STRUCTURAL CHURCHMANSHIP

Romanism, as seen through Calvin's eyes, was essentially clerical. A clericalism concerned about the interior realities, sensitive to the inner call of the Holy Spirit, fed on the Word of God, consecrated without calculation to the pastoral work of the church, this kind of clericalism Calvin could have understood. Calvin says that what he experienced in Roman Catholicism was not a concern for interior realities or consecration without calculation, but an unabashed concern for the structure, for the bare bones by which it was held together, for the scaffolding which gave form to its facade.

[202] *ibid.*, 17, 46.

[203] *ibid.* Under the force of circumstances, which he could not control, Calvin had to modify his demands as regards the frequency with which the Eucharist ought to be celebrated. He began by asserting that it should be celebrated at least once a week, then once a month, and finally four times a year (Christmas, Easter, Pentecost, and the first Sunday of September). Cf. OS I:371; CR 10A:25; *Inst.*, IV, 16, 43.

This structure had no need to justify itself, did not stand under judgment, had, seemingly, no other purpose than to preserve itself. Self-preservation and self-perpetuation were its *raison d'être*. The structure was not to be doubted and not to be questioned, and, most of all, not to be disturbed, because it was the heavenly Jerusalem let down from heaven before its time, the Platonic image of the eternal reality made incarnate in history. Because it was an eternal reality the structure had one answer to all doubters and detractors: apostolic succession. There was no theological problem, no scriptural difficulty, no historical ambiguity to which apostolic succession was not the answer. The individual who sought assurance of comfort in this life and salvation in the next had only to become part of the structure. Faith was not important, nor penitence, but to be a cleric was. And the cleric's business was to say mass and preserve the established disorder. Seen against such a background it can be a matter of small wonder that Calvin's ecclesiology was strongly influenced by Bucer's stress on discipline and union with Christ.

The gilded sinecure

To seek a pastoral office was, in Calvin's mind, to be entrusted with a responsibility. It was not primarily an honor, and certainly not a legal fiction by which one could lay claim to a comfortable income. "Those ordained are not to think themselves promoted to an honor but charged with an office which they are with solemn attestation obligated to discharge. But the Roman masters (who think that nothing ought to be taken care of in religion except the belly) first interpret the title as meaning an income sufficient for their support."[204]

There is something essentially evil about a pastoral situation in which the pastoral offices are given "not to benefit the churches but those men who receive them."[205] Those

[204] *ibid.*, IV, 5, 4.   [205] *ibid.*, 5, 6.

147

who are promoted to ordination "are more concerned about their own advantage than about the upbuilding of the church."[206] Those so ordained exploit the Eucharist for their financial support. They "hire out their daily labor in celebrating masses or chanting, and earn a living, so to speak, by the fees they collect for this."[207] This is a perversion of the pastoral office, which is essentially ordained to service, to instruction, and to discipline. The pastors "have been set over the church not to have a sinecure, but, by the doctrine of Christ, to instruct the people in true godliness, to administer the sacred mysteries and to keep and exercise upright discipline."[208]

Because the office of pastor is seen as a sinecure, the priests have attempted to wring from it the utmost advantage. Exploiting the piety and religious generosity of the people, they assure themselves a comfortable living, and, not out of their own pockets, but with alms meant for the poor, they erect, extend, enrich, and embellish the externals of religion, and this while neglecting pure doctrine and the pastoral duty of instructing the people. Nothing is able "to satisfy the voraciousness of the priests. For while they try to spare themselves, they induce the people by superstition to apply what should have been distributed to the poor, to constructing churches, erecting statues, buying vessels, and providing sacred vestments. Thus are daily alms consumed in this abyss."[209] There is no excuse given for this passion for display. On the contrary, "they say that the dignity of the Church is decently sustained by this magnificence."[210]

Calvin knows that he is not alone in protesting against this heaping of gold on gold, and ornament on ornament. "Jerome also, when he inveighs against excessive splendor of churches, honorably mentions Exuperius, bishop of Toulouse in his day, who carried the Lord's body in a wicker basket and his blood in a glass vessel, but suffered no poor man to hunger."[211] Calvin's protest here is against an excessive pre-

206 *ibid.,* 3, 7.   207 *ibid.,* 5, 9.   208 *ibid.,* 3, 6.
209 *ibid.,* 5, 18.   210 *ibid.,* 5, 17.   211 *ibid.,* 4, 8.

occupation with gilded churches and golden copes; but it is also against the neglect of the poor. The temples of stone are decorated and filled with statues, relics, altars, plaques, and this without thought of moderation. But "so far are they from taking due care of living temples that they would rather let many thousands of the poor die of hunger than break the smallest cup or cruet to relieve their need."[212]

And the abuse of the pastoral office is not confined to the lower orders of the clergy, nor even to the ignorant among the bishops. "If any [bishops] are more learned—of this, however, instances are rare—they deem the bishopric nothing but a title of splendor and magnificence."[213] Is this, then, the structure for which they claim apostolic origins? Is this, then, the pastoral office, "to glow with pride in the delicacies of the table, splendor of apparel, a great retinue of servants and magnificent palaces?"[214] The bishops have forgotten the injunction from antiquity that "the glory of the bishop is to provide for the poor."[215] When the clergy are so taken up with benefices, titles, the building of churches, and the other externalities of religion it cannot be a matter of surprise that "today the courts resound with more lawsuits over priestly offices than almost anything else."[216] These lawsuits show the basically secular, monetary consideration as the basis of the pastoral office realized in Roman Catholicism. "How foolish it is to seek church order here!"[217]

Mechanistic apostolic succession

"To defend such a disordered government" they put forward the name of Christ.[218] Specifically they say: "We are the pillars of the church, the leaders of religion, the vicars of Christ, the heads of believers; for the apostolic power has come to us by succession."[219] It is to this claim, that of apos-

---

[212] *ibid.*, 5, 18.   [213] *ibid.*, 5, 13.   [214] *ibid.*, 5, 17.
[215] *ibid.*, 5, 19.   [216] *ibid.*, 5, 6.   [217] *ibid.*, 5, 19.
[218] *ibid.*, 5, 13.
[219] *ibid.* Apostolic succession was also bound up with the objectivization of the Spirit. Cf. Haas, *op.cit.*, 518.

tolic succession, that they repeatedly return, as though it were
the answer to all questions. When their rule is accused of des-
potism "they unfailingly mention that it is that venerable hier-
archy often praised by great and holy men," as though "this
formless chaos" was "handed down to them from the apostles."[220] It is ultimately this claim which insures that the structure will not, indeed cannot, perish, though it is rotten with
abuses and corruption. Apostolic succession has become for them
the excuse for such abuses as pluralities. "They cloak such
abominable foulness with the name of church in order that
they may escape from all rebuke! But also, if it please God,
in this villainy is contained that most holy 'succession,' whose
merit—they boast—ensures that the church does not perish."[221] This boast is an attempt to bind God to a given
structure without thought for his sovereignty. If the Old Testament temple was abandoned, why not that which has only
"the title and appearance of the church." "If that Temple, which
seemed consecrated as God's everlasting abode, could be
abandoned by God and become profane, there is no reason
why these men should pretend to us that God is so bound to
persons and places, and attached to external observances, that
he has to remain among those who have only the title and
appearance of the church."[222]

Calvin rejects the notion that the "church exists wherever
bishops succeed one another."[223] This is much too organizational a concept of apostolic succession, too mechanistic, too
preoccupied with mere structural continuity, and not sufficiently preoccupied with that deeper continuity which is
founded in purity of doctrine. "Especially in the organization
of the church nothing is more absurd than to lodge the succession in persons alone to the exclusion of teaching."[224]
However much they insist on apostolic succession, however
often they repeat their claim, "it is clear that the order they
have is neither from Christ, nor from his apostles, nor from
the fathers, nor from the ancient church."[225]

[220] *Inst.*, IV, 5, 13.   [221] *ibid.*, 5, 7.   [222] *ibid.*, 2, 3.
[223] *ibid.*   [224] *ibid.*   [225] *ibid.*, 5, 14.

Economics of churchmanship

The structure is maintained in existence and, at the same time, given a semblance of religious purpose by the ordination of priests who support themselves by saying mass. In this way the pastoral office is stripped of all its essential functions and becomes that inward-looking clericalism which is no longer ordained to the people of God but to perpetuating itself. "I say briefly, if it be the presbyter's office . . . to feed the church, and administer the spiritual Kingdom of Christ, all such sacrificers who have work or wages only in the hawking of masses not only fail in their office, but have no lawful office to exercise. For no place is given them for teaching; they have no people to govern. In short, nothing is left to them but the altar on which they sacrifice Christ."[226] The whole of the pastoral office is seen in terms of ritual Pelagianism. "For what ministry to the church can they perform? They have cast off as burdens too troublesome the preaching of the Word, the care of discipline, and the administering of the sacraments. For what do they have left by which to boast they are true presbyters? Well, they have singing and ceremonial pomp."[227] The whole of the pastoral office is, for them, contained in the word "sacrifice." "For they ordain no one, except to perform sacrifice."[228] "They create by their ordination not presbyters to lead and feed the people, but priests to perform sacrifices."[229] The whole structure is dominated by the idea of sacrifice and ceremony, even the lower orders. "Similarly, when they consecrate deacons, they do nothing about their true and proper office, but ordain them only for certain rites concerned with chalice and paten. . . . They charge them only with ministering at the altar, reading or chanting the gospel and goodness knows what other trifles."[230]

The continuing structure, together with its inevitable sacrifice, was seen as so necessary and so comfortable that priests

[226] *ibid.*, 5, 9.   [227] *ibid.*, 5, 10.   [228] *ibid.*, 5, 5.
[229] *ibid.*, 5, 4.   [230] *ibid.*

were ordained for whom there was no vacancy. And against these "indiscriminate ordinations" Calvin raised his voice.[231] "Is it not always absurd to appoint a presbyter to whom you assign no place? For they ordain no one, except to perform sacrifice."[232] Calvin reminds his Roman friends that the Council of Chalcedon had laid down that "there should be no ordinations free of pastoral obligations, that is, that a place be assigned to the person ordained where he is to exercise his office."[233] But what is even more absurd, Calvin contends, is the practice of ordaining monks to the priestly office and then forbidding the monks to exercise pastoral rights. Not that Calvin is in favor of monk-pastors. "Let this now be enough: in the purer church it was considered a great absurdity for a monk to function in the priesthood."[234] It was a contradiction in terms because the "presbyter's duty is to rule his own church," while the monks, by reason of their vocation, do not rule a church. "Some of the mendicants preach; all the rest of the monks either chant or mutter masses in their dens."[235] The absurdity is carried further because "when they are ordained they are expressly forbidden to do the things that God has enjoined upon all presbyters. . . . It is an open mockery of God when anyone is made a presbyter with the purpose of abstaining from his true and genuine office."[236]

Nonpreaching preachers

Calvin's bitter language is partly due to the large role the sacrifice of the mass played in ritual Pelagianism, liturgical clericalism, and structural churchmanship, but most of all he was bitter over the neglect of the people; they were left unnoticed, uninstructed, and undisciplined. "For Christ commanded that stewards of his gospel and sacraments be ordained, not that sacrificers be installed. He gave a command to preach the gospel and feed the flock, not to sacrifice victims. He promised the grace of the Holy Spirit not to enable

[231] *ibid.*, 5, 4.   [232] *ibid.*, 5, 5.   [233] *ibid.*, 5, 4.
[234] *ibid.*, 5, 8.   [235] *ibid.*   [236] *ibid.*

them to make atonement for sins, but duly to engage in and maintain the government of the church."[237] The ministry is not a matter of receiving honor or a place in a structure, but of preaching the Word of God. "We are not concerned about some hereditary honor which can be given to men while they are sleeping, but about the office of preaching, from which they so strenuously flee."[238] There is "scarcely one man in a hundred who once in his whole life mounted any pulpit."[239] The examination which takes place in the ordination ceremony is not about ability to preach the gospel, but they are asked "whether they can read their masses, whether they can decline some common noun that occurs in the lesson, whether they can conjugate a verb."[240] The bishop who is ordaining is hardly better prepared for his office than the men he ordains. Bishops are not chosen for their learning or their ability to preach; and when learning is elevated to the episcopal office, it is not the learning of a theologian or a preacher but of a canon lawyer. "The practice of having an examination of learning has, to be sure, become too old-fashioned. But if learning is held in any regard, they choose a lawyer who knows how to plead in a court rather than how to preach in a church."[241] The pastoral instinct is wholly wanting where there is no apostolic structure.

Pastoral insensitivity

Roman Catholicism has also manifested a lack of pastoral sensitivity in relating its structure to the needs of the soul. There is in man the need for assurance. "If there is anything in the whole of religion that we should most certainly know, we ought most closely to grasp by what reason, with what law . . . forgiveness of sins may be obtained! Unless this knowledge remains clear and sure, the conscience can have no rest at all, no peace with God, no assurance or security."[242] But when the Romans prepare to go to communion they must first ascertain whether or not they are in the state of

[237] *ibid.*, 19, 28. [238] *ibid.*, 5, 13. [239] *ibid.*, 5, 12.
[240] *ibid.*, 5, 5. [241] *ibid.*, 5, 1. [242] *ibid.*, III, 4, 2.

grace. "They interpret 'in the state of grace' to mean to be pure and purged of all sin. Such a dogma would debar all the men who ever were or are on earth from the use of this sacrament."[243]

For two reasons this is not possible. First the Pelagian presupposition which supports such a dogma: we labor "mightily in pursuit of worthiness . . . we expiate our unworthiness by contrition, confession, and satisfaction."[244] Worthiness is not moral probity but faith and love; not the sincere contrition but the Lord's mercy.[245] Secondly, "since no definite assurance of our worthiness appears, the door will always remain locked by that dread prohibition which decrees that they who eat and drink unworthily eat and drink judgment upon themselves."[246] To demand a knowledge of our worthiness is to demand what souls, weak or strong, cannot give, and as a result "miserable consciences are tormented."[247] "They torture souls with many misgivings, and immerse them in a sea of trouble and anxiety."[248]

Calvin here speaks as a pastor of souls and he contends that the Roman Catholic confessional practice based on contrition, confession, and satisfaction, which are human acts, is not sufficient to give souls the security and assurance they need to approach the table of the Eucharist. "I say that these remedies are too feeble and fleeting for consciences dismayed and dejected and stricken with the horror of their own sin."[249] If man is to have that assurance necessary for him to approach his God with confidence, then this assurance cannot be based on any act of man. "For when will anyone dare assure himself that he has applied all his powers to lament his sins?"[250] "It makes a great difference whether you teach forgiveness of sins as deserved by just and full contrition, which the sinner can never perform; or whether you enjoin him to hunger and thirst after God's mercy to show him—

---

[243] *ibid.*, IV, 17, 41.   [244] *ibid.*
[245] Cf. *ibid.*, III, 4, 3; *ibid.*, IV, 17, 42.   [246] *ibid.*, 17, 41.
[247] *ibid.*, III, 4, 2.   [248] *ibid.*, 4, 1.   [249] *ibid.*, IV, 17, 41.
[250] *ibid.*, III, 4, 2.

through the recognition of his misery, his vacillation, his weariness, and his captivity—where he ought to seek refreshment, rest, and freedom."[251] Only an act of God's mercy can give man that peace of conscience he needs to eat the body of Christ without fear of eating judgment. To encourage man to seek his security in contrition, confession, and satisfaction is to encourage him to pursue an illusion and can only lead him to "desperation."[252] A pastoral practice based on this Pelagian assumption not only leads to despair, but drives "all men from approaching this most holy Supper."[253] Indeed the demands the Romans make of their penitents make the Eucharist superfluous. They "require such perfection in receiving the sacrament as would make the sacrament void and superfluous. For it is a sacrament ordained not for the perfect, but for the weak and feeble."[254] And when they have sufficiently dismayed weak souls, they set all things right with a little exercise in ritual Pelagianism: "But where they seem to have wounded hearts deeply, they heal all the bitterness with a light sprinkling of ceremonies."[255]

[251] *ibid.*, 14, 3.   [252] *ibid.*, 4, 3.   [253] *ibid.*, IV, 17, 42.
[254] *ibid.* The whole of *Inst.*, IV, 17, 42 is a remarkable testimony to Calvin's pastoral involvement and to his pastoral sensitivity.
[255] *ibid.*, III, 4, 1.

IV. The Transcendent God as a Sacramental and Ecclesiological Concern: Calvin's Eucharistic Preoccupations, I

Calvin's Dialectical Method: The Shifting Centralities

THE ROMAN CATHOLIC who approaches the theology of Calvin, comes to it with a distinct disadvantage. If the Catholic is also a scholastic theologian, his difficulties are multiplied. He is accustomed to the precisions of a theology which presupposes highly developed philosophical skills in a kind of linear logic. He is no stranger to mystery or to the inexplicable, but, within the confines of a reverence for that which cannot be explained, he arranges the material of revelation in propositions which are meaningful, but which he realizes are not exhaustive. He is a logician at the same time that he is a theologian, and his logical sense is sometimes more easily offended than his theological sense. In his methodology he is deductive.

Such a theological preparation can prepare the Catholic theologian for a critique of Calvin, but it can also lead him into endless difficulties in his attempt to understand Calvin. In Calvin the Catholic scholastic finds a collection of terminologies: biblical, Augustinian, nominalist, *devotio moderna*, humanist, reformation, scholastic, together with that taken from Bernard. These stand alongside one another, sometimes in opposition to one another, and the Catholic scholastic is dismayed that Calvin is not disturbed by these sometimes contradictory elements.[1]

[1] Cf. L. G. M. Alting von Geusau, *Die Lehre von der Kindertaufe bei Calvin*, Mainz, 1963, 80; Karl Reuter, *Das Grundverständnis der Theologie Calvins*, Neukirchen, 1963, 20-22; 24; 28-35; 37-47; 55-66; 208-210; Eduard de Moreau *et al., La crise religieuse du XVIe siècle*, vol. 16, *Histoire de l'église*, eds. Augustine Fliche and Victor Martin (no place given), 1950, 215.

The logical element found in scholastic theology, this linear logic, is also found in Calvin. As will be seen in the next two chapters, there is an inner logic to Calvin's eucharistic theology. And it was his rigid adherence to this logic which, as will be seen, gave rise to the accusation of rationalism, and here the accusation was applied to both methodology and content. However, linear logic is not that which characterizes Calvin's theological system. Without implying that Calvin's methodology is simply applied juristics, he can be described as a dialectician applying to theology the *concordia discordantium* which he learned as a jurist.[2]

There is in Calvin's theological system no material principle from which he derived his doctrine.[3] He has not built a speculative system. Nor should the precise sense of order and the clarity of his formulations be mistaken for a highly refined systematics.[4] Rather he has gathered, somewhat in the manner of an eclectic, a great number of theological particulars, elements, component parts, and *opposita* which stand one alongside the other, one over against the other, and are worked into a theological unity by the formal dialectical method.[5] Instead of a central doctrine, in the systematic sense of a universal principle of systematization, there is a series of central doctrines which stand over against one another, each a central concern, and each demanding the attention accorded to an absolute or near absolute.[6] Because

[2] Cf. Hermann Bauke, *Die Probleme der Theologie Calvins*, Leipzig, 1922, 13, 14; Peter Barth, "Die Erwählungslehre in Calvins Institutio von 1536," *Theologische Aufsätze*, ed. E. Wolf, Munich, 1936, 432; Alexandre Ganoczy, *Calvin théologien de l'église et du ministère*, Paris, 1964, 59-68; Rupert E. Davies, *The Problem of Authority in the Continental Reformers*, London, 1964; W. Kolfhaus, *Christusgemeinschaft bei Johannes Calvin*, Neukirchen, 1939, 14, 15.

[3] Bauke, *op.cit.*, 31.

[4] To give an example in just one area of Calvin's systematics, T. F. Torrance, a very sympathetic student of Calvin, repeatedly calls attention to inconsistencies in Calvin's teaching on man. Cf. *Calvin's Doctrine of Man*, London, 1949, 8, 19, 20, 36, 66, 88, 93, 106.

[5] Cf. Bauke, *op.cit.*, 31.

[6] Paul Jacobs objects to A. Schweizer's (*Die Glaubenslehre der evangelisch-reformierten Kirche*, Zürich, 1844) attempt to make predestination the

of this Calvin will not only admit paradoxes, but actively seeks them, placing paradox alongside of paradox, each asserting its own particular truth and clarifying the paradox which stands opposite.[7] The one paradox does not cancel out the other paradox, though it appears to render the others contradictory. By means of the play of one centrality against another centrality, one nucleus against another nucleus, Calvin achieves a certain unity and order. The unity is not tidy and neat, nor without embarrassing gaps, but it is an impressive unity. And beneath the unity and order, the paradoxes, the various centralities, and the lesser contrasts remain.[8] For Calvin, theology is not the clarification of a principle but rather the clarification of a mystery which is set forth in a dialogic form, where each pole of the mystery speaks an imperative, which is spoken back by the other pole of the mystery, but in terms of its own absolute. The two voices of the dialogue form the *foci* of an ellipse, each of which is unyielding, and from this tension comes clarification and, ultimately, unity.[9]

Within the great lines of this ellipsoidal logic Calvin will often think in terms of strict linear logic. Here he can be as linear as any scholastic. But his system as system, in its large outline, is built on the dialectical tension of the ellipsoidal, not on the precision of the linear.

---

central doctrine, in a systematic sense, of Calvin's theology. Jacobs asserts that such an attempt presupposes that the faith is a system comparable to a philosophical system. Cf. *Prädestination und Verantwortlichkeit bei Calvin*, Neukirchen, 1937, 17. Jacobs rejects what must be rejected, but for the wrong reason. Calvin's theology, like all theology, is an ordering of the data of faith, to put it crudely. Theologizing is, at least in part, a human activity concerned with revealed truth. Jacobs rightly remarks that the faith is not given as, and is not comparable to, a philosophical system. But Schweizer and other Calvin scholars were attempting to find a central doctrine, not in the faith, but in Calvin's theology. This attempt is legitimate, but, as a matter of fact, vain. Such a central doctrine does not exist in Calvin's systematics because of his dialectical method by which he plays one centrality against another.

[7] Cf. Reuter, *op.cit.*, 46.   [8] Cf. *ibid.*, 209, 210.

[9] Cf. Bauke, *op.cit.*, 16.

Those who would reproduce Calvin's theological unity cannot do so by selecting one of Calvin's central concerns and erecting it into a principle of systematization, in the dogmatic sense, so that the one central doctrine is always seen as Calvin's point of departure and the tool of his systematization.[10] The centralities shift within the confines of the whole systematics. In a given dogmatic area two centralities, biblical themes, will stand over against each other, as mutually unyielding opposites. These centralities become normative and exercise their rights of centrality, only to be later shifted into the background when Calvin moves to another dogmatic area, where another set of centralities moves forward to assert its imperium.[11] There is a great deal of flexibility to these pairs of shifting centralities and sometimes they overlap, one set moving momentarily into the imperium and tension of another set of centralities.

At the very beginning of the *Institutes*, indeed in the very first sentence, Calvin employs this bipolarity.[12] "Nearly all the wisdom we possess, that is to say, true and sound wisdom, consists of two parts: the knowledge of God and of ourselves. But, while joined by many bonds, which one precedes and brings forth the other is not easy to discern."[13] As shall be seen, Calvin uses this methodology in his sacramental theology as well as in his theology of grace and law, of

[10] Cf. *ibid.*, 31, 32.

[11] For this reason Bauke can speak with justice of four principal doctrines in Calvin's theology. Cf. *ibid.*, 58-95. It is interesting to note that M. Scheibe speaks of predestination as being a central doctrine for a limited number of other doctrines, for example, the doctrine of God and ecclesiology. Cf. *Calvins Prädestinationslehre*, Halle, 1897, 85f. Cadier also speaks of the various centralities in Calvin's system. Cf. *La doctrine Calviniste de la sainte cène*, Montpellier, 1951, 15.

[12] Cf. Reuter, *op.cit.*, 9-27. Reuter notes the strong influence of Bernard in certain aspects of Calvin's dogmatics and methodology. Cf. also Peter Barth, "Calvin," RGG[2] where the author calls attention to the dialectical method with which Calvin handles the doctrines of grace, law, election and predestination. Cf. also August Lang, *Johannes Calvin*, Leipzig, 1909, 89; Josef Bohatec, "Calvins Vorsehungslehre," *Calvinstudien*, ed. J. Bohatec, Leipzig, 1909, 353; G. Gloede, "Calvin," *Evangelisches Kirchen-Lexikon*, Göttingen, 1956.

[13] *Inst.*, I, 1, 1.

election and predestination, and in his teaching on the Trinity and the Holy Spirit.[14]

There is much in Calvin's intellectual pre-history to account for the dialectic: Platonism, the neo-Platonism of the Augustinian tradition, the imperatives of nominalism (for example, Bradwardine's dilemma of divine participation and man's sinfulness), and, not to be forgotten, the biblical witness.

A Catholic theologian, and especially a scholastic theologian, is unaccustomed to the theological elasticity which a dialectical method affords and he is prone to jump to erroneous conclusions.[15] The linear logic of the scholastic theologian is apt to consider the ellipsoidal logic of the dialectic theologian a matter of philosophical confusion. In studying Calvin and in giving a presentation of Calvin's theological convictions he will be tempted to reject one of the two opposing centralities, one of the *opposita* which stand together in Calvin's systematics, convinced that since Calvin taught the one, he cannot have seriously been convinced of the other. Whether, in every case, the *opposita* can objectively stand together is another question, and he who writes a critique of Calvin can justly raise the question. But the two do in fact stand together in Calvin's theology, rightly or wrongly, and no presentation of Calvin's thought can claim any validity which ignores these *opposita*, or attempts to cancel out one of them. One of the centralities in Calvin's theology is the sovereignty of God.

The Unconditioned Sovereignty

THE TRANSCENDENTAL GOD AND THE
ROMAN IDOLS

The instinct in Calvin for the transcendental, and his life-long struggle to preserve the complete "otherness" of God intact, is not unrelated to the Roman church he experienced.

---

[14] Cf. Werner Krusche, *Das Wirken des Heiligen Geistes nach Calvin*, Göttingen, 1957, I.

[15] Cf. von Geusau, *op.cit.*, 62, 63.

Though such transcendentalism was not foreign to the history of theology prior to Calvin—Duns Scotus, William of Occam, Thomas Bradwardine, and Gregory of Rimini gave expression to it—his own experience of Catholicism and his judgment upon it could not have but given added impetus to a thoroughly biblical patristic and philosophic preoccupation with the transcendent God.[16] The casual objectivizing of divinity and the naked empiricism in sacramental impersonalism, the domestication and manipulation of God in sacramental idolatry, the proud and aggressive presuppositions of ritual Pelagianism, the reductionism of structural churchmanship by which dedication to the sovereign Lord meant a comfortable sinecure and the perpetuating of the structure, could only have strengthened that instinct for the transcendental without which Christianity has no meaning.

The judgment Calvin spoke over Roman Catholicism was a judgment concerning idolatry. There is no other word which sums up so completely Calvin's conception of Rome, and no other word explains so clearly the vehemence and venom with which he rejected and condemned Roman Catholicism. The medieval church was the church of idolatry.[17] How clearly this idea stood in the foreground of his consciousness is seen in Calvin's elaboration of his doctrine of God, of his *Gottesbegriff*.

In the *Institutes* Calvin does not give a formal and detailed discussion of the nature, existence, and attributes of God. Only when he writes of the Trinity does he appear to be writing a strictly theological treatise. Those chapters given to the doctrine of God (I: 11-13) are divided into two parts. Chapters 11 and 12 are directed toward uprooting idolatry, not idolatry in general, but the idolatry of Rome.[18]

---

[16] Cf. Erwin Iserloh, *Gnade und Eucharistie in der philosophischen Theologie des Wilhelm von Ockham*, Wiesbaden, 1956, 67. Iserloh also discusses the question of Pelagianism in Occam. Cf. *ibid.*, 126-133. Cf. also Reuter, *op.cit.*, 152, 153.

[17] Cf. Louis Bouyer, *The Spirit and Forms of Protestantism*, Westminster, 1956, 60, 61.

[18] Cf. B. B. Warfield, *Calvin and Augustine*, Philadelphia, 1956, 178.

Chapter 13 is also polemic in nature and is directed against the antitrinitarianism of his day. He does not set out to write an abstract treatise, but to expose and condemn the great medieval sin, idolatry. He writes more as a pastor than as a theologian for his interest is in the needs of souls. For this reason these sections are permeated by a deep religious feeling. The great danger is idolatry, specifically Catholic idolatry, and therefore his exposition of the doctrine of God is handled indirectly, and in relation to that true worship of God. Method and language here are not unrelated to that of the *devotio moderna.*

The idolatry which is Catholicism, therefore, largely determines his exposition of the doctrine of God. The doctrine of God gives Calvin an opportunity to write on true worship, which is worship without images, pictures, and all the paraphernalia by which "the superstitious have thought he [God] will be near them."[19] Behind the passions of idolatry is the desire to visualize and localize God: "For just as soon as a visible form has been fashioned for God, his power is also bound to it. Men are so stupid that they fasten God wherever they fashion him."[20]

This temptation to give God visible form and to localize him will play a large role in Calvin's eucharistic doctrine. Though the Eucharist is not specifically treated in these sections, Calvin does relate the idolatry against which he fights to the true Eucharist. "And by the dreadful madness that has heretofore occupied the world almost to the total destruction of godliness, we have experienced too much how the ensign of idolatry is, as it were, set up, as soon as images are put together in churches. For men's folly cannot restrain itself from falling headlong into superstitious rites. But even if such danger were not threatening, when I ponder the intended use of churches, somehow or other it seems to me unworthy of their holiness for them to take on images other than those living and symbolical ones which the Lord has

[19] *Inst.,* I, 11, 1.   [20] *ibid.,* 11, 9.

consecrated by his Word. I mean Baptism and the Lord's Supper. . . ."[21]

THE SOVEREIGN IMPERATIVE IN ITSELF

To the housebroken God of Catholicism, to this tame image of the imageless, Calvin opposes the sovereign Lord who is the "entirely other," who transcends all things human and dwells in light inaccessible. Such a God can only reveal himself as the hidden God. The God who reveals remains hidden, and the hidden God is only partly revealed; only the back side of God is seen. Such a God cannot be domesticated, given visual form, localized, summoned at a clerical command, and dismissed by the chemistry of stomach acids. "Let us willingly leave to God the knowledge of himself. For, as Hilary says, he is the one fit witness to himself, and is not known except through himself."[22] The absolutely transcendent God is the absolutely sovereign God, he who determines all and is determined by none.[23] It is indeed this God who breaks through time and enters history. This coming down of God is a sign also of the essential distance which separates men from God.[24] There is no religion, no piety, and no worship unless this distance is recognized, and, to a degree, preserved. "Horrible is the divine majesty."[25]

For all the religious and philosophical transcendence of Calvin's God, he is neither a Stoic necessity, nor a Scotistic reduction to naked will, nor a metaphysical abstraction. The sovereignty of God is always that of a father who "wishes us to look to him, to put our trust in him, to worship and call upon him."[26] Those who would create a deistic image of God "do not at all taste God's special care, by which alone his fatherly favor is known."[27] God is, for Calvin, always

---

[21] *ibid.*, 11, 13.   [22] *ibid.*, 13, 21.

[23] Cf. Yves Congar, "Calvin," *Catholicisme*, Paris, 1949.

[24] Cf. Heinz Otten, *Calvins Theologische Anschauung von der Prädestination*, Munich, 1938, 39.

[25] *Inst.*, III, 20, 17.   [26] *ibid.*, I, 5, 6.

[27] *ibid.*, 16, 1.

Lord and Father, and his sovereignty can never be used to diminish the essential fatherly character of his power.

An essential note of this sovereignty is the necessity of God remaining the only cause. Here Calvin stands in the tradition of Bradwardine. In inanimate creation the providence of God is not that of "a general principle of confused motion . . . but one that is directed toward individual and particular motions."[28] "To make God a momentary Creator, who once for all finished his work, would be cold and barren, and we must differ from profane men especially in that we see the presence of divine power shining as much in the continuing state of the universe as in its inception."[29] Though he rejects all pantheism, Calvin holds that life in the animal kingdom is not a definitive gift but needs continual "inspiration," so that the death of an animal is not merely a thing of nature, but occurs when God withdraws his Spirit.[30]

The sovereignty of God is betrayed when, to explain evil, men introduce the permissive will of God. Calvin is not going to concede any more to man than was Gregory of Rimini. Calvin will have none of the permissive will, "as if God sat in a watchtower awaiting chance events, and his judgments thus depended upon human will."[31] Predestination is essentially a guard of the sovereign Lord who is himself undetermined, but who determines all. In typical dialectic fashion Calvin asserts that God is the only cause, and that men are nonetheless responsible for their actions and incur guilt, for which they are justly punished. Reprobation is also conceived in terms of the absolute freedom of the sovereign God; God is the author of reprobation, but also, in the strict sense, its cause. "I confess a hundred times that God is the author of it [reprobation]."[32]

This unmitigated predestinarianism is reminiscent of Gregory of Rimini. The whole world order and its history, both secular and religious, is led to its proper end by him

[28] *ibid.*, 16, 3. [29] *ibid.*, 16, 1.
[30] Cf. CR 43:162; *ibid.*, 47:479; *ibid.*, 48:414.
[31] *Inst.*, I, 18, 1. [32] *ibid.*, III, 23, 3.

who is the cause and ruler of creation, and of the new creation, and is the Lord of history.[33] This God of utter mysteriousness, who is beyond all, and in all, who is separated from all things earthly by a measureless gulf, who is the first cause and at every moment the continuing cause of every creature, who is the sole author and the sole agent of holiness, who is himself the essence which cannot be imaged, who gives his glory to no creature—this God Calvin opposes to the attendant God of Roman ecclesiasticism. Calvin's interest here is to establish the sovereignty of God as it is in itself, not merely in its relation to us. Luther's God was all in the order of efficient causality, but, seemingly, man was all in the order of final causality; Calvin's God is all in the order of means and of ends.[34] In spite of his great pastoral concern, man does not stand in the center of the stage. In the presence of such a God Calvin feels an imperative which is both metaphysical and theological, and, for himself personally, in some sense, experiential. He felt himself seized by the sovereignty of God and consecrated to its service, an implacable instrument of the glory of God.[35]

THE GOD WHO CHOOSES IS ALWAYS FREE

There will be difficulties translating such an exalted and deeply religious doctrine of God into a viable Christology, ecclesiology, and sacramental theology, and, because of the difficulties involved, Calvin will not always find his views acceptable to his contemporaries. It was, in fact, these transcendental premises which were at the root of the majority of his theological controversies.[36]

Especially when the sovereign God, who determines all and is determined by none, is related to secondary causes, more specifically causes having to do with the sanctification and salvation of man, such as the sacraments, will there be

---

[33] Cf. Wilhelm-Albert Hauck, *Vorsehung und Freiheit nach Calvin*, Gütersloh, 1947, 18; Hauck, *Die Erwählten*, Gütersloh, 1950, 21.
[34] Cf. Bouyer, *op.cit.*, 60.   [35] Cf. Congar, "Calvin," *Catholicisme.*
[36] Cf. Wendel, *op.cit.*, 111.

difficulties. The problem will be to harmonize, if not contradictory elements, at least elements which stand at the opposite poles of theological reality, to harmonize effective secondary causes with the absolute sovereignty of God.

It has been remarked how often Calvin speaks of inferior means when treating of the acts of God's providence.[37] God indeed often works through instruments or through secondary causes.[38] He does not always act immediately through the Holy Spirit.[39] But the use of secondary causes does not mean that he in any way is obliged to use them.[40] He uses bread as a means because he chooses to use bread, and though the bread is an apt symbol of nourishment, the significance of the means is not so much that it is bread, as that it is chosen. There is something almost accidental in the choice of this particular means.[41]

Though God chooses to use bread as an instrument, he remains, in an absolute sense, independent of the instrument. Though the cases in which Calvin speaks of a direct, unmediated act of God in reference to man are not frequent, they show that for Calvin the freedom of God with reference to his instruments is a truth of the theological order which is in fact verified in the existential order. The freedom of God in relation to his instruments is first a metaphysical necessity and then an existential fact. It is not sufficient to assert that God can save man without using the means which he has ordained to salvation, but we must add that God has actually saved many men without using the secondary causes.[42]

God uses bread to nourish us because he chose to do so, but he does not in any sense remain bound to objects even after having chosen them.[43] Nor does he give to them a power which is proper to himself.[44] To feed man unto salvation is a work of God and the sacraments never possess

---

[37] Cf. Krusche, *op.cit.*, 25.   [38] Cf. CR 44:206.   [39] Cf. *ibid.*, 44:184.

[40] Cf. *ibid.*, 24:240.   [41] Cf. *ibid.*, 40:116.   [42] Cf. *Inst.*, IV, 16, 19.

[43] Krusche notes that evidently Calvin never thought that God could bind himself; cf. *op.cit.*, 343.

[44] Cf. CR 24:102.

this as an immanent power. The Eucharist is never an object, but a personal instrument. The Eucharist does not have, either from nature or from God, a power of nourishing spiritually which it possesses in a definitive sense. There is no power given to the eucharistic bread so that the bread possesses that power now and need not again, and ever again, receive the power to nourish spiritually.

Because the relation of God to the Eucharist is not a "once for ever" relationship, not a relationship of discontinuity but of continuity, not the relationship of a completed fact, but of an ever-actual initiator and, in a somewhat literal sense, inspirator, the bread is nourishing. God does not need bread to nourish us spiritually. He does not even need bread to nourish us physically.[45] Whatever comes from the mouth of God and is diffused by the Spirit nourishes us, and this both physically and spiritually. It is not bread alone that nourishes but what comes forth from the mouth of God.

RESTORING DIVINITY TO GOD

Calvin sees the way to safeguard the freedom of the sovereign God by insisting that the sacraments never become immanent subjects of causality. There is in them no immanent power of causality, though they are in a manner of speaking secondary causes. There is to be no surrendering of power on the part of God, no giving over of an independent actuating force. God does not save by proxy. When God chooses bread and wine as means of nourishing us, they are in actuality nourishing only because God breathes into them his power.[46] To be chosen is not enough.

There are several reasons why Calvin gives marked emphasis to the unconditional freedom of the sovereign God over against the secondary causes and instruments. Above all he wants to assure that the sovereignty of God suffers no restriction and is not conditioned either by man, for whom the instruments are means of sanctification, or by the instruments themselves. The sovereign is above the laws which he

[45] Cf. *ibid.*, 24:240.   [46] Cf. *ibid.*, 40:550.

makes; Calvin asserts this as a matter of principle for the civic order.[47] What is valid in the second instance, that of the earthly order, is valid by metaphysical necessity in the first instance, that of the cosmic order and the order of salvation.[48] There is no dependence one can predicate of God in any manner, no dependence on man or sacraments, no dependence either in the real order or in the logical order, but, on the contrary, he has and is the empire and dominion of sovereignty, the supreme intelligence over all intelligences, the supreme will over all wills.[49] God does not surrender any of his sovereignty to the sacraments.

The Roman Catholicism he experienced convinced him that it was precisely the sovereignty of God which men had forgotten. To attribute to the church an exaggerated supernatural character, as though she herself were divinity, to endow the sacraments with an importance such that without them salvation was not possible and with them salvation thinkable only in reference to them, to encourage and abet the sacramental will-to-power of sacramental activity, to approve of rendering divinity to a thing in transubstantiation, to legislate the crassest theological materialism in which God is summoned by a formula and dismissed by digestion, to bind men's consciences with ritual posturings of human invention in which salvation is supposedly contained, and to prostitute service of God's glory to a benefice and to an assurance that the established disorder will continue in perpetuity, all of this was to sin against the sovereignty of God. The sovereignty and divinity had not only been sinned against, but had been appropriated. And it was the goal of Calvin's theological endeavor to restore divinity to God.

There is also a pastoral reason for Calvin's unrelenting efforts to uphold the unconditional freedom of the sovereign

---

[47] Cf. Bohatec, *Calvins Lehre von Staat und Kirche*, Breslau, 1937, 41.

[48] Cf. CR 37:47.

[49] Cf. August Lecerf, *Introduction à la dogmatique réformée*, vol. 2, *Du fondement de la specification de la connaisance religieuse*, Paris, 1938, 245.

God. Here Calvin wanted to give weak souls assurance and even a measure of certitude, without which the Christian life is not possible.[50] The sacraments are, by definition, seals of assurance and certitude. Whether God works through the sacraments, or whether he works directly, he gives to man assurance of his good will toward him, and the assurance that he will nourish him. Though he works often through the sacraments, he does not need them to bring nourishment to man. In reference to the ever-effective Holy Spirit, baptism is not necessary for the God who wishes to save, although we must ourselves seek baptism; and in reference to God's ever-effective power, the Eucharist is not necessary for the God who wishes to nourish, although we must eat the bread he gives.[51] God is not bound by the sacraments, but we are. In this way the devout are always assured of nourishment, even when it is not possible to receive the Eucharist. God can and will give the life that sustains even outside of the sacraments. In this way the freedom of God is maintained, the devout have the assurance that the necessary nourishment will not, in any case, fail, and theology is preserved from a cold formalism. This is not to lessen respect for the sacraments or free man from the obligation to receive them. It is simply to assert that we should not so theologize that we translate man's obligation to receive them into God's obligation to use them. Our Father in heaven is a father without compare, and he is not, as an earthly father, bound to determined means, so that without them he fails his children. "God declares himself a father in that he subsists through the virtue of his Spirit."[52]

Lordship of Christ

ELECTED IN CHRIST

The sovereign God, who determines all and is determined by none, freely elects those whom he will, and by this elec-

[50] Cf. *Inst.*, III, 4, 2.   [51] Cf. Krusche, *op.cit.*, 30, 31.
[52] CR 34:130.

tion "the elect are so united in Christ that as they are dependent on one Head, they also grow together into one body."[53] The election is not only made in reference to Christ, but it is made in Christ.[54] This in a double sense: because Christ took part in the decree of election as the Second Person of the Trinity and because Christ is the effective agent of the decree in his office of mediator.[55] Further, the predestined find their salvation only in Christ. He himself is their salvation. No matter from where one starts, he who decrees, or he who effects, or he who is salvation, one always returns to Christ.

Election and predestination have not only a Christological but also an ecclesiological orientation. Election in Christ is the basis of the church, and it is this basis which establishes the lordship of Christ in the church, and is the guarantee that in the church neither ecclesiological divinization nor sacramental divinization, with its inevitable sacramental Pelagianism and structural churchmanship, has any validity.[56] Election in Christ is a pure expression of the sovereignty of God and the lordship of Christ in the church. The lordship of Christ belongs to the essential structure, is built into that which gives the church substance and form. And it is not as though the church were set up, as some construct, independent, effective, and self-determining, which then must be made to submit to the lordship of Christ. The lordship of Christ is a theological truth of the first order and the church finds her own essence and meaning by remembering that this theological truth does not belong to a theological periphery. It was specifically this truth which Rome had forgotten and for this reason it finds a large place in Calvin's polemics and systematics.

[53] *Inst.*, IV, 1, 2. On the lordship of Christ cf. Alfred Göhler, *Calvins Lehre von der Heiligung*, Munich, 1934, 111-113.

[54] Cf. *Inst.*, III, 25, 5; CR 8:114.

[55] Cf. François Wendel, *Calvin, The Origins and Development of His Religious Thought*, New York, 1963, 208.

[56] Cf. Wilhelm Niesel, *The Theology of Calvin*, Philadelphia, 1956, 189, 190.

Outside of this lordship, the individual Christian has no existence. And when the individual Christians are multiplied and taken together as the whole body of believers, the whole gathering which makes up the human denominator of the church, this totality also has no existence apart from the lordship of Christ. The totality is, in a religious sense, of no more worth apart from Christ than the single individual. In the economy of salvation one does not arrive at greater worth by multiplication. Specifically as church we are as nothing and he is all.[57]

The church which sets itself up as an absolute, not only above judgment but equal with the judge, rendering judgment, canonizing and anathematizing, as by a power which she possesses inwardly, as a self-contained atomized source, has nothing to do with the church of Christ. Indeed, the church, though she is the body of Christ, cannot make laws which bind in conscience; this is a divine prerogative which the church cannot usurp. She can and must witness to and proclaim God's laws, but she herself has no power to bind consciences.

The assurance and certitude of salvation she imparts cannot be anything proper to herself; she mediates them but they are not hers. The assurance of salvation and the certitude that God has saved us is found in the first instance in that absolute act of election in Christ by which the church is constituted. "Our salvation rests upon sure and firm supports, so that even if the whole fabric of the world were overthrown, the church could neither totter nor fall. First, it stands by God's election, and cannot waver or fail any more than his eternal providence can. Secondly, it has in a way been joined to the steadfastness of Christ."[58] She is strong because she has no strength and no power proper to herself. Her strength is that of her Lord. She consoles the comfortless and gives certitude to the unsure because she herself is nothing and has nothing. She can give only the comfort of

[57] Cf. *ibid.*   [58] *Inst.*, IV, 1, 3.

Christ and the steadfastness of Christ. The lordship of Christ is effective in her only on condition of her unconditional poverty. The lordship of Christ stands over against all human presumptions, all self-redemption, all ritual exhibitionism, and all ecclesiasticism. It stands over against a sacramentalism which has taken over God's aseity and has set up its kingdom.

ONLY ONE LORDSHIP IN THE CHURCH

The lordship of Christ, if it is to have its full meaning in the ecclesiological dimension, must be reduced from the purely theological order to the existential order. The order and government of the church must give evidence that Christ reigns in it. "The right way to lead the church can be learned nowhere else than from its Lord."[59] Calvin could not take this injunction indifferently, because if the lordship of Christ is a truth of the first order, then Calvin's declaration that the right way to lead the church must be found in Christ, in the Christ whose body is the church, cannot be only one of the vague gentilities of moral exhortation, only a derivative postscript, but rather is central.[60] The individual soul and the whole community must bring their faith to the confession that the sovereign Christ exercises his lordship insofar as they are one with the body of Christ, that he alone is the head, that they are subject to him and he alone rules and is master in the church, that there is no office of lordship in the church other than that of Christ, but only offices of service.[61] The church must resist the temptation to form herself in the image of a power of this world which stands completed and self-justified, whose structure is related to Christ as something external to him, professing to serve him, but serving him at her own leisure and in her own time, and serving him with means of her own choosing and in a man-

[59] CR 13:284.   [60] Cf. Niesel, op.cit., 189.
[61] Cf. Inst., IV, 6, 10.

ner of her own making. Such an image of the church is based on the attempt to separate the head from the body.[62]

"Wherever we see the Word of God purely preached and heard, and the sacraments administered according to Christ's institution, there, it is not to be doubted, a church of God exists."[63] It is through these two means, preaching and the administration of the sacraments, that the church experiences Christ because in them the lordship of Christ is announced and realized. And where the lordship of Christ is actualized there is his church. No greater service is renderable by a pastor of the church than his zeal for the preached Word, baptism, and the eucharistic table.[64] Those who announce the coming of the kingdom and the presence of the lordship of Christ must not so identify themselves with that kingdom and lordship as though to appropriate it. Nor is the announcement of this lordship by those in the service of Christ to be taken as an occasion for the pastors to establish a lordship of their own over the community, to assume pretentious proprietary claims. They are to remain instruments of the Holy Spirit and their function in the community of the faithful is service.[65]

These marks of the true church, preaching and the administration of the sacraments, must be understood within a wider framework, namely the recognition of the lordship of Christ. Calvin says explicitly that it belongs to the mark of the true church not only to preach the Word of God, but that the Word of God be heard, and, to be specific, that it be heard by the church. "Wherever we see the Word of God preached and heard . . . there a church of God exists." The true church is not necessarily found where there is much religious speaking and preaching and where the sacraments are often celebrated and the name of Christ is often spoken.[66] Rather the church of Christ is there where Christ in his Word and sacrament is recognized and held in high honor

---

[62] Cf. CR 13:283.   [63] *Inst.*, IV, 1, 9.   [64] Cf. *ibid.*, 3, 4.
[65] Cf. CR 24:274.   [66] Cf. Niesel, *op.cit.*, 194.

as the only Lord and as the only sanctifier. This has to do with the church itself and not only the individual hearer: "This is the mark of the true church, by which it is to be distinguished from all other gatherings which falsely claim to speak in the name of God and presume to pass themselves off as churches; where the lordship and priesthood of Christ is earnestly recognized; but where Christ is not recognized as king and priest, there is nothing else but chaos."[67] In the last analysis there can be no truer mark of the church of Christ than the mark Christ himself gave when he said, "My sheep hear my voice." Simply to be instituted and founded is not enough; nor is it enough to be a religious gathering of impressive proportions.[68] Ultimately the question must be, "Whom does it hear?" . . . "Whom does this gathering honor?" "The church of God distinguishes itself from all other damnable sects in that she alone hears his Word and in that she alone permits herself to be guided by his command."[69] The body of Christ has ears only for the Words of Christ, and she gives recognition to no other voice and to no other command.

ECCLESIOLOGY OF LORDSHIP, NOT OF PIETY

Calvin did not, as did some of his contemporaries and as did the later confessional writings of the Calvinist tradition, erect discipline as one of the marks of the church.[70] To have done so would have made the existence of the church dependent on man's fidelity and would be to measure the church with a human rule. We have assurance, security, and comfort in the knowledge that in spite of all scandals, all the vices of her sinning members, the church is there where his

[67] CR 39:69.
[68] Cf. Niesel, *Die Theologie Calvins*, 2nd edn., Munich, 1957 194. (Not all sections of Niesel's German text were translated for the English edition.)
[69] CR 48:569.
[70] Cf. A. Adam, "Kirche," RGG³. While it is true that for Calvin discipline is not one of the marks of the church, this dogmatic position is present in the teaching of Calvin's contemporaries, namely Peter Martyr and Martin Bucer. Cf. Joseph McLelland, *The Visible Words of God*, Edinburgh, 1957, 125. Cf. also Wendel, *op.cit.*, 301.

lordship is announced and heard through Word and sacra-ment.[71] The truth of the church is not to be found in moral probity, though the moral consciousness and moral achieve-ment of discipline "serve as its sinews."[72] To seek the truth of the church there would be to bring the faithful into per-petual insecurity. Calvin rejected the spiritualist ideal of a sinless church and also denied the right to leave a church simply because of its moral inadequacies.[73] The church is not built upon the piety of the congregation but upon the Lord who rules. And when the faithful within the church seek forgiveness of their sins it is not to be found in their contri-tion and satisfaction, but rather in the Lord's mercy.[74] He who belongs to the church should be calm in the knowledge that he is not only sanctified by God, once and for all, but that he is also daily justified by the Lord's mercy. The same Christological, Christocentric reasons for which Calvin em-phasized the lordship of Christ made him hesitant about building his ecclesiology on the basis of the general priest-hood in the church. His ecclesiology proceeds rather from the dogmatic assumption that the church is the body of Christ, and in this way he brings the Christocentric frame-work of his whole theology into sharper relief. However, Calvin's doctrine of the mystical body proceeds not from the Incarnation but from election in Christ.

As if to safeguard the assumptions of such an ecclesiology he will go a long way toward identifying what the church does with what Christ does. Commenting on Isaiah 45:14 Calvin writes: "When he says that the Israelites shall be victorious over all the nations, this depends on the mutual relation between the head and the members. Because the only begotten Son of God unites to himself those who be-lieve in him, so that they are one with him. It frequently happens that what belongs to him is transferred to the church which is his body and fullness. In this sense, rule also is attributed to the church, not so as to obscure by haughty

[71] Cf. Niesel, *The Theology of Calvin*, 199.   [72] *Inst.*, IV, 12, 1.
[73] Cf. *ibid.*, I, 13.   [74] Cf. *ibid.*, III, 4, 2; *ibid.*, IV, 1, 20.

domination the glory of her head, or even to claim the authority which belongs to him, or in a word, so as to have anything separate from her head; but because the preaching of the gospel which is committed to her is the spiritual scepter of Christ, by which he displays his power. In this respect no man can bow down submissively before Christ without also obeying the church, insofar as the obedience of faith is joined to the ministry of doctrine, yet so that Christ their head alone reigns, and alone exercises his authority."[75] It is evident from this quotation that there is a measure of identity between Christ and the church; but it is also evident that Christ gives his lordship to no one, not even to the church. Nor does he give his lordship to the sacraments.

The church must never act as though Christ has bound himself to her in any definitive way so that the church has Christ at her disposal, summoning him when she wills and dismissing him at leisure.[76] Even her very real authority and the efficacy of her sacraments cannot be upheld in such a way as to indicate that in these matters Christ has had his say, and these are now the concerns of the church. Christ is not bound. He is lord over the church and over the sacraments. For this reason Calvin labels as a gross error the supposition that participation in the sacraments is essential to salvation or to communion with the body of Christ. There is an "uninterrupted communication of the flesh of Christ," which is effective quite apart from the Eucharist, which communion Calvin calls the "perpetual manducation of faith."[77] The Lord of faith will not be bound to the instruments of faith, nor will he be defined by their limits. Christ is Lord not only in the church and in the sacraments but also over and beyond the sacraments.

[75] CR 37:140, 141.

[76] Cf. Ronald S. Wallace, *Calvin's Doctrine of the Word and Sacrament*, Edinburgh, 1953, 236.

[77] CR 47:154, 155. Yves Congar comments on this communication of the flesh of Christ prior to sacramental union. Cf. *Vraie et fausse réforme dans l'église*, Paris, 1950, 434.

V. Union with Christ as a Sacramental
and Ecclesiological Concern:
Calvin's Eucharistic Preoccupations, II

The Moment in Faith

AMONG SCHOLARS there is little doubt that union with Christ constitutes one of the centralities,[1] an emphasis for which Calvin is in large part indebted to Martin Bucer. Both Calvin's thought and his piety are deeply impregnated with union with Christ, and for this he has various expressions; union, communion, communication, participation with Christ, grafted into Christ, inserted into Christ, Christ dwelling within us. Without an understanding of this union with Christ one will easily misunderstand Calvin's teaching on justification, sanctification, his ecclesiology and sacramental theology, as well as his personal piety. Especially in regard to his eucharistic doctrine is union with Christ important as it forms that larger background, spoken or unspoken, without which neither his polemic against the Lutherans, Zwinglians, or the Roman Catholics, nor a positive presentation of his doctrine, can be grasped in any depth.

Union with Christ has its first roots in the decree of election of God—the Father, Son, and Holy Spirit. Because of his trinitarian theology Calvin will speak interchangeably of the election by God and the election by Christ.[2] To be elected is not identical with being planted in Christ, but both occur at the same time. Faith, the work of the Holy Spirit, depends on election. Faith, election, and to be planted in Christ are all closely related so that each carries resonances of the other; what the one does not say, the other says. For Calvin, faith

---

[1] Cf. Peter Brunner, *Vom Werk des heiligen Geistes*, Tübingen, 1935, 38. Cf. also Werner Krusche, *Das Wirken des heiligen Geistes nach Calvin*, Göttingen, 1957, 266; W. Kolfhaus, *Christusgemeinschaft bei Johannes Calvin*, Neukirchen, 1939, 11-23.

[2] Cf. Paul Jacobs, *Prädestination und Verantwortlichkeit bei Calvin*, Neukirchen, 1937, 74.

is not a teaching and not a simple announcement of good news, no matter how heavy with scriptural texts and inspiration, but the announcement of good news in a person and his work.[3] This personalist view will be met in Calvin's doctrine of grace and Eucharist. Nor is faith just confession; it must also be union. Indeed faith is sanctifying only to the degree that we are planted in Christ. Faith "does not reconcile us to God at all unless it joins us to Christ. . . . How can there be a saving faith except insofar as it engrafts us in the body of Christ?"[4]

What precisely is the relationship of faith to union with Christ? Can one simply identify faith and union with Christ, or is faith something more than union with Christ? Calvin took pains to make clear that for him faith was not the same as union with Christ.[5] For him union is an effect of faith. This was not to erect a causal relationship, nor even a temporal posteriority, as though one had faith and then one was united to Christ. Faith was rather a dimension of union and participation, faith and being planted in Christ occurring in the one and same act, so that the one is never without the other.[6]

All of this is seen more clearly in Calvin's disagreement with Zwingli, when he asserted that eating is not identical with faith but rather the fruit and effect of faith.[7] Calvin is not insisting on a real distinction between the two, but he is insisting on what he considers a safeguard against a purely intellectual concept of faith, faith as knowledge, or faith as a body of knowledge. Seen historically, Calvin's polemic here is inspired by his rejection of Zwingli's spiritualism. Eating is an interpretation of faith insofar as it guards against an intellectualization of faith and, also, because it gives realism to the assertion that in faith we have a real communion with the glorified Lord, with his body and blood, and this through

[3] Cf. Brunner, *op.cit.*, 38; Krusche, *op.cit.*, 265; L. G. M. Alting von Geusau, *Die Lehre von der Kindertaufe bei Calvin*, Mainz, 1963, 103, 104.
[4] *Inst.*, III, 2, 30.   [5] Cf. *ibid.*, IV, 17, 5.
[6] Cf. Kolfhaus, *op.cit.*, 36.   [7] Cf. the whole of *Inst.*, IV, 17, 5.

the power of the Holy Spirit. This makes it clear that eating is not specifically a eucharistic act, not an act which is limited to altar and cup. The Eucharist cannot claim this real participation in the body of Christ as well as with the soul of Christ as its own specific domain.[8] For Calvin, as for Luther, there is no specific eucharistic gift, no object, person, effect, or grace given in the Eucharist which is not given in faith outside of the Eucharist. The "perpetual eating," which is equivalent, with the qualification mentioned above, to a perpetual communication or perpetual participation, precedes the institution of the Eucharist as is evident in John 6: 53f, for at the time Christ spoke these words the Eucharist had not yet been instituted.[9] The mode of eucharistic eating is, then, an expression of, a moment in, the mode of perpetual eating which takes place in faith. No specific content is to be attributed to this moment. Though having no specific content, the Eucharist does have a specific function: to interpret more precisely and more concretely that union we have with Christ, a union not just with the Godhead of Christ, but rather a union with him who took our flesh, a flesh that is now the instrument of eternal life.[10]

A comparison of Calvin's teaching on the union with Christ which takes place in faith through the power of the Holy Spirit, with the union with Christ which takes place in the Eucharist, also through the power of the Holy Spirit, will show how Calvin subsumed the eucharistic eating under the larger moment of faith, the perpetual eating. When speaking of the union with Christ in faith Calvin speaks, usually, of a communion or communication with Christ, or in Christ, or we are inserted into Christ or grafted onto

---

[8] Cf. Krusche, *op.cit.*, 270.   [9] Cf. *ibid.*, 270.

[10] Cf. *Inst.*, IV, 17, 7-9; CR 9:470. Otto Ritschl conceives of the union with Christ by reason of the Eucharist, as taught by Calvin, as a higher level of union. This is to mistake the special function of the Eucharist, that of concretizing, for a special or higher level of union with Christ. Cf. *Dogmengeschichte des Protestantismus*, vol. 3, *Theologie des 16. und 17. Jahrhunderts in ihrer Entstehung und Entwicklung*, Göttingen, 1926, 241.

Christ.[11] When speaking of the union with Christ through the means of the Eucharist he speaks rather of the communication of, or participation in, the body and blood of Christ. But in both cases he speaks of a union with, or participation in, the substance of Christ. When speaking of the Eucharist he will say that we are united to the substance of his flesh and blood,[12] and when speaking of the union through faith he says simply that we are united to the substance of Christ.[13] And in both cases it is the Holy Spirit who effects the union, and in both cases we are united to the substance of Christ. Clearly, Calvin considers the substantial participation which we have in the Eucharist to be a precision of that substantial participation which we have with Christ through union in faith. What Calvin says about our substantial union with Christ by reason of the Eucharist, can be said about our union with Christ quite apart from the Eucharist.

For the theologian who wishes to understand Calvin's eucharistic doctrine within the terms of Calvin's systematics this subsuming of the union with Christ through the Eucharist under the more general union with Christ through faith should not be used as means of canceling out all eucharistic realism, and more especially of canceling out real presence in any proper sense of the term. The *opposita* must remain.

It would be hazardous to erect a direct relationship between Calvin's doctrine of union with Christ—more specifically the want of any specific eucharistic gift—and his polemic against Rome. However, this polemic belongs to the historical and theological tradition by which Calvin was in part formed and to which he gave expression, and it cannot have been without theological influence. To have granted a specific eucharistic gift would have opened the door to all the exaggerations of sacramental divinization: the Eucharist as independent cause of salvation, the sacraments as the instruments of a sacramental imperialism, claiming to be the exclusive means of salvation. To specify Christ in this unique

[11] CR 47:151.   [12] Cf. *Inst.*, IV, 17, 19.   [13] Cf. CR 25:658.

way, that of a specific eucharistic gift, would be to suggest the possible validity of sacramental idolatry with its paradings and prostrations, and to sanction the presumptions of a ritualism which, because it could summon its God, and dismiss him, could also redeem itself. To specify the eucharistic gift in this way would be immediately to clericalize it, for a gift which is so specified will immediately be ritualized and codified, both clerical preoccupations.

The Ecclesial Moment

ECCLESIOLOGY OF INWARDNESS

Calvin's great ecclesiological concern was to build a theology of the church which is marked by a pervading inwardness and interiority, an interiority which finds its roots in Christology and Pneumatology, and finds its simplest expression in the union with Christ. This was Calvin's answer to the divinization of ecclesiasticism and sacramentalism, to ritualism and ritual Pelagianism. The Roman preoccupation with the mere structure of the church, with the ecclesiastical anatomy, with the organizational, ceremonial, and decorative aspects of the church, moved him to create an ecclesiology and sacramental theology where that which was most inward, union with Christ, was normative. In this context Christology and Pneumatology, as two centralities, move forward, speak their absolutes, and exercise their imperium. Already in Humbert of Silva Candida, Christology and Pneumatology were used as points of departure for building a eucharistic theology.

To attain this inwardness, all initiative must be ascribed to the sovereign God. Men do not join themselves to the church because they see that it is proper to do so, or because they see that it is necessary. Rather the Son of God gathers his church and he himself joins members to himself: "Christ aggregated to his body that which was alienated from the hope of life: the world which was lost and history itself."[14] Man cannot

[14] *ibid.*, 55:219.

take the initiative because he is a slave and, therefore, he is not free. He is free only when he is given freedom, and this he received from Christ when he was incorporated in the body of Christ: "'The Son has made you free.' With these words Christ makes it clear that to him alone belongs the fullness of freedom, that all others are freed only by his grace, indeed that all others are born slaves. For that which belongs to him as of its nature, he communicates to us through being received as children, when we are incorporated in him through faith and are made his members."[15]

There is no ecclesiology possible apart from this interior union which Christ in the Holy Spirit effects. The essence of the church grows directly out of our being grafted into Christ, which is the work of the Holy Spirit. "All the elect are so united in Christ that as they are dependent on one Head, they also grow together into one body, being joined and knit together as are the limbs of a body. They are made truly one since they live together in one faith, hope and love, and in the same Spirit of God."[16]

The role of the Holy Spirit is unitive. It is the Holy Spirit who grafts those elected from eternity into the body of Christ, brings about a pneumatic union of Head and members, and through this union of Head and members creates a pneumatic communion of the members in relation to one another.[17] The unity of Head and members effected by the Holy Spirit is not a metaphorical unity but that of a body which is none other than the body of Christ. Not only does the Holy Spirit join members to the Head, but within that body of Christ with its Head and members it has a further unitive function. It communicates the gifts and the life of the Head to the members.[18] The Holy Spirit is the principle of unity also insofar as it is the Spirit of adoption by which each can cry "Abba, Father."

Insofar as all are members, the Holy Spirit is the common, constitutive gift. And insofar as he is the constitutive gift,

[15] *ibid.*, 47:204.   [16] *Inst.*, IV, 1, 2.   [17] Cf. CR 49:667.
[18] Cf. *Inst.*, II, 15, 2.

all share in him alike. In this context there is no such thing as one who is more member than another. The difference between member and member cannot be found in that which is of the essence of membership. The difference is to be found rather in that which is over and above membership, and that is in the various gifts of the Spirit. These gifts are not the gifts of the Spirit as over against the gifts of Christ. In Christ is found the Spirit without measure, and the anointing of Christ at baptism is nothing else than the anointing of the Head for the sake of the members.[19] It is the Holy Spirit who distributes the gifts of the Head to the members.

The pneumatic accent given to ecclesiology must not be interpreted to mean that Calvin intended to create a pneumatic community where there was the freedom of the Spirit but not the order of the Spirit. Besides the general priesthood, which is bound up with the Spirit of adoption, there are the spiritual offices, whose responsibility it is to teach and to rule. What distinguishes member from member is not priesthood and nonpriesthood, nor even degrees of the priesthood, since the common priesthood is founded on the common Spirit of adoption, but members are distinguished by the charisms which are given by the Spirit over and above the common priesthood. The spiritual offices in the church are seen only in the light of charisms; indeed the definitive legitimation of a spiritual office is the gifts of the Spirit.[20] The spiritual office is, then, seen in a pneumatic-charismatic context, and, further, since the church is under the sovereignty of the Spirit, one can speak of the rule of the church as a pneumatocracy.

All of this stands in opposition to the triumphalism of ecclesiasticism and juridicism and to the fixity of the Platonic image let down from heaven. For Calvin the church is not something closed and finished, which was simply to be delivered over to the next generation, but rather a union of Head and members in love under the Spirit. It was not a sys-

[19] Cf. CR 36:236.
[20] Cf. *Inst.*, IV, 19, 28. Cf. also CR 47:439; *ibid.*, 48:601.

tem, even a system of sanctification, but a union of Head and members. Nor had Calvin any patience with an ecclesiology which grows out of official "churchness" and, on the pastoral level, issues in "church people," or "church folks." For Calvin there was only the people of God under the sovereign Spirit.[21]

No supper without union with Christ

The same inwardness which he attempted to create in ecclesiology through his Christology and Pneumatology, an inwardness of which union with Christ is the highest expression, he repeated in his eucharistic doctrine. Here too the two centralities, Christology and Pneumatology, move forward and become dominant, and union with Christ is that end to which Christology and Pneumatology are subservient. How these two dogmatic areas exercise their dominance and how this sacramental inwardness was created is discussed in Chapters VI and VII. The present concern is to show how this inwardness was experienced and expressed in the eucharistic, worshiping community.

Though Calvin did not consider the sacraments as necessary means of salvation, and though union with Christ was not considered as dependent on the sacraments—as is also the case in Roman Catholicism—he did consider union with Christ as quite unthinkable apart from the sacraments. Union with Christ was not considered without reference to the Eucharist, or to baptism for that matter, just as union with Christ was not considered without reference to faith.[22] The Eucharist, on the other hand, is possible only in view of a preceding and present union with Christ. The grafting into Christ, of which Calvin speaks, is at the same time a grafting into the body of Christ, a grafting into the body of the

21 Cf. Kolfhaus, *op.cit.*, 100, 106.
22 Cf. CR 9:17.

church.[23] Grafting into Christ cannot be separated from being grafted into the church.[24] The Eucharist is the visible expression of this present and enduring union with Christ, a union which is in his body, the church. The Eucharist does not first give us the union with Christ, but is rather the pledge of this union, a strengthening of the union we have with him through faith, a witness which attests to a union which was present before the eucharistic fact. "I come to the Eucharist in order to seek a witness that Jesus Christ is my life and that I am incorporated in him and that the life I have from him will be eternal."[25] "The holy Eucharist is a witness of the union which we have with Jesus Christ."[26]

To be grafted into the church is not an affair of isolated individuals, and therefore no private persons can administer baptism. Baptism should be performed in the presence of the church: "Whenever anyone is to be baptized, present him to the assembly of believers, and, with the whole church looking on as witness and praying over him, offer him to God."[27] The emphasis here is on the local church.

The taking of the Eucharist is also not a private act, much less a multitude of private acts performed together. If the Eucharist is the visible expression of a present and enduring union with Christ, the eucharistic gathering is the church, in Christ and his Spirit, made visible.[28] Here too the emphasis is on the local church. "The Lord so communicates his body to us there that he is made completely one with us and we with him. Now, since he has only one body, of which he makes us all partakers, it is necessary that all of us also be made one body by such participation. The bread shown in

---

[23] Cf. *ibid.*, 39:46.
[24] Cf. Krusche, *op.cit.*, 317. Calvin speaks of being grafted into Christ in CR 49:665; *ibid.*, 49:106; *ibid.*, 52:12, of being grafted into the body of Christ in *ibid.*, 44:141; *ibid.*, 45:606; *ibid.*, 45:776; *ibid.*, 46:740; *ibid.*, 47:376, of being grafted into the body of the church or into the church in *Inst.*, IV, 16, 9; *ibid.*, 16, 22; *ibid.*, 1, 2; *ibid.*, 1, 21.
[25] CR 48:594.   [26] *ibid.*, 9:751.   [27] *Inst.*, IV, 15, 19.
[28] Cf. Jan Weerda, "Ordnung zur Lehre zur Theologie der Kirchenordnung bei Calvin," *Calvin-Studien 1959*, Neukirchen, 1960, 169.

the Sacrament represents this unity."[29] Since the Eucharist is the sign of the unity which we have in the body of Christ, no one but those "who in truth belong to the body of Christ" should come to the eucharistic table.[30]

This was one of the compelling reasons why Calvin rejected the reception of the true body by unbelievers. The Eucharist is simply the pledge of the union with Christ. If the Eucharist is the means of growing in faith and confirming our union with the Head, how can an unbeliever who is not united to Christ, receive it?[31] And if the unbeliever—in Chapter VII we shall see that in Calvin's thought unworthiness is the lack of faith and love—cannot, in his unbelief, be united to Christ, how can he gather with the believers around the eucharistic table? "Although they [unbelievers or unworthy] are divided and separated by hatred and ill will from their brethren, that is, from the members of Christ, and thus have no part in Christ, they still testify that this alone is salvation—to partake of Christ and be united with him."[32] Those who are not united to Christ and therefore do not really belong to the local church should not and cannot partake of the sign of unity. The Eucharist makes it evident to all who it is who belongs to the worshiping community, the local church.[33]

Therefore, also, Calvin attached great importance to excommunication. Though discipline did not become a mark

[29] *Inst.*, IV, 17, 38.   [30] CR 7:77.

[31] Cf. Kolfhaus, *op.cit.*, 120, 121. There are aspects of Calvin's eucharistic doctrine which are difficult to grasp and which admit of varying interpretations. However the corporate nature of the Eucharist is so clearly stated in Calvin—it was the sins of the Roman Catholics against the corporate and social character of the Eucharist which prompted much of his indignation— that it cannot be a matter of dispute among scholars. It is therefore painful and embarrassing to find a scholar of Gregory Dix's stature asserting: "The real eucharistic action is for Calvin individual and internal, not corporate. It is one more example of the intractability of the scriptural sacraments to the protestant theory, and the impossibility of adapting to a 'religion of the spirit' and pure individualism the institutions of a 'religion of incarnation' which presupposes the organic community of the renewed Israel." *The Shape of the Liturgy*, rev. edn., London, 1952, 633.

[32] *Inst.*, IV, 17, 40.   [33] Cf. Weerda, *op.cit.*, 169, 170.

of the church for Calvin, as it did for Bucer and Peter Martyr, he did consider that the right to exclude impenitent sinners was one of the prerogatives of the true church. To this right he devoted a whole chapter in his *Confession of Faith*.[34] Excommunication was the cornerstone of his whole system of discipline, but it would be a mistake to look upon it purely as a tool of ecclesiastical coercion. Calvin situated the right of excommunication first of all in an ecclesiological context, that of the local church. "Since the church itself is the body of Christ, it cannot be corrupted by such foul and decaying members without some disgrace falling upon its Head."[35] Then Calvin situated it sacramentally. "Here also we must preserve the order of the Lord's Supper, that it may not be profaned by being administered indiscriminately."[36]

The meaning of excommunication is not that the culprit is subjected to a more rigid disciplinary process, though this element is also present, but rather that the unworthy ought not to appear there where Christ offers himself to his own. That Calvin himself did not consider all of this matter of secondary importance is seen from the long struggle he had with the secular authorities over the right of the church to excommunicate, a right for which he fought both in Strassburg and in Geneva. Rather than give up this right he was willing to resign his pastoral duties.

No supper except in common: communion of the sick

The ecclesiological significance of the Eucharist as a sacrament is repeated when the Eucharist is considered as rite and celebration. Calvin's insistence on the ecclesial, corporate, local, character of the Eucharist, which he inherited largely from Bucer, can best be seen in those circumstances when the temptation is to underestimate or neglect this ecclesial character, namely, the communion of the sick. Calvin did not consider the communion of the sick absolutely necessary.[37] Nor did he consider it to be without dangers, as seen

[34] Cf. OS I:424.　　[35] *Inst.*, IV, 12, 5.　　[36] *ibid.* Cf. also CR 12:76.
[37] . . . non ita praecise necessario. . . . CR 20:201.

in the idolatry which the carrying of the Eucharist through the streets had occasioned in Roman Catholicism.[38] There was also a great deal of opposition to the practice of giving communion to the sick, as is evident from Calvin's lack of success in having the practice introduced in Geneva. Since it could not be introduced without a great deal of contention, and because the customs of the various churches differed, Calvin did not force the issue.[39] However he made it clear that he was quite unhappy about the lack of opportunity for the sick to communicate, and it was his wish that the want of this eucharistic practice in Geneva be not held up as the norm after his death. "It displeases me that we do not have the custom of administering the Supper to the sick; but it is not I who have deprived those departing this life from enjoying this consolation."[40]

What he objected to in the Roman practice was the private character of communion of the sick. The Eucharist is essentially ecclesial, corporate, and local, and these essential qualities cannot be set aside even for the convenience and comfort of the sick. The union with Christ in sacrament, as in faith, can take place only in the community which is his body.[41] This is not a matter of arbitrary legislation, nor of Calvin's whim, but a matter of Christ's explicit will.[42] Calvin's emphasis on the local church in its eucharistic life comes from biblical roots. Therefore any rite for the communion of the sick must maintain an ecclesial character. As a norm which is without exception, Calvin declared that "although there is no legitimate Supper unless it is held in common (*nulla sit legitima coena, nisi communis*), yet such a Eucharist as is given to the sick [Calvin here presupposes that friends and relatives gather in the sick room to make a common celebration] will not be considered false because it will

[38] Cf. *ibid.*, 20:200.

[39] Sed quia mos diversus invaluerat, ut sine magna contentione impetrari non posset mutatio, paci consulere malui . . . *ibid.*, 17:311, 312. Acquiesco quia utile non esset contendere. *ibid.*, 20:200.

[40] *ibid.*, 17:311, 312.   [41] Cf. *ibid.*, 20:201.   [42] Cf. *ibid.*

not be private."[43] "Therefore in order that the [eucharistic] action may not be foreign to or depart in the slightest from the institution by Christ, it is my wish that it take place only in the gathering of the faithful and only when accompanied with instruction and by means of a public rite."[44] This norm is not violated in giving communion to the sick when it is given as a part or appendix to a public cultic act. Note also the union of Word and sacrament. The sacramental action is to be accompanied with an instruction. There must always be the proclamation of the Gospel when the community gathers for the eucharistic action. If the Eucharist is the body of Christ it is also the Word of Christ.

Calvin notes that when Paul upbraided the Corinthians, asking them if they did not have houses in which they could eat and drink, he did not mean to exclude the Supper from private houses. "For Paul, while admonishing the Corinthians that each is to eat and drink in his own home, does not exclude the Supper in a private home but only makes a distinction between the spiritual mystery and ordinary meals so that the one will not be confused with the others."[45] What is forbidden is not celebrating the Eucharist in a private home, but celebrating the Eucharist privately, which is something quite different. To avoid celebrating the Eucharist privately, without a local "church," Calvin suggests that friends, acquaintances, and neighbors gather in the home of the sick man so that the Eucharist can be celebrated according to the command of Christ, that is communally. "It is therefore fitting that a congregation assemble, made up of relatives, friends and neighbors, so that distribution may be made according to the command of Christ; and so let the [eucharistic] action be joined with the explanation of the mystery."[46] The same injunction holds for giving communion to prisoners. All that Calvin insisted upon was that the prisoners, properly prepared to receive, should receive the

[43] *ibid.*   [44] *ibid.*   [45] *ibid.*

[46] *ibid.*, 10A:213, 214. Cf. also Jean Cadier, *La doctrine Calviniste de la sainte cène*, Montpellier, 1951, 18, 19.

Eucharist in what should really be a communion, namely that the Eucharist be celebrated in an assembly or company of believers.[47] Because the Eucharist is essentially an act of the local church, it cannot be stored or reserved. And even the communion of the sick cannot disregard the act quality and local quality of the Eucharist.

Since the Eucharist is a normal part of the church's life, not an event of rare occurrence, the community should give frequent expression to its essentially eucharistic character.[48] "It is certain that a church cannot be regarded as well ordered and governed if the holy meal instituted by our Lord is not often celebrated and well attended."[49] "Baptism should be, as it were, an entry into the church, and an initiation into faith; but the Supper should be a sort of continual food on which Christ spiritually feeds the household of his believers. . . . The Supper is repeatedly distributed, that those who have once been drawn into the church may realize that they continually feed upon Christ."[50] In spite of all the emphasis which Calvin placed upon the Word and upon preaching, and in spite of the word character of the sacrament, the Eucharist was not to be deprived of *a central* role. In worship as in theology there are various centralities, and the one does not cancel out the other. The Eucharist, as Calvin well knew, is peculiar to the church's corporate worship. While the pastor administers the Word both to individuals as well as to congregations, the Eucharist was essentially and uniquely corporate worship.[51] To this Calvin would allow no

[47] Cf. Mitchel Hunter, *The Teaching of Calvin*, Glasgow, 1920, 185, 1n. Hunter simply cites his source as "Letter, 1558." I take it that Hunter has access to a source not available to me since I could not find this letter under the year 1558.

[48] "Yet in spite of Calvin's emphasis on the Word, which he held to have been wickedly neglected for centuries in the Church, he also considered the Church to be essentially a eucharistic fellowship." Gedes MacGregor, *Corpus Christi*, London, 1959, 52.

[49] CR 10A:6. The whole problem of the frequency of celebration is handled by William Maxwell, *The Liturgical Portions of the Genevan Service Book*, Edinburgh, 1931, 201-205. Cf. also MacGregor, *op.cit.*, 53, 2n.

[50] *Inst.*, IV, 18, 19.

[51] Cf. *ibid.*, 52. Gerard van der Leeuw remarks that since the period im-

exception. He would not easily forget the tirades he directed against liturgical clericalism, especially as it was expressed in the private mass. There was no occasion on which it was proper to neglect the unity of the worshiping community of which the Eucharist is the symbol. Calvin would not open the door, ever so little, to the possibility that the Eucharist be isolated from its ecclesiological setting. The Eucharist is, and should remain, the act of the local church, not just of the local clergy.

An exposition of the inwardness Calvin attempted to achieve in his eucharistic doctrine must give place not only to the closeness of our union with Christ, but also to a limiting qualification of this union. The union with Christ achieved in the Eucharist must not give way to any cheapening of the transcendence of God. It is precisely the function of the Holy Spirit to guard against sacramental immanence.[52] By means of his doctrine of the Holy Spirit, Calvin attempts to avoid, and this in a radical way, any sacramental substitutes for God's transcendence. There is in Calvin a real sacramental mysticism, but he will not tolerate what he considers a fuzzy sacramental mysticism which forgets the distance between God and man, which recognizes no boundaries, no barriers. Here the work of the Holy Spirit is the work of a jealous God; he will not give God's transcendence to a creature. Here too the *opposita* must be maintained: union-distance.

The Social Dimension: *Communio Sanctorum*

THE BODY OF CHRIST, THE CHURCH, AS SOURCE OF ETHICAL CONCERN

Calvin once defined the church as "the society of all the saints which is spread through all the world and through all

---

mediately following the reformation, the Eucharist has been considered an appendage to worship. This seems not to have been the case during the reformation period itself. Cf. *Sakramentales Denken*, Kassel, 1959, 65.

[52] Cf. Kolfhaus, *op.cit.*, 115.

ages, but gathered together by the one doctrine of Christ and by the one Spirit, observing and cultivating the unity of faith and fraternal concord."[53] To this he added: "We deny that we have ever left this society, but rather we revere her as a mother and we desire to remain in her bosom."[54] Calvin's declaration that he had never left this society was more than a clarification of his relation to the Roman church. He was rather making a declaration with regard to his ultimate salvation. "Such as forsake the church . . . wholly alienate themselves from Christ."[55] Outside of the church "there can be neither salvation nor truth."[56] To leave the unity of faith found in the society of the saints, to destroy the bonds by which the body of Christ, the church, was bound together, was to sin against Christ himself, and to declare oneself beyond salvation. To disrupt the fraternal concord found in the society of the saints, to put at variance the members of the same body, was also to sin against Christ. It was not possible to sin against a member of Christ without sinning against Christ. The union with Christ is the basis of that ordered unity by which members are bound to one another.

Calvin's ethical doctrine finds its roots in that which binds together the members of the society of the saints which is the body of Christ. There can be no other source of ethical concern, no other norm of moral action than this community, this society of the saints. The community is itself the source and fountain of ethical concern, not as a sociological phenomenon—Calvin was not here concerned with the specific sociological aspects of his ecclesiology—but, quite simply, because the community is the body of Christ.[57] To sin against a brother is to sin against Christ. The Christian knows no other norm of ethical action. Calvin's ethics are ethics of the union with Christ and have a strong ecclesiological orientation.

Our ethical relationship to one another is, therefore, deter-

---

[53] OS I:466.   [54] *ibid*.   [55] CR 55:133.
[56] *ibid*., 37:199. Cf. also *ibid*., 40:281.   [57] Cf. Jacobs, *op.cit*., 91.

mined by our relationship to Christ. "We must be incorporated in Christ so that we are all bound together."[58] Our relationship to him is essentially a community relationship, a member-body relationship, and there can be no private bonds, no exclusive and esoteric nexus, which binds us to Christ apart from the other members. "When we are bound to him it is certain that we belong to all whom he has joined to his body."[59] These are the unmistakable ecclesiological presuppositions and accents found in Calvin's ethics.

THE ETHICAL CONCERN IN ITS EXISTENTIAL, EUCHARISTIC EXPRESSION

When Calvin reduces his ecclesiology from teaching to act, from the church as she is conceived dogmatically to the church as witnessing to her oneness with Christ in the eucharistic act, from the broad ecclesiological view to the narrower, concrete, local church gathered as the body of Christ in eucharistic worship, he brings with him his ethical concern. In fact when Calvin speaks of the Eucharist in detail in the fourth book of the *Institutes*, as well as elsewhere, a not inconsiderable amount of space is devoted to ethical problems. This Calvin does quite naturally since his ethics is a *Gemeinschaftsethik*. It is, as Jacobs explains, in the eucharistic act that the community, the local church, gives visibility to its twofold character: subjectively considered, through the congregation, and objectively considered, through the body of Christ.[60] It is in this eucharistic context that Calvin develops his doctrine of discipline, that is, the question of keeping the body of Christ undivided and unpolluted. Both when Calvin acts as a systematic theologian writing a theological treatise, and when he acts as a pastor of souls, these ethical questions are seen in the context of the church at eucharistic worship.[61] Therefore his insistence on the church's right to

[58] CR 49:464.

[59] *ibid.*, 51:514. Cf. also the excellent sermon of Calvin on Ephesians IV: 1-5 in *ibid.*, 51:523.

[60] Cf. Jacobs, *op.cit.*, 91.   [61] Cf. *ibid.*, 91, 92.

excommunicate, and the assurance that this is not just a tool of ecclesiastical dictatorship. The church at worship must really be the church, and the communicants must really belong to the body of Christ. The ethical question is not only a matter of guilt or lack of guilt, but it is a question of the body of Christ seen ecclesiologically and, because ecclesiologically, sacramentally. It goes without saying that in Calvin the Eucharist is not the exclusive point of departure for things ethical. There are large areas in his ethical writings where it does not appear. The eucharistic viewpoint is one of several centralities within Calvin's ethical thought.

Jacobs notes that the ethical questions, as teaching, are developed by Calvin within the framework of his soteriology, where, as teaching, they belong systematically. But ethics, as manner of life and conduct, is treated within the framework of the church.[62] Since the church is the place where the ethical concern is reduced to particularity, ethics as conduct belongs to this ecclesiological framework. His ethics, therefore, looks to his ecclesiology for clarification and for meaning, and his ecclesiology is given an ethical orientation. His doctrine of the eucharistic community is his ecclesiology concretized and localized, is his ethics in its highest cultic expression.[63]

When speaking of ethical concern in these eucharistic terms, it should be remembered that when Calvin speaks of eucharistic worship, he is not speaking of something apart from the Word. The Word, as preaching or doctrine, is for him an essential part of the Eucharist. There could no more be a Eucharist without doctrine than there could be a Eucharist without bread or without community.[64] The ethical questions are therefore also related to the theology of the Word.

Calvin's clearest expression of an ethical concern in a eu-

---

[62] Cf. *ibid.*

[63] Jacobs also notes the strong eschatological orientation of Calvin's ethics; cf. *op.cit.*, 112.

[64] Cf. CR 20:201.

charistic context is found in the *Institutes* IV:17, 38. In spite of its extended length, it is given here almost in full:

> For the Lord so communicates his body to us there [the Lord's Supper] that he is made completely one with us and we with him. Now, since he has only one body, of which he makes us all partakers, it is necessary that all of us also be made one body by such participation. The bread shown in the Sacrament represents this unity. As it is made of many grains so mixed together that one cannot be distinguished from another, so it is fitting that in the same way we should be joined and bound together by such great agreement of minds that no sort of disagreement or division may intrude. I prefer to explain it in Paul's words: "The cup of blessing which we bless is a communicating of the blood of Christ; and the bread of blessing which we break is a participation in the body of Christ. . . . Therefore . . . we . . . are all one body, for we partake of one bread." We shall benefit very much from the Sacrament if this thought is impressed and engraved upon our minds; that none of the brethren can be injured, despised, rejected, abused, or in any way offended by us, without at the same time, injuring, despising, and abusing Christ by wrongs we do; that we cannot disagree with our brethren without at the same time disagreeing with Christ; that we cannot love Christ without loving him in the brethren; that we ought to take the same care of our brethren's bodies as we take of our own; for they are members of our body.

The community in its eucharistic worship determines the Christian life and is, as the body of Christ, the source of that life. The teaching on the union with Christ in faith is here experienced sacramentally, and the elect knows experientially that his neighbor, with whom he received the body of Christ, is a member of Christ. Any act which puts him in relation to this neighbor puts him in relation to Christ. And in this relation to Christ he finds both his ethical motivation and the ultimate ethical judgment. Here Zwingli's concept of communion-fellowship receives its due, since Calvin develops it beyond the strictly sanctuary Eucharist.[65]

Calvin uses this ethical argument to reject the Roman practice of communicating only once a year. The Eucharist is the food of fraternal love. And to nourish this fraternal love we should frequently, not just once a year, receive the body of Christ. Among Roman Catholics, Calvin complains, the Eucharist is received only once a year, and that perfunctorily. Such is not the will of Christ. "Rather it was ordained to be frequently used among all Christians in order . . . to nourish mutual love, to give witness among themselves to this love, and to discern its bond in the unity of Christ's body. For as often as we partake of the symbol of the Lord's body, as a token given and received, we reciprocally bind ourselves to all the duties of love in order that none of us may permit anything that can harm our brother, or overlook anything that can help him, where necessity demands and ability suffices."[66]

The Pastoral Dimension

ASSURANCE OF SALVATION

The impersonality of ecclesiastical life and of sacramental life, the concern for the outward forms, and the automatic continuity of the ecclesiastical order and the elaborate but dedicated attention given to the mechanics of this continuity, together with the emphasis on the external sign of the sacrament and the objectivization of the sacrament, moved Calvin, together with Luther, to give a greater role to the personal and to the transcendent. The ecclesiastical journeyman, Calvin was convinced, could not put the faithful in personal contact with God because official Rome sought salvation in rites and structures. Nor could this practitioner

---

[65] Paul Wernle, *Der Evangelische Glaube nach den Hauptschriften den Reformatoren*, vol. 3, *Calvin*, Tübingen, 1919, 109. Cf. also Yngve Brilioth, *Eucharistic Faith and Practice: Evangelical and Catholic*, London, 1930, 157, 158.

[66] *Inst.*, IV, 17, 44.

give to the faithful, who were filled with doubts and beset with fears and temptations, the assurance of salvation and the personal joy which comes with the certitude that their sins are forgiven. From a machine or structure or a sacramental "thing" one cannot receive assurance, which in the religious sphere is always personal.

It becomes clear in Calvin that he, following, as he not without reason thought, St. Augustine, St. Bernard, and Luther, was preoccupied with building a theological system in which the assurance of salvation would not be based on any external forms or rites, nor on a sacramental thing, nor on anything human or created. "Now if we ask in what way the conscience can be made quiet before God, we shall find the only way to be that unmerited righteousness be conferred upon us as a gift of God. . . . Let even the most perfect man descend into his conscience and call his deeds to account, what then will be the outcome for him?"[67] It is in this light that we must judge Calvin's rejection of all introspection and soul searching, the examination of one's good and bad qualities, and this from a man who by no means condoned moral laxity. Such soul searching is based on a theology which would find salvation in man.

Calvin will build his theology on a foundation which no human frailty or weakness could undermine, and this was the pure will of God and his decrees. These were beyond facades and ceremonial etiquette and were subject to no earthly or ecclesiastical law, and therefore give an unimpeachable certitude.

Calvin was against any prying into the eternal decrees of God. To ask for particular personal assurance of salvation was highly dangerous and rash.[68] But there was a more general assurance to which all have a right, an assurance which is bound up with election and union with Christ and is founded not on special revelations but on the Word of God.[69]

[67] *ibid.*, III, 13, 3. Cf. also F. C. Baur, *Lehrbuch der christlichen Dogmengeschichte*, Tübingen, 2nd edn., 1858, 283.

[68] Cf. Wernle, *op.cit.*, 294.   [69] Cf. *Inst.*, III, 21, 1.

This assurance of salvation is not assurance in the usual sense. It is not a static state or possession, which is once received and possessed in undisturbed perpetuity. The Christian who has assurance is always "on the way," and he is always threatened by temptation and doubt.[70] The assurance of salvation is, like bread, given daily, and must daily be asked for and daily received. When this assurance is taken for granted, or is deprived of the tensions of faith, it becomes an illusion.

Assurance of salvation is in no sense assurance unless it is founded on God himself and unless it gives a divine certitude. "God is invincible. We know that our salvation is therefore certain."[71] This invincibility is made known to us in election, which has as its goal to make us children of God. Indeed, assurance is only another expression for being children of God.[72] "Now what is the purpose of election but that we, adopted as sons by our Heavenly Father, may obtain salvation and immortality by his favor?"[73] We are not made sons of God by some independent decree, but only in Christ. "Those whom God has adopted as his sons are said to have been chosen not in themselves but in his Christ."[74] Since Christ is in his person the ground of assurance of election and assurance of salvation, there can be no assurance apart from Christ, not even in the Father, seen in isolation from Christ. "But if we have been chosen in him, we shall not find assurance of our election in ourselves; and not even in God the Father, if we conceive him as separated from his Son."[75] Since it is into the body of Christ that the Father has destined those to be engrafted whom he will call his own, "we have a sufficiently clear and firm testimony" that we are of that number "if we are in communion with

[70] Cf. Wilhelm Hauck, *Die Erwählten*, Gütersloh, 1950, 77, 79.
[71] CR 8:100.   [72] Cf. Hauck, *op.cit.*, 75.   [73] *Inst.*, III, 24, 5.
[74] *ibid*.

[75] *ibid*., III, 24, 5. This passage should be kept in mind when Calvin is criticized for not keeping his doctrine of predestination in a Christological framework.

Christ."[76] For Calvin, then, there is assurance of salvation only in relation to Christ. Only this assurance can withstand the trials of faith and the burdens of temptation. This places the basis of our assurance beyond ourselves in God and gives it its certitude. Not only has election, on which our assurance rests, come from God, also our predestination, our inner call, enlightenment, justification, being born again, and the gift of perseverance—stages in the complete unfolding and revelation in time of election—also come from God. All are necessary for our salvation, all come from God in Christ, and because each is a pure gift from God, each is an added sign of the assurance of salvation.[77] The certitude is invincible because it is founded on God the invincible.

The role which assurance of salvation plays in Calvin's theology, systematic and pastoral, can be seen most clearly in his doctrine of predestination.[78] The doctrine of double predestination was taught by Calvin as a fact of revelation. He was profoundly disturbed by the doctrine of negative predestination, but it was in the source of revelation, as he read it, and to this he bowed. Religion for Calvin was before all else submission to the sovereign God, bowing before deep spiritual realities, pleasant or unpleasant. Predestination to hell was a great mystery which he did not pretend to understand and therefore he preferred neither to dwell upon it nor to write about it at any length. This is clearly seen in his nonpolemic writings, namely his exegetical works and his sermons, where negative predestination receives scant attention.[79] There is in Calvin's sermons no trace of a morbid eagerness to thunder from the pulpit the eternal damnation of God's negative predestination. Calvin, indeed, did not consider negative predestination as material for homiletic proclamation.[80] From the attention which Calvin gave to

[76] *ibid.*, 24, 5.   [77] Cf. *ibid.*, 24, 6.

[78] Bauke holds that predestination was rather the application of the ràtional-dialectic method to a religio-historical situation than a speculative elaboration. Cf. *Die Probleme der Theologie Calvins*, Leipzig, 1922, 83.

[79] Cf. Jacobs, *op.cit.*, 148-152.   [80] Cf. *ibid.*, 152.

negative predestination in his sermons and nonpolemic works, a more accurate estimate can be made of the role this doctrine should, in Calvin's mind, take in a theological exposition whose form and content are not determined by polemic considerations.

Contemporaries of Calvin denied double predestination, and for polemic reasons Calvin expanded on negative predestination in his systematic works, so that in the *Institutes* it takes up, quantitatively, more space than Calvin would have allotted to it had he been free from polemic considerations to develop his systematics according to purely dogmatic norms.[81] Calvin answered his critics with great vigor and force and at great length—he considered the doctrine of reprobation had close connection with the teaching on God, and to deny the one was to deny the other. To deny negative predestination was to deny the teaching on God's absolute freedom, his sovereign lordship, the necessity of his being unconditioned and the only cause. The closer a declaration of faith is bound to the doctrine on God, the more central and the more unassailable it is.[82]

Calvin's teaching on predestination is an expression of his teaching on God, but it has a functional role in the life of faith: that of assuring consciences of salvation.[83] The salvation which is founded on God, on his love and mercy, is a free grace, freely given. And God does not repent of his gifts. Of such salvation there can be no doubt. Such a salvation can only be a matter of peace and joy, and therefore predestination gives strong support to the assurance of salvation.[84] Calvin speaks of "the very sweet fruit" of predestination.[85] A look at Calvin's sermons is convincing proof that when he acted as pastor he preached predestination as the reason for great joy.[86] The certitude of predestination is the certitude of eternal peace and beatitude.

---

[81] Cf. *ibid.*, 148.   [82] Cf. Hauck, *op.cit.*, 20.

[83] For the role assurance of salvation has played in the interpretation of Calvin's doctrine of predestination cf. Jacobs, *op.cit.*, 17, 26, 28, 29, 35.

[84] Cf. O. Weber, "Calvin," RGG[3].   [85] *Inst.*, III, 21, 1.

[86] Cf. Johannes Calvin, *Predigten über das 2. Buch Samuelis*, ed. Hanns

THE EUCHARIST AS PLEDGE OF SALVATION

To counteract any remnants of sacramental imperialism and its sacramental will-to-power, Calvin states that "assurance of salvation does not depend upon participation in the sacrament, as if justification consisted in it. For we know that justification is lodged in Christ alone, and that it is communicated to us no less by the preaching of the gospel than by the seal of the sacrament, and without the latter can stand unimpaired."[87] Calvin can say this because for him the meaning of the Eucharist resides in the promises, which he, like Luther, identifies with the words of institution. It is the promises which stand behind the sacraments, which fortify the faithful and give them assurance. "It is not, therefore, the chief function of the Sacrament simply and without higher consideration to extend to us the body of Christ. Rather, it is to seal and confirm that promise by which he testifies that his flesh is food indeed and his blood is drink, which feed us unto eternal life."[88] The sacrament adds nothing to the promises as such, so that it can be said that Calvin's attention is directed not to the body and blood of Christ but to the fulfillment of the promises.[89]

Having insisted that assurance of salvation does not depend on the sacraments, Calvin then proceeds to show that it is the specific task of the sacraments to give that assurance. The sacrament takes its place at the side of the Word as the means of leading the faithful to assurance of election and of salvation.[90] When Calvin introduces the subject of the Eucharist in Chapter 17 of the fourth book of the *Institutes* he devotes the first two sections to the assurance of which the

---

Rückert, Neukirchen, 1936-1961, 184f, 212f, 351, 352, 483. Cf. also CR 28:677, 678; *ibid.*, 49:159-162. Calvin stresses more the certitude of salvation found in predestination and the joy we obtain from such certitude than directly the joy of predestination.

[87] *Inst.*, IV, 14, 14.   [88] *ibid.*, 17, 4.

[89] Cf. W. Boudriot, "Calvins Abendmahlslehre," *Reformierte Kirchenzeitung*, vol. 79 (1929), 91.

[90] Cf. August Lecerf, *Etudes Calvinistes*, Neuchâtel, 1949, 40.

Eucharist is the seal and food. In these two introductory sections of Chapter 17 he speaks of assurance five times. And here, as when speaking of assurance of election, Calvin locates the assurance of salvation not just in the reception of the body and blood of Christ, but in union with Christ—the same Christological method by which he situated assurance of election.[91] "Godly souls can gather great assurance and delight from this Sacrament; in it they have a witness of our growth into one body with Christ such that whatever is his may be called ours. As a consequence, we may dare assure ourselves that eternal life, of which he is heir, is ours."[92] To receive the sign of our union with Christ, the body and blood, is to give us assurance that "the Kingdom of Heaven, into which he has already entered, can no more be cut off from us than from him."[93]

The Eucharist is the pledge of that wonderful exchange by which Christ, taking upon himself our mortality, "has conferred his immortality upon us."[94] The Eucharist is also that food by which the Father gives to his sons the pledge to assure us of his continuing liberality. In the Eucharist "Christ attests himself to be the life-giving bread, upon which our souls feed unto true and blessed immortality."[95]

The Word is also assurance of salvation. It gives the "hope of immortality."[96] But he who hears the Word may still need assurance. "For how little assurance would you grasp, if you heard that the Word of God (from which you are far removed) contains in itself fullness of life, but in and round about yourself nothing but death meets you and moves before your eyes? But when the Source of life begins to abide in our flesh, he no longer lies hidden far from us, but shows us that we are to partake of him. But he also quickens our very flesh in which he abides, that by partaking of him we may be fed unto immortality."[97]

Calvin's pastoral efforts with regard to the Eucharist were

---

[91] Cf. *Inst.*, III, 24, 5.   [92] *ibid.*, IV, 17, 2.   [93] *ibid.*
[94] *ibid.*   [95] *ibid.*, 17, 1.   [96] *ibid.*, 17, 8.   [97] *ibid.*

directed toward making this pledge of immortality more accessible. To do this he attempted to quiet the consciences of the faithful with regard to the problem of worthiness, and he attempted to increase the number of times the Eucharist would be celebrated. As has been seen in Chapter III, Calvin considered the demands made upon the people in the matter of worthiness excessive. The Romans "torture and harass pitiable consciences in dire ways."[98] By their examination of conscience they attempted to ascertain whether or not they were in the state of grace, for Calvin both a theological and pastoral impossibility. "For if it is a question of our seeking worthiness by ourselves, we are undone; only despair and deadly ruin remain to us."[99] Such seeking certainly has a Pelagian ring.

Though he would demand that each man prove himself worthy in regard to his faith and love, Calvin gives much attention to the necessity of being assured and of having a quiet conscience so that one can make a generous response to Christ. While at Strassburg, Calvin had each person who was to take communion announce that fact to the pastor beforehand. His purpose, in part, was to give greater solemnity to the Eucharist, but also to exclude the unworthy from it. He also talked privately with the persons who presented themselves so that those "who have an encumbered conscience" could receive the aid they needed.[100] In a letter to Farel he further explains that in such conversations the ignorant can be instructed so that they will be better prepared for communion, those in need of special admonition can receive it, and that those tormented with a troubled conscience can receive consolation.[101] In all of this the pastoral emphasis was upon the Supper as the medicine of the sick, the food for the weak. "This sacred feast is medicine for the sick, solace for sinners, alms to the poor. . . . For since in it Christ is given to us as food, we understand that without him we would pine away, starve, and faint."[102] This sacrament is

[98] *ibid.*, 17, 41.   [99] *ibid.*   [100] *ibid.*, III, 4, 13.
[101] Cf. CR 11:41.   [102] *Inst.*, IV, 17, 42.

"ordained not for the perfect, but for the weak and feeble, to awaken, arouse, stimulate, and exercise the feeling of faith and love, indeed, to correct the defect of both."[103] Those who are disturbed in conscience because of some moral fault should be assured that the worthiness demanded for the reception of the sacrament is faith and love, a worthiness which comes from God and therefore gives assurance to approach the table with confidence.

If one asks what worthiness man can bring to the Supper, then the answer must be, "Only his own unworthiness." "This is the worthiness—the best and only kind we can bring to God—to offer our vileness and so to speak our unworthiness to him so that his mercy may make us worthy of him; to despair in ourselves so that we may be comforted in him; to abase ourselves so that we may be lifted up by him. . . . We shall think that we, as being poor, come to a kindly giver; as sick, to a physician; as sinners, to the Author of righteousness; finally, as dead, to him who gives us life."[104] The assurance of eternal life of which the bread of life is a sign does not come from man—nor does the assurance of worthiness necessary to approach and receive the bread of life. Both assurances are pure gifts, and because the two gifts proceed from God's sovereign love and mercy, they are infallibly given to the humble and repentant. Neither salvation, nor the approaches to salvation find their basis in man, and therefore they are certain, assured.

Calvin's own attempts to have communion celebrated once a week were not successful, and Niesel notes that the regular celebration of the Lord's Supper every Sunday has nowhere established itself.[105] Under pressure from the civil authorities he, for a time, advocated communion once a month, and ultimately had to adopt the custom of Berne of celebrating the Supper four times a year.[106] Ultimately Calvin had Zwingli

---

[103] *ibid*.   [104] *ibid*.

[105] Cf. Niesel, "The Order of Public Worship in the Reformed Churches," *Scottish Journal of Theology*, vol. 2 (1949), 387.

[106] Cf. OS I:371.

to blame for this custom of quarterly communion as the Berne custom was introduced by Zwingli. At one time Calvin admitted that the congregations were not spiritually ready to celebrate the Eucharist weekly.[107] But this was an existential fact, and neither a universal pastoral nor a dogmatic norm. Quite the opposite. The guiding pastoral norm was Johannine: "I am the bread of life." And the bread of life is to be eaten frequently. As opposed to the Roman Catholic practice of receiving communion once a year, he recalled that in the early church "it became the unvarying rule that no meeting of the church should take place without the Word, prayers, partaking of the Supper, and almsgiving," and that this order "remained in use for many centuries."[108] He also quoted Chrysostom with approval. "Whoever does not partake of the mysteries is wicked and shameless to be present there. . . . Would it not be better for you not to have been present?"[109] On the other hand, though "all are to be urged and aroused" to receive communion, none is "to be forcibly compelled" to the Lord's table."[110] The Roman custom of receiving once a year was plainly inadequate and Calvin labeled it "a veritable invention of the devil."[111] The immediate effect of the reformation, both in Switzerland and in Germany, was to restore the practice of more frequent communion.[112]

[107] CR 10A:213.   [108] *Inst.*, IV, 17, 4.
[109] *ibid.*, 17, 45. Cf. also PL 62:29.
[110] *ibid.*, 17, 46.   [111] *ibid.*
[112] Cf. H. J. Wotherspoon, J. M. Kirkpatrick, *A Manual of Church Doctrine*, 2nd edn., London, 1960, 46. The fathers of the Council of Trent "recommended that the faithful receive communion each time they came to Mass, a notion far removed from the practice of the day." Joseph A. Jungmann, *The Mass of the Roman Rite*, New York, 1950, vol. 1, 138.

VI. The Eucharist in Its Christological Context: Calvin's Eucharistic Doctrine, I

The Mystery Cannot Be Measured

THE THEOLOGIAN who stands before the mystery of Christ in his eucharistic presence, or indeed, before any of the Christian mysteries, must come to terms with the certainty that what he is called upon to explain is ultimately beyond explanation, that the mystery, though above reason, is not against it, and that, finally, the mystery can to a degree be penetrated. In the face of these theological norms, the theologian who is precise where there is no precision, who gives tidy summations as exhaustive and definitive formulations, who hides his incompetence behind a noisy appeal to the incomprehensibility of the mystery, is a sad theologian.

Calvin, too, experienced theological hesitations, and he despaired of adequately expressing the inaccessibilities which had been only partly grasped. But even when the truths were dialectical in character he would not allow the truths which he considered theological certainties to be lost or obscured in imprecision. Without attempting to hide the basic inadequacy of the theologian before the mystery, and without consciously seeking in purely subjective propensities certainties which could not be found in an ordered theology, he did not fail to recognize how far the mystery was beyond man's comprehending: "Now, if anyone should ask me how this [presence of Christ in the Eucharist] takes place, I shall not be ashamed to confess that it is a secret too lofty for either my mind to comprehend or my words to declare. And to speak more plainly, I rather experience than understand it. Therefore, I here embrace without controversy the truth of God in which I may safely rest."[1] Note here the unabashed role Calvin assigns to religious instinct or experience: "I rather experience than understand it."

[1] *Inst.*, IV, 17, 32.

Calvin knew a mystery when he saw one, and he knew that the mystery was beyond man's measuring: "I therefore freely admit that no man should measure its sublimity by the little measure of my childishness."[2] Calvin admits his own personal limitations and urges those who can to go beyond him. One will note here a deeply personal and religious attitude, an almost mystical submission to the magnitude of the mystery: "I urge my readers not to confine their mental interest within these too narrow limits [that is, 'the little measure of my childishness'], but to strive to rise much higher than I can lead them. For, whenever this matter is discussed, when I have tried to say all, I feel that I have as yet said little in proportion to its worth. And although my mind can think beyond what my tongue can utter, yet even my mind is conquered and overwhelmed by the greatness of the thing. Therefore, nothing remains but to break forth in wonder at this mystery, which plainly neither the mind is able to conceive nor the tongue to express."[3] Calvin's inadequacy before the mystery is that common to man, indeed, even to an apostle: "It would be extreme madness to recognize no communion of believers with the flesh and blood of the Lord, which the apostle declares to be so great that he prefers to marvel at it rather than to explain it."[4] In a letter to the King of France, Calvin writes that the Eucharist, being the mystery of faith, can be understood only by faith: "This mystery transcends in its depth the measure of our capacity and the whole order of nature. In one word, inasmuch as it is celestial, it can be apprehended only by faith."[5]

But the insistence on the element of mystery is no reason for foregoing an explanation: "Knowledge of this great mystery is most necessary, and, in proportion to its importance, demands an accurate exposition."[6] Neither does the enduring mystery give an excuse for introducing absurdities, an assertion Calvin cast in the form of a syllogism. "A doctrine carrying many absurdities with it is not true. The

[2] *ibid.*, 17, 7.   [3] *ibid.*   [4] *ibid.*, 17, 9.
[5] CR 9:719.   [6] *Inst.*, IV, 17, 1.

doctrine of the corporeal presence of Christ is involved in many absurdities; therefore it follows that it is not true."[7] This is not to say that the ultimate judge is reason: "We declare that we reverently embrace what human reason repudiates. We only shun absurdities abhorrent to piety and faith."[8] Against Westphal, who had said that Calvin was so bound to reason as to be unable to grant to God other than a power proper to the order of nature, Calvin answered that his solution was also not without an element of the incredible: "There is nothing more incredible than that things severed and removed from one another by the whole space between heaven and earth should not only be connected across such a great distance but also be united, so that souls may receive nourishment from Christ's flesh."[9] Though Calvin would not admit that he was measuring the divine by the human, he did insist that even in these mysteries reason and common sense had a role. Calvin distinguished three kinds of reason: "There is a reason naturally implanted which cannot be condemned without insult to God, but it has its limits which it cannot overstep without being immediately lost. Of this we have sad proof in the fall of Adam. . . . There is another kind of reason which is vicious, especially in a corrupt nature, and is manifested when mortal man, instead of receiving divine things with reverence, would subject them to his own judgment. . . . But there is a third kind of reason which both the Spirit of God and the Scripture sanction."[10] It is this third kind of reason which Calvin invokes to prove whether a theological statement has passed beyond the confines of the mystery and has become involved in absurdities. This third kind of reason functions within the faith, and permits no theological declarations with regard to one doctrine which are out of harmony with, or in contradiction to, theological declarations with regard to other doctrines. To be more specific, eucharistic doctrine must be in harmony with Christology, Pneumatology, and ecclesiology.

Calvin took no little pride in his eucharistic doctrine,

[7] CR 9:233.   [8] *ibid.*, 9:514.   [9] *Inst.*, IV, 17, 24.   [10] CR 9:474.

especially with regard to its clarity. "In this doctrine of the sacraments, their dignity is highly extolled, their use plainly shown, their utility sufficiently proclaimed, and moderation in all things duly maintained; so that nothing is attributed to them which ought not be attributed, and nothing denied them which they ought to possess."[11] He was scrupulous, he says, in avoiding ambiguous expressions and invites his opponents to imitate his clarity, suggesting that they will not dare accept this challenge, for to do so would necessitate their acceptance of Calvin's eucharistic doctrine.[12]

To attain this clarity he will not suffer "deceitful subtleties" such as the scholastics employ. "They [the schoolmen] do nothing but indulge in deceitful subtleties. They grant that Christ is not there contained in any circumscriptive or bodily fashion. But they devise a mode which they neither understand themselves nor can they explain it to others."[13] No explanation can be theologically acceptable which does not begin with mystery and end with mystery, and the clarity attained is in thinking around the sacrament, not in thinking through it. The ultimate norm, then, is that "this mystery transcends in its depth the measure of our capacity and the whole order of nature. In one word, inasmuch as it is celestial, it can be grasped only by faith."[14] Of this mystery "it is more proper to wonder than to speak."[15]

Calvin is in no special need to justify his assertion that the eucharistic fact is essentially mystery. Tradition had, however, prepared the reformation Christian to accept mystery. The revived Augustinianism, the intuitionalism of Platonism, the bold supernaturalism of the nominalists, all conspired to maintain the numinous in doctrine.

[11] *Inst.*, IV, 14, 17.   [12] Cf. CR 9:21.

[13] *Inst.*, IV, 17, 13. Calvin's accusation is not without some justification, but in defense of the schoolmen it must be added that the same accusation can be leveled against any theological explanation of this mystery, Calvin's included. The rule of orthodoxy is not clarity, however desirable, but conformity to the source of revelation. More than one theologian has sinned by being clear where there is no clarity.

[14] CR 9:719.   [15] *Inst.*, IV, 17, 9.

The Christological Dialectics in Eucharistic Doctrine

CHRISTOLOGICAL ORIENTATION

Contrary to first appearances, Calvin does not start out with the problem of elements. Calvin's doctrine asserts the validity of the promises made in connection with the Eucharist quite apart from the problem of the elements. The promises stand in the foreground, not the problem of the elements.[16] His first concern is not, then, the problem of the physical elements but is a Christological concern. "We have already taught (IV, 14, 5) that they [the sacraments] are seals by which God's promises are sealed, and moreover, it is very clear that no promise has ever been offered to me except in Christ. Consequently to teach us about any promise of God, they must show forth Christ. To this pertains that heavenly pattern of the Tabernacle and of worship under the law, which was put before Moses on the mountain."[17] So Christ is the end of the sacraments of the Old and New Testaments; in the one, Christ is promised, while in the other, attestation is given that Christ has already been revealed.

When treating more specifically of the real presence, Calvin again situates the problem in its wider Christological context. "But we must establish such a presence of Christ in the Supper as may neither fasten him to the element of bread, nor enclose him in bread, nor circumscribe him in any way (all which things, it is clear, detract from his heavenly glory); finally, such as may not take from him his own stature, or parcel him out to many places at once, or invest him with boundless magnitude to be spread through heaven and earth. For these things are plainly in conflict with a nature truly human. Let us never (I say) allow these two limitations to be taken away from us: (1) Let nothing be withdrawn from Christ's heavenly glory—as happens when he

---

[16] Cf. CR 47:151; *Inst.*, IV, 17, 8-34. Cf. also Paul Jacobs, *Prädestination und Verantwortlichkeit bei Calvin*, Neukirchen, 1937, 89.

[17] *Inst.*, IV, 14, 20.

is brought under the corruptible elements of this world, or bound to any earthly creatures. (2) Let nothing inappropriate to human nature be ascribed to his body, as happens when it is said either to be infinite or to be put in a number of places."[18] The truth which Calvin is here defending is precisely a Christological truth. He stood in defense of "the truth of the human nature on which our salvation rests,"[19] and this against Lutheran Christology, and for similar reasons against the Roman Catholic Christology.[20] To admit either the Lutheran or the Roman view of the Eucharist was to destroy the humanity of Christ, and this was to invalidate our redemption. Any theory of eucharistic doctrine must safeguard the integrity of Christ's humanity. "It is the true nature of a body to be contained in space, to have its own dimensions and its own shape. Away, then, with this stupid fiction which fastens both men's minds and Christ to bread."[21] Against the ubiquity teaching of the Lutherans, Calvin said that the Lutherans, who based their doctrine on the omnipotence of God, should not expect that the omnipotence of God should turn flesh into spirit. Calvin thought that the teaching of the spiritualists and the Lutherans were on the same level. Both endanger the integrity of Christ's humanity.

Calvin's arguments took their inspiration not from rationalism, of which he was accused, but from a biblical theology of revelation. God has revealed himself in the flesh, and therefore God becomes an object-subject for us, and, with the help of our conceptual tools, we can make statements about this object-subject.[22] When one declares, as Cal-

---

[18] ibid., 17, 19.   [19] CR 9:208.

[20] It is at times difficult to know against whom Calvin is writing. The arguments used against the Lutherans are quite valid, from Calvin's point of view, when used against the Roman Catholics. Both positions necessitated a kind of local presence.

[21] Inst., IV, 17, 29.

[22] Wilhelm Niesel, *Calvins Lehre vom Abendmahl*, 2nd edn., Munich, 1935, 68, 72. Cf. also Ronald S. Wallace, *Calvin's Doctrine of Word and Sacrament*, Edinburgh, 1953, 21-24. Calvin answers the accusation of rationalism in *Inst.*, IV, 17, 24; CR 9:48, 74, 94, 194, 196. Cf. Jean Cadier's

vin accuses the Lutherans of asserting, that the flesh of this object-subject (Logos become man) is no longer the same as our flesh, then one endangers the revelation in the mediator, Jesus Christ, and thereby also our redemption.

CALVIN, A NESTORIAN?

Having insisted on the integrity of the humanity of Christ in heaven after the resurrection, Calvin goes on to say that though "the flesh of Christ is like a rich and inexhaustible fountain that pours into us the life springing forth from the Godhead into itself,"[23] yet the flesh of Christ does not have of itself the power to give us life: "But the flesh of Christ does not itself have a power so great as to quicken us, for in its first condition it was subject to mortality; and now, endowed with immortality, it does not live through itself."[24] For Calvin the body of Christ, as also the human nature of Christ, is only a means by which the Logos attains its ends, so that the body of Christ even after its assumption by the Logos and union with the Logos, does not have the life-giving power as a property of its own substance.[25] Using the example of a spring, Calvin says that "water is sometimes drunk from a spring, sometimes drawn, sometimes led by channels to water the fields, yet it does not flow forth from itself for so many uses, but from the very source, which by unceasing flow supplies and serves it. In like manner the flesh of Christ is like a rich and inexhaustible fountain that pours into us the life springing forth from the Godhead into itself."[26] Calvin does speak of the body of Christ as "life-giv-

---

comments on Calvin's defense. *La doctrine Calviniste de la sainte cène*, Montpellier, 1951, 37.

[23] *Inst.*, IV, 17, 9. Cf. also CR 49:110. Wallace notes that Calvin prefers to say that we are saved in Christ rather than by Christ, "for the former phrase has more expressiveness and force and denotes the union with Christ which is such a necessary part of the Gospel." *Calvin's Doctrine of the Christian Life*, Edinburgh, 1959, 17, 18.

[24] *Inst.*, IV, 17, 9.

[25] Cf. Helmut Gollwitzer, *Coena Domini*, Munich, 1937, 120.

[26] *Inst.*, IV, 17, 9. Cf. also Joachim Beckmann, *Vom Sakrament bei Calvin*, Tübingen, 1926, 146.

ing," but this is mostly a manner of speaking: "Nevertheless, since it [the body of Christ] is pervaded with fullness of life to be transmitted to us, it is rightly called 'life-giving.' "[27]

There is a Nestorian tendency in Calvin as in Zwingli, though more pronounced in the latter. Calvin gave a Nestorian emphasis to his Christology in his reaction against Luther and also because of his desire to maintain the essential distinction of the two natures and those properties special to each nature. Luther had taken the unity of the person of Christ and proceeded through the use of communication of idioms to extend the ubiquity of the divine person to the human nature of Christ. Calvin took the immutability and incommunicability of the divinity and proceeded to rather different Christological conclusions.[28] In the heat of controversy lines were drawn that might not otherwise have been drawn, and formulas were set up which bear the imprint of the battle front. This must be kept in mind when judging the Christological formulations of Calvin, especially his classical text, which came to be known as the *Extra Calvinisticum*: "Even if the Word in his immeasurable essence is united with the nature of man into one person, we do not imagine that he was confined therein. Here is something marvelous: the Son of God descended from heaven in such a way that, without leaving heaven, he willed to be born in

[27] *Inst.*, IV, 17, 9.

[28] Cf. François Wendel, *Calvin, The Origins and Development of His Religious Thought*, London, 1963, 168. There is a general tendency among Calvin scholars to make note of his Nestorian tendency. Max Dominice, "Die Christusverkündigung bei Calvin," *Jesus Christus im Zeugnis der Heiligen Schrift und der Kirche*, Beiheft 2, *Evangelische Theologie*, Munich, 1936, 243; Joseph Ternus, "Chalkedon und die Entwicklung der protestantischen Theologie," *Das Konzil von Chalkedon*, vol. 3, *Entscheidung um Chalkedon*, eds. A. Grillmeier, H. Bacht, Würzburg, 1954, 532; H. Bauke, "Christologie," RGG²; Max Thurian, "The Real Presence," *Christianity Divided*, eds. Daniel J. Callahan *et al.*, New York, 1961, 210; F. W. A. Korff, *Christologie, De Leer van Het Komen Gods*, Nijkerk, 1940, vol. 2, 262, 263. On the other hand Seeberg and Grass give greater emphasis to the essential orthodoxy of Calvin's Christology. Reinhold Seeberg, *Lehrbuch der Dogmengeschichte*, vol. 4/2, *Die Fortbildung der reformatorischen Lehre und die Gegenreformatorische Lehre*, 5th edn., Darmstadt, 1953, 582; Hans Grass, *Die Abendmahlslehre bei Luther und Calvin*, Gütersloh, 1954, 214.

the virgin's womb, to go about the earth, and to hang upon the cross; yet he continuously filled the world even as he had done from the beginning."[29] The Christological dialectic is clearly stated within a Platonic framework: the Godhead fully committed in the Incarnation remains the Godhead uncommitted; the Godhead unmixed, present everywhere, is the Godhead undivided, present in his humanity.

There are three factors in Calvin's Christology which need to be considered in weighing the influence of his Christology on his eucharistic doctrine: his vigorous and unhesitating rejection of Nestorius; the essential Nestorian manner of thinking apparent in his Christology, as seen especially in his doctrine of the communication of idioms; and the basic orthodoxy of his Christology.

Calvin's rejection of Nestorius is conscious and undoubted: "We therefore hold that Christ, as he is God and man, consisting of two natures united but not mingled, is our Lord and the true Son of God even according to, but not by reason of, his humanity. Away with the error of Nestorius, who in wanting to pull apart rather than distinguish the natures of Christ devised a double Christ! Yet we see that Scripture cries out against this with a clear voice. . . . Hence, just as Nestorius had justly been condemned at the Synod of Ephesus, so Eutyches was afterward justly condemned. . . . For it is no more permissible to commingle the two natures in Christ than to pull them apart."[30]

If words have any meaning then we must take Calvin's protestations here seriously. He rejected Nestorius and he adhered to the formulations of Chalcedon. He earnestly sought to find a middle way between Nestorianism and Eutychianism, and in this attempt he was not entirely suc-

[29] *Inst.*, II, 13, 4. For the eucharistic relevance of the *Extra Calvinisticum* cf. Jacobs, "Die Gegenwart Christi im Abendmahl nach reformiertem Verständnis und das römisch-katholische Gegenbild," *Gegenwart Christi*, ed. Fritz Viering, Göttingen, 1959, 24, 25.

[30] *Inst.*, II, 14, 4.

cessful.[31] Calvin shied away from the ontological influence of one nature upon the other. He failed to see that the whole reality of human nature is in a more eminent way contained in the divine nature and that the divine nature in the person of the Word is ontologically present to, and contained in, though not limited to, human nature, and that human nature is, by reason of this grace of union, sanctified. He was convinced that to concede this ontological presence of one nature to the other would be to cast aside that which is primary in revelation and in the Christian consciousness, namely, the tension between the unmixed and undivided, between complete commitment and the uncommitted. The dialectic is not just a method; it is revelation.

We can see this tendency to separate the two natures in Calvin's doctrine of the redemptive value of the Passion. He declared that the Passion of Christ was, in itself, of no particular value or efficacy; what value the Passion had was bestowed upon it by the divine will when it accepted the Passion as sufficient. It was this acceptance which gave the Passion its redemptive value. "Apart from God's pleasure Christ could not merit anything; but did so because he had been appointed to appease God's wrath with his sacrifice, and to blot out our transgressions with his obedience. To sum up: inasmuch as Christ's merit depends upon God's grace alone, which ordained this manner of salvation for us, it is just as properly opposed to all human righteousness as God's grace is."[32] The accent on the will of God and on the *acceptatio divina* makes one wonder to what degree Calvin is here indebted to the nominalist tradition.

The doctrine of the ontological union of the two natures would therefore be suspect in Calvin's mind as a mixing of the natures, although a union of natures is not necessarily a mixing and can be achieved without losing the integrity of

---

[31] Cf. Johannes L. Witte, "Die Christologie Calvins," *Das Konzil von Chalkedon*, vol. 3, 510.

[32] *Inst.*, II, 17, 1. Cf. also CR 10A:160-165.

either nature.[33] Calvin's thought processes concentrated rather on the indivisible unity of the person of Christ. By reason of the indivisible unity of the person of Christ one attributes to human nature what belongs to the divine nature, and vice versa. It should be noted that Calvin speaks of an omnipresence of God through his Godhead or divinity, but that he also speaks of the omnipresence of the person of the God-man, the Mediator: "Although Christ, who is God and

[33] As examples of this tendency in Calvin texts taken from his commentary on the fourth Gospel have been chosen. The fourth Gospel was chosen because of the divinization of the humanity of Christ which forms part of the evangelist's Christology. Cf. William Grossouw, *Revelation and Redemption, a Sketch of the Theology of St. John*, Westminster, 1955, 60-63. Especially in those passages where John accents the unity of the Word become flesh, one sees Calvin's reluctance to take the occasion to treat of the same subject. On John XIV: 8-14: *Quod ego in patre, et pater in me.* Haec verba non ad divinam Christi essentiam refero, sed ad modum revelationis. Christus enim quoad arcanam suam deitatem nihilo nobis notior est quam pater. Verum dicitur esse expressa Dei imago, quia se totum in illo patefecit Deus: quatenus illic immensa eius bonitas, sapientia et virtus in solidum apparet. Neque tamen perperam veteres, qui hinc testimonium sumunt pro asserenda Christi divinitate. Sed quia non simpliciter disputat Christus, quis sit in se, sed qualis debeat agnosci a nobis, virtutis potius quam essentiae elogium est. Pater ergo in Christo esse dicitur, quia in eo habitat plena divinitas et virtutem suam exserit. Christus vicissim dicitur esse in patre, quia divina virtute se unum cum illo esse ostendit. CR 47:326. The best example of Calvin's tendency to shy away from any ontological influence of one nature on the other, and also of the soteriological direction of his Christology, is seen in his exegesis of John XVII: 21: *Ut omnes unum sint, etc.* Caeterum tenendum est, quoties unum se cum patre esse in hoc capite pronuntiat Christus, sermonem non haberi simpliciter de divina eius essentia, sed unum vocari in persona mediatoris, et quatenus caput nostrum est. Sic quidem praecise multi ex patribus interpretati sunt, Christum unum esse cum patre, quia aeternus sit Deus. Sed huc eos abripuit contentio cum Arianis, ut concisas sententias in alienum sensum torquerent. Longe autem aliud Christi consilium fuit, quam ad nudam arcanae suae divinitatis speculationem nos evehere. Si quidem a fine ratiocinatur, ideo nos debere unum esse, quia alioqui inanis et infructuosa esset quam habet cum patre unitas. Ergo ut rite comprehendas quo pertineat istud, Christum et patrem unum esse, cave ne Christum exuas mediatoris persona, sed eum potius considera, ut est ecclesiae caput, et membris suis coniunge: ita optime stabit contextus, ne irrita sit vel inutilis filii cum patre unitas, eius virtutem oportere in totum piorum corpus diffundi. Unde etiam colligimus, nos unum cum Christo esse, non quia suam in nos substantiam transfundat, sed quia spiritus sui virtute nobiscum vitam suam et quidquid accepit a patre bonorum communicet. CR 47:387. Cf. also *ibid.*, 45:456; *ibid.*, 45:643; *ibid.*, 47:18; *ibid.*, 47:376; *ibid.*, 47:387.

man, mediator between God and man, whole and undivided as he is, fills heaven and earth, but with respect to his flesh he is only in heaven."[34] For Calvin the communication of idioms is not to be found in the ontological union of two integral natures but exclusively in the office of Christ as the Mediator. "Insofar as he is God, he cannot increase in anything, and does all things for his own sake; nothing is hidden from him; he does all things according to the decision of his will, and can be neither seen nor handled. Yet he does not ascribe these qualities solely to his human nature, but takes them upon himself as being in harmony with the person of the Mediator."[35]

Calvin gives a further restriction. He considers the communication of idioms in the Mediator only in relationship to the saving work of that Mediator: "Until he comes forth as judge of the world, Christ will therefore reign, joining us to the Father as the measure of our weakness permits. But when as partakers in heavenly glory we shall see God as he is, Christ, having then discharged the office of Mediator, will cease to be the ambassador of his Father, and will be satisfied with that glory which he enjoyed before the creation of the world. . . . He [Christ] then returns the lordship to his Father so that—far from diminishing his own majesty—it may shine all the more brightly. Then, also, God shall cease to be the Head of Christ, for Christ's own deity will shine of itself, though as yet it is covered by a veil."[36] Though the

[34] *ibid.*, 9:246. Cf. also *ibid.*, 9:220. However, Calvin never developed these ideas on the omnipresence of the person of the God-man, the Mediator, in any systematic way. Cf. Werner Krusche, *Das Wirken des Heiligen Geistes*, Göttingen, 1957, 150.

[35] *Inst.*, II, 14, 2.

[36] *ibid.*, 14, 3. Cf. also *ibid.*, IV, 17, 9; CR 75:376; *ibid.*, 75:387. With these texts in mind one would have to modify the opinion of Grass that there is no communication of idioms from one nature to another in Calvin. Cf. *op.cit.*, 261.

Witte has mistranslated the Latin text and therefore draws false conclusions. Nam et tunc desinet caput Christi esse Deus is translated into German as "dann wird Christus auch aufhören Haupt zu sein." Basing his conclusions on this false translation, Witte declares, "Calvin scheint hingegen der Ansicht

Son of God will still retain the assumed humanity after the whole economy of redemption has been accomplished, he will cease to be a Mediator. His mission fulfilled, he surrenders his office. There is a marked *ad Patrem* movement to this aspect of his Christology. With the economy of salvation completed, his office fulfilled, Christ lays all at the foot of the Father.

Calvin's stress upon the unity of the person and upon ascribing what is proper of one nature to another nature only because of the unity of the person does not mean that he never speaks of the communication of idioms in a more traditional manner. This is to say that he goes beyond ascribing the properties of one nature to the person of Christ and ascribes the properties of one nature to another: "What is done in human nature is transferred—improperly, but not without reason—to the divinity."[37] Calvin's concern was to defend the incommunicability of the two natures and in his doctrine of the communication of idioms it was this aspect of the problem which he considered to be the occasion of the theological sins of the Lutherans and Romans. Because of this preoccupation, his doctrine of the communication of idioms falls short of the patristic doctrine.[38] However, any judgment on Calvin's doctrine of communication of idioms

---

zu sein, dass der Sohn Gottes nach dem Tage des letzten Gerichts seine menschliche Natur ablegen werde." "Die Christologie Calvins," *Das Konzil von Chalkedon*, 503, 504. The office of mediator is not eternal in Calvin's estimation; but we cannot conclude from this that Calvin thought the cessation of the office meant the cessation of the humanity of Christ.

[37] *Inst.*, II, 14, 2. Cf. also OS I:79.

[38] Joseph Ternus says that Calvin's concept of the communication of idioms is not that of the fathers. Cf. "Chalkedon und die Entwicklung der protestantischen Theologie," *Das Konzil von Chalkedon*, 497. Witte says that he took over the patristic meaning. Cf. "Die Christologie Calvins," *Das Konzil von Chalkedon*, 496. The Calvinist theologian E. Emmen is of the same mind. Cf. *De Christologie van Calvijn*, Amsterdam, 1953, 47f. The Harvard thesis of E. David Willis, now in the process of publication, should give a clearer insight into this and related Christological problems in Calvin, especially Calvin's Christology in its patristic roots. I did not have an opportunity to examine the work of this theologian.

must be made with the polemic background in mind. There is good reason why Calvin had difficulty here.

NOT HERESY, BUT DIALECTICAL ATTITUDE

Nestorianism is a heresy, and heresy is a very strong word, as evidenced by Calvin's own abhorrence of it. "The saving doctrine of Christ is the soul of the church," and to pervert doctrine is to destroy the church.[39] A tempting solution to the problem would be to adopt Krusche's position, namely, that Calvin's rejection of Nestorius in II, 14, 4-6 is proof only that Calvin did not want to be a Nestorian, and is not proof that he was not, in fact, a Nestorian.[40] This would mean that a theologian of Calvin's stature did not rightly understand what he was rejecting, and further did not understand Chalcedon, a position it would be difficult to document.

Calvin's Christology bears the marks of the battlefield, but it remains within the bounds of orthodoxy. His Nestorian tendency is just that. It is a manner of looking at things, a frame of mind, an underlying attitude, a theological disposition which characterizes his movements within the boundaries of Christological orthodoxy. However much he prefers to stress the dialectics of the heavenly and the earthly rather than their union, his doctrine can hardly be considered heretical. His dialectical attitude, which is both doctrine and a persistent, permeating theological disposition, is orthodox. Calvin has preserved and stressed elements which belong to the deposit of faith in his Christology—the Antiochian element of the "unmixed," the Leonine element of "saving the properties of both natures." Calvin's stress on these elements never goes so far as to formally contradict the definition of Chalcedon. If he insists upon distinction, he also insists upon no separation. His rejection of the divinization of the humanity of Christ is in sharp contrast to the

[39] *Inst.*, IV, 12, 1. Cf. also J. H. Kromminga, "Calvin and Ecumenicity," *John Calvin Contemporary Prophet*, ed., Jacob T. Hoogstra, Grand Rapids, 1959, 151; Peter R. McKenzie, "The Invisibility of the Church for Luther and Calvin," typewritten thesis, University of Edinburgh, 1952, 133, 134.

[40] Cf. *op.cit.*, 146, 109n.

theology of the early church and the theology of the Fourth Gospel, especially as regards the "divinization" of the humanity, yet Calvin did not fail to give consideration to the peculiar concerns of Chalcedon, and the final judgment must be that Calvin is true to Chalcedon and that he is not a Nestorian, conscious or unconscious.[41]

There is much that is admirable in Calvin's Christological formulation, for instance, an *ad Patrem* movement. All leads back to the Father. Calvin's Christology is characterized by a realism to the point of fault, which is seen in the large place he gives to the emphasis on the "unmixed" and on the "saving the properties of both natures." There is a determination to safeguard the humanity of Christ, and, in Wendel's phrase, to safeguard the divinity from contamination by the humanity, even to the extent that he neglects the divinization of the humanity.[42]

It is his realism in handling the humanity and divinity of Christ which brings about a want of realism in the union of the two natures. At this level, Calvin substitutes dialectical tension for realism. The ambiguity of his realism in Christology will be reflected in his ecclesiology and in his sacramental theology.[43] The element of his Christology most markedly represented in his eucharistic doctrine is the frame of mind, or underlying attitude, that theological disposition which prompts him to shy away from any ontological influence of one nature upon the other, any fusion of natures remaining unmixed and integral.

[41] Cf. Witte, "Die Christologie Calvins," *Das Konzil von Chalkedon*, 529. Wendel also notes the pronounced aversion in Calvin to any divinization of the humanity. Cf. *op.cit.*, 165, 168. Peter Martyr was also against such a divinization of the humanity. Cf. Joseph McLelland, *The Visible Words of God, An Exposition of the Sacramental Theology of Peter Martyr Vermigli*, Edinburgh, 1957, 104.

[42] Cf. McLelland, *op.cit.*, 165.

[43] Catholic authors point out the effect Calvin's tendency to shy away from an ontological influence of one nature on the other has in ecclesiology. Cf. Witte, "Die Christologie Calvins," *Das Konzil von Chalkedon*, 522. Cf. also E. Schillebeeckx, *Christ the Sacrament of the Encounter with God*, New York, 1963, 185-189; Yves Congar, *Vraie et fausse réforme dans l'église*, Paris, 1950, 433, 434, 436-438.

The tension already found in the unmixed and integral of Chalcedon is given a new formulation in what has come to be called the *Extra Calvinisticum*, already quoted. Calvin is on the defensive against any attempt to mix the two natures. The Godhead of Christ fills all things, and although it is joined to the humanity and dwells in it, the Godhead is not bound to the humanity. One can predicate no dependence of the divinity on the humanity, not even in the smallest degree. The divinity has not "left heaven to hide itself in the prison house of the body."[44] The divinity, unmixed and undivided, does not limit itself to the humanity, but while dwelling there, remains also entirely outside of the humanity. Here the Heidelberg Catechism is a faithful interpreter of Calvin. Question 48 sets up the problem: "Will not, however, the two natures in Christ be separated in this way from each other, as a human nature is not able to be present wherever the Godhead is?"[45] And the answer: "Not at all, because as the Godhead is incomprehensible and ubiquitous, it needs must follow that it is indeed outside its assumed human nature and nevertheless is also in it [the human nature] and remains united to it."[46] Calvin posits two centralities: complete commitment and the uncommitted.

The *Extra Calvinisticum* is not dualistic in its insistence on the dialectics of commitment and the uncommitted; nor does it have anything to do with either rationalism or spiritualism in their reformation meaning. Further, Calvin has no intention of depreciating the historical commitment in the incarnation, but rather he wishes to see the God-man and also the church and sacraments in the tension of an ellipsoidal dialectic. Neither the commitment nor the uncommitted cancels out the other. The two dogmatic facts, the

[44] *Inst.*, IV, 17, 30.
[45] *Bekenntnisschriften und Kirchenordnungen*, ed., Wilhelm Niesel, 2nd edn., Zürich, 1949, 160.
[46] *ibid*.

two centralities, stand over against one another, each speaking its absolute to the other, each unyielding. The incarnation is not a dogmatic fact in repose, but an event which involves the play of forces between the complete commitment and the uncommitted. The dynamics of the unmixed and the undivided must be maintained. Any adequate affirmation of this event must give expression to its bipolarity and also to the continuing tension of the *opposita*. The distinct but not separate realities are not two isolated Christological facts. In both Christology and sacramental theology they are related in ellipsoidal tension.

Calvin has not created here a few *concordia oppositorum,* but has further developed and given a new formulation to what was already present in Chalcedon, if not directly from Chalcedon, then through the Christological controversy between Duns Scotus and Thomas Aquinas.[47] However, the occasion for Calvin's formulation, and the purpose for which it was created is polemic, and, what is of greater interest here, a eucharistic polemic. It is found in the first edition of the *Institutes* where it is used as a tool against the Lutheran doctrine of the Eucharist.[48] The *Extra Calvinisticum*, then, is essentially eucharistic in origin and in overtones, and this gives added validity to its normative value in Calvin's eucharistic theology.[49]

Calvin himself applied the dialectic of the commitment and the uncommitted to eucharistic doctrine. Here the tension is between the heavenly (which includes Christ's glorified humanity) and the earthly, between the signified and the sign. Having stated the *Extra Calvinisticum*, Calvin then proceeds:

> There is a commonplace distinction of the schools to which I am not ashamed to refer: although the whole Christ is

[47] Cf. Jacobs, "Die Gegenwart Christi im Abendmahl," *Gegenwart Christi*, 26.
[48] Cf. OS I:141.
[49] Cf. Jacobs, "Die Gegenwart Christi im Abendmahl," *Gegenwart Christi*, 26. Grass is certainly wrong when he states that the Christological teaching of Calvin was not developed with the eucharistic polemic in mind. Cf. *op.cit.*, 259.

everywhere, still the whole of that which is in him is not everywhere. And would that the Schoolmen themselves had honestly weighed the force of this statement. For thus would the absurd fiction of Christ's carnal presence have been obviated. Therefore, since the whole Christ is everywhere, our Mediator is ever present with his own people, and in the Supper reveals himself in a special way, yet in such a way that the whole Christ is present, but not in his wholeness. For, as has been said, in his flesh he is contained in heaven until he appears in judgment.[50]

If in a somewhat different form, here again is complete commitment and the uncommitted.

The tension of the unmixed and undivided will be found in Calvin's eucharistic doctrine in the relationship he established between Calvary and the Lord's Supper, the once-for-all and the true memorial, the subject of God in Christ and the subject of the faithful Christian, the divine fullness and completion in Christ and the eucharistic rights and power of the church, the body of Christ and the elements of bread and wine, real presence and the integrity of bread and wine.[51] These same patterns of tension are also to be found in his ecclesiology, where Calvin shies away from an identification between Christ and the visible church, the church as structure, though the church remains the body of Christ.

Christ Among Us

CALVIN BETWEEN THE REFORMERS

It is in the context of these Christological presuppositions, then, that we understand Calvin's doctrine of the real presence, local presence, and his concept of substance. With the fact of real presence, Calvin had no difficulty: "Westphal insists upon the presence of the flesh in the Supper. We do not deny it."[52] "The controversy with us is not as to the reception

[50] *Inst.*, IV, 17, 30.
[51] Cf. Jacobs, "Die Gegenwart Christi im Abendmahl," *Gegenwart Christi*, 32.
[52] CR 9:73.

but only as to the mode of reception."[53] It is with the mode of this presence, with the "how" rather than the "what," that he came into conflict with Lutherans and Romans alike. And though he had no hesitations in setting forth the "what" of the Eucharist, he professed a proper restraint in setting forth the "how."[54] Rather than denying the real presence, as he has been accused of doing, he presupposes it.[55] None of the reformers defended it more forcibly than Calvin. To reject the Roman Catholic and the Lutheran explanation of the real presence, as he did, is not to deny the real presence; it is rather to reject an explanation of a dogmatic fact. And Calvin rejects the explanation of the dogmatic fact, not the fact itself.

It is indeed the desire to preserve the real presence, which Calvin feels is threatened by consubstantiation, that motivates Calvin to reject the Lutheran explanations. Having rejected the Roman Catholic and Lutheran explanations on the one hand, and the Zwinglian explanation on the other, Calvin was at pains to elaborate an explanation which only incidentally stands between the two traditions.[56] That he acted as a mediator between the two groups did not arise out of his desire to stand in the middle. Rather because he was in the middle, he desired to mediate. There are two traditions represented in Calvin's doctrine, the symbolist-virtualist tradition and the realist tradition. The students of Calvin have attempted to place him either in the symbolist-virtualist tradition, asserting that his theological home is essentially

[53] *ibid.*, 9:74. Cf. also *ibid.*, 9:31, 32.

[54] Cf. *Inst.*, I, 17, 32; *ibid.*, 17, 7; CR 9:31.

[55] ". . . Calvin denied the real presence; but he maintained that in the Lord's Supper there was a genuine communion of the Body and Blood of Christ." George H. Tavard, *Protestantism*, London, 1959, 41. Father Tavard has correctly understood the theological élan of Calvin's eucharistic doctrine, but he does not give Calvin full credit for his sacramental realism. Beckmann calls attention to the fact that the real presence was so firmly established in Calvin's mind that he never even discussed it. Cf. *Vom Sakrament bei Calvin*, Tübingen, 1926, 15.

[56] Cf. L. Staehelin, *Johannes Calvin*, Elberfeld, 1863, vol. 1, 212; John T. McNeill, *Unitive Protestantism*, New York, 1930, 186.

Zwinglian, or in the realist tradition, asserting that he is theologically related more to Lutheran dogmatic.[57] The impulse to label, always a dubious inclination, is more than usually misleading in the case of Calvin because of the complexity of his theological and pastoral motivations, and, his own opinion to the contrary notwithstanding, of the complexity of his eucharistic doctrine.[58] And he who would choose one of the centralities in Calvin's eucharistic thought to the neglect of the other centralities, will most certainly place a false tag upon him.

DIALECTICAL OPPOSITA IN REAL PRESENCE

As has been seen, Calvin's point of departure is a Christological dialectic: "I reject only absurd things which appear to be either unworthy of Christ's heavenly majesty, or incompatible with the reality of his human nature, since they are in necessary conflict with God's Word; for it also teaches Christ was so received into the glory of the Heavenly Kingdom as to be lifted above all worldly estate, and no less carefully sets off in his human nature those things which are proper to true humanity."[59] The humanity of Christ is in heaven; to assert this is to deny that he is in another place. "Flesh must therefore be flesh; spirit, spirit—each thing in

[57] There is no agreement as to which side Calvin is more closely bound. Some say he stands closer to Luther. Cf. Hermann Sasse, *This Is My Body*, Minneapolis, 1959, 297; Paul Wernle, *Der evangelische Glaube nach den Hauptschriften der Reformatoren*, vol. 3, *Calvin*, Tübingen, 1919, 105; Wendel, *op.cit.*, 251; Gerardus van der Leeuw, *Sakramentales Denken*, Kassel, 1959, 70; Niesel, *op.cit.*, 33; Seeberg, *op.cit.*, 607, 608. Among others Ritschl and Congar think he approximates more closely the position of Zwingli. Cf. Otto Ritschl, *Dogmengeschichte des Protestantismus*, vol. 3, *Theologie des 16. und 17. Jahrhunderts in ihrer Entstehung und Entwicklung*, Göttingen, 1926, 160, 230; Yves Congar, "Calvin," *Catholicisme*, Paris, 1949.

[58] "Sein Sakramentsbegriff ist ausserordentlich Kompliziert." van der Leeuw, *op.cit.*, 68.

[59] *Inst.*, IV, 17, 32. Many of the Christological factors found in Calvin's eucharistic doctrine are found in a more explicit and developed form in Peter Martyr. His theology is much more philosophically structured. Cf. McLelland, *op.cit.*, 105, 106. Though their theologies differ in emphases Calvin attested to the fact that they were in substantial agreement. Cf. CR 9:490.

the state and condition wherein God created it. But such is the condition of flesh that it must subsist in one definite place, with its own size and form."[60] Though Christ is with us "according to the presence of his majesty," he is not with us "according to the presence of his flesh," and it was of this presence of the flesh of which Christ spoke when he says "You will not always have me."[61] Calvin's preoccupations here are two; to take nothing away from the glorified Christ, and to maintain the integrity of Christ's humanity, and more the second than the first. "Let us never (I say) allow these two limitations to be taken away from us: (1) Let nothing be withdrawn from Christ's heavenly glory—as happens when he is brought under the corruptible elements of this world, or bound to any earthly creatures. (2) Let nothing inappropriate to human nature be ascribed to his body, as happens when it is said either to be infinite or to be put in a number of places at once."[62] Here again are the *opposita*.

Because the body of Christ has its place in heaven, it cannot have its place on earth. Calvin held that heaven was to be spoken of as a place, for it was to this place that the body of Christ was taken at the Ascension: "When it is said that Christ is taken up into heaven there is clear mention made of the spatial differences. . . . It is evident that the heaven whereunto Christ was received is opposite from the frame of the world; therefore it necessarily follows that if he be in heaven, he is beyond the world."[63]

Calvin's emphasis on Christ's body having its place in heaven can be misleading. He did not think of Christ's body being assigned to a definite place in heaven. This would be speculation, and for speculation Calvin has little more than contempt: "Shall we therefore, someone will say, assign to Christ a definite region of heaven? But I reply with Augustine that this is a very prying and superfluous question: for us it is enough to believe that he is in heaven."[64] "Not that

[60] *Inst.*, IV, 17, 24.   [61] *ibid.*, 17, 26.   [62] *ibid.*, 17, 19.
[63] CR 48:13. Cf. also *ibid.*, 9:79; *ibid.*, 20:75.
[64] *Inst.*, IV, 17, 26.

it is literally a place beyond the world, but we cannot speak of the Kingdom of God without using our ordinary language."[65] He is quite aware that there is not a celestial circumscription reserved to the divinity and the glorified creatures, that the glorified body of Christ is not bound by the Aristotelian category of place. Christ is not in a place in heaven, but he is there as in a space of place.[66]

The idea of local presence is repugnant to Calvin because it is contrary to the sovereignty of Christ. Any descent as implied in local presence is opposed to the lordship of Christ because it puts the body of Christ at the disposal of a man. This, for Calvin, is simply absurd. God is never at the disposal of man, at his beck and call. It is especially because of what Calvin considers an attack on the sovereignty of God and the lordship of Christ that he rejects the Catholic doctrine of transubstantiation. Local presence is also repugnant to Calvin because it would mean that Christ's body is at the same time in heaven and on the altar, and this implies a Docetic view of Christ's humanity.[67]

Any explanation of the real presence would have to safeguard this sovereignty and lordship, while at the same time giving due consideration to both the biblical and patristic realism. And it was to the task of maintaining these centralities in tension and union which Calvin set himself.

ANALOGICAL RELATIONSHIP BETWEEN
SIGN AND SIGNIFIED

For Calvin the mystery stands or falls with the analogy between the sign and the signified. Here, too, the Christological tensions must be maintained. Though "the symbol

[65] CR 20:75.

[66] Cf. Cadier, *op.cit.*, 44. Cf. also Heinrich Janssen, "Die Abendmahlslehre Johannes Calvins," *Die Eucharistie im Verständnis der Konfessionen*, ed. Thomas Sartory, Recklinghausen, 1961, 213; Krusche, *op.cit.*, 142. Both Sartory and Wendel stress too much the local meaning of place in this context. Cf. Thomas Sartory, "Eucharistisches Gedankengut bei unseren getrennten Brüdern," *Die Eucharistie im Verständnis der Konfessionen*, 392; Wendel, *op.cit.*, 266.

[67] Cf. CR 1:121.

differs in essence from the thing signified . . . the name of the visible sign is . . . given to the thing signified."[68] This is the sacramental mode of thinking, says Calvin, which is proper to the sacred Scriptures: "Christ declares that the bread is his body. These works relate to a sacrament; and it must be acknowledged that a sacrament consists of a visible sign, with which is connected the thing signified, which is the reality of it. It must be well known, on the other hand, that the name of the thing signified is transferred to the sign; and therefore, no person who is well acquainted with Scripture will deny that a sacramental mode of expression ought to be taken metonymically."[69] The name of Christ's body is given to that which in fact remains bread.[70]

This is not to say that we do not receive the body of Christ. The sign is distinguished from the reality, but not separated: "Many think that we make no distinction between the sign and the truth signified, unless we separate them entirely, to make God like a mountebank, who exhibits delusive representations by sleight of hand."[71] God does not lie, and neither do his signs. What is signed is given. It is the Christ who instituted the sign, who speaks through it and acts in it: "We believe . . . that both in baptism and the Lord's supper, God in reality bestows on us and accomplished by effects what is there symbolized, and moreover we receive with the signs the real possession and enjoyment of what is there presented to us. And thus it is that those who bring to the sacred table of Jesus Christ a pure faith, as it were a vessel, receive what the symbols represent."[72] The act of God and the act of man in the sacrament are so close that they form a dialogic reality. What belongs to God exclusively is ascribed to man, but there is no doubt as to the real agent. God alone produces whatever we obtain from the sacraments. God it is who acts in the sacraments, and because it is he who acts, the sacra-

[68] *Inst.*, IV, 17, 21.   [69] CR 45:706.
[70] Cf. *ibid.*, 49:455.   [71] *ibid.*, 12:422.
[72] *ibid.*, 9:719. There is an excellent text in which Calvin speaks more clearly of Christ acting in the sacraments. This text concerns baptism. Cf. *Inst.*, IV, 15, 14.

ments have a certain infallibility: "God truly performs whatever he promises and figures by signs; nor are signs without effect, for they prove that he is their true and faithful author."[73] These sacraments, signs of God's acts, are not signs of an act of God in the past, but of the God of history acting now, in the present.[74] It is to safeguard the act of God in the present that Calvin insists upon metonymy, that is using the name of one thing for another associated with it. Only in this way is the sacrament a real act of God, and only in this way is the reality of what is signified given. Only in this way are the total commitment and the uncommitted kept intact.

Calvin will have nothing to do with transubstantiation because it destroys, he says, the tension between sign and signified. Transubstantiation is essentially eucharistic monophysitism; the dialectic is destroyed. If you take away the sign—as happens in transubstantiation—you take away the reality. The earthly element, in Christology and in eucharistic doctrine, is that instrument by which we receive the heavenly. Only if the bread remains bread is there an instrument, and only then does the sacrament give us the body of Christ: "In the Supper the flesh of Christ is not truly and fittingly promised to us to be truly food unless the true substance of the outward symbol corresponds to it."[75] By the doctrine of transubstantiation they have the sign made out to be only the shadow of bread, only its appearance. Since the sacrament only gives what it signifies, it cannot give us Christ as our food when the substance of the bread has been taken away. What is left is only the shadow, the accidents. And the sacrament which is only a shadow cannot sign reality and cannot give reality. Only when the bread remains bread is there a correspondence between the sign and its reality. The Romans, by their doctrine of transubstantiation, have destroyed the symbol, and they have thereby destroyed

[73] ibid., 14, 17.
[74] Cf. W. Kolfhaus, *Christusgemeinschaft bei Johannes Calvin*, Neukirchen, 1939, 108.
[75] *Inst.*, IV, 17, 15.

the reality.[76] Without the reality of the sacrament you have no real presence, and therefore transubstantiation is a denial of the real presence.

Between the reality and the sign there is a parallel relationship one to the other, while the reality and the sign stand in an immediate relationship to the believer, so that, according to Calvin, the believer receives the body and blood of Christ when he receives the bread and wine.[77] This parallel relationship is not unrelated to the dialectics of Calvin's Christology. In his Christology he took every means to exclude any "intermingling" or "confusion of substance," and insisted on the elements of the "distinct but not separate," of the "unmixed," and on the "saving the properties of both natures."[78] Calvin no doubt had the Chalcedonian formula in mind, with his own strong dialectic interpretation, when he wrote of the sacraments: "The sacraments of the Word should not and cannot be at all separated from their reality and substance. To distinguish, in order to guard against confounding them, is not only good and reasonable, but altogether necessary; but to divide them, so as to make the one exist without the other is absurd."[79] "The body with the bread is a thing of heaven with a thing of earth; to hold that the bread is the body is nothing else than to confound heaven and earth together."[80] To assert that bread is body is to destroy the dialectics, to lose the total commitment and the uncommitted in sacramental confusion. In the relationship be-

[76] Cf. CR 49:487. Cf. also van der Leeuw, *op.cit.*, 63; Beckmann, *op.cit.*, 107; Cadier, *op.cit.*, 34.

[77] Cf. Niesel, *op.cit.*, 67. Calvin's teaching on sacramental efficacy is similar to the Scotist pact theory. The "occasionalism" of the Scotist theory is wanting in biblical and patristic realism, but it is still, as far as the official teaching of the church is concerned, an acceptable explanation of sacramental causality.

[78] McLelland gives a summary history of the Christological argument based on the analogical relationship of the person of Christ to the Eucharist. Cf. *op.cit.*, 104, 105.

[79] OS I:509. Cf. also Wallace, *Calvin's Doctrine of the Word and Sacrament*, 168.

[80] CR 9:210. It is interesting to see how a modern Calvinist develops this thought. Cf. T. F. Torrance, "Concerning the Ministry," *Scottish Journal of Theology*, vol. I (1948), 198.

tween the sign and the signified, the tensions of the unmixed and the undivided must be maintained, otherwise that error fatal to Christology, to sacramental theology, and therefore to redemption is given credence, namely the confusion of natures. To safeguard against the confusion of natures, the heavenly and the earthly, the *opposita* must remain. Transubstantiation destroys the *opposita*.

If the realities of which Calvin is speaking are biblical realities, his categories here are greatly influenced by Plato. The dialectic here is between the earthly and the heavenly, between the image and the intelligible reality. It is by means of the earthly sign that one participates in the heavenly body of Christ. The earthly sign assures us that we participate in the heavenly reality even though it must of necessity remain in heaven. The Platonic categories assure both the imperative of the Ascension and that of Christ's words: "This is my body." Transubstantiation destroys the Platonic tension: sign becomes signified, the intelligible reality becomes the image, heaven comes to earth.

If the bread must remain bread, yet gives us the body of Christ, then the mode of Christ's real presence is attained through representation. Since Calvin excludes all local presence—because Christ's body is no longer here in our world and will not come back until the Second Coming—the mode of his presence must be that of representation. "For Christ is not visibly present, and is not beheld with our eyes, as the symbols are which excite our remembrance by representing him. In short, in order that he may be present to us, he does not change his place, but communicates to us from heaven the virtue of his flesh as though it were present."[81] The presence of Christ as our food is signed by the bread and is given or effected through the power of the Holy Spirit. The Holy Spirit effects the presence of Christ when the sign representing the effect is communicated to the believer. It is in these terms that we must understand Calvin's assertion: "We maintain no other presence than that of a relationship."[82]

[81] CR 49:489.   [82] *Inst.*, IV, 17, 13.

Christ Substantially Among Us

ABSURDITIES AND SACRAMENTAL
MATERIALISM EXCLUDED

It is granted that Calvin's use of the word "substance" is not without ambiguity.[83] He both rejects the term and accepts it. In the first edition of the *Institutes* he rejected the term in one place and used it in a somewhat imprecise sense in another.[84] This ambivalent attitude toward the term remained with Calvin, and to understand his rather fluid use of the term, three different meanings which he attached to the term must be described.[85]

1. The scholastic meaning. This is the sense of the term common to the schoolmen and to hylomorphism. In this sense substance means the nature of the thing, and in a eucharistic context, the true and natural body of Christ, or the *substantia corporis*, the subjective genitive. And it is in this sense that Calvin rejected the concept of substance and rejected the term at every stage of his theological career, early and late.[86]

2. Christ is himself the substance of the sacraments. It is Christ himself who, through faith, is received in personal union. "By bidding us take, he indicates that it is ours; by bidding us eat, that it is made one substance with us."[87] "I say that Christ is the matter of all the sacraments, or if you wish, the substance of all the sacraments, since all the sacraments have their solidity in him, and promise nothing beyond him."[88] "I have always called Christ the substance of Baptism and the Lord's Supper."[89]

3. The substance which is given to us when we receive Christ. This sense is more in the virtualist tradition. From the body of Christ we receive all the fruits, the power and life of Christ himself. It is, in other words, the spiritual sub-

[83] Cf. Grass, *op.cit.*, 249.
[84] Cf. OS I:142.
[85] Cf. Gollwitzer, *op.cit.*, 120, 121.
[86] Cf. OS I:142; *Inst.*, IV, 17, 14.
[87] *ibid.*, 17, 3.
[88] *ibid.*, 14, 16.
[89] CR 37:718.

stance of the body of Christ, which flows from the body of Christ into our souls.[90]

The two acceptable meanings of substance can easily be deceptive. Calvin does not teach that we receive the sub-strata of some invisible material, nor a fluid material, nor some celestial essence.[91] Having made his distinctions, he tends to strain them. He presses the idea of substantial presence as far as possible within the context of these strained distinctions. His concern is only to exclude what he calls theological absurdities, that Christ is present everywhere, as found in the ubiquity teaching of Luther, that Christ is present in a number of places at one time, as in the transubstantiation of the Roman Catholics, that his presence is crassly physical. "But when these absurdities have been set aside, I freely accept whatever can be made to express the true and substantial partaking of the body and blood of the Lord, which is shown to believers under the sacred symbols of the Supper—and so to express it that they may be understood not to receive it solely by imagination or understanding of mind, but to enjoy the thing itself as nourishment of eternal life."[92] "I confess that our souls are truly fed by the substance of Christ's flesh."[93] "Those who exclude the substance of vivifying flesh and blood from the communion defraud themselves of the use of the supper."[94] "That we really feed in the Holy Supper on the flesh and blood of Christ, not otherwise than as bread and wine are the nourishment of our bodies, I freely confess."[95] "When, therefore, we speak of the communion which believers have with Christ, we mean that they communicate with his flesh and blood no less than with his spirit, so as to possess thus the whole Christ."[96]

Here should be recalled the free use Calvin made of the term "substance" in regard to union with Christ by reason of faith, which was discussed in Chapter V. When speaking of union with Christ in faith, Calvin speaks of communion

[90] Cf. *ibid.*, 37:712, 730.
[92] *Inst.*, IV, 17, 19.
[94] *ibid.*, 9:76.
[96] OS I:435.

[91] Cf. Wendel, *op.cit.*, 260.
[93] CR 9:70.
[95] *ibid.*, 20:73.

with the substance of Christ. When speaking of union with Christ in the Eucharist he speaks also of union with the substance of Christ. In both cases, union in faith and union in the Eucharist, what we receive is the substance of Christ. Calvin's use of the term in his eucharistic passages must be kept in the framework of his larger theological thought on the union with Christ in faith. Calvin can use the term "substance" in what appears to be a completely ambiguous sense, because he proceeds from his doctrine of union with Christ in faith. However, these considerations should not be taken to mean that Calvin rejected a real presence in any realistic sense.

Calvin's enemies were not satisfied with his explanation, which they considered unclear and ambiguous. His further precisions are found in his elaboration of the relation of substance to conversion, of substance as an act of the Holy Spirit, and his insistence that the body is really given, not just an effect of the body.

CONVERSION: ONE DOES NOT PREACH TO BREAD

Though it is difficult to get a more precise meaning of substance in Calvin, yet his use of the term indicates what he meant and what he did not mean. This is true of the term "conversion" with regard to the words of consecration. Calvin would admit the use of the term provided that it was correctly understood: "Indeed, I admit that some of the old writers used the term 'conversion' sometimes, not because they intended to wipe out the substance in the outward sign, but to teach that the bread dedicated to the mystery is far different from common bread, and is now something else."[97] With the term he has no quarrel as long as it is understood to mean that "the bread, which had been appointed for the nourishment of the body is chosen and sanctified by Christ to a different use, so as to begin to be spiritual food."[98] There is then a difference between the bread before consecration, and the bread after consecration; and the difference is to be

[97] *Inst.*, IV, 17, 14. [98] *ibid.*

found in the function of the bread after consecration, namely to be a true instrument of presenting us with the reality which it signifies.[99] But the bread remains bread after the consecration.

Calvin further specifies the meaning of the term "conversion" when he uses it in connection with baptism. He says quite explicitly that the term "ought to signify nothing more in the Supper than in baptism."[100] "For the church fathers here also affirm a wonderful conversion when they say that the spiritual washing of the soul is made from a corruptible element, yet no one denies that the water remains."[101] Though Calvin does not deny a certain propriety in the use of the term with regard to the elements, namely the bread takes on a different function, yet his attention is drawn to the spiritual effect of the effective sign. "No other conversion occurs than with respect to men, inasmuch as to them they [the earthly elements] are seals of the promises."[102] It is because of this conversion in the hearts of men that Calvin insists that the "words of consecration" are directed not to the elements but to the faithful: "But this principle was hidden from them [the Romans], that the bread is sacrament only to those persons to whom the word is directed."[103] One does not preach to bread.

It is clear from Calvin that the words of consecration are not a formula in a static sense which is commonly thought of as the Roman Catholic position, but are rather the word of faith which we preach, or preaching on the mystery of faith. There must be some giving of doctrine, either through preaching or through reading of the scriptures: "God does not bring forward signs without the Word, for what would a sacrament be if we beheld nothing but the sign? It is doctrine alone that makes the sacrament, and therefore let us know that it is mere hypocrisy where no doctrine is taught, and that the Papists act wickedly when they lay aside

---

[99] Cf. Thurian, "The Real Presence," *Christianity Divided*, 206, 207.
[100] *Inst.*, IV, 17, 14.   [101] *ibid.*
[102] *ibid.*, 17, 15.   [103] *ibid.*

doctrine, and give the name of sacrament to empty ceremonies."[104]

As is seen in the liturgy of 1542, the giving of the doctrine
is not seen as a formula, since there is in this form of service
no repetition of the words which could take on the significance of the Roman Catholic sacramental formula of consecration.[105] Calvin is not greatly concerned with what precisely must be said, but with what must be done. The Word
must be preached and the sacrament must be given.

Calvin's thinking here is clearly dominated by a reaction
against sacramental mechanism—sacramental mechanism
and sacramental impersonalism.[106]

We must hold that bread is not consecrated by whispering and breathing, but by the clear doctrine of faith. And
certainly it is a piece of magic and sorcery, when the consecration is addressed to a dead element; for the bread is
not made for itself but for us, a symbol of the body of
Christ. In short, consecration is nothing else than a solemn
testimony, by which the Lord appoints to us for a spiritual use an earthly and corruptible sign. This cannot take
place unless his command and promise are distinctly heard
with the purpose of edifying the faithful. It is therefore
evident that the low whispering and breathing of the Papists are a wicked profanation of the mystery. Now if Christ

[104] CR 36:351. Cf. also Beckmann, *op.cit.*, 8.

[105] Cf. A. Lecerf, *Etudes Calvinistes*, Paris, 1949, 48. Cf. also William Maxwell, *The Liturgical Portions of the Genevan Service Book*, Edinburgh, 1931,
121-126. The manner in which the words of consecration are incorporated
into the exhortation show clearly that they were not used as sacramental
words in a consecratory sense.

[106] Cf. Adolph Franz, *Die Messe im deutschen Mittelalter*, Freiburg, 1902,
407-728. "The complaints raised by the Reformers, especially by Luther,
were aimed accurately and quite relentlessly against questionable points in
ecclesiastical praxis regarding the Mass." Joseph A. Jungmann, *The Mass
of the Roman Rite*, New York, 1950, vol. 1, 132. Cf. also Franz Xaver
Arnold, "Vorgeschichte und Einfluss des Trienter Messopferdekrets auf die
Behandlung des eucharistischen Geheimnisses in der Glaubensverkündigung
der Neuzeit," *Die Messe in der Glaubensverkündigung*, eds., Franz Xaver
Arnold, Balthasar Fischer, 2nd edn., Freiburg, 1953, 123-129.

consecrates the bread, when he declares to us that it is his body, we must not suppose that there is any change of the substance, but must only believe that it is applied to a new purpose.[107]

By his emphasis on doctrine, on the word character of the sacrament, Calvin seeks to counteract the ritualistic mechanism and sacramental empiricism he sees in Roman Catholicism; his stress on the act of faith of the believer who hears the Word is directed against the passivity of sacramental magic, an attempt to restore personalism to piety; and his nominalistic, antisubstantialist affirmations are directed against the same gross sacramental materialism, the eucharistic empiricism, which St. Thomas so determinedly rejected, but which was a persistent element of late medieval popular piety.[108] Whatever one's judgment on these emphases as a total theological attitude, there can be little doubt that as emphases they were historically justified, indeed, necessary.

LOCAL PRESENCE AND SACRAMENTAL EMPIRICISM

The same materialism and empiricism which prompted Calvin to reject conversion in the sense taught by the scholastics of his time (as he understood them) prompted him to reject local presence, which he considered a consequence of a substantialist view of conversion. Local presence involves a number of absurdities. To affirm it is to deny the reality of

[107] CR 45:706.

[108] Cf. Otto Karrer, "Die Eucharistie im Gespräch der Konfessionen," *Die Eucharistie im Verständnis der Konfessionen*, 356; Gerhard Kretz, "Calvins Auseinandersetzung mit der katholischen Kirche," typewritten thesis, University of Tübingen, 1962, 84; Jungmann, "Liturgy on the Eve of the Reformation," *Worship*, vol. 33 (1959), 514; Jungmann, *The Mass of the Roman Rite*, vol. I, 131; Paul Doncoeur, "Lessons of Eucharistic History," *Worship*, vol. 23 (1949), 355; Ernest Benjamin Koenker, *The Liturgical Renaissance in the Roman Catholic Church*, Chicago, 1954, 101. Also of importance is Francis Clark, *Eucharistic Sacrifice and the Reformation*, Westminster, 1960, 209-226. Clark's volume is a valuable contribution and the question cannot be discussed without reference to it. Unfortunately the book is dominated by reformation attitudes, by the relics of an ancient polemic, and by a tone which is a little too triumphant.

Christ's humanity since a body cannot be in several places at the same time. Christ assumed our nature, ascended into heaven with it, but he did not change its nature.[109] Local presence demands annihilation of the substance of bread, which Calvin held with Wyclif is absurd.[110] Pastorally, the doctrine of local presence is an invitation to all the idolatries of Roman eucharistic devotion, especially exposition of the Eucharist.[111] Finally, there is, as shall be seen more fully later, a strong eschatological motive to Calvin's objection to local presence. "For in his flesh he is contained in heaven until he appears in judgment."[112] Local presence is an anticipation of the Second Coming and therefore deprives the Christian life of its essential eschatological tension.

Calvin had studied his Thomas and he knew that Thomas, too, rejected local presence. "They grant that Christ is not there contained in any circumscriptive or bodily fashion."[113] The related problem of a substantial presence, where sacramental materialism, impersonalism, and empiricism is ever a danger, was, as taught by Thomas, clearly not understood by Calvin. In this area his thinking was dominated by empirical rather than metaphysical categories. This made it extremely difficult for Calvin, as it is also difficult for us today, to rightly understand the meaning of the great scholastics. There was no real meeting of minds here. Thomas spoke of substance in metaphysical terms, and Calvin interpreted him in empirical terms.[114] Therefore the reproaches Calvin levels against Thomas are not valid for Thomas himself, but do retain a certain validity when directed against the later scholasticism, and also when directed against the popular eucharistic piety.

[109] Cf. OS I:521.

[110] Cf. *ibid.*, V:357. St. Thomas also rejected the annihilation of the substance of bread. Cf. *Summa Theologica*, III, 75, 3, ad 3.

[111] Cf. OS I:522.   [112] *Inst.*, IV, 17, 30.

[113] *ibid.*, 17, 13. If Christ is not present circumscriptively or in a bodily fashion, then, from a theological point of view, Thomas cannot be accused, on this point, of teaching local presence or sacramental empiricism.

[114] Cf. Henry Chavannes, "La présence réelle chez saint Thomas et chez Calvin," *Verbum Caro*, vol. 13 (1959), 166.

SUBSTANCE AS ACT OF HOLY SPIRIT

Studying, against this background, Calvin's strong opposition to any substantial inclusion of the body of Christ in the elements makes understandable his position that the real presence is to be found in the act of the Holy Spirit. The real presence is not simply a fact (simply a substance) but it is an act, a reality, which is not a past act or reality, but a present act and reality. In the meeting of the Holy Spirit and faith, according to the promises and the order established by God, which takes place in the reception of the sacramental signs, is found the presence of the life-giving body of Christ. This, for Calvin, is the real presence. Indeed, as shall be seen, real presence, *manducatio spiritualis* and the communication of the body and blood of Christ are only different expressions for one and the same act. All of these find their center in the reception of the sacrament in which the Holy Spirit realizes and effects the communication of the life-giving and sanctifying body and blood of Christ. More precisely, we are concerned here not with a substance in a substance but an act in act.[115] The real presence is realized through the hidden power of the Holy Spirit, and the eating and drinking of the body and blood of Christ are accomplished through the power of the same Holy Spirit. The presence is not, then, substantial, and the eating is not substantial, but rather a representation by the Holy Spirit, an effecting of the presence of Christ and the eating of his flesh and blood in the same Holy Spirit. Calvin does not propose a pure spiritual presence, nor a presence related only to man's spirit, but rather a presence which is spiritual only because it is effected by the Holy Spirit. The bond between real presence and eating is not a substantial bond, but a real joining by means of which the substance of Christ is received. The body and blood are really given, really received, not just union with Christ.[116]

Having said this it must be granted that Calvin's concern

[115] Cf. Beckmann, *op.cit.*, 151.
[116] *ibid.*, 103.

was not the narrow concern about real presence, but the larger and broader concern about union with Christ. Though he insisted on real presence, it was not, viewing his sacramental doctrine in his whole theological system, his dominant preoccupation, not even his dominant eucharistic preoccupation. What preoccupied him was union with Christ. He also contended that there was no gift proper to the Eucharist.[117] Though this is a weakening of Calvin's eucharistic realism, it belongs logically to his system both because of his preoccupation with union with Christ rather than with real presence, and because of his rejection of local presence with its attendant drawing down of the body of Christ and the body's inclusion under the elements. Calvin saw no contradiction between his rejection of a gift proper to the Eucharist and his realistic teaching on the real presence.

Not only is Christ given in the sacrament, but it is precisely his body and blood which is given. To say that the Eucharist gives us a participation in the Spirit of Christ is not enough. Calvin rejects any formulation which would limit our union with Christ to something of a spiritualistic communion: "I am not satisfied with those persons who, recognizing that we have some communion with Christ, when they would show what it is, make us partakers of the Spirit only, omitting mention of flesh and blood. As though all these things were said in vain: that his flesh is truly food, that his blood is truly drink: that none have life except those who eat his flesh and drink his blood."[118] It will be noted that Calvin here calls on biblical realism to assert the necessity of believing in a sacrament which truly gives flesh as food and blood as drink. His rejection of transubstantiation does not lead him to doubt that it is, indeed, the body of Christ which feeds: "If it be true that the visible sign is given to us to seal the gift of the invisible substance, we ought to enter-

---

[117] Cf. *Inst.*, IV, 17, 26; *ibid.*, 17, 28. Cf. also Janssen, "Die Abendmahlslehre Johannes Calvins," *Die Eucharistie im Verständnis der Konfessionen*, 218; Niesel, *op.cit.*, 97; Krusche, *op.cit.*, 272.

[118] *Inst.*, IV, 17, 7.

tain a confident assurance that in receiving the symbol of his body, we at the same time truly receive the body itself."[119] The specific gift of the sacrament is Christ in his totality, and this totality cannot be found aside from his flesh, for it is only here that we find righteousness and salvation. There is no salvation in a half-Christ: "Even though they [the sacraments] direct our faith to the whole Christ and not to a half-Christ, they teach that the matter of both righteousness and of salvation resides in his flesh."[120]

EFFECT OF BODY OR BODY ITSELF?

There is still the question whether the sacrament gives the substance of Christ's body, or gives some power or effect which flows from the substance of Christ's body. In other words, can we say that Calvin is a "virtualist" in his teaching on substance? Grass suggests that Calvin's insistence that we are substantially fed on the body and blood of Christ in the Eucharist must be taken with a grain of salt.[121] It is not the substance of the flesh itself we receive but something which comes from this flesh, namely life and power. According to Grass, when Calvin says that we receive the substance of Christ's flesh, he really means that the flesh is the source of the power of life.[122] Calvin himself says as much in no uncertain terms: "I frankly confess that I reject their teaching of the mixture, or transfusion, of Christ's flesh with our soul. For it is enough for us that, from the substance of his flesh Christ breathes life into our souls—indeed, pours forth his very life into us—even though Christ's flesh itself does not enter into us."[123] As early as 1536 he had said that it was "not the very substance of his body or the true and natural body of Christ . . . but all the benefits which Christ in his body provided for us," which we receive.[124]

[119] *ibid.*, 17, 10.   [120] *ibid.*, III, 11, 9.
[121] Cf. Grass, *op.cit.*, 230, 238, 239.
[122] Cf. *ibid.*, 233. Hermann Sasse says that the substance of the body is actually not more than its power or the benefits connected with that body. Cf. *op.cit.*, 327, 54n.
[123] *Inst.*, IV, 17, 32.   [124] OS I:142.

What Calvin means to exclude here is only a crass notion of substance. For him, substance in the Eucharist is not a "material substance," and he wants to avoid giving credence to the belief that in the sacramental presentation of the body and blood there is "anything earthly or material."[125] While the body of Christ feeds us it remains at a great distance from us and is not mixed with us. Though Christ descends to us, he "descends to us by his virtue."[126] He speaks also of "the spiritual efficacy which emanates from the body of Christ."[127] All of these expressions are directed against any kind of sacramental materialism and sacramental impersonalism, any inclusion of the physical body of Christ within earthly limitations, any transfer of the body of Christ from its place of heavenly glory.

But Calvin has already said that his purpose is to exclude absurdities, and having done so, he by no means wanted to give the impression that he was "substituting something different [that is, from the body] which is to have the effect of abolishing the gift of the body."[128] It is nothing other than the natural body which is given to us. In a letter to Peter Martyr Vermigli, Calvin deplores the fact that the arguments of John à Lasco always end up in the assertion "that the natural body of Christ is not given us to eat. As though we could gain life from any other source than the natural body of Christ."[129] To his opponents, who had said that the merits or benefits of Christ's body are not the body itself, Calvin answered that he had never equated merits and the

---

[125] CR 55:110.   [126] *ibid.*, 9:72.
[127] *ibid.*, 55:110.   [128] *ibid.*, 9:72.

[129] *ibid.*, 15:388. There is no contradiction between Calvin's declaration in OS I:142 that it is "not the very substance of his body or the true and natural body of Christ," that we receive, and his assertion in CR 15:388 that it is the natural body which we receive. In the first case he is speaking against sacramental materialism, a religious empiricism. In the second, he defends the biblical realism against à Lasko who would say that the sacramental gift is not the body of Christ. Calvin counters with an implied question. And if we do not receive the natural body, then what body do we receive? Is there, then, more than one body? No, indeed not. It is the natural body of Christ which is the gift and the source of life.

body of Christ. What he held was that we receive food and nourishment from the very body of Christ.[130] He further specifies that we receive the benefits only because we have first received the substance.[131] Calvin says explicitly that we receive more than the effect of Christ's body; we receive the body itself: "Christ does not simply present to us the benefit of his death and resurrection but the very body in which he suffered and rose again."[132]

Before one makes a hasty judgment in favor of a "virtualist" interpretation of Calvin, his doctrine of the efficacy of the sacramental signs should be recalled. When God says that we should eat his flesh and drink his blood, then he means this and nothing less. When he says that we are to take and eat, for this is his body, we cannot believe that we receive anything but what his mouth tells us and the signs proclaim to us. God is true and he neither lies to us nor speaks lightly. "Unless a man means to call God a deceiver, he would never dare assert that an empty symbol is set forth by him. Therefore, if the Lord truly represents the participation in his body through the breaking of bread, there ought not to be the least doubt that he truly presents and shows his body."[133] What he promises he accomplishes. Christ "does the very thing which he shows and ratifies what he does."[134] The sacraments then are not merely psychological aids depicting something before our eyes, a truth which God does not want us to forget, but they are instruments in the economy of salvation, instruments, by virtue of which what is represented, is presented.

Calvin's somewhat nominalistic terminology, his antisubstance declarations, his rejection of any kind of sacramental

---

[130] Cf. *ibid.*, 9:72, 73. Grass is doubtful that Calvin really solves the difficulty here. Cf. *op.cit.*, 253.

[131] Cf. *Inst.*, IV, 17, 11. Calvin is not always clear in this matter. Though he distinguishes between the merits or benefits and the body, he appears at times to equate "flesh" or "body" with the power of the body. "Thus where the substance of Christ's body in its virtue and vitalizing properties is active and efficacious, there, in effect, is the Body of Christ." Gwyn Walters, "The Doctrine of the Holy Spirit in John Calvin," typewritten thesis, University of Edinburgh, 1949, 251.

[132] CR 49:487.   [133] *Inst.*, IV, 17, 10.   [134] CR 9:184.

empiricism should not lead us to assert that he was a "virtual-ist," without some kind of qualification.[135] In this instance, above all, the Platonic framework of Calvin's biblical doctrine must be kept in mind. By means of the concepts of image and participation, Calvin can insist that the heavenly reality remains in heaven and that the body of Christ is really given. The *opposita* of the dialectic must be maintained in union and tension. A pure virtualist interpretation does not do justice to either the content or framework of Calvin's eucharistic doctrine; indeed it reduces the Supper to little more than a phantom of Christ's body. Neither can one say, even after giving due consideration to the "word" character of the sacraments in Calvin, that the Eucharist has only a noetic function.[136] In order to underline the reality of the reception of the body and blood of Christ, Calvin showed a preference for realistic expressions. With a certain abandon he used the realistic expressions "truly," "really," "substantially," "essentially," "bodily," and to a certain extent also the corresponding adjectives and substantives, most especially *substantia*.[137] What is to be rejected are only those philosophical notions implicit in the Lutheran and Roman Catholic views. Calvin himself faces the problem and solves it.

> Only when we obtain Christ himself do we come to be partakers of his benefits. . . . I attend to the import of the words, for Christ does not simply present to us the benefit of his death and resurrection, but the very body in which he suffered and rose again. Christ's body is really, that is truly, given to us in the supper, to be wholesome food for our souls. Our souls are nourished by the substance of the body that we may be truly made one with him, or what amounts to the same thing, that a life-giving virtue from

[135] Cf. Luchesius Smits, *Saint Augustin dans l'oeuvre de Jean Calvin*, Louvain, 1957, vol. I, 31; Sasse, *op.cit.*, 327, 54n.

[136] ". . . das Sakrament hat nur eine noetische, erklärend-deutende Funktion für die Zukunftsverheissung. . . ." Wim Boelens, "Die Arnoldshainer Thesen," typewritten thesis, University of Würzburg, 1963, 265. Cf. also van der Leeuw, *op.cit.*, 69.

[137] Cf. Grass, *op.cit.*, 248.

Christ's flesh is poured into us by the Spirit, though it is at a great distance from us and is not mixed with us.[138]

It should be noted that Calvin sees no opposition between the assertion that "Christ's body is really . . . truly given to us in the Supper," and his assertion that the "life-giving virtue from Christ's flesh is poured into us by the Spirit." Here, too, we meet Calvin's dialectics, but beyond that there is here an ambiguity implicit in the imperatives of a Christology of Nestorian tendencies.[139] He who in Christology tends to separate the humanity from the divinity in Christ, will also tend to separate sign from signified in sacramental theology, bread from body, and wine from blood. Such a one will also have difficulties giving a theological explanation of the relation of the Eucharist to the person of Christ which is in harmony with biblical and patristic realism.[140] The ambiguity is part of Calvin's theological system, and one cannot eliminate the ambiguity in an attempt at a synthesis which is not present in Calvin's sacramental doctrine, an attempt to tidy up what Calvin, perhaps consciously, left untidy, and then think that one has faithfully reproduced his theology. He asserts that Christ is not substantially present in the elements, that we receive the power of Christ's body, that Christ is not present under the elements, that Christ's body is received, that it is not just an effect of Christ's body which we receive. The question arises, is the realism of the total commitment and the uncommitted, seen separately, so great that the realism of their union is not given sufficient attention? This seems to have been true of his Christology, and

[138] CR 49:487.

[139] A study of the eucharistic doctrine of the Nestorians shows that they experienced the same difficulties in their eucharistic doctrine as did Calvin, and that, in fact, there is a surprising similarity between their eucharistic doctrine and that of Calvin. These similarities should not be taken to mean that Calvin was in fact a Nestorian, but rather that he gave preference to a juxtaposition of the two natures instead of to their realistic union because of his theological attitudes. Cf. Wilhelm de Vries, *Sakramententheologie bei den Nestorianern*, Rome, 1947, 212-220.

[140] Cf. Thurian, "The Real Presence," *Christianity Divided*, 215, 216.

one is not surprised to meet it here again in his eucharistic doctrine.

Also for Beza, Calvin's biographer and successor, with whom Calvin was in agreement, the presence is not just an effect of Christ's body.[141] If substantial presence in the Catholic or Lutheran sense is too much, the presence merely of an effect is not enough. "The oral presence in Calvin is not the presence of an absence."[142]

SUBSTANCE AS SOTERIOLOGICAL PERSONALISM

This is not to say that we do not receive also the effects of Christ's body and blood, but rather to insist that neither the work is separated from the person of Christ nor the person separated from his work or effect. We cannot receive the heavenly benefits apart from the person of the Mediator. And when man receives what Christ has effected, then he must first of all be joined to his person, and more than that, must be joined to his body and blood. Without close union with Christ, with the God-Man, there is no holiness; without the body of Christ there is also no effect. Calvin gave particular emphasis to this personal union with the Mediator.[143]

Calvin's concern then is not to define what is given in the Eucharist in terms of substance, though he uses the term frequently, but rather to disengage us from the philosophical notion of substance and lead us to the notion of person. To receive his person is to receive the whole Christ—body, blood, and divinity. To receive Christ is not to receive an abstraction.

If one wanted to characterize the doctrine of Calvin, one would say that for him the concept of substance is essentially soteriological. This is a consequence of his Christology which is soteriological in character. So decidedly do the concepts of the Mediator and Redeemer dominate his idea of substance that Calvin avoids speaking of the heavenly or glorified body

141 Cf. CR 17:494. Cf. also Gollwitzer, *op.cit.*, 117, 3n.
142 Max Thurian in a private interview, Taizé, 15 August 1962.
143 Cf. CR 9:842.

of Christ being given in the Eucharist and prefers to speak rather of communion with the Mediator and Redeemer.[144] "By declaring that his body is given for us and his blood shed for us, he teaches that both are not so much his as ours. For he took up and laid down both, not for his own advantage but for our salvation. And, indeed, we must carefully observe that the very power and almost entire force of the sacrament lies in these words: " 'which is given for you,' . . . 'which is shed for you.' The present distribution of the body and blood of the Lord would not greatly benefit us unless they had once for all been given for our redemption and salvation."[145] "For Christ would not have been the bread of life for us if he had not been born and had not died for us, and if he had not arisen for us."[146] " 'The bread which I shall give you is my flesh, which I shall give for the life of the world.' By these words he doubtless means that his body will be to us as bread for the spiritual life of the soul, for it was to be made subject to death for our salvation."[147] Not only is substance defined—or more properly described—in soteriological terminology, but also the famous effects: "I call Christ with his death and resurrection the matter, or substance. But by the effect I understand redemption, righteousness, sanctification, and eternal life, and all the other benefits Christ gives to us."[148]

Calvin's concept of substance then is self-consciously not philosophical but rather biblical, and signifies the profound reality of a being or of a thing, and more precisely the profound reality of the person of the Redeemer and Mediator.[149] The concept is, when compared to the scholastic, much less abstract. In the forefront stands that redemptive self-

---

[144] Cf. Niesel, *The Theology of Calvin*, Philadelphia, 1956, 219.

[145] *Inst.*, IV, 17, 3.   [146] *ibid.*, 17, 5.   [147] Cf. *ibid.*

[148] *ibid.*, 17, 11. Cf. also Seeberg, *op.cit.*, 607, where the author calls attention to the difference between Calvin and Luther in this matter.

[149] Cf. Cadier, *op.cit.*, 23; Thurian, "The Real Presence," *Christianity Divided*, 206. Kretz also mentions the centrality of the Redeemer to the concept of substance. It is, however, going a little too far to say that body and blood for Calvin are only biblical expressions, as though the body and blood were not really present and given. Cf. *op.cit.*, 303, 1n.

giving of God in Christ, and this in various forms. The Christ of the Eucharist is the Mediator, the God-Man who acts for us. He is the Redeemer, the God-Man given for us. And he is the God-Man Emmanuel, the God with us.[150] The concept of substance in Calvin, then, is soteriological, personal, and actual.

[150] Cf. Niesel, *Calvins Lehre vom Abendmahl*, 49-51.

VII. The Eucharist in Its Pneumatological Context: Calvin's Eucharistic Doctrine, II

Pneumatological Prolegomena

FROM TENSIONS OF THE EXTRA CALVINISTICUM TO PNEUMATOLOGICAL TENSIONS

CALVIN held it as axiomatic that "Christ is not to be separated from the Spirit."[1] And this is as valid for the Mediator as for the eternal Son.[2] However, as Krusche—to whom this section is largely indebted—has pointed out, when the relationship of the Spirit to the eternal Son and the relationship of the Spirit to the Mediator are examined with reference to extratrinitarian works, creation for instance, there is a difference of considerable importance.[3] First, the Spirit as proceeding from the eternal Son. As the eternal Son or Logos, through whose power—the power being the Holy Spirit—the world was created, Christ is everywhere present, breathing in the power of the Spirit and sustaining life.[4] There is in creation no life, further, no continuing existence, unless the eternal Son through the sending of the Spirit sustains that life and existence. Without this sustaining act of the eternal Son through the Spirit, all would fall back into nothingness.

The Holy Spirit also proceeds from the incarnated Son, from the Mediator. And the conserving in existence through the Spirit who proceeds from the eternal Son is not an act which ceases or is interrupted when the eternal Son becomes the incarnated Son, otherwise creation would fall back into nothingness. The incarnated Son is not only he who receives the Spirit, but also he who sends the Spirit, and sends it specifically as Redeemer. When the eternal Son sends the Spirit to creation, he sends him to all creation, but when

---

[1] CR 49:491. [2] Cf. *ibid.*, 36:138.
[3] Cf. Werner Krusche, *Das Wirken des Heiligen Geistes nach Calvin*, Göttingen, 1957, 127, 128.
[4] Cf. CR 50:63; CR 41:62.

the incarnated Son, as Redeemer, sends the Spirit, he sends him only to the elect, to the new creation.[5] Indeed, the Mediator-Redeemer never manifests himself without the Spirit of sanctification. There are, then, two works of the Holy Spirit, which are not posterior, one to the other, but simultaneous, with the one ordered to the other: the work of sustaining and of redeeming, the work of providence and of predestination.[6]

It becomes evident that in Calvin's systematics, Christology can only be considered pneumatologically, and this gives validity to Grass' observation that the Eucharist in Calvin can only be considered pneumatologically.[7] The same dialectic found in his Christology is found in his Pneumatology, though not so completely developed, the same tension between the complete commitment and the uncommitted. The second person of the Trinity does not cease, after the Incarnation, to animate the universe and to sustain it in existence through the power of the Holy Spirit. But the Holy Spirit, who works everywhere and is everywhere effective, does not work everywhere unto salvation, but only there where he proceeds from the incarnated Redeemer.[8] Here the *filioque* is seen from the viewpoint of the preexistent Son and the incarnated Son.[9] In the works *ad extra* the Spirit who proceeds from the preexistent Son is effective in all of first creation, but the Spirit who proceeds from the incarnated Son is effective only there where the Son is Redeemer. The Spirit does not give new life to all, but only to the elect; here again, the complete commitment and the uncommitted.

The *Extra Calvinisticum* and the distinguishing of the *filioque* into the preexistent and the incarnated Son form a systematic unity.[10] The preexistent Son goes into the flesh and is the receiver of the Spirit, but he is not absorbed by the flesh nor merged in the flesh, but remains he who sends the

---

[5] Cf. *ibid.*, 9:515.   [6] Cf. Krusche, *op.cit.*, 128.
[7] Cf. *ibid.* 24. Cf. also O. Weber, "Calvin," RGG[3].
[8] Cf. CR 9:515.
[9] Cf. *Inst.*, III, 1, 2.
[10] Cf. Krusche, *op.cit.*, 120.

Spirit.[11] Seen Christologically the λόγος ἔνσαρκος does not cease to be the λόγος ἄσαρκος. The preexistence of the eternal Logos is not canceled out nor absorbed by the existence of the Logos become man. The eternal Son preexists also after the Incarnation and he exists at the same time. This simultaneous existence should not be taken to mean that there are two Sons or two Logoi, but rather that the tension between the preexistent and the existent should not be lost.

Seen pneumatologically, these Christological facts mean that the Holy Spirit proceeds, during the course of time, from the eternal Logos through whom the world was created, and the Holy Spirit sustains and conserves in being every creature in every time and age. The Holy Spirit, continues Krusche, however, proceeds not only from the Logos, who remains outside of the flesh, that is from the λόγος ἄσαρκος, but he also proceeds from the incarnated Logos, from the λόγος ἔνσαρκος.[12] The difference in the concept of procession here consists in the procession, in the second case, from a Mediator, a Mediator who is God joined to a human nature in the unity of a person. And as Mediator, according to his human nature, he is the receiver of the Holy Spirit, so is he, as Son, he who is and remains, also in the person of the Mediator, of the same essence as the Father, the Giver and Sender of the Holy Spirit—in this case, however, with regard to the work of sanctification, not with regard to the work of sustaining or conserving. Insofar as the *filioque* is related to the incarnated Son, the procession of the Holy Spirit is related to the work of sanctification. Through this sending, the Spirit does not work in regard to everybody, but only in regard to those for whom Christ is the effective Redeemer. The work of sanctification through the sacraments, the Eucharist in particular, will bear the imprint of this close relationship between Christology and Pneumatology, and the dialectics of the complete commitment and the uncommitted in Pneumatology will leave its imprint on that all-important eucharistic problem, the communion of the un-

[11] Cf. *ibid.*, 129.　　　　　[12] Cf. *ibid.*

worthy. The application of Christology and Pneumatology, specifically the *Extra Calvinisticum* and the *filioque*, to eucharistic doctrine will illustrate again the shifting centralities within Calvin's thought.

IMPERSONALISM WITHIN PNEUMATOLOGICAL

PERSONALISM

Of the criticisms one could make of Calvin's Pneumatology, three are of special importance for the matter at hand: the slight tendency toward modalism, the resulting tendency toward impersonalism in Pneumatology, the apparent confusion of the work of Christ and that of the Holy Spirit.

In Calvin's pneumatological vocabulary the Holy Spirit is spoken of as *virtus, vigor, vis, potentia, energia, effectus, impulsus, instinctus, motus, influxus.*[13] The question arises, "Is the Holy Spirit a power, a quality, or is he (it) a person?" When speaking of the inner-trinitarian life, Calvin's categories are those of a power or quality. Commenting on Genesis I: 26 Calvin writes that "Within God something distinct is found so that certainly his eternal wisdom and power reside in him."[14] Speaking of God making a consultation, he says that God consulted with his eternal wisdom and power, that is with the Son and the Holy Spirit.[15] In the inner-trinitarian life *virtus* is not merely an attribute which characterizes the manner of the Holy Spirit's existence, but is rather identified with this existence.

Also, when the works of the Trinity *ad extra* are examined, power and efficacy are not only ascribed to the Holy Spirit by appropriation, but rather the Holy Spirit is identified with this power. ". . . To the Holy Spirit is assigned power and efficacy of action," because the Holy Spirit is "the power by which he [God] executes the decrees of his plan."[16] The Holy Spirit is the essential power of God.[17] Krusche notes that when Calvin speaks of the hidden power of God,

[13] Cf. *ibid.*, 9.   [14] CR 23:25.
[15] Cf. *ibid.*, 34:134.   [16] Cf. *Inst.*, I, 13, 18.
[17] Cf. CR 45:31.

he thinks of the Holy Spirit not as the proper subject of a divine act, but rather as the active force of a divine act.[18]

There can be no doubt that Calvin, as a theologian of the Trinity, believed that the Holy Spirit was a person.[19] This must be said with all clarity. However, within an undoubted personalism there is a strain of impersonalism, and this strain of impersonalism will come to the fore in Calvin's eucharistic doctrine. Perhaps a second question can, in Calvin's defense, be asked. "If the Holy Spirit is a power, a quality, does that exclude his (it) being a person?" If he is guilty of modalism, it is only a slight modalism.[20] His doctrine is purer than his *Sprachgebrauch*.

When this doctrine of the Holy Spirit with its strain of impersonalism is applied to the Eucharist, the vocabulary remains impersonal and instrumental. In regard to his eucharistic role the Holy Spirit is compared to the sun shedding its beams upon the earth, thereby casting something of its substance upon the earth.[21] More precisely, the Holy Spirit is "like a channel through which all that Christ himself is and has is conveyed to us."[22] It is this citation from Calvin which prompts Bizer to accuse Calvin of a "materialism of the Spirit."[23] This impersonal vocabulary is all the more surprising since it is Calvin's intent to restore personalism to the-

---

[18] Cf. K. F. Noesgen, *Geschichte der Lehre vom Heiligen Geist*, Gütersloh, 1899, 158.

[19] Cf. Edmon Grin, "Quelques aspects de la pensée de Calvin sur le Saint-Esprit et leurs enseignements pour nous," *Theologische Zeitschrift*, vol. 3 (1947), 279. Cf. also Max Thurian, "The Real Presence," *Christianity Divided*, eds. Daniel J. Callahan *et al.*, New York, 1961, 213.

[20] Cf. Ernst Wolf, "Deus Omniformis," *Theologische Aufsätze*, ed. Ernst Wolf, Munich, 1936, 448; Louis Goumaz, *La doctrine du salut d'après les commentaires de Jean Calvin sur le nouveau testament*, Paris, 1917, 238; B. B. Warfield, *Calvin and Augustine*, Philadelphia, 1956, 230.

[21] Cf. *Inst.*, IV, 17, 22.

[22] *ibid.*

[23] Cf. Ernst Bizer, *Studien zur Geschichte des Abendmahlsstreits im 16. Jahrhundert*, Gütersloh, 1940, 285. Cf. also Paul Tschackert, *Die Entstehung der lutherischen und der reformierten Kirchenlehre*, Göttingen, 1910, 401. Thurian notes that Calvin himself was not entirely satisfied with the explanation of the mystery which he gave. Cf. "The Real Presence," *Christianity Divided*, 208.

ology and to the pastoral aspects of the Eucharist, an intent which is not without a measure of success.[24]

Finally, the close relation between Christology and Pneumatology—no pneumatological statement without its corresponding Christological statement, and vice versa—has led some to accuse Calvin of confusing the work of Christ and the work of the Holy Spirit.[25] Calvin's position is that the subject of the Eucharist is the Lord, and there is no Christ without the Spirit, and no Spirit without Christ. The Holy Spirit has no proper work.[26] Not to have a proper work is precisely the work of the Holy Spirit. The accusation is interesting here, not because it is true, but because one can see how easily a theologian could make such a judgment. Carried to its logical conclusion the accusation of confusing the work of Christ and the Spirit leads to the accusation that the Eucharist represents not the real presence of Christ, but rather the real presence of the Holy Spirit.[27] The Holy Spirit becomes the proper sacramental reality and the body and blood become the "irrational remnant."[28] This, too, must be rejected, though the relation of the Holy Spirit to the eucharistic body makes such accusations understandable even when not justified.

DEVOTIONAL PRESUPPOSITION AND POLEMIC MOTIVATION

After Calvin had asserted his belief in the reality of Christ's presence and before he treated of the manner in which this presence is brought about, namely through the

---

[24] Cf. Thurian, "The Real Presence," *Christianity Divided*, 213. Thurian notes here the de-personalizing of the Holy Spirit in the application of Pneumatology to eucharistic doctrine, but fails to note that in Calvin's Pneumatology itself, quite apart from its application to the Eucharist, there is this element of impersonalism.

[25] Cf. Krusche, *op.cit.*, 24.   [26] Cf. *ibid.*

[27] Cf. Wilhelm Niesel, *Calvins Lehre vom Abendmahl*, 2nd edn., Munich, 1935, 99. Cf. also Wim Boelens, "Die Arnoldshainer Thesen," typewritten thesis, University of Würzburg, 1963, 271.

[28] It must be remembered that Calvin's Pneumatology, as his Christology, is a *Schutzlehre*. As his Christology guards against sacramental mechanism, so his Pneumatology guards against sacramental materialism and sacramental imperialism.

Holy Spirit, he prefaced his elaboration on the role the Holy Spirit plays with a remarkable declaration of faith in which he professes that he does not understand the mystery, that he experiences it rather than understands it, and once again insists in realistic terms that the body is really eaten, the blood really drunk, that the sacramental signs are, in fact, efficácious signs in which Christ acts and gives what is signed. The declaration is remarkable not only for its dogmatic content but for its deeply devotional character:

> Now, if anyone should ask me how this [real presence] takes place, I shall not be ashamed to confess that it is a secret too lofty for either my mind to comprehend or my words to declare. And, to speak more plainly, I rather experience than understand it. Therefore, I here embrace without controversy the truth of God in which I may safely rest. He declares his flesh the food of my soul, his blood its drink. I offer my soul to him to be fed with such food. In his Sacred Supper he bids me take, eat, and drink his body and blood under the symbols of bread and wine. I do not doubt that he himself truly presents them, and that I receive them.[29]

Both the doctrinal content and the deeply devotional character of this passage make it clear that in assuming the difficult task of explaining how the mystery is accomplished, he wishes from the beginning to declare in unmistakable terms that there is more than a spiritual relationship between Christ and ourselves, that it goes beyond some supposed psychological moment in which we apprehend what Christ has done for us and what Christ has given us. The insistence here is upon bodily involvement. The eucharistic mystery involves the body and blood of Christ, that body in which he suffered and died and rose again, and that blood which he shed for us. It is this body which is exhibited to us in the sign, and is, in fact, given to us to be really eaten. In spite of all that he objects to in the term "substantial," he uses it to

[29] *Inst.*, IV, 17, 32.

designate that real joining between Christ and the recipient of the Eucharist.[30] In the Eucharist, Christ "is obtained, I affirm, not only when he dwells in us—when he is one with us—when we are members of his flesh—when, in fine, we are incorporated with him (so to speak) into one life and substance. . . . Christ does not simply present to us the benefit of his death and resurrection but the very body in which he suffered and rose again."[31] Whatever the theological difficulties he would encounter, the essential biblical and realistic quality of Calvin's devotional life would not be satisfied with anything less than a strong, realistic eucharistic doctrine.

Also to be noted is the polemic motivation behind the role Calvin assigns to the Holy Spirit in his eucharistic doctrine. This is not to invalidate it, but to understand why Calvin, in his historical situation, attributed so much importance to it. There is little doubt that the role Calvin assigns to the Holy Spirit is motivated, in large part, by the protest against the Roman and Lutheran dogmatics, in which the elements contain and give the body of Christ. One of Calvin's eucharistic preoccupations is to insist that, as far as the elements go, the body of Christ is not a "givenness."[32] There is no need for such a relationship between the body of Christ and the elements since

> . . . the Lord bestows this benefit upon us through his Spirit. . . . For as we do not doubt that Christ's body is limited by the general characteristics common to all human bodies, and is contained in heaven (where it was once for all received) until Christ return in judgment, so we deem it utterly unlawful to draw it back under these corruptible elements or to imagine it to be present everywhere. *And there is no need to do this for us to enjoy a participation in it*, since the Lord bestows his benefit upon

[30] Cf. Ronald S. Wallace, *Calvin's Doctrine of the Word and Sacrament*, Edinburgh, 1953, 151.

[31] CR 49:487.

[32] Cf. Niesel, "Das Calvinische Anliegen in der Abendmahlslehre," *Reformierte Kirchenzeitung*, vol. 82 (1932), 51.

us through his Spirit. . . . The bond of this connection is
therefore the Spirit of Christ, with whom we are joined
in unity and is like a channel through which all that Christ
himself is and has is conveyed to us. . . . [Paul] teaches that
the Spirit alone causes us to possess Christ completely and
have him dwelling in us.[33]

It was, then, partly to find a way to explain the realism of his
eucharistic doctrine without falling into "that feigned inclusion of the body itself under the element," that Calvin assumed the position that "it takes place by the power of the
Holy Spirit."[34] There was no need for including the body of
Christ under the species of bread and wine, a thought which
to Calvin's mind was quite literally unthinkable, when all
the demands of biblical and patristic realism could be fulfilled by the body of Christ being given to us through the
power of the Holy Spirit. His invocation of the Holy Spirit
and his elaboration of the large role played by the Holy
Spirit is anti-Roman and anti-Lutheran in motivation, but it
is precisely the role of the Holy Spirit, together with his
biblical categories and the Platonic concepts of image and
participation, which makes it possible to retain a sacramental
realism. It was to retain this realism while rejecting transubstantiation and consubstantiation that he developed his doctrine of the eucharistic role of the Holy Spirit.

This is not, of course, to say that polemics were his only
motivation. He saw justification for his doctrine in Romans
VIII: 9. Nor, as has been shown, was Calvin an innovator
in this matter. Calvin found the doctrine of the Holy Spirit
as the bond of our union with Christ in the Eucharist in a
sermon Erasmus attributed to John Chrysostom, which
Erasmus inserted into an edition of Chrysostom's works
published at Basel in 1530.[35] To assign the Holy Spirit an important eucharistic role is, of course, hardly foreign to the

[33] *Inst.*, IV, 17, 12. Italics added.
[34] *ibid.*, 17, 26.
[35] Cf. Niesel, *Calvins Lehre vom Abendmahl*, 92.

eucharistic traditions of either East or West.[36] To speak of only a few Western theologians, a eucharistic role is assigned to the Holy Spirit by Augustine, Isidore of Seville, Humbert of Silva Candida, Rabanus Maurus, and Ratramnus.

Dialectics and Personalism

HOLY SPIRIT AS CERTITUDE AGAINST OBJECTIVIZATION

We have noted the deeply personal quality of Calvin's eucharistic doctrine. It was, in part, by means of his teaching on the eucharistic role of the Holy Spirit that Calvin sought to bring this personal element to the fore.[37] By means of his teaching on the Holy Spirit, Calvin sought to avoid every possibility of making a "thing" of the sacrament. From an historical point of view this is quite understandable when we remember his polemic against sacramental impersonalism, and when we consider the rather frequent objectivization which can be found both in the theology and the devotional life of the Middle Ages.[38]

Calvin was deeply concerned to show that in his system it was not a thing which gave holiness; what gives holiness is the reception of the body and blood of Christ through the power of the Holy Spirit. The reality of the sacrament is the person of Christ in his body and blood, and this can be received only through the power of the Holy Spirit. Only a divine power can give a divine person, only a divine power can give that which is in heaven, the body and blood of Christ. This a material thing can never do.

Here too Calvin's Christology enters in. Calvin will have

---

[36] The problem of the *epeklesis* is witness to the eastern tradition. And it is found also in St. Thomas. *Sicut autem se habet virtus Spiritus Sancti ad aquam baptismi, ita se habet corpus Christi verum ad speciem panis et vini. Summa Theologica.* III, 73, 1, ad 3.

[37] Calvin also stressed the personal element through the relationship of Word to sacrament. E. Schillebeeckx recognizes this element of personalism in Calvin but gives it a somewhat negative and restrictive character. Cf. *Christ the Sacrament of the Encounter with God*, New York, 1936, 185, 186.

[38] Johannes L. Witte, "Die Christologie Calvins," *Das Konzil von Chalkedon*, vol. 3, *Entscheidung um Chalkedon*, eds. A. Grillmeier, H. Bacht, Würzburg, 1954, 528.

nothing to do with a divinization of the humanity of Christ and the sanctification of human nature which comes from its ontological union with divine nature, a union which takes place without confusing or mixing of the natures. This too, in Calvin's mind, would be a species of objectivization, making of divinity "a thing." And if the divinity is objectivized in this way in the humanity of Christ, then the whole process of salvation and sanctification falls under objectivization, is degraded to the realm of "a thing" or "things," for what is true in Christology, will, in its measure, be true in sacramental theology, and vice versa. Because the humanity of Christ is not joined to the divine nature in this ontological union, in sacramental theology the causal relationship between sign and signified is developed in terms of the Holy Spirit.[39]

There is a definite systematic, in the methodological sense, to Calvin's handling of the doctrine of the Holy Spirit. In his ecclesiology he holds that there is no church, no ministry of the Word, no sacraments outside of the Holy Spirit, just as there is no salvation outside the church.[40] By means of the doctrine of the Holy Spirit, Calvin has established a symmetry between his doctrine of baptism and Eucharist and has brought them in close relationship with the Word. Here the Spirit gathers all three gifts into unity: "For first, the Lord teaches and instructs us by his Word. Secondly, he confirms it by the sacraments. Finally, he illumines our minds by the light of his Holy Spirit and opens our hearts for the Word and sacraments to enter in, which would otherwise only strike our ears and appear before our eyes, but not at all affect us within."[41] The Spirit, too, is sovereign. When he wants, and ostensibly it is often, God can work through instruments or through mediate causes.[42] God is by no means bound to act always immediately through the Spirit, but can

[39] Cf. *ibid*.

[40] Cf. Gwyn Walters, "The Doctrine of the Holy Spirit in John Calvin," typewritten thesis, University of Edinburgh, 1949, 255.

[41] *Inst*., IV, 14, 8.

[42] Cf. CR 44:206.

use a variety of means, without however being committed to or bound by such means.[43] And when it pleases God to act through the sacraments he does so without compromising his lordship. "So far, then, is God from resigning the grace of his Spirit to the sacraments that all their efficacy and utility are lodged in the Spirit alone."[44] His sovereignty demands that a "division between Spirit and sacraments" be made so that "the power to act rests with the former, and the ministry alone is left to the latter—a ministry empty and trifling apart from the action of the Spirit, but charged with great effect when the Spirit works within and manifests his power."[45] This division between Spirit and sacraments is the dialectic between total commitment and the uncommitted in Calvin's Pneumatology.

One sees how carefully Calvin guards against any "divinization" of the sacramental means God has ordained. Here too Calvin's Christology as well as Pneumatology is normative.[46] The divinization Calvin would not attribute to Christ's humanity he is not about to attribute to the sacraments, no matter what qualifications save such a theology from a species of sacramental monophysitism. The divinization of the Eucharist in Roman Catholicism was all the more undesirable because it was accompanied by objectivization.

HOLY SPIRIT AND ASCENSION IN ELLIPSOIDAL · UNION AND TENSION

The Christ who was taken up into heaven is made present on earth in the giving of the eucharistic elements through the power of the Holy Spirit. The physical transfer of the body of Christ from earth to heaven and the whole theology of

---

[43] Cf. *ibid.*, 44:184; CR 24:240. Calvin asserts in CR 9:118 that even when God chooses to use the sacraments his choice does not prevent his grace from sometimes preceding, sometimes following the use of the sign.

[44] *ibid.*, 25:54. It should be noted that when Calvin uses the word *spiritus* he means the third Person of the Trinity. Cf. Niesel, "Kirche und Sakrament," *Evangelische Theologie*, vol. 2 (1935), 108.

[45] *Inst.*, IV, 14, 9.

[46] Cf. T. F. Torrance, *Kingdom and Church*, Edinburgh, 1956, 143, 144.

the Ascension play a large part in Calvin's theology, as they had in the whole eucharistic tradition since Augustine. The Ascension of Christ and the coming of the Holy Spirit are antithetically, dialectically, related; the one demands and presupposes the other, and stand as two centralities in ellipsoidal union and tension. "Surely, the coming of the Spirit and the ascent of Christ are antithetical; consequently, Christ cannot dwell with us according to the flesh in the same way that he sends his Spirit."[47] The Ascension then is the determining factor in the manner of Christ's eucharistic presence. "For if we would place him under the corruptible elements of this world, besides subverting what Scripture tells us in regard to his human nature, we annihilate the glory of his Ascension."[48] During his earthly life Christ was present really, by reason of a human and corporal presence. After his Ascension and the sending of the Holy Spirit, his presence is still a real presence, but it is a spiritual presence.[49] These terms "spiritual presence," so easily misunderstood as used by Calvin, do not mean a spiritualistic presence in which the body is really not received.[50] They do not stand in opposition to less real, nor do they denote an immaterial presence. They are not synonymous with a species of psychological presence. Once again, the presence of Christ in the

[47] *Inst.*, IV, 17, 26. Peter Martyr also argues from such an antithesis. Cf. Joseph McLelland, *The Visible Words of God*, Edinburgh, 1957, 117.

[48] OS I:521, 522.

[49] Cf. Krusche, *op.cit.*, 143.

[50] The question has often been asked whether Calvin's doctrine is a species of sacramental spiritualism. Cf. Otto Ritschl, *Dogmengeschichte des Protestantismus*, vol. 3, *Theologie des 16. und 17. Jahrhunderts in ihrer Entstehung und Entwicklung*, Göttingen, 1926, 168; Gerardus van der Leeuw, *Sakramentales Denken*, Kassel, 1959, 68; Joachim Beckmann, *Vom Sakrament bei Calvin*, Tübingen, 1926, 162; Jean Cadier, *La doctrine Calviniste de la sainte cène*, Montpellier, 1951, 22; Helmut Gollwitzer, *Coena Domini*, Munich, 1937, 119, 120; Thomas Sartory, "Eucharistisches Gedankengut bei unseren getrennten Brüdern," *Die Eucharistie im Verständnis der Konfessionen*, ed. Thomas Sartory, Recklinghausen, 1961, 393; Sartory, "Das Mysterium der Kirche in reformatorischer Sicht," *Mysterium Kirche*, eds., Ferdinand Holböck, Thomas Sartory, Salzburg, 1962, vol. 2, 995; Heinrich Janssen, "Die Abendmahlslehre Johannes Calvins," *Die Eucharistie im Verständnis der Konfessionen*, 209; Niesel, *Calvins Lehre vom Abendmahl*, 39, 79, 99.

Eucharist is called spiritual because the presence is effected by the Holy Spirit.

As though to remove all doubt that he was compromising sacramental realism by the concept of "spiritual presence," Calvin places the idea of substance and spiritual presence side by side in his summation at the end of the *Short Treatise on the Lord's Supper*. The summation is an affirmation that we are partakers of the proper substance of the body and blood and that spiritual presence is presence effected by the power of the Holy Spirit. "We all then confess with one mouth, that on receiving the sacrament in faith, according to the ordinance of the Lord, we are truly made partakers of the proper substance of the body and blood of Jesus Christ. ... We must hold that it [the presence] is made effectual by the secret and miraculous power of God, and that the Spirit of God is the bond of participation, this being the reason why it is called spiritual."[51]

Though, as shown in the previous chapter, the idea of substance is by no means excluded from the Calvinist definition of presence, the definition, to be true to Calvin, must be conceived not in substantialist terms, but rather in terms of the Holy Spirit. A substantialist definition could not stand together with the Ascension. To cast the definition in substantialist terms would, in Calvin's mind, risk the danger of reducing the Eucharist to "a thing," a danger of which Calvin is ever aware, and one can see the parallel measure he takes in Christology to avoid it. Calvin's definition of real presence is essentially dynamic, personalistic, and actual. For him the presence of Christ in the Supper is an act of the Holy Spirit.[52]

This pneumatic emphasis should not lead one to suppose that Calvin taught a Docetic presence. The Ascension is not a Docetic experience. Spiritual presence does not mean that we receive a spiritual distillation or essence of the heavenly Christ.[53] "Those who exclude the substance of vivifying flesh and blood from the communion defraud themselves of the

[51] OS I:529, 530.   [52] Cf. Cadier, *op.cit.*, 65.
[53] Cf. Beckmann, *op.cit.*, 131.

use of the supper."[54] And Calvin will not be satisfied with anything less than the whole Christ. "When, therefore, we speak of the communion which believers have with Christ, we mean that they communicate with his flesh and blood not less than with his Spirit, so as to possess thus the whole Christ."[55] The role of the Holy Spirit, then, in Calvin's eucharistic doctrine is not directed toward any spiritualization of the body of Christ.

Calvin's use of the Holy Spirit in a eucharistic context, though polemically motivated, is not, as he rightly pointed out, a denial of mystery.[56] Rather it involved the assertion of an absolute divine miracle.[57] There is a vast distance between God and man, between heaven and earth. For Calvin this distance is first of all metaphysical and it is distance in this metaphysical sense which became one of the centralities of his systematics. However there is in his eucharistic doctrine also an unmistakable local sense. "What, then, our mind does not comprehend, let faith conceive: that the Spirit truly unites things separated in space."[58] For Calvin, the Ascension experience has to do with body, space, movement from an earthly here to a heavenly there.

One cannot interpret Calvin's eucharistic doctrine without this strong spatial element, restricting oneself only to the metaphysical sense of distance, the distance between our world and the world of God.[59] The role of the Holy Spirit is not a rationalistic device, invoked to free us from the bur-

[54] CR 9:76. [55] OS I:435.

[56] Cf. *Inst.*, IV, 17, 10; *ibid.*, IV, 17, 24.

[57] Cf. Niesel, *Reformed Symbolics*, Edinburgh, 1962, 273.

[58] *Inst.*, IV, 17, 10.

[59] Niesel holds that distance here is not to be taken in the ordinary local sense, but rather in the sense in which man's world is distant from God's world. It is true that this metaphysical concept of distance is primary in Calvin's thought and is a systematic instrument in forming his theology. But over and above this metaphysical sense there is an unmistakable local sense in his eucharistic doctrine. "What, then, our mind does not comprehend, let faith conceive: that the Spirit truly unites things separated in space." *Inst.*, IV, 17, 10. This is clearly more spatial than metaphysical and Niesel's position must therefore be rejected. Cf. *Calvins Lehre vom Abendmahl*, 92. Cf. also CR 49:488.

dens of faith. More precisely, the place of the Holy Spirit in eucharistic doctrine does not free us from the necessity of bowing down before a miracle. "Those who do not understand that such a thing cannot happen without several miracles are more than stupid."[60] The miracle Calvin places before us is not the Roman miracle of transubstantiation, not the Lutheran miracle of consubstantiation, but it is nonetheless a miracle, and before it Calvin invites us to bow. He gave what he thought was a better explanation (by means of the Holy Spirit the body of Christ penetrates to us— *penetret ad nos*), and in this explanation the moment of the miracle is not dispensed with, but merely shifted, transferred to another theological level.

DIALECTICS IN FAITH

Calvin's Pneumatology is normative as he works out the problems of faith and time in relation to the Eucharist. The Holy Spirit is never so committed to the works of sanctification, the Eucharist for example, that he ceases to be the uncommitted. Also, there are traces here of an intimate connection between Pneumatology and Christology. The Spirit is Sanctifier only there where Christ is Redeemer.

Having explicitly set aside the Roman Catholic and Lutheran explanations, which draw the body of Christ back "under these corruptible elements," or imagine "it to be present everywhere," Calvin continues:

And there is no need of this for us to enjoy a participation in it, since the Lord bestows this benefit upon us through his Spirit so that we may be one in body, spirit, and soul with him. The bond of this connection is therefore the Spirit of Christ, with whom we are joined in unity, and is like a channel through which all that Christ himself is and has is conveyed to us. For if we see that the sun, shedding its beams upon the earth, casts its substance in some measure upon it in order to beget, nourish, and give growth to

[60] *Inst.*, IV, 17, 24.

its offspring—why should the radiance of Christ's Spirit be less in order to impart to us the communion of his flesh and blood? On this account, Scripture, in speaking of our participation with Christ, relates its whole power to the Spirit. But one passage will suffice for many. For Paul, in the eighth chapter of Romans, states that Christ dwells in us only through his Spirit. Yet he does not take away that communion of his flesh and blood which we are now discussing, but teaches that the Spirit alone causes us to possess Christ completely and have him dwelling in us.[61]

In this passage Calvin places the whole of our relation to Christ, eucharistic and non-eucharistic, under the sovereignty of the Holy Spirit, and this in opposition to the Roman and Lutheran eucharistic positions. And on the other front, he had already rejected Zwingli's position, which made of the Eucharist an act of the believing man.[62] The Eucharist, in Calvin's view, is more than the act of a man who lives by faith. It is an act of the Holy Spirit who moves us by faith.

The Eucharist as an act of the Holy Spirit is more than a safeguard against the enemies of transcendence. Rather Calvin employs the concept of the sovereignty of the Holy Spirit as a centrality of his systematics as he develops his sacramental theology. The act of faith is an act of the sovereign Spirit. The Spirit not only creates faith in the heart of man, but gives this faith its content and its fulfillment, Jesus Christ. In the act of faith the Holy Spirit does not overcome transcendence, but rather inserts the Christian into an economy where transcendence and incarnation each assert its absolute. Transcendence and incarnation are embodied in Christ as the content of faith.

This act of faith is not an act of our own efforts, and neither the act proper nor its effects can be compassed by the human dimension. "Faith is the principal work of the Holy Spirit. . . . Faith itself has no other source than the Spirit. . . .

[61] *ibid.*, 17, 12.

[62] Cf. Niesel, "Das Calvinische Anliegen in der Abendmahlslehre," *Reformierte Kirchenzeitung*, vol. 82 (1932), 50, 51.

We have said that perfect salvation is found in the person of Christ. Accordingly, that we may become partakers of it he baptizes us in the Holy Spirit and fire."[63] Faith is the "unique gift of the Spirit."[64] The sovereignty of the Spirit is not exhausted in the act of initiating faith and the Spirit does not resign this sovereignty when once man has been brought to faith. "The Spirit is not only the initiator of faith, but increases it by degrees, until by it he leads us to the Kingdom of Heaven."[65]

This general role of the Holy Spirit in the economy of salvation is further specified in the Eucharist. Here too the Spirit creates the faith, gives the gift, and unites the giver and receiver. Since saving faith is dependent upon election and results from election, the Holy Spirit maintains his sovereignty. There is here no sacramental divinization, no sacramental mechanism. No unworthy man, and for Calvin an unworthy man is an unbelieving man, can usurp the gift or negate the grace given with it. Here the subjective efficacy of the sacrament remains bound to the faith which depends on election.[66] Indeed the manner of eating, worthy or unworthy, stands in the closest relationship to election and faith.[67] This must not be construed to mean that the real presence arises out of the act of faith of the believers. Rather the Holy Spirit who effects the presence of Christ also gives the faith which makes a man worthy. This is sacramental objectivity of a high order, though it is neither the sacramental objectivity of the Lutheran nor the Roman.

Never does the Spirit lose his sovereignty. The Spirit delegates the sovereignty to no creature, whether that be a creature, bread and wine, designated by God to signify food of life and the source of grace, or whether the creature be a

[63] *Inst.*, III, 1, 4.
[64] *ibid.*, 2, 8.
[65] *ibid.*, 2, 33.
[66] Cf. Mitchel Hunter, *The Teaching of Calvin*, Glasgow, 1920, 108. Reinhold Seeberg, *Lehrbuch der Dogmengeschichte*, vol. 4/1, *Die Entstehung des protestantischen Lehrbegriffs*, 5th edn., Darmstadt, 1953, 604.
[67] Cf. Beckmann, *op.cit.*, 16, 17.

sacred person who dispenses this sign. Sovereignty cannot here be reduced to an aspect of transcendence. It is essentially dialectic, the sovereignty of the uncommitted and the sovereignty of the total commitment in the economy of salvation and sanctification, here specifically sanctification through the Eucharist. This in contrast to the domestication of God in Catholicism, where, in Calvin's view, he is committed to the extent that he ceases to be the uncommitted.

DIALECTICS IN TIME

The Spirit is sovereign not only over bread and wine, and over the hearts of men, but also over time and history. The flesh of Christ was eaten by the Jews in the desert who followed the Rock, although the flesh of Christ did not yet exist. Commenting on First Corinthians X: 4, Calvin writes, "How could the Jews be partakers of the spiritual meat and drink, when there was as yet no flesh of Christ that they could eat? I answer that though his flesh did not as yet exist, it was, nevertheless food for them. Nor is this an empty subtlety or sophism, for their salvation depended on the benefit of his death and resurrection. . . . The reception of it was the secret work of the Holy Spirit, who brought it about that Christ's flesh, though not yet created, was made efficacious in them."[68] The total commitment is not such that the Spirit is trapped in either the sacrament or in time. The Spirit who is sent by the Mediator as well as by the eternal Word—because he proceeds from the Mediator as well as from the eternal Word—works sanctification wherever Christ is Redeemer. Christ is Redeemer for the Jews in the desert; through faith they are joined to the Redeemer's death and resurrection. The space-time limitations of bread and wine and history are not the measure of the uncommitted. The gift of the Spirit, the faith dimension, is also not measured by either space or history.

The intervention of the Holy Spirit in the Supper should not be thought of in only a temporal sense, as though the

[68] CR 49:455.

Holy Spirit, in some unmeasured moment, disarranged nature and effected the eucharistic miracle. This is a sovereignty too modest and too furtive to be that of which Calvin speaks. The act of the Holy Spirit is not something that can be experienced in the temporality of the fleeting moment, so that the act no longer continues to exist. The act of the Holy Spirit in the Eucharist is a moment in that sovereignty of which we spoke above. The sovereignty endures though the eucharistic moment passes. The act of the Holy Spirit cannot, therefore, be simply identified with the eucharistic action.[69] Through the act of the Holy Spirit in the Eucharist, we are shown again the promises of Christ, and this showing is a sealing of the promises, the assurance that we are given what is signed. The union with Christ signed in the eucharistic symbols extends beyond the eucharistic act, and for this reason Calvin says that the act of the Holy Spirit also extends beyond the Eucharist.[70] In this context Calvin's teaching that there is no specific sacramental grace is more easily understood. The grace given in the Eucharist is the same grace which is given in the sermon and in prayer.[71] To be more precise, there is nothing which can be said of the eucharistic event which cannot be said of the teaching of our union with Christ.[72] The gift is the same. There is no other union with Christ than that which is given to the believer in the devout hearing of a sermon, or prayerful reading of the scripture, or in prayer.[73] This is not, in Calvin's mind, to cancel out sacramental realism, much less the sacramental reality. The *opposita* must remain.

[69] Cf. Niesel, *Calvins Lehre vom Abendmahl*, 95, 96.

[70] Cf. CR 9:232.

[71] Cf. Niesel, *Calvins Lehre vom Abendmahl*, 97; Beckmann, *op.cit.*, 132.

[72] Cf. Krusche, *op.cit.*, 271.

[73] Cf. Niesel, *Calvins Lehre vom Abendmahl*, 97, 98. Paul Althaus accuses Calvin of assigning the Holy Spirit a mythological role in his eucharistic doctrine. Cf. *Die lutherische Abendmahlslehre in der Gegenwart*, Munich, 1931, 36. Calvin's rejection of sacramental mechanism was replaced by an impersonalism in Pneumatology which makes such an accusation possible though not entirely justified.

ZWINGLI DISSOLVES SACRAMENTAL DIALECTIC

Calvin, with an understatement quite uncharacteristic of him, introduces the question of the relation of eating to faith by dryly remarking, "there is no unanimity as to the mode of partaking of him."[74] Then he proceeds: "For there are some who define the eating of Christ's flesh and the drinking of his blood as, in one word, nothing but to believe in Christ."[75] For Zwingli, then, to eat is to believe. Calvin does not reject the expression, though he is clearly unhappy with it. "I do not utterly disallow that expression, but only deny that it is the full interpretation, if they mean to define what it is to eat Christ's flesh."[76] For Calvin, the expression is defective not because of what it asserts but because of what it fails to assert. "But it seems to me that Christ meant to teach something more definite, and more elevated, in that noble discourse in which he commends to us the eating of his flesh. It is that we are quickened by the true partaking of him . . . no one should think that the life that we receive from him is received by mere knowledge. . . . I say that we eat Christ's flesh in believing, because it is made ours by faith."[77] Because it is true that there is no other eating than the eating which takes place through faith, and because the eucharistic act is an act of the Holy Spirit in regard to the humanity of Christ, the eucharistic elements cannot be an empty sign, but must have realization and reality. There is for Calvin no eucharistic body which is accepted in faith, but not in reality. The Eucharist, indeed, is not divorced from faith, but the Eucharist is more than naked faith. It is also reality. Calvin rejects Zwingli because Zwingli has solved the mystery and dissolved the dialectic of an objective presence by choosing one of the poles of the sacramental dialectic. This Calvin will not abide. The *opposita* must remain.

Calvin's discontent with Zwingli and the consequent insistence that eating is not to be identified with naked faith

---

[74] *Inst.*, IV, 17, 5.   [75] *ibid.*   [76] *ibid.*, 17, 6.
[77] *ibid.*, 17, 5. Note the rejection here of a purely noetic function.

apart from the reality, should not be taken as evidence that the substance of Christ, in either the Roman or Lutheran sense, is given or received in the Eucharist. Both local presence, that is Christ substantiated in, under, and with the bread, and the eating of this substance by unworthy Christians, are rejected. To wish to mix the substance of Christ's flesh with the soul of man—or with his body—involves only absurdities.[78] Neither the norms of Pneumatology nor of Christology could countenance such a doctrine.

Having seen the danger in pushing Calvin's rejection of Zwingli to mean his acceptance of a substantialist position, the same caution must be taken in his rejection of the Roman and Lutheran substantial eating. His rejection of these positions is hardly civil, and Calvin makes no attempt to hide his contempt. The Roman and Lutheran positions are, quite simply, unspeakable nonsense. However strong his rejection of these substantialist positions, he is not rejecting a real eating of the body of Christ. He is not rejecting sacramental realism.[79]

The Holy Spirit in Act

OBJECTIVITY BECAUSE OF THE HOLY SPIRIT

To assert that the flesh of Christ is received by the believer through faith, that the believer receives it spiritually, is not necessarily to fall into subjectivism. In so formulating his doctrine Calvin had no intention of denying a real presence, nor did he propose a presence which would be limited to the good dispositions of the faithful, even though these good dispositions arose from faith.[80] To say that the believer receives the body and blood through faith is to say that he receives them through the Holy Spirit who gives faith. Calvin did not think that to receive the flesh of Christ through the power of the Holy Spirit, a manner which he called spiritual, was to reduce all to subjectivism. Spiritual is not an equivalent for subjective.[81]

---

[78] Cf. CR 9:31.   [79] Cf. *ibid.*, 9:79.   [80] Cf. Cadier, *op.cit.*, 56.
[81] Cf. A. Lecerf, *Etudes Calvinistes*, Paris, 1949, 50.

Calvin is not against every kind of eucharistic objectivity, but only that kind of objectivity which makes of Christ's body a "givenness," which renders it the object as in sacramental impersonalism, which encloses it in the elements or asserts that it is present everywhere.[82] And he would also reject that objectivity which he sees implied in the Catholic doctrine of *ex opere operato*. Having made these objections, he insists on the objective character of the sacraments. Calvin asserts, for instance, that the validity of baptism, whose true character was hidden from the receiver or who neglected it, remains intact unless it had been deliberately renounced.[83]

For Calvin the objectivity of the sacraments is bound up with the sovereignty of the Spirit; to deny the sacraments their rightful objective character is to call in question the rightful sovereignty of the Spirit and also the lordship of Christ. Sacramental validity is not dependent on the visible church, though only those who belong to the body eat the body.[84] Nor is its objective character compromised by the condition or choice of him who receives it. "What I have said is not to be understood as if the force and truth of the sacrament depended upon the condition or choice of him who receives it. For what God has ordained remains firm and keeps its own nature, however men may vary. For since it is one thing to offer and another to receive, nothing prevents the symbol consecrated by the Lord's Word from being actually what it is called, and from keeping its own force. Yet this does not benefit a wicked or impious man."[85]

The worthiness or unworthiness of the minister of the sacrament does not enter the question of the objective character of the sacraments. "Now, suppose what we have de-

[82] Ernst Troeltsch, in characterizing Calvin's theology, mentions, among other traits, "a very strong and definite emphasis upon the sacraments as objective Divine means of grace." Cf. *The Social Teaching of the Christian Churches*, vol. 2, *Church History*, London, 1951, 580.

[83] Cf. *Inst.*, IV, 15, 17.

[84] Cf. Beckmann, *op.cit.*, 19, 82.

[85] *Inst.*, IV, 14, 16.

termined is true—that a sacrament must not be judged by the hand of the one by whom it is ministered, but as if it were from the very hand of God, from whom it doubtless has come. From this we may then infer that nothing is added to it or taken from it by the worth of him by whose hand it is administered. . . . It ought to be enough for us to recognize the hand and seal of our Lord in his sacraments, whatever carrier may bring them."[86]

The presence of Christ in the Eucharist is an objective reality and as such is bound to faith, but it is not subjectively dependent on faith. Rather it leads to faith. Faith is not a condition of sacramental objectivity, but another gift which precedes and accompanies the eucharistic gift.[87] That faith is not a condition is seen in the assurance that the flesh and blood of Christ are given no less truly to the unworthy than "to God's elected believers."[88] "Christ proffers this spiritual food and gives this spiritual drink to all."[89] Because the promises of God cannot be annulled and because God is faithful to his promises even when man is not faithful to his, the gift of the body and blood is given to all.

The objectivity of the sacraments is, then, founded in their actualization through the power of the Holy Spirit, and the subjectivity is guaranteed by the role of faith, which is also a gift of the Holy Spirit. To safeguard this objectivity Calvin stressed their personal instrumental character, an instrumentality related to the heavenly Christ working through his Spirit. For Calvin, the personal instrumental character remains only when the grace is not enclosed within the sign and when the grace is not joined to the sacrament in some mechanical way. The type of objectivity found in the Roman doctrine of *ex opere operato*, which is for Calvin the

[86] *ibid.*, 15, 16.

[87] Cf. Paul Jacobs, "Die Gegenwart Christi im Abendmahl nach reformiertem Verständnis und das römisch-katholische Gegenbild," *Gegenwart Christi*, ed. Fritz Viering, Göttingen, 1959, 29. Cf. also Otto Karrer, "Die Eucharistie im Gespräch der Konfessionen," *Die Eucharistie im Verständnis der Konfessionen*, 368.

[88] *Inst.*, IV, 17, 33.

[89] *ibid.*

objectivity of a thing, cannot be valid precisely because it lacks the note of personalism, and because the commitment is such that the uncommitted ceases to be.[90]

The sacraments, and the Eucharist particularly, are the personal free acts of God. God sanctifies no one by proxy and he saves no one by proxy. Christ acts through the instrumentality of signs by means of the power of the Holy Spirit, and this instrumentality has validity and authenticity only as long as it does not usurp the immediate and the personal character of the divine act. Sanctification is union with the person of Christ, a union brought about only by the power of the Holy Spirit. The person of Christ is united to the person of man through the power of the Holy Spirit. The instrumentality of the sacraments is an instrumentality of this person to person relationship. When the sacraments become things, or static objects, or independent realities, or impersonal forces, when they lose the immediacy of a person, more particularly of a personal act, on the divine level involving Christ and the Holy Spirit, on the human level involving man, they lose their meaning in the economy of salvation.[91] The instrumentality of the sacraments and their objective character can be safeguarded only within the confines of this theological personalism.

It should be stressed that for Calvin this personalism is more than psychological. This is the personalism of faith, and within this personalism of faith—personalism is here not subjectivism—the sacraments find their greatest guarantee of objectivity. Beyond the objectivity of the Spirit in act there is, in the sacramental economy, no objectivity.[92]

WORTHINESS: ACT OF HOLY SPIRIT, NOT MORAL PROBITY

Writing in his commentary on First Corinthians in 1546, Calvin asserted that the question of whether the wicked receive the body of Christ is not, in his opinion, an essential point.[93] And this from a man who did not customarily con-

---

[90] Cf. Beckmann, *op.cit.*, 39. Cf. also CR 7:701.   [91] Cf. CR 12:127.
[92] Cf. Schillebeeckx, *op.cit.*, 188.   [93] Cf. CR 49:491.

sider his stand a matter of opinion. Reading through the vast amount of material which Calvin wrote on the Eucharist and noting the very large place he gave to this question, the unyielding passion with which he upheld his position, the easy contempt with which he labeled the Roman and Lutheran positions theological enormities—the use of contempt and a vulgar righteousness were by no means wanting in either Roman or Lutheran writings—leads one to conclude that when Calvin wrote this line in 1546, he conceded more than was his custom to concede. The whole temper of his eucharistic writings would indicate that here was a point of first importance, a point of the greatest necessity.

That the unworthy do not receive the body of Christ must be attributed to the sovereignty of the Spirit and the infallible fruitfulness of the body of Christ. The Spirit gives the mouth of faith and the Spirit gives the gift. The unworthy do not receive because they cannot. They cannot receive because they are unbelieving. Calvin, on this point, stands in the tradition of Paschasius Radbertus, Rabanus Maurus, Ratramnus, Berengarius, and, so he thought, of Augustine.

It should be noted how strongly Calvin stressed the religious nature of worthiness. What he sought in the communicants was far more a religious disposition than a moral disposition. And the religious disposition is faith and love. "Worthiness itself consists in faith and love."[94] The sacrilege of the unworthy who approach the communion table is that they receive the sign of faith without faith, their unworthiness consisting essentially in the fact "that they do not believe that the body is their life."[95] Because the unworthy man is a man without faith and without love he does not, cannot receive the body of Christ which is offered to him. Because the efficacy of the sacrament comes from the power of the Holy Spirit and because this power is manifested in the communicant through faith and love, which are works of the Holy Spirit, there cannot be any eating of the body on the

[94] *Inst.*, IV, 17, 42.   [95] *ibid.*, 17, 40.

part of the unworthy.[96] Because the unworthy man is a man without faith and without love, he does not, cannot receive the body of Christ which is offered to him. What is objectively offered to him cannot be received, not because he lacks moral righteousness, but because he is devoid of an objective religious gift and disposition: faith and love, which are acts of the Holy Spirit. Each man takes from the sacrament only that which he gathers in the vessel of faith, says Calvin borrowing from Augustine. The man who does not have the vessel receives nothing.

The faith which constitutes worthiness is not mere assent to the gospel history, or assent to a body of truths. Those who come with such chaste intellectual equipment, merely the logic of faith, are counted among the unworthy and they receive only an empty sign. "Without a lively feeling of faith," there is no worthiness, and therefore no reception of the sacrament is possible.[97]

There is a duty for each man to examine himself, to test his worthiness. Each man should "descend into himself, and ponder within himself whether he rests with inward assurance of heart upon the salvation purchased by Christ; whether he acknowledges it by confession of mouth."[98] These are the internal, religious dispositions, dispositions both deeply theological and deeply personal, which are the essence of worthiness. The examination has to do with faith. Where does he seek salvation? Does he seek the assurance of salvation in Christ? The duty of each man to prove himself according to the norms of this essential religious quality of worthiness does not dispense him from proving himself in relation to a moral concern, in relation to moral striving. Each should examine himself to ascertain "whether he aspires to the imitation of Christ with the zeal of innocence and holiness; whether, after Christ's example, he is prepared to give himself for his brethren and to communicate himself to those with whom he shares Christ in common; whether, as he is counted a member by Christ, he in turn so holds all

---

[96] Cf. Cadier, *op.cit.*, 56.   [97] CR 49:492.   [98] *Inst.*, IV, 17, 40.

his brethren as members of his body; whether he desires to cherish, protect, and help them as his own members."[99] Note the large place in this examination to social sensitivity. Apart from concern for one's brothers in Christ there can be no true morality. Probity is not the confrontation of each Christian with Christ, but the confrontation of each Christian with the body of Christ, which is the church.

If the examination shows that we are not yet perfect in these matters, we should not be unduly disturbed. What is of importance here is that these outward expressions of our faith, expressions of an ascetic and social order, should "day by day increase our faith" which we have received as a gift. "Not that these duties both of faith and of love can now be made perfect in us, but that we should endeavour and aspire with all our heart toward this end in order that we may day by day increase our faith once begun."[100]

Calvin was no laxist but rather a man who risked his position and his authority to keep unworthy men from the communion table. Calvin would rather, however, demand too little than too much in the way of a moral disposition, and wants above all to avoid the tortured, harassed, and pitiable conscience he seems to find in Roman Catholicism and also among the Anabaptists.[101] It would be to defeat the meaning and purpose of the sacrament if too much were demanded, for the sacrament was instituted "not for the perfect, but for the weak and feeble, to awaken, arouse, stimulate, and exercise the feeling of faith and love, indeed, to correct the defect of both."[102] When we are concerned with worthiness of a moral order then "this is worthiness—the best and only kind we can bring to God—to offer our vileness and (so to speak)

[99] *ibid.*

[100] *ibid.*

[101] Cf. *ibid.*, 17, 41. On Calvin's stand with regard to excommunication from the reception of communion cf. John T. McNeill, *The History and Character of Calvinism*, New York, 1954, 80f, 140, 145, 164, 177. Hunter notes that "the crowning proof of his esteem for the sacrament is provided by his making excommunication, i.e. deprivation of the right to communicate, the supreme ecclesiastical penalty." *op.cit.*, 185.

[102] *Inst.*, IV, 17, 42.

our unworthiness to him so that his mercy may make us worthy of him."[103]

As concerns both the religious disposition and the moral disposition, Calvin does not demand either a perfect faith or a perfect moral life, but asks of the communicant that he look only to Christ for the assurance of salvation, that he seek in the promises given in the Eucharist the means of moral growth.[104] A religious consciousness and a religious sensitivity and an authentic moral earnestness are required, but not perfection. "It is not a perfect faith or repentance that is required. . . . But if you aspire to the righteousness of God with an earnestness of purpose, and humbled, in view of your misery, you completely lean upon Christ's grace and rest upon it, know that you are a worthy guest to approach that table."[105]

OBJECTIVITY AND WORTHINESS AS SOTERIOLOGICAL
AND PNEUMATOLOGICAL EXPRESSIONS

When Calvin's eucharistic doctrine is discussed, a great deal of attention is given to Calvin's teaching that the unworthy do not receive the body of Christ but only an empty sign. Seldom is sufficient attention given to those declarations of Calvin's which assure an objective character to the Eucharist by asserting that the body is offered to all. The gift is given but it is not received because of the lack of faith. This lack of faith does not nullify the objective nature of the giving. Calvin denies that "the trustworthiness of God's promises can be diminished or fail through men's ungratefulness . . . the power of the mystery remains intact, no matter how much wicked men try to their utmost to nullify it."[106] Far from denying the objective nature of the sacrament, his doctrine is rather based upon it: "This is the integrity of the sacrament . . . that the flesh and blood of Christ are no less truly given to the unworthy than to God's elect believers. . . . He [God] is ready to give to the unworthy what they reject,

[103] *ibid.*
[105] CR 49:493.

[104] Cf. Bizer, *op.cit.*, 288-290.
[106] *Inst.*, IV, 17, 33.

indeed, offers it freely."[107] Calvin insists that there is no question here of the sacraments being without efficacy or God being unfaithful to his promises. "Since Christ's body is presented to the wicked no less than to the good, this is enough so far as concerns the efficacy of the sacrament and the faithfulness of God."[108] The certainty that the body of Christ is given does not destroy the certainty that the body of Christ is not received by the unworthy.

Two theological principles govern Calvin's thought here: the Spirit is efficacious only where Christ is Redeemer, and the objective efficacy of Christ's body. "Christ cannot be disjoined from his Spirit. Hence . . . his body is not received as dead or even inactive, disjoined from the grace and power of his Spirit. . . . Now in what way could the man who is altogether destitute of a living faith and repentance, having nothing of the Spirit of Christ, receive Christ himself?"[109] From the point of view of giving the body of Christ, it is the will of Christ that his body be the food of life for all and in the power of the Spirit he gives it as food to all. He does not give to the unworthy something neutral or different, something other than the body of Christ. To them are offered the body in reality and truth.[110] That the unworthy do not receive what they are offered is not due to any deficiency on the part of the giver or of the gift. The unworthy man cannot receive the body because of his obduracy in unbelief.

From the point of view of receiving the body of Christ, the Spirit is sent by the Redeemer only to those for whom he, Christ, is in all reality the Redeemer, namely, to the elect. Since Christ does not send his Spirit to the unworthy, they cannot receive the body of Christ. Christ cannot be separated from his Spirit. Where Christ is not really Redeemer, there

---

107 *ibid*.

108 CR 49:492. One cannot speak, as Wim Boelens does, of Calvin proceeding from the uncertainty of sanctification through the sacraments. Cf. "Die Arnoldshainer Thesen," typewritten thesis, University of Würzburg, 1963, 263.

109 CR 49:491.

110 Cf. Otto Weber, *Grundlagen der Dogmatik*, Neukirchen, 1962, vol. 2, 713.

is no Spirit, no faith, and therefore the unworthy cannot receive the body which is in reality extended to them. Here again is evidence of the strong soteriological character of Calvin's doctrine. The Eucharist is, in fact, an expression of soteriology.

The objectivity of the sacrament remains, but it is not the objectivity of a thing. This is another manifestation of Calvin's abiding fear of making the means of grace "things." He will not tolerate what he feels to be a false immediacy between the substance of the Eucharist and those who take part in it, an immediacy which is present when the sacrament becomes a "thing."[111] This is, of course, to reject a type of objectivity, and he makes the rejection without regret. But he retains another kind of objectivity, that objectivity which arises out of the inseparable unity between Christ and his Spirit. The Eucharist is also an expression of this pneumatological fact. Calvin will not separate the reception of Christ from the reception of his Spirit. And apart from the reception of the Holy Spirit there can be no reception of Christ.[112] "All of those who are devoid of Christ's Spirit can no more eat Christ's flesh than drink wine that has no taste."[113] "Christ cannot be disjoined from his Spirit. Hence . . . his body is not received as dead or even inactive, disjoined from the grace and power of his Spirit."[114]

Calvin also uses another line of argument to prove that though the unbelievers are offered the body of Christ they do not receive it. This argument stems from the efficacy of Christ's flesh. Christ's body and blood infallibly effect holiness; they cannot be received without effecting holiness. To maintain that unbelievers taste the body of Christ but receive it without benefit is simply not tenable, since it questions this infallible sanctifying quality of Christ's body. He who does not taste the flesh of Christ with benefit, does not taste the flesh of Christ at all. "No one can eat his very flesh without any benefit."[115]

[111] Cf. Niesel, *Reformed Symbolics*, Edinburgh, 1962, 274.
[112] Cf. D. W. Kreck, "Abendmahl," RGG³.
[113] *Inst.*, IV, 17, 33.   [114] CR 49:491.   [115] *Inst.*, IV, 17, 33.

"The Living Experience of His Death"

THE BODY WHICH HAS BEEN SACRIFICED

Calvin's eucharistic writings are largely determined by polemics. The controversies over the Eucharist and predestination were the two dogmatic areas in which he was almost continually carrying on some kind of theological warfare. Had Calvin been able to approach the eucharistic problem a little more dispassionately, with less of the defender of the faith's zeal and more of the disinterested but not uncommitted thoroughness of a dedicated theologian in peaceful possession of the faith, Calvin's eucharistic doctrine might have given larger place to the Eucharist as a sacrifice, as memorial, as a covenant, and as thanksgiving. These elements are not entirely missing, but they do not play a large part in Calvin's eucharistic consciousness.

Whether Calvin approached the eucharistic doctrine of sacrifice as found in contemporary Roman Catholicism on the essentialist level or on the level of the devotional life of the people, he found much that provoked him, and provoked him even to bitterness, as we saw in Chapter III. The provocation was probably the reason why some aspects of eucharistic doctrine were neglected.[116] On the essential level he was deeply disturbed by the Roman concept of sacrifice as applied to the Eucharist because it implied sacramental Pelagianism, giving something to God.[117] It was bad enough that man attempts to give something to God, and it was even worse that what man attempted to give, had, once and for all, already been given: a propitiatory sacrifice.[118] On the level of normal Roman devotional and liturgical life, as Calvin himself had seen and experienced it, the sacrifice had become highly clericalized: it was the priest who offered and it was the priest who, with the exception of once a year, received

[116] Cf. Geddes MacGregor, *Corpus Christi*, London, 1959, 188.

[117] Cf. Pierre-Yves Emery, "The Teaching of Calvin on the Sacrificial Element in the Eucharist," *The Reformed and Presbyterian World*, vol. 26 (1960), 110.

[118] Cf. *Inst.*, IV, 18, 3.

the fruits of the sacrifice, communion.[119] And Calvin wondered what all these ceremonies, usually carried out by a solitary priest, had to do with the worship of the people of God. The clericalization went further. The priest could and did offer the sacrifice without the participation of the people in the now notorious private masses, thus giving expression to liturgical clericalism.[120] It was in a very real sense the priest's mass. Worship was, for Calvin, essentially ecclesial, and without the participation of the church there could be no worship in the Christian sacramental sense.[121]

It was not that Calvin rejected the idea of sacrifice, or denied that it had any relationship to the Eucharist. Calvin grants that the New Testament speaks of sacrifice, not only in general, but specifically in connection with the Eucharist.[122] In the New Testament there is no other expiatory sacrifice than the sacrifice of the cross. The Eucharist itself is sacrificial only to the extent that what we are offered to eat is the body which was offered up on the cross. Calvin did more than concede this sacrificial content; he insisted upon it: "It is not the chief function of the sacrament simply and without higher consideration to extend to us the body of

[119] On clericalization cf. E. L. Mascall, *The Recovery of Unity*, London, 1958, 4, 5.

[120] Cf. CR 45:705.

[121] For Calvin's attitude toward both liturgy and ceremonies cf. J. D. Benoit, *Initiation à la liturgie de l'église reformée de France*, Paris, 1956; Benoit, *Liturgical Renewal*, London, 1958, 29-36; G. D. Henderson, "Calvin and Worship," *Transactions of the Scottish Ecclesiological Society*, vol. 12, part 2, 1938, 69-74; Niesel, "The Order of Public Worship in the Reformed Churches," *Scottish Journal of Theology*, vol. 2, 1949, 386, 387; J. Paquier in *Ways of Worship*, eds., Pehr Edwall *et al.*, London, 1951, 241-248; William Maxwell, *An Outline of Christian Worship*, 3rd edn., London, 1960, 112-119; Maxwell, *The Liturgical Portions of the Genevan Service Book*, Edinburgh, 1931, 3-52; Rudolf Stählin, "Die Geschichte des christlichen Gottesdienstes von der Urkirche bis zur Gegenwart," *Leiturgia*, vol. 1, *Geschichte und Lehre des Evangelischen Gottesdienstes*, eds., Karl Ferdinand, Walter Blankenburg, Kassel, 1954, 64-66.

[122] Cf. Paul Wernle, *Der evangelische Glaube nach den Hauptschriften den Reformatoren*, vol. 3, *Calvin*, Tübingen, 1919, 110f. Peter Martyr, in this case, will not go as far as Calvin in recognizing the idea of sacrifice in the New Testament as applied to the Eucharist. Cf. McLelland, *op.cit.*, 242, 249.

Christ."[123] To receive the body of Christ, purely and simply, might be religiously elevating, but it, in fact, has nothing to do with the Eucharist. "For the Lord does not present his body to us simply, and without any additional consideration, but insofar as it has been sacrificed for us."[124] If we want to know the meaning of the Eucharist, then, we can only find it on the cross. "The sacrament sends us to the cross of Christ."[125] Man cannot embrace the eucharistic Christ unless he also embraces the crucified Christ.[126]

MERE MEMORIAL IS NOT ENOUGH

There is little development in Calvin of the memorial aspect of the Eucharist. Seen historically, the large place given in Calvin's eucharistic doctrine to sacramental realism is bound up with his neglect of the memorial aspect. Zwingli and others had said that the Lord's Supper was a memorial of the redemptive fact, Calvary, but only a memorial. For Calvin this was not enough. The Lord's Supper is, in truth, memorial, but not just memorial. It is also the reality of Christ's body and blood. In his insistence on what the spiritualists denied, namely, the real presence, he failed to give much attention to what he held in common with them, that is, the Lord's Supper as memorial.

The Christological and pneumatological dialectics are here again in evidence. The commitment in the memorial sacrifice is never such that the memorial is identified with the sacrifice of the uncommitted. There is unity, but also the tensions of the unmixed and the undivided.

Calvin's concern is not with the historical fact of Christ's death, but, in a characteristic pastoral way, with the meaning of the historical fact.[127] Commenting on the words "for the remission of sins" of Mark XIV: 24, he writes that

---

[123] *Inst.*, IV, 17, 4. [124] CR 49:488.
[125] *Inst.*, IV, 17, 4. [126] Cf. CR 49:489.
[127] Cf. Yngve Brilioth, *Eucharistic Faith and Practice: Evangelical and Catholic*, London, 1930, 167. Peter Martyr has some remarkable reflections on the Eucharist as the memorial of the Lord's death and of the whole mystery of our redemption. Cf. McLelland, *op.cit.*, 283.

"these words direct us to the sacrifice of the death of Christ, without the remembrance of which the Lord's Supper is never observed in a proper manner."[128] "And indeed, it is impossible for believing souls to be satisfied in any other way than by being assured that God is pacified toward them."[129] And then he adds a pastoral note. The assurance of God's good favor can be found only in the commemorative, reflective character of the Eucharist. The assurance is not in the body of Christ, as such, but in the eucharistic body as memorial of the passion. The relation between the Eucharist and the sacrifice is neither accidental nor casual. Commenting on the words "On the night in which he was betrayed," Calvin wrote: "For the Lord might have committed this covenant-seal to the apostles at some previous time, but he rather waited until the time of his oblation, that the apostles might soon after see accomplished in reality in his body what he had represented to them in the bread and the wine."[130] The relation between the Eucharist and the sacrifice of Calvary is not an embellishment but belongs to the essential nature of what the Eucharist is. Had the body not been sacrificed for us, it would avail us nothing to receive it: "It must be carefully noted that the most conspicuous, indeed almost the whole power of the sacrament resides in these words 'which is given for you,' . . . 'which is shed for you.' For otherwise it would be of no avail that the body and blood of the Lord should be administered, had they not once for all been sacrificed for our redemption and salvation."[131] "Just as this crucified flesh will be of no value to us unless we eat it with faith, so the bare eating of it has no meaning unless it is done in reference to the sacrifice which was once offered."[132] And, though Calvin does not maintain the necessity of the sacraments in a Roman sense, he does not hesitate to say that the sacramental contact with the sacrifice of the cross through the eucharistic memorial was a necessity: "For

[128] CR 45:711.
[129] *ibid.*
[130] CR 49:484.
[131] *Inst.*, IV, 17, 3.
[132] CR 45:710.

it would be of no avail to us that the sacrifice was once offered, if we did not now feast on that sacred banquet."[133] That sacrifice, offered once and for all, unrepeated and unrepeatable—this past sacrifice is related to the living present in the eucharistic elements insofar as the sign shows his death.[134] "We do not deny that the sacrifice of Christ is so shown to us there that the spectacle of the cross is almost set before our eyes—just as the apostle says that Christ was crucified before the eyes of the Galatians when the preaching of the cross was set before them."[135]

In a passage remarkable for its sacrificial orientation, Calvin upholds the unity between the sacrifice of the cross and the eucharistic memorial of that sacrifice, a memorial brought about by the figures or signs of bread and wine. We are so grafted into Christ, so united to him that the sacrifice which he offered belongs to us as though we had ourselves offered it. "The cup and also the bread must be sanctified in accordance with this practice, in order that the wine may be a figure of the blood of our Lord Jesus Christ and the bread of his body, in order to show that we have truly fed upon him, and being as it were grafted into him may have a common life, and that by the virtue of the Holy Spirit may be united to him, in order that the death and passion that he has undergone may belong to us and that that sacrifice, by which we are reconciled to God, may be attributed and imputed to us now as if we had offered it ourselves in person."[136] Calvin's concern here is clearly to define man's participation in the sacrifice of Christ. His concern is obviously personal involvement in that sacrifice which is "attributed and imputed" to us as if we had offered it ourselves. Such an involvement is possible only when the Eucharist in some way puts us in contact with the sacrifice of the cross. The special attention given in this passage to participation in the

[133] *ibid.*, 47:153.

[134] Cf. Wernle, *op.cit.*, 106.

[135] *Inst.*, IV, 18, 11. Calvin attaches specific sacrificial importance to the breaking of the bread. Cf. CR 49:488.

[136] *ibid.*, 49:665.

Eucharist, and through it in the sacrifice of the cross, is not so surprising when we remember that Calvin's attack was directed mainly against private masses, mass without the communion of the faithful. For him the private mass seemed to be a repetition of the sacrifices and not a participation in the sacrifice of Calvary, not a feeding upon that sacrifice through the church's feeding upon its benefits.[137]

The involvement of which Calvin speaks is not only ritual but also personal. And here we see the deep devotional character of Calvin's eucharistic piety. For all the long years of polemics, the attacks and counterattacks, the problem presented by the Eucharist was not just a theological bone to be fought over. The problem was more than intellectual, more than dogmatic; it was a problem which touched the devotional life in its deepest roots. "For we do not eat Christ duly and unto salvation unless he is crucified, when in living experience we grasp the efficacy of his death."[138] "The Lord's body was once for all so sacrificed for us, that we may now feed upon it, and by feeding, feel in ourselves the working of that unique sacrifice."[139] "For the command to us to 'declare the Lord's death till he come' in judgment means nothing else than that we should by the confession of our mouth declare what our faith recognizes in the sacrament: that the death of Christ is our life."[140]

It is possible to construct a rather remarkable theology of sacrifice from texts, and not isolated texts, from Calvin's writings. Such a theology would not invalidate the polemic Calvin directed against the Roman theology of sacrifice. But it would be totally misleading to think that this more positive approach to sacrifice is characteristic of Calvin's eucharistic teaching. The texts are there, as are the beginnings of a more complete theology of sacrifice as applied to the Eucharist, but they are left undeveloped, and they stand on the

[137] Cf. Thurian, *The Eucharistic Memorial*, part 2, *The New Testament*, London, 1961, 81, 3n.
[138] *Inst.*, IV, 17, 4.
[139] *ibid.*, 17, 1.
[140] *ibid.*, 17, 37.

periphery of Calvin's eucharistic preoccupations, possibly because of the strong stand he felt he must take against the Roman position.

EATING THE COVENANT-BODY

The involvement in the sacrifice is both ritual and personal because the Eucharist is a covenant. In New Testament times the covenant pre-dates the sacrifice of Calvary and is founded rather in the sacrificial will of Christ, present in every moment of his life, but the covenant is identified with the body offered on Calvary as its most characteristic and highest expression.

The sacraments in general are defined in terms of the covenant: a sacrament is a seal by which God's covenant, or promise, is sealed.[141] It should be noted that Calvin's doctrine of the promise is here equated with his doctrine of the covenant. Only God can make a promise of grace, and only God can initiate a covenant. Each promise is given a seal which is a sacrament. There can be no other sacraments than those for which there is a promise of grace. Since these promises are specifically covenant promises, initiated by God and testified to by his Word, there can be no sacrament initiated by and testified to only by the church. The covenant promise must be found in the Word and neither customs nor rites, having an extended ecclesiastical history and tradition nor a supposed faith of the church, can supply to a covenant a promise not found in the Word. The covenant promise which is not found in the Word does not exist.

The Eucharist is the ratification of the covenant made on the cross. It was also by this relationship that Calvin reaffirmed the unity of the sacrifice of the cross and the eucharistic sacrifice. The unity of the sacrifice of the cross and the eucharistic sacrifice is not to be found in any repetition of the sacrificial act, nor even in the application of the sacrifice of the cross to man through the Eucharist, but is founded rather on the covenant. The covenant is reaffirmed in the

[141] Cf. *ibid.*, 19, 2.

body of Christ offered sacrificially on the cross, and we, by eating the bread which shows forth the cross, are made participators of the reconciliation effected on the cross. The unity between the sacrificial covenant of the cross and the eucharistic covenant is not maintained by any perpetuating of the sacrificial act, much less by a renewal of that sacrificial act, but by the one covenant-body, once offered and now eaten. "On Paul's and Luke's authority I understand the bread to be Christ's body, because it is the covenant in his body."[142] Because we can now eat that body which had been sacrificed for us, thereby sharing in that reconciliation effected through the body, we can say that "in the Supper we have both the covenant and a reinforcing of the covenant."[143] What is true of the body is also true of the blood. "He also calls the cup 'the covenant in his blood.' For he in some measure renews or rather continues, the covenant which he once for all ratified with his blood (as far as it pertains to the strengthening of our faith) whenever he proffers that sacred blood for us to taste."[144]

ALL IS THANKSGIVING

Calvin was less uncomfortable with the Eucharist as thanksgiving than with the Eucharist as sacrifice. Though the Eucharist cannot be a propitiatory or expiatory sacrifice, it can be and is a sacrifice of praise. It is a sacrifice of praise because in celebrating the Eucharist "we commemorate and declare his death, and give thanks," and this is to "do no other than offer the sacrifice of praise."[145] To offer this sacrifice of praise we must be priests, but the priesthood must not be clericalized to the point of a special sacramental priesthood. There is only one priest, Christ. He it is who offers the sacrifice of praise. "The Mediator interceding for us is Christ. He is our Pontiff, who has entered the heavenly

[142] *ibid.*, 17, 20.
[143] CR 49:489.
[144] Cf. *Inst.*, IV, 17, 1. Cf. also CR 49:489.
[145] *Inst.*, IV, 18, 17. The doctrine of Peter Martyr is cast in almost identical terms. Cf. McLelland, *op.cit.*, 110.

sanctuary and opens a way for us to enter."[146] There is only one priest, Christ, and "in him we are all priests, to offer praises and thanksgiving, in short to offer ourselves and ours to God."[147] Our priesthood in him is not to be separated from his priesthood, nor our eucharistic sacrifice separated from his. "We do not appear with our gifts before God without an intercessor. . . . He is the altar upon which we lay our gifts, that whatever we venture to do, we may undertake in him. He it is, I say, that has made us a kingdom and priests unto the Father."[148]

There is no specific thanksgiving character to the Lord's Supper which distinguishes it from the general thanksgiving character of the Christian life. "Under the second class of sacrifice, which we have called that of εὐχαριστικόν are included all the duties of love."[149] To embrace the brethren with love and with deeds of love is to act with thanksgiving. "Also included are all our prayers, praises, thanksgivings, and whatever we do in the worship of God."[150] Sacrifice of praise in this sense belongs to the very definition of the church. "This is so necessary for the church that it cannot be absent from it."[151] And just as the sacrifice of praise in this general sense belongs to the definition of the church, so it belongs to the definition of the Lord's Supper. "The Lord's Supper cannot be without a sacrifice of this kind, in which, while we proclaim his death and give thanks, we do nothing but offer a sacrifice of praise."[152] And because this sacrifice concerns the church as a whole, so all Christians are called to exercise their priesthood in its offering. "From this office of sacrificing, all Christians are called a royal priesthood."[153]

[146] *Inst.*, IV, 18, 17.
[147] *ibid.*, 19, 28.
[148] *ibid.*, 18, 17.
[149] *ibid.*, 18, 16.
[150] *ibid.*
[151] *ibid.*
[152] *ibid.*, 18, 17.
[153] *ibid.* It goes without saying that there is no question of Calvin's meaning an intercessory or propitiatory sacrifice when he uses the term "sacrifice of praise." Cf. *ibid.*, 18, 14.

"UNTIL HE COMES"

There is some disagreement among the interpreters of Calvin's eucharistic doctrine as to the importance of the eschatological dimension. Cadier maintains that Calvin gave it very little attention, while Weber maintains that he gave it strong emphasis.[154] And Janssen feels that the eschatological orientation in Calvin is stronger than in Luther.[155] Calvin nowhere treats of the Eucharist in an eschatological context at any length. And given the right occasion Calvin can disappoint one by not rising to it.[156] But the eschatological instinct is present, and it is evident when one studies the broader outlines.

The eschatological instinct is essentially Christological and rises out of the Christian's union with Christ in faith. Union with Christ is that kernel in which what is hoped for and what will ultimately be revealed is already contained.[157] He who is planted in Christ must have the same movement in time toward the Father as Christ, and must receive of the same reward given to Christ. To be joined to Christ is to be put in relation with the mystery of Christ, his death, Resurrection, Ascension, and Second Coming. Calvin's point of view is not that of the Mysterium theology of Odo Casel. His efforts are not directed to showing how we live through these mysteries of Christ with Christ, but rather to showing the meaning of these mysteries as far as the benefits we receive from them are concerned—by reason of our union with Christ through faith and the sacraments.[158]

When speaking of these mysteries in a eucharistic context, Ascension holds a central place, so much so that Calvin himself asks the question "Why do we repeat the word 'As-

---

[154] Cf. Cadier, *op.cit.*, 83; O. Weber, "Calvin," RGG³.

[155] Cf. "Die Abendmahlslehre Johannes Calvins," *Die Eucharistie im Verständnis der Konfessionen*, 216.

[156] Cf. CR 49:490.

[157] Cf. Heinrich Quistorp, *Calvins Eschatologie*, Gütersloh (no date), 12.

[158] Having spoken of the death and resurrection of Christ in *Inst.*, IV, 17, 4, Calvin proceeds to apply these mysteries to man through faith and the sacraments in *ibid.*, 17, 5.

cension' so often?"[159] The answer, of course, is to maintain a "spiritual presence," that is a presence in the Eucharist effected through the power of the Holy Spirit. Through the power of the Holy Spirit we are raised to heaven, and this raising up to heaven is the condition of receiving Christ and participating in his body and blood. "In order that we may be capable of participating we must rise heavenwards."[160] But it goes beyond this. The obstinacy with which he maintains the physical presence of Christ in heaven is bound up with the relevancy he sees in this mystery for the other Christological mysteries also essential to revelation, that is, the mysteries of the two natures in Christ, his Resurrection, the Ascension, and finally his return at the end of time.[161] Once again, his rejection of local presence is eschatological in character.

Ascension, because so obviously an end of one stage of the economy of salvation and the beginning of another, serves as a point of reference for the other mysteries, backward to the Resurrection and forward to the Second Coming. Because Christ has ascended, his body is in heaven, and therefore it cannot be included under the elements, as both Lutherans and Roman Catholics would wish. To include the body of Christ under the elements would be to bring back the body of Christ to earth before the Second Coming, which is the complement of the Ascension. "For in his flesh he is contained in heaven until he appears in judgment."[162] On the other hand the Eucharist is a foretaste of the *eschaton* and draws us toward it. How much of a *Heilsgeschichte* can be found in Calvin is still problematic but there are at this point and in other areas of his theology at least the beginnings.[163]

[159] *ibid.*, 17, 27.   [160] CR 49:488.
[161] Cf. Cadier, *op.cit.*, 44.   [162] *Inst.*, IV, 17, 30.
[163] The first to call attention to the presence of history of salvation ideas, at least in their beginnings, was Wernle, *op.cit.*, 275. G. Schrenk notes its presence in Calvin's commentary on Genesis. Cf. *Gottes Reich und Bund im älteren Protestantismus, vornehmlich bei J. Cocejus*, Gütersloh, 1923, 45. Hans Heinrich Wolf would concede crude beginnings, not as regards the substance of the covenant, but in the changing administration of the one unchanging covenant. Cf. *Die Einheit des Bundes*, Neukirchen, 1958, 65.

The Ascension, then, is a point of departure for Calvin.[164] "For if we would place him under the corruptible elements of this world, besides subverting what Scripture tells us in regard to his human nature, we annihilate the glory of his Ascension."[165] Christ cannot be corporally present in the elements because the Ascension has introduced a spatial element.[166] But beyond this spatial imperative implicit in the doctrine of the Ascension, there is also implicit an eschatological imperative, a parousial disquiet. There are two moments in this eschatological imperative: the vertical and upward, which is the *sursum corda*, and the horizontal and forward, which is the parousial expectancy proper. These two moments are related to each other not as static, independent instants in a given history, but rather as living events in the movements of history: the first, the *sursum corda*, as an enduring élan which carries the motion of time up and is drawn forward to the second moment, the Parousia, where it finds its fulfillment and meaning. The eschatological imperative ultimately destroys the spatial imperative.

First the Ascension as invitation to raise up our hearts: "For though he has taken his flesh away from us, and in the body has ascended into heaven, yet he sits at the right hand of the Father—that is, he reigns in the Father's power and majesty. . . . If we are lifted up to heaven with our eyes and minds, to seek Christ there in the glory of his Kingdom, as the symbols invite us to him in his wholeness, so under the symbol of bread we shall be fed by his body, under the symbol of wine we shall separately drink his blood, to enjoy him at last in his wholeness."[167] Calvin goes beyond calling attention to the fact that the Ascension means that the body which

---

T. F. Torrance holds a similar position. Cf. *op.cit.*, 155, 156. Cf. also Niesel, "Das Abendmahl und die Opfer des alten Bundes," *Theologische Aufsätze*, ed. Ernst Wolf, Munich, 1936, 178.

[164] "The crucial point for Calvin in a doctrine of the Sacrament is the Ascension and all that the Ascension implies." Torrance, *op.cit.*, 130.

[165] OS I:521, 522.

[166] Cf. CR 48:13.

[167] *Inst.*, IV, 17, 18.

was here on earth is now in heaven and that we should therefore seek him there. He calls to witness, if one can be ex-
cused a crude expression, the mechanics of the Ascension,
that we are to lift up our hearts to him in heaven. "When he
is borne high into the air, and teaches us by means of the
cloud beneath him that he is no longer to be sought on earth,
we safely infer that his abode is now in heaven—just as Paul
also declares, and bids us look for him from heaven."[168]

What relevance for a Christian does the *sursum corda*
have if it is nothing more than a vertical moment, an upward
movement? The full mystery of our union with Christ, even
of our union with the ascended Christ, is not complete unless
this *sursum corda*, which moves upward with Christ's Ascension, also moves forward with Christ's history. A *sursum
corda* is truncated which goes up to Christ but not forward
to Christ. Interpreting the words of the angels to the
apostles, Calvin says, "It is as if they said: received into
heaven in your very sight he has claimed his heavenly empire: it remains for you patiently to wait until he comes
again as judge of the world. For he has now entered heaven,
not to possess it by himself, but to gather you and all godly
people with him."[169] The *sursum corda* would be fragile if
Christ's body had not first risen and ascended into heaven
in our flesh. That he is flesh of our flesh, yet "bore it up to
heaven," is the pledge that "we have hope of our resurrection and of our ascension. How weak and fragile that hope
would be, if this very flesh of ours had not been truly raised
in Christ, and had not entered into the Kingdom of
Heaven."[170]

There is then a movement in Christ's history which invites
us to lift up our hearts: "Ascension follows resurrection:
hence if we are the members of Christ we must ascend into
heaven, because he, on being raised up from the dead was
received up into heaven that he might draw us with him."[171]
The eucharistic mystery is precisely the mystery of Christ as

[168] *ibid.*, 17, 27.   [169] *ibid.*
[170] *ibid.*, 17, 29.   [171] CR 52:117.

he draws our hearts upward to his body and forward to the return of that body at the Second Coming when our redemption is complete. The Eucharist cannot be defined as to its theological content or its pastoral function unless it is seen in that tension where the spatial imperative is normative but ever threatened with destruction by the eschatological imperative. Calvin gives expression to this tension in the form used in administering communion: "Let us raise our hearts and minds on high where Jesus Christ is in the glory of his Father, and from which we look for him at our redemption."[172]

[172] OS II:48. The form for giving communion is somewhat long and the above quotation is only a small part of the form.

VIII. Open Questions

Purpose and Scope

THE TEACHING of Calvin on the Eucharist has ecumenical interest today. It is not that the ecumenical dialogue should never go beyond the reformation situation—this would be sad for both Protestants and Catholics. Rather it means that some of the fears which motivated Calvin are the fears which motivate many modern Protestants. And the task Calvin set himself—whether successfully fulfilled or not is another question—is in part the task which modern Protestant theologians set for themselves. In this chapter some of the accusations Calvin raised against Roman Catholics are examined in the light of the present stage of theological development. The subject matter is limited by the accusations which Calvin raised: thus, transubstantiation will be considered only from the point of view of Calvin's accusation of empiricism; the faith context of the sacraments only from the point of view of sacramental impersonalism; the efficacy of the sacraments (*ex opere operato*) from the point of view of mechanism; the presence of Christ in grace (by reason of faith) and in the Eucharist only in relation to sacramental imperialism; the church's role in the eucharistic act only in relationship to ecclesiological divinization; and the sacramental formula only under the aspect of ritualism.

What is offered here is not a comparison between Calvin's doctrine and modern Catholic thought. This would be, from the methodological point of view, unjustifiable. Since Calvin's objections form the point of departure, the traditional categories, especially in the section on transubstantiation, have for the most part been kept, instead of using the categories of more recent theology. Further, what is here presented is not meant to be an exhaustive exposition of the topics treated, but rather indications of the direction such open questions can take. Nor is it my purpose to show what various theologians since Calvin's day have said. The specifically historical remarks are made only as introductory and to clarify the present theological situation. In short, this section is addressed to the task of indicating not what *has* been said but what *can* be said in using Calvin's objections as a point of departure.

Sacramental Empiricism

IS TRANSUBSTANTIATION THE ONLY SOLUTION?

The problem of transubstantiation is more than an ecumenical problem; it is an inner church problem for Catholics. There is room here for differences of opinion, and a broad area remains open for discussion.[1] Transubstantiation is a rational explanation of the mystery,[2] but it is a rational explanation which has as its purpose not to lay bare the mystery but to make an affirmation in the most forcible terms with regard to the mystery. If it succeeds in making the categorical affirmation but fails to clarify the mystery to everybody's satisfaction, then it has fulfilled its function. No philosophical explanation, whether logical or ontic, can touch the mystery and expose its inner meaning to the complete satisfaction of either believer or unbeliever. A certain light can be thrown on the mystery, something can be said about it in a rational way, but the explanation falls far short of the reality. Even after the rational explanation fails, as fail it must, there remains the protest: what was bread is now body.

If transubstantiation is a defined dogma, and it is, it need not be considered the only acceptable explanation. Nor is it necessary to say that the protest directed at transubstantiation is essentially dependent on a philosophical system. His-

[1] Cf. Karl Rahner, "Die Gegenwart Christi im Sakrament des Herrenmahls nach dem katholischen Bekenntnis im Gegenüber zum evangelisch-lutherischen Bekenntnis," *Die Eucharistie im Verständnis der Konfessionen*, ed. Thomas Sartory, Recklinghausen, 1961, 350.

[2] Max Thurian's observations need a slight modification. Transubstantiation is a rational explanation but it is more especially a categorical affirmation. "It was not intended to be a rational explanation of the mystery but a categorical affirmation of the reality of the presence of Christ." "The Real Presence," *Christianity Divided*, eds. Daniel J. Callahan, *et al.*, New York, 1961, 204.

torically it has been quite dependent on hylomorphism.[3] The Council of Trent considered the doctrine of transubstantiation defined. But when it said that transubstantiation was most apt, it was referring not to the dogma as such, though Trent approved of the dogma, but to the aptness of the term to express what took place.[4]

It is not possible for theologians who are handing down a tradition which has been defined to "correct" it. They are, however, free to improve it. Even Councils have improved defined dogmas, as for example Chalcedon's improvements on the Christological decrees of Ephesus. An improvement in this sense does not correct but merely expresses better what has to be said. The church leaves the door open and theologians who accept the doctrine of transubstantiation are free to seek other explanations of the dogmatic fact of the real presence. It is possible for Protestants to accept the truth of a formulation, such as transubstantiation, without accepting the purely philosophical presuppositions which stand behind such a formulation.[5] One need not be a Thomist in order to be saved.

THE SPIRITUALIST TRADITION
AND THE MATERIALIST REACTION

Down through the Middle Ages there was a spiritualist tradition having Augustine as its inspiration, which used a spiritualist vocabulary. The spiritualist vocabulary was not intended to overthrow the reality of the presence in the Eucharist. It was rather a means of excluding all materialism

[3] Grass thinks that the doctrine of transubstantiation has been so bound up with Aristotelian categories that it can no longer free itself. Cf. "Abendmahl," RGG[3].

[4] Cf. Denz. 1652.

[5] Cf. Peter Lengsfeld, "Die Einheit der Kirche und die Wiedervereinigung der getrennten Christen in katholischer Sicht," *Una Sancta*, vol. 18 (1963), 10. Karl Rahner expresses the same thought, though with a slight modification. Cf. "Die Gegenwart Christi im Sakrament des Herrenmahls," *Die Eucharistie im Verständnis der Konfessionen*, 333.

Cf. also Michael Schmaus, *Katholische Dogmatik*, vol. 4/1, *Die Lehre von den Sakramenten*, 5th edn., Munich, 1957, 295.

in conceiving the reality of the eucharistic presence.[6] This spiritualist vocabulary was the common heritage of the 9th to the 11th centuries, notwithstanding the divergencies of doctrinal emphasis of those who used the common terminology.[7] The writings of Ratramnus are especially abundant in spiritualist terminology: "To taste the Lord! Is it to feel something corporal. The Spirit invites one therefore to experience the relish of spiritual taste and invites one to think that in this drink and bread there is nothing corporal but invites one to feel the whole spiritually because the Lord is a spirit."[8] "There is nothing here to be felt corporally but spiritually. It is the body of Christ, but not corporally, and it is the blood of Christ, but not corporally. Under the veil of corporal bread and corporal wine exists the spiritual body and the spiritual blood."[9] These formulas were not invented by Ratramnus but were common in the Augustinian tradition. In this same tradition Florus wrote: "This bread of the most holy oblation is the body of Christ, not by reason of matter or of a visible appearance, but by reason of a spiritual virtue and power."[10] Aelfric of Canterbury, who inherits Ratramnus' spirit, repeats that the bread and wine of the sacrifice are changed into the spiritual body and into the spiritual blood, and that this change is itself of a spiritual order.[11] He also insists on the distance which separates the body in which Christ suffered from his spiritual body which we call the Eucharist.

From the 9th to the 11th centuries *spiritualis* is used to determine a mode of presence. The *corpus spirituale* is the body which is in *spiritualibus sacramentis*, which is celebrated *in spiritualibus mysteriis*, which one offers *in sacrificio spirituali*. It is at the same time the body which, contrary to the victims of pagan sacrifices, *non corporali mectatione sed spiritale*[sic] *ratione celebratur*, and the body

---

[6] Cf. Henri de Lubac, *Corpus Mysticum, l'eucharistie et l'église au moyen âge*, 2nd edn., Paris, 1948, 155.

[7] Cf. *ibid.* .

[8] PL 121:151.

[9] *ibid.*, 121:152.

[10] *ibid.*, 119:77.

[11] Cf. de Lubac, *op.cit.*, 158.

which is not only conceived through the Spirit, but which is offered through the Spirit.[12] At the beginning of the 12th century Odo of Cambrai sums up the spirit of this spiritualist tradition which retains sacramental realism but rejects sacramental materialism. "This host is pure, because although true flesh and blood, it is however spiritual and incorrupt. . . . This host is flesh, not carnal but uncontaminated light. It is body and not corporal but spiritual light."[13] Berengarius, basing himself on Ratramnus and quoting Augustine, Ambrose, and Jerome, asserted that one could not condemn him without rejecting the whole previous tradition. Concentrating on the old spiritualist themes with an exclusiveness alien to representatives of this spiritualist tradition, and repeating the spiritualist themes in an atmosphere completely different from that which had prevailed earlier, he gave occasion to a reaction whose best—and worst—representative is Cardinal Humbert's formulation of 1059, a formulation our Protestant friends will not let us forget. That such a declaration of eucharistic faith, so patently motivated by a crude materialism, was possible shows the vehemence of the reaction. In keeping with the reaction, eucharistic miracles, often crude and ultrarealistic, are multiplied towards the middle of the 11th century—in the time of Berengarius' activity. The reality of substantial change at the moment of consecration is also officially defined. The whole controversy led to a devaluation of the sign and the displaced attention was diverted to sacramental efficacy. Symbolism becomes something artificial and accessory. Fortunately the language of Cardinal Humbert's formulation never received general acceptance and was replaced by the formula of 1079.

THE TERMINOLOGY: FLUID OR FIXED?

The term "transubstantiation"

The term transubstantiation itself comes out of the theology of the 12th century and can be found in Magister Rol-

[12] Cf. *ibid.*, 159, 160.
[13] PL 160:1064.

and (1150), in Stephen of Tournai (1160), and in Peter Comestor (1170).[14] The 1079 confession of Berengarius speaks of the bread being *substantialiter converti*.[15] The sense here is not yet Aristotelian. The first use of the term in papal documents is found in a letter of Innocent III (1202) and is found in official conciliar documents of the 4th Lateran Council (1215).[16] When the term was first used it meant the changing of one substance into another.[17] The term was in use before Aristotelianism had a firm hold and therefore it lacked the precise philosophical content it later took on. Its use at the 4th Lateran Council was, then, nonphilosophical and was meant to mark only the profound objective reality of the change effected by the consecration, notwithstanding the permanence of the sensible aspects. The term was, however, interpreted in the Aristotelian sense by St. Thomas and most scholastic theologians. St. Thomas did not raise the tools of substance and accidents—Aristotelian precisions—to the level of a dogma. He knew that the tools were philosophical categories in the service of theology. Though the doctrine of transubstantiation was fortified by these tools, the Aristotelian physics were not incorporated by St. Thomas into the doctrine itself.[18] Trent, though strongly provoked by the reformation situation, did not canonize the hylomorphic conception or any philosophical theory.[19] From the discussions which took place at the Council it is clear that though they were satisfied with the term, and said so, their concern was not for the term itself but for the affirmation of

[14] Cr. Rahner, "Die Gegenwart Christi im Sakrament des Herrenmahls," *Die Eucharistie im Verständnis der Konfessionen*, 333; Hans Jorissen, *Die Entfaltung der Transsubstantiationslehre bis zum Beginn der Hochscholastik*, Münster, 1967, 7. However in a lecture given in Rome in December 1965 E. Schillebeeckx asserted that it was first used between the years 1100 and 1130.

[15] Cf. Denz. 700.   [16] Cf. Denz. 784, 802.

[17] Cf. J. de Baciocchi, "Eucharistie," *Catholicisme*, 1959.

[18] Cf. *ibid*. Cf. also a biblical treatment of the Eucharist by the same author. "Le mystère eucharistique dans les perspectives de la bible," *Nouvelle Revue Théologique*, vol. 77 (1955), 570.

[19] Cf. Cyril Vollert, "The Eucharist: Controversy on Transubstantiation," *Theological Studies*, vol. 22 (1961), 392.

the profound change which took place. The great Thomist theologian Melchior Cano, at the session of September 9, 1551, while insisting on the aptness of the term, remarked that the term did not appear to be of faith since the previous councils had not presented it as being of faith.[20] In this regard it should be remembered that Trent did not have the intention of giving a full and exhaustive exposition of the whole of the church's sacramental doctrine, but only of distinguishing the Catholic sacramental concept from the Protestant.[21]

Previous to Trent, in both the Middle Ages and Renaissance, some theologians became involved in speculation with regard to the physics of the Eucharist, speculations of a dubious nature. And this tradition of physicists had representatives down to the time of the reformation. The reformers reacted against the excesses of the "physicist" theologians and gave more emphasis to the symbolist tradition, which will be discussed further. This reaction is understandable in the reformation situation. However, it is also instructive for the current ecumenical conversations. The partners in the dialogue are both concerned with gaining hold of the Christian reality and the Christian experience. This experience and reality are incarnated in the temporal and contingent, in the very movement of history. Not every development in this history is desirable or to be approved. What is historical and temporal can always be defective. To concentrate on a development which both agree to be defective and to be rejected, seems a great loss of ecumenical effort. No Catholic theologian today would uphold the first confession of faith which Berengarius was forced to sign. Nor would any theologian today subscribe to the eucharistic speculations of the physicist theologians of the Middle Ages and the Renaissance.

[20] Cf. D. G. Ghysens, "Présence réelle eucharistique et transsubstantiation dans les définitions de l'église Catholique," *Irénikon*, vol. 32 (1959), 425.

[21] Cf. Hubert Jedin, *A History of the Council of Trent*, vol. 2, *The First Session at Trent, 1545-47*, New York, 1961, 386.

Substance and accidents as defined dogma?

When a contemporary man thinks of substance he thinks of matter which has a certain homogeneity, possessing an ensemble of sensible characteristics and physio-chemical, biological properties. This physical, chemical, organic notion of substance differs radically from what the medieval theologians ascribed to the term. For them substance had to do with the complete and concrete being, corporal or not, seen in its fundamental and constitutive unity, the ultimate intrinsic word of its being. Substance in this sense was to be attained only through the intellect.[22] Substance in this sense is obviously not that of the contemporary man, whose concept is scientific. Nor is it substance in a vulgar sense, which is cruder and less differentiated. As used by the Council of Trent it does have a common or vulgar sense. In the decrees of the Council the concept is still vague and undetermined. In this sense the substance of bread is simply bread, that by which bread is really bread; the sense is general but fixed and means the profound fundament of a thing. The philosophical determination of the concept of substance as *ens in se* and *subsistens per se* is not envisaged in the decrees of the Council.[23]

Nor is it to be thought that the Council defined substance and accidents as part and parcel of the dogma. The Council had no intention of raising what Aristotle and Thomas meant by substance and accidents to the level of dogma. On the other hand, the Council clearly said that the doctrine of transubstantiation is attached to the idea of substance and that one cannot, without temerity, reject it. It appears that the Council went out of its way to avoid canonizing the term "accidents." Certain theologians proposed that the word *accidentibus* instead of *speciebus* be used in the phrase . . .

[22] Cf. *ibid*. Cf. also de Baciocchi, "Le mystère eucharistique dans les perspectives de la bible," *Nouvelle Revue Théologique*, vol. 77 (1955), 571.

[23] Cf. Rahner, "Die Gegenwart Christi im Sakrament des Herrenmahls," *Die Eucharistie im Verständnis der Konfessionen*, 341, 16n. Cf. also Otto Karrer, "Die Eucharistie im Gespräch der Konfessionen," *ibid*., 364.

manentibus dumtaxat speciebus panis et vini of canon 2.[24]
The Fathers rejected this suggestion lest the introduction of
the term *accidentibus* be taken to mean that the use of the
companion term *substantia* was to be interpreted in the sense
common to the Aristotelians.[25] This is an indication that the
doctrine of transubstantiation need not be expressed only in
the framework of substance and accidents,[26] and is also an
indication of the reserve the Council exercised lest it appear
to canonize a school of philosophical thought—a reserve not
always respected or imitated.

There is little doubt as to the valuable service the terms
substance, accidents, and transubstantiation have rendered
the church. However, in an ecumenical dialogue their value is
diminished. The terms have meaning within a given frame
of reference, either the nonphilosophical frame used by the
Council or the philosophical frame used by Thomas and the
Thomists. Here they are understandable and are still service-
able for those trained in the tradition. But for those without
scholastic training they can be misleading and dangerous. In
a scientific age men are always reading the meanings of
physics and chemistry into a transphysical term. Even the
simple translation of *substantia* into substance is misleading.
And accidents is by no means a felicitous translation of the
scholastic term *accidens*.[27] It has been suggested that the term
substantia be avoided because of the equivocal meanings attached to it.[28] This seems to be especially true in an ecumenical
exchange. Even Catholic theologians among themselves have
profound difficulties because of the illusive nature of the
term. It must be admitted that Catholic theologians do not
have an adequate idea of substance and that they are faced

24 Cf. Denz. 1652.

25 Cf. Ghysens, "Présence réele," *Irénikon*, vol. 32, 427.

26 Cf. Alois Winklhofer, "Eucharistie als Opfer, Speise und Anbetung,"
Aktuelle Fragen zur Eucharistie, ed. Michael Schmaus, Munich, 1960, 94, 95.

27 Cf. de Baciocchi, "Le mystère eucharistique," *Nouvelle Revue Théologique*, vol. 77, 572.

28 Cf. de Baciocchi, "Presence eucharistique et transsubstantiation," *Irénikon*,
vol. 32 (1959), 159.

with the temptation of being precise where there is no precision.[29]

All of this is not to suggest that the whole traditional framework in which transubstantiation has been expressed should be rejected. This would be to have a poor sense of history and would also be to set aside valuable insights, clarifications, and precisions which can be of service also in ecumenical discussions. While retaining these, cannot theologians seek new ways of explaining the old truth? Transubstantiation has traditionally been tied to hylomorphism, but is it necessarily tied to it?

THE SACRAMENTAL MODE VERSUS THE EMPIRICAL

The common preoccupations of Thomas and Calvin

Calvin recognized that neither St. Thomas nor Peter Lombard approved of the confession of 1059 which was given to Berengarius to sign. Indeed, he recognized that "the schoolmen, having a horror of such barbarous impiety, speak more modestly."[30] It is remarkable to note how both Thomas and Calvin depart from the same presuppositions. Both wish to safeguard the real presence; both wish to exclude cross materialism. Both insist that there can be no change of place,

---

[29] Cf. J. Coppens, "Miscellanée bibliques," *Ephemerides theologicae Lovanienses*, vol. 33 (1957), 495-498. Coppens holds that in any attempt to explain transubstantiation, the point of departure must be the bread and wine and not the body and blood of Christ, because Christ himself is not attained directly by the power of the sacramental words, and the glorious body of Christ is immutable. The sacramental action effects something in the bread which escapes sense perception in such a way as to leave unchanged the sensible qualities. It is this something which is substance. Since we do not have a perfectly adequate notion of substance we should not attempt to make the concept too precise. Cf. F. Selvaggi, "Il concetto di sostanza ne dogma eucharistico in relazione alla fisica moderna," *Gregorianum*, vol. 30 (1949), 7-45. After examining a chemical analysis of bread he came to the conclusion that there was no reason for thinking that the minute particles, which in the flour make up heterogeneous substances, are so united to form a single substance in bread. Neither chemically nor philosophically can we speak properly of the substance of bread. The various substances which go to make up that whole is what we commonly call bread. The bread and wine are therefore not a continuous whole but a mass of many substances.

[30] *Inst.,* IV, 17, 13.

that the body of Christ remains in heaven, that Christ cannot be present on the altar or table as in a place.[31] Both are concerned about sacramental personalism.

If St. Thomas would have to choose between two possibilities, presence in a naked sign or local presence in the strict physical sense, then he would be forced to say that Christ is present only in the naked sign because local presence is absolutely excluded. The body of Christ is true body and this body is in heaven. Exclusion of any kind of local presence is a central concern for both Calvin and Thomas. But there are not, for Thomas, two possibilities but three, the third possibility being presence *in sacramento: non solum in significatione vel figura, sed etiam in rei veritate*.[32] *Veritas* is often a substitute for *substantia*. The mode in which Christ is present *in rei veritate* is the sacramental mode. St. Thomas comes to the conclusion that Christ is present substantially in the sacramental mode almost, as it would seem, by excluding the other two possibilities, either annihilation of the bread or resolution into a pre-existing material.[33] It is precisely in order to deny a material presence that St. Thomas affirms that the body and blood of Christ are present under the accidents of bread and wine according to the mode of a substance.[34]

Thomas has the same preoccupations as Calvin. He is a realist but not an ultrarealist. At no time in the eucharistic mystery is it a matter of the natural Christ, that is, Christ in his natural condition. He is not present *in propria specie* but *in specie aliena*.[35] St. Thomas is not speaking of the natural life of Christ, but of representative life. The eucharistic body and blood of Christ represent the body of Christ and the blood of Christ in their natural state.[36] There is, more-

[31] Cf. *Summa Theologica*, III, 76, 5.

[32] *ibid*. Cf. also *ibid*., 75, 1.

[33] Cf. *ibid*., 75, 3.

[34] Cf. Henry Chavannes, "La présence réelle chez saint Thomas et chez Calvin," *Verbum Caro*, vol. 13 (1959), 159.

[35] *Summa Theologica*, III, 76, 5, ad 1.

[36] Cf. Abbot Vonier, *The Collected Works of Abbot Vonier*, vol. 2, *The Church and the Sacraments*, Westminster, 1952, 286.

over, no change in the person of Christ at any moment of the eucharistic event. The body of Christ is not in the sacrament according to the mode proper to dimensions but rather according to the mode of a substance.[37] The mode of being of Christ in the sacrament is the mode of being of a substance. Substance here must be cleansed of all sensible elements. We should not think that the substance here intended is that which is under the covering of the accidents, as the kernel is under the husk. The substance, as here understood, is accessible only to the intellect.[38] Neither the senses nor the imagination can attain it. The reality is metaphysical, not empirical.

Christ in the sacrament is not in the ordinary sense of the term subject to movement or change. The body of Christ is not broken when the host is divided nor is the body of Christ moved when the host is carried in a procession. It is clear that all anthropomorphic ideas must be dismissed. When it is said that Christ is present according to the mode of a substance, what is meant is something which has nothing to do with natural presence. The presence of Christ in the Eucharist is not a natural presence which is hidden under a thin disguise. The sacramental presence belongs to an order which has nothing in common with natural presence. How could Christ, in his natural reality, be both in heaven and on earth? There will be no end to difficulties if one insists on applying concepts of the natural order to the sacramental order. It is because the two orders are so different that it is possible for Christ to be present in heaven in his natural state and in the Eucharist in his sacramental state.[39] Although material, as is every body, the body of Christ as it now exists in heaven exists in the fashion of a spiritual substance—a point Calvin could not understand, thinking that this was a denial of the humanity of Christ. As the soul in the body, the body

[37] Cf. *Summa Theologica*, III, 76, 5.

[38] Cf. the commentary on *Summa Theologica*, III, 76, 3 and 4 in *Die Deutsche Thomas-Ausgabe*, vol. 30, *Das Geheimnis der Eucharistie*, Salzburg, 1938, 501, 502.

[39] Cf. Vonier, *op.cit.*, 327.

of Christ is substantially present whole and indivisible in the entire bread and in every part of it.[40] While the body of Christ in heaven retains its proper dimensions, the body is not present according to these dimensions in the sacrament because the presence is sacramental not natural.

The spiritual tradition maintained

The eating of the sacrament is for Thomas, as for Augustine, a spiritual eating. This is not meant to exclude a real eating, but simply to exclude a material eating.[41] In all of his dogmatic assertions, Thomas guards against that which Calvin fears—a species of sacramental realism which is in fact not at all sacramental but quite clearly crude religious materialism. Much attention has been given to the realism in St. Thomas' eucharistic doctrine, and with justification; similar attention has not been given to the spiritual element in his teaching. That St. Thomas must be absolved of all accusations of sacramental empiricism is clear also to Protestant students of his thought.[42]

In the heat of the reformation controversy, theologians, such as that remarkable man Kaspar Schatzgeyer (1463-1527), were saying that Christ·is not present in the sacrament in his natural form, but in a spiritual way, *in mysterio*. He dared to use this terminology even in the reformation situation, though he had no thought of weakening the reality of the presence.[43] Trent took care to preserve these elements of spiritualism. It declared that the sacramental mode of existence is to be distinguished from the natural mode of existing.[44] However, all theologians were not as truly sacramental in their thinking and proposed a crude empiricism which St. Thomas had previously condemned. St. Thomas

[40] Cf. Matthias Joseph Scheeben, *The Mysteries of Christianity*, St. Louis, 1946, 470, 471.

[41] Cf. *Summa Theologica*, III, 75, 1, ad 1.

[42] Cf. Francis Clark, *Eucharistic Sacrifice and the Reformation*, Westminster, 1960, 417, 21n.

[43] Cf. Erwin Iserloh, *Der Kampf um die Messe*, Münster, 1952, 39-46, 57, 58.

[44] Cf. Denz. 1636.

had warned against approaching the sacrament with the imagination—here used in his technical sense.[45] There was and is the danger of using sacramental terms which are filled with empiricial content. Some wanted to substitute Christ under the thin skin of the sensible appearances and in the same volume.[46] Descartes thought that the soul of Christ was united to the material particles of bread in the manner analogous to the manner in which our soul animates the constitutive elements of our body.[47] The Cartesian Maignan imagined the complete substitution of Christ for the bread and wine which rendered the sacramental signs pure subjective impressions miraculously produced on our senses by God.

These are clearly deviations from the Catholic tradition, and are so recognized and thoroughly rejected. It will not advance ecumenical conversations to resurrect these and similar absurdities which are rejected by all. Contemporary theologians, as well as St. Thomas, cannot concede any local displacement of the body of Christ so that it comes down from heaven.[48] The real and corporal presence of Christ in the sacrament is nonspatial, noncarnal.[49] Through the consecrated bread the glorious Christ is shown and given to the church in all that constitutes his personality, his body included. The breaking of the host, the eating and digestion (or corruption) of the consecrated bread does not affect the glorious body of Christ but only the sign through which Christ offers himself entirely to God and gives himself entirely to the church. The eucharistic banquet has nothing in common with cannibalism, nor with the pagan banquet-sacrifices in which the victim is destroyed by being consumed. It should be remembered that Christ does not become bread

[45] Cf. *Summa Theologica*, III, 76, 7.

[46] Cf. de Baciocchi, "Le mystère eucharistique," *Nouvelle Revue Théologique*, vol. 77, 570.

[47] Cf. *ibid*.

[48] Cf. A. Michel, "Transsubstantiation," *Dictionnaire de théologique catholique*, Paris, 1946.

[49] Cf. de Baciocchi, "Eucharistie," *Catholicisme*.

and wine, but that bread and wine become the body of Christ, which is something quite different.[50] Nor is the sign adored when the host is carried in procession or exposed for benediction. What is adored is the signified. Not to adore the signified would be impiety and the negation of sacramental signification.

The Council of Trent rejected the teaching that Christ is present only in the use of the sacrament.[51] However there is a core of truth in the *in usu* teaching which Catholic theologians, following the lead of the Council, should not neglect, namely that the Eucharist is instituted in order to be consumed: *Institutum . . . ut sumatur.*[52] To state it in other terms, the first sentence of eucharistic doctrine is "This is my body" not "Under these appearances I am present."[53]

The eating of the Eucharist is a spiritual eating. As has been seen, both Thomas and Augustine meant to exclude by this term not a real eating but a material eating. St. Thomas explains himself further by adding that Christ can be eaten spiritually in two ways.

> In one way as he exists in his proper species, and in this way the angels eat Christ spiritually, insofar as they are united with him in the enjoyment of perfect charity and in the clear vision (which sort of bread we also expect to find in heaven), such union not being by faith only, as we have it here on earth. The other way of eating Christ spiritually is as he is under the appearances of the sacrament, insofar, namely as a man believes in Christ with a desire of receiving the sacrament; and this is not only eating Christ spiritually, but also eating the sacrament itself, a thing that does not belong to the angels; and therefore, though it behooves the angels to eat Christ spiritually, it does not behoove them to eat the sacrament spiritually.[54]

[50] Cf. *ibid.*

[51] Cf. Denz. 1654, 1639.

[52] Cf. Denz. 1643.

[53] Cf. Rahner, "Die Gegenwart Christi im Sakrament des Herrenmahls," *Die Eucharistie im Verständnis der Konfessionen*, 353.

[54] *Summa Theologica*, III, 80, 2.

St. Thomas is a spiritual theologian and, far from being an ultrarealist, he resembles St. Augustine in many ways. St. Thomas and the other great scholastics, above all St. Albert the Great and St. Bonaventure, represent a definite spiritual conception of the Eucharist, a position taken over against the crude, even sensual, materialism of eucharistic doctrine as found in the high Middle Ages. The contrast between the spiritualism of Thomas' teaching and the eucharistic materialism of the high Middle Ages was great enough to prompt the dying Thomas to exclaim, on receiving the Eucharist as Viaticum, "If I have ever expressed myself erroneously on this sacrament, I submit to the judgment of the holy Roman church. . . ."[55]

No mistake, however, should be made about this spiritual eating. St. Thomas is not talking of that pious practice of spiritual communion but of a real sacramental communion which presupposes faith and love. The flesh of Christ profits nothing if it is only physically eaten and not eaten spiritually, that is, with faith and love. Though Calvin and Thomas approach communion somewhat differently, on this point they are in agreement. Without faith and love, no man can profit by the sacrament.

FAITH AND THE EMPIRICAL FACT

Since on the level of experience, both vulgar and scientific, consecration changes nothing, one can call the consecrated host "bread" from both the vulgar and scientific point of view. The senses do not deceive us when they tell us that what we see is bread since here the senses attain their object. And since the physical and biological properties of the bread remain, it has been suggested that the word "consecration" be translated somewhat in the manner in which the Fathers spoke of "sanctifying" the elements.[56] Neuner-Roos suggests

[55] Cf. Martin Grabmann, *Thomas Aquinas*, New York, 1928, 15, 16. Cf. also Vonier, *op.cit.*, 273. For a history of the broad outlines of the problem cf. Jorissen, *op.cit.*

[56] Cf. Karrer, "Die Eucharistie im Gespräch der Konfessionen," *Die Eucharistie im Verständnis der Konfessionen*, 366

Weihe for German speaking peoples.[57] These attempts have nothing to do with detracting from the reality of what the word transubstantiation attempts to say. They are rather means of avoiding that materialism which is always a danger in sacramental realism.

Because at the level of experience, vulgar and scientific, nothing changes, contemporary theologians are not likely to panic when scientists tell them that matter consists of extremely complicated articulations of microscopic subatomic particles. Quite simply, this leaves the teaching of transubstantiation unaffected. No matter in what way scientists explain the structure of matter, the structure is imbedded in matter itself so that we can say of something that it is coal, and of another thing that it is wood, and of another thing that it is bread, and of another that it is soft. Everything has its own proper essence, an essential being that may exist in various states, but does not itself cease with the cessation of such states or conditions. This basic being is what changes in transubstantiation.[58] Partly because of the delayed impact atomic thinking had on theologians there was, immediately after the war, a long series of articles written on transubstantiation.[59] In regard to this discussion Pius XII said: "We can continue to seek scientific explanations and interpretations, but these should not, so to say, expel Christ from the Eucharist and leave behind in the tabernacle only the eucharistic species preserving a so-called real and essential relation with the true Lord who is in heaven."[60] The reality of the presence is more than a real and essential relation.

Possibly the presence of empiricism in the Catholic tradition makes it difficult for Protestants, and possibly for interested nonbelievers, to take a sympathetic view of transubstantiation. The appeal can be made to reason for light, but

[57] Cf. *Der Glaube der Kirche in den Urkunden der Lehreverkündigung*, eds. Joseph Neuner *et al.*, 6th edn., Regensburg, 1961, 296.

[58] Cf. Schmaus, *Katholische Dogmatik*, vol. 4/1, 296:

[59] Cf. Vollert, "The Eucharist: Controversy," *Theological Studies*, vol. 22, 380-421.

[60] *Acta Apostolicae Sedis*, vol. 48 (1956), 720.

ultimately only a believing Christian, Catholic or Protestant, can bow before this mystery. Faith recognizes what the senses cannot, what neither physics nor chemistry can affirm, indeed what these disciplines must deny. These mysteries do not fall under the metaphysics of pure reason, under the metaphysics of the schools. They erect a system of a new, supernatural metaphysics which is related to natural metaphysics much in the way natural metaphysics is related to physics.[61] This is difficult to submit to, but even this is not the end. For the scientist, as scientist, and for the nonbeliever it is illogical to affirm this mystery. It is a mystery of an entirely different order about which the human sciences have, in the strictest sense, nothing to say either for or against. Even while the search for new formulations goes on, it must be recognized that no biblical or philosophical insights, much less any new scientific teaching, can make this mystery acceptable to the scientist as scientist, or to the nonbeliever. The nonbeliever, if he is to remain a nonbeliever, must remain firm in his denial.[62] This is also true of the scientist as scientist.

Finally, transubstantiation is not a proof. Proof is possible where there is question of truth merely of the intellectual order. What is capable of being grasped in this mystery can be grasped only by the intellect. We can say something positive about the mystery, and negatively we can show that the truth is not incompatible with reason. But there are inaccessibilities here which surpass the intellect because they belong to a different order of reality.[63] Transubstantiation is not proof but witness. It is a protest made in faith that what Christ says is true: "This is my body."

[61] Cf. Scheeben, *op.cit.*, 478.

[62] Cf. Coppens, "Miscellanée bibliques," *Ephemerides theologicae Lovanienses*, vol. 33, 495-498.

[63] Cf. Gertrude Reidick, "Zur Diskussion über die Arnoldshainer Abendmahlsthesen," *Die Eucharistie im Verständnis der Konfessionen*, 324, 325. Cf. also David Michael Stanley, "The Conception of Salvation in Primitive Christian Preaching," *Catholic Biblical Quarterly*, vol. 28 (1956), 248.

TRANSIGNIFICATION AND THE
ENCYCLICAL "MYSTERIUM FIDEI"

In the years before the appearance of the encyclical *Mysterium Fidei*, September 3, 1965, there was some theological dissatisfaction with eucharistic theology and the problem of transubstantiation was again being discussed. The causes of the unrest were manifold: the textbook theology presupposed a medieval concept of bread as a particular kind of substance, which is no longer acceptable since bread is universally recognized to be a number of substances; the dominance of hylomorphism structured the sacraments in terms of immutable essences instituted by Christ so that the institution of the rite was given more importance than the meaning of the rite; the hylomorphic framework is foreign to contemporary existential phenomenology which is concerned with personal existence and with the personalist concept of man and his relationship to God; the tendency to isolate transubstantiation and make it an end in itself and to ignore the broad biblical, theological, and liturgical context; an impatience with the neglect of the actual presence of Christ in the eucharistic community, and the tendency in some circles to use transubstantiation to objectify Christ, to make him "a thing"; the wish to get away from a purely noetic, cognitive concept of sign and to use the phenomenological and anthropological insights into sign realities and sign-making; the desire to avoid a sensualist, physicist explanation based on atoms and molecules by using the *sacramentum-signum* as the point of departure. These were the grievances, real, understandable, and justified, and it is not surprising that they gave impetus to a restructuring of the doctrine, whatever the deficiencies of this restructuring.[64]

The restructuring took various forms; only four of them are mentioned here. The Jesuit professor, P. Schoonenberg,

---

[64] Cf. "Controversy on the Real Presence," *Herder Correspondence*, vol. 2 (1965), 388-392. Cf. also E. Schillebeeckx, "Transubstantiation, Transfinalization, Transignification," *Worship*, vol. 40 (1966), 324-338.

took the risen Christ as his point of departure.[65] The presence of Christ is the presence of the resurrected Lord. This presence does not mean, in the first instance, presence of Christ in the sign, but in the eucharistic community. He distinguishes two kinds of presence: local, which is the impersonal presence of a thing, and personal, which means an intensive reciprocal communication bringing those involved to a unity. God is only freely and personally present. In the historical Christ, God was locally and personally present; after the Resurrection he is present only spiritually and personally. Christ is spiritually and personally present in the eucharistic community before the consecration. The presence of Christ under the sign of bread and wine is characterized as real because the presence of Christ is realized in us through the sign. The sign offers us the risen body of the risen Christ. Transubstantiation does not mean that Christ comes down bodily from heaven, but means that the bread has a new meaning, a new finality, a new significance. Therefore one speaks of transfinalization or transignification. The physical reality of the bread must remain after the consecration so that it can fulfill its function as a sign.

The English theologian, Charles Davis, also spoke in phenomenological terms.[66] The bread has unity and intelligibility only in its relation to man, not in itself. Christ now gives to this same set of physical substances a new meaning, purpose, function, and relation to man. By reason of His words, the bread becomes the sign of His active presence and self-giving.

Luchesius Smits, a student of both Augustine and Calvin, came to the conclusion that transubstantiation grew out of a polemic situation with the result that the presence came to be conceived in terms excessively static.[67] His point of departure is the hypostatic union. Just as 'man becomes God' in Christ

[65] Cf. "De Werkelijke Tegenwoordigheid," *Verbum*, December (1964); "Eucharistische Tegenwoordigheid," *De Heraut*, vol. 95 (1964), 333-336; "Nogmaals: Eucharistische Tegenwoordigheid," *De Heraut*, vol. 96 (1965), 48-50.

[66] Cf. "The Theology of Transubstantiation," *Sophia*, vol. 3 (1964), 12-24.

[67] Cf. "Van oude naar nieuwe transsubstantiatieleer," *De Heraut*, vol. 95 (1964), 330-344.

so that what is human no longer has its own independence but is taken up into a higher existence, so bread and wine no longer have their own independence but are taken up into higher manner of existence proper to the risen Lord. The consecrated bread is not in itself the body of Christ, but is rather that bread which the Lord has taken. Precisely because it is taken by the Lord is the bread the body of Christ.

E. Schillebeeckx contributed an article to the controversy.[68] He casts doubts on the methodological procedure of describing the Tridentine dogma in phenomenological terms. He asserted that transubstantiation as a formulation of a natural philosophy could be set aside (the exterior garment of the dogma), but insofar as it is an expression of an ontological conversion it must be retained.

The problem raised again by these new formulations, to which the encyclical *Mysterium Fidei* especially addresses itself is that of the reality of the eucharistic conversion. "As a result of transubstantiation the appearances of bread and wine undoubtedly take on a new meaning and a new finality. For they no longer remain the appearances of ordinary bread and ordinary wine, but become the sign of something sacred, sign of a spiritual food. However, the reason they take on this new significance and this new finality is simply because they contain a new 'reality' which we may justly term ontological."[69] The encyclical thus insists that the change touches the bread ontologically.

Note should be made that the encyclical does not use the Thomistic word *accidens* but limits itself in this context to the broader and more vague term *species* or appearance. This would seem to indicate that for all its traditionalism, the encyclical wishes to adopt Trent's stand of theological non-commitment as regards any given theological explanation of the dogma.[70] The encyclical is giving rather the theological

68 Cf. "Christus' Tegenwoordigheid in de Eucharistie," *Tijdschrift voor Theologie*, vol. 5 (1965), 136-172.

69 *Acta Apostolicae Sedis*, vol. 57 (1965), 766.

70 Cf. Colman O'Neill, "What is 'Transignification' All About?" *Catholic World*, vol. 202 (1966), 205.

data of the dogma which must be maintained in any eucharistic theory. This would indicate that the encyclical also uses the term *substantia* in the sense in which Trent used it, that is, the non-Aristotelian, pre-philosophic sense or the profound reality of a thing. If one is to cast the eucharistic event in terms of *substantia*, it would seem best not to fill this term with Aristotelian content, but keep to its nontechnical, pre-philosophic meaning.

Nothing has been asserted in the encyclical which would give any credence to a physicist concept of the sacrament. The conversion which is of the entire substance of bread into the body of Christ still has nothing to do with the constituent elements of bread, neither as atoms or molecules. The conversion is a religious and metaphysical event, not a physical event. This is not a mere concession to science but a demand of the sacramental state. "The eucharistic sacramentality," says E. Schillebeeckx, "demands precisely that the physical reality does not change, otherwise there would no longer be any eucharistic sign."[71] The material elements look the same, have the same chemical properties, act in the same way, and have the same effect—nourishing the body. This partially answers the objection Calvin raised against transubstantiation, namely that if one destroys the physical reality of bread, it can no longer sign the heavenly reality; it can no longer give the body of Christ. Only on condition that the materiality of bread remains can there be a eucharistic reality.

Two absolutes of the doctrine are: at the level of the material elements nothing is changed, or whatever is experimentally observable or open to scientific investigation is left unchanged; the conversion touches the bread metaphysically, ontologically. The encyclical here gives expression to the spiritualist tradition of Augustine and the realist tradition of Ambrose. The bread is the sign of the body of Christ, but the sign is not just a symbol of Christ's active presence, nor is it just a relation to man to be explained merely phenomenologically, nor is it any kind of extrinsic attribution, but

[71] Schillebeeckx, "Transubstantiation," *Worship*, vol. 40, 337.

the bread is touched and transformed ontologically. The conversion, however, takes place within the sacramental framework. The encyclical is wary of explaining the mystery by restricting the real presence to the limits of symbolism. What is rejected here is a presence which is real in symbol but not in ontological reality. The encyclical obviously does not mean to deprive the Eucharist of its very sacramentality. This would lead only to absurdities. The sacrament remains in a sacramental category—*in genere signi*—and is not placed in a physical category. Though the change touches the bread ontologically, transubstantiation cannot take the Eucharist out of the sign category. This is not to diminish either the reality or profundity of what takes place in transubstantiation, but to insist that the Eucharist is, and remains, a sacrament.

As long as a theologian accepts the Eucharist in the biblical sense, accepts the Tridentine dogma, the ontological nature of the conversion, he can propose other affirmations alongside of transubstantiation. Even given the strictures of *Mysterium Fidei*, there is no suggestion that transfinalization or transignification are inappropriate denominations as long as the constants of the dogma are kept. Rather than abandon a phenomenological approach, it would seem that phenomenology and the broader biblical framework have the most to offer in carrying on the task of clarifying the meaning and the power of Christ's body in the Eucharist.[72]

THE CONDENSED CHRIST AND FALSE ULTIMATES

The disputes—long, heated and often without charity—which transubstantiation occasioned have often given non-Catholics a false impression. Transubstantiation is not a doctrine of the first rank. For a Catholic the doctrine that the body and blood are given is a truth of the first rank.[73] This is the mystery about which we are primarily concerned.

[72] A good example of such an attempt is Joseph M. Powers, "Mysterium Fidei and the Theology of the Eucharist," *Worship*, vol. 40 (1966), 17-35.
[73] Cf. Vonier, *op.cit.*, 315.

Transubstantiation is an explanation of a fact; it is not the fact itself. It is an after-thought, proposed because the fact was threatened.[74] Though the sacramental fact, the real presence, is a truth of the first rank, it is not an absolute. Rather it is a relative. The sacramental state is a temporal state belonging to the time of man's pilgrimage. The sacramental state does not have the quality of eternity in its essential being. Though we must adore there the Eternal and the Absolute, the sacramental form of the Eternal and Absolute is relative. It is relative to offering, eating and drinking; it is relative to union with Christ.

There is a tendency to isolate the sacrament from its use because of the insistence on transubstantiation. The Eucharist is not present only in the act of being administered—*tantum in usu*—but it is instituted to be used: *Institutum est . . . ut sumatur*. It is not just a question of bread and wine being transubstantiated into body and blood but of bread and wine being transubstantiated into the body and blood which are true food and true drink. The concern to avoid an exaggerated spiritualist vocabulary or a Capharnite vocabulary should not obscure the use of the sacrament. It is to be offered and to be eaten and drunk.

The long and tedious disputes over the "physics" of the real presence should not divert Christians from the purpose of the real presence—union with Christ. The history of eucharistic theology is a sad witness to the manner in which controversy, while fostering precision—not always an unadulterated blessing—orients attitudes toward false ultimates. The true ultimate here is not matter and form, nor substance and accidents, nor even the body of Christ, but union with Christ. One should not set aside 1900 years of history; the history of the people of God is also a type of revelation, and the truths of this history must be kept. Having said this, it must also be said that the surest guide to true ultimates is the biblical witness. The antidote to a eucharistic history often given to the materialities of a condensed Christ is the

[74] Cf. *ibid.*, 314.

Word of God witnessing to that deep personal giving of the total Christ, that meeting of Person and person in the eucharistic moment. Transubstantiation fails in its protest if this true ultimate is lost sight of.

Transubstantiation is the only explanation of the mystery of the real presence which has received official definition. This need not mean that it is the only explanation possible. As long as the truths of which transubstantiation is the protest are safeguarded and transubstantiation itself is not rejected, other solutions can be sought. Transubstantiation cannot be corrected, but it can be improved. In matters of real presence it is sometimes difficult to say what we believe and what we do not believe so that the problems here weigh heavier upon the Catholic theologian than upon the Protestant.[75] Part of the difficulty is to be found in not knowing with precision where the dividing line is between the teaching of the church in the strict sense on the one hand, and on the other, the school theology and theories about what the church teaches.[76] Protestant theologians often experience the frustration of never being able to come to grips with the problem, the boundaries of which are not agreed upon by Catholic theologians. Here the myth of monolithic Catholicism dies easily.

In an ecumenical situation this divergence of theological opinion within Catholicism points out the necessity of safeguarding at least that degree of latitude which is conceded, sometimes in begrudging toleration, to Catholic theologians. What is granted to Catholic theologians should not be denied to Protestant theologians. A greater degree of agreement than obtains among Catholic theologians should not be expected of Protestant theologians. The points of difference which divide schools of theology within the church should not be a cause of separation among Christians.[77] The ecu-

---

[75] Cf. Rahner, "Die Gegenwart Christi im Sakrament des Herrenmahls," *Die Eucharistie im Verständnis der Konfessionen*, 330, 331.

[76] Cf. *ibid.*, 331.

[77] Cf. Hans Küng, *The Council and Reunion*, London, 1961, 171.

menical conversations have as their goal one faith, one church; they do not have as their goal one school of theology. Catholic theologians should therefore not demand of others what they do not demand of themselves. When a teaching is a matter of free opinion it should not be propounded as defined dogma. And dogmas are not to be multiplied.

Sacramental Impersonalism

THE SACRAMENT AS "THING"

One of Calvin's enduring fears, a fear which helped form his Christology as well as his sacramental doctrine, was the fear of impersonalism. Impersonalism is always a danger where religious activity, especially sanctifying activity, is bound up with things—bread, wine, oil, water. The material aspects of the sacraments can easily claim more than their share of attention. Even when the material aspect is seen in relation to a sacramental act, our sacramental thinking can easily be dominated by categories from the physical world, and, more precisely, from the mechanical world. When this happens the sacraments are conceived as automatic dispensers of salvation: cause, act, effect. A sacrament is not the celebrated vase, which, without effort on our part and without our knowing it, stores up a definite quantity of grace. When Catholic theologians say that sacraments contain grace this has nothing to do with storage. Grace cannot, of course, be stored. To contain grace is a technical theological phrase, admittedly not a happy one, which is used to express the realism with which God works in and through the sacrament, also in and through the specific material element of the sacrament. Grace is not poured into the sacrament as water into a vase, ready then for use. It is perhaps time that vases be excluded from the theological and catechetical vocabulary of sacramental theology.

Sacraments are not things and they do not confer grace upon us as if we were "things," but upon us as men endowed with free will.[78] Nor do the sacraments relieve us of the duty

[78] Cf. P. F. Fransen, *Faith and the Sacraments*, London, 1958, 18.

of loving God in order to attain salvation, as Father Schillebeeckx once remarked. Nor is the church free to dispose of
the sacraments as she wills. To acknowledge that the sacraments were instituted by Christ, whether generic or specific,
does not suffice to escape the danger of magic.[79]

The Eucharist, above all, is not a "thing." It is the sacramental mystery of Christ's presence among us. It is not an
object but a subject in act. It is the act of the God-Man by
which he engages man in dialogue. The body-person man,
enters into an existential relationship with the divine body-
person, Christ. The mere repetition of communions is not
sanctifying. What is sanctifying is the personal meeting and
dialogue and union with Christ and the communion with
other believers in Christ. The eucharistic sacrifice, by virtue
of transubstantiation, has immediately to do with the body
and blood of Christ, not with his whole person, but the representative nature of the sacrifice necessitates that it terminate
in the person, Christ.[80]

FAITH AS PERSONALIST EUCHARISTIC CONTEXT

One of the temptations of religious controversy, a temptation to which both sides have succumbed, is that of making a caricature of the other's position. There is truth in the
caricature, but it is a twisted truth. The contours of the
other's doctrine are falsified to highlight that which is peculiar
to it, a falsification motivated by a polemical attitude. The
ideal should be to present the other's position without dis-
tortion, so that one's partner in the dialogue can recognize
his position. The capsulized truth should not only be doctrinally correct, recognizable as the true position of the other,
but the manner of stating it should not be such as to give a
false impression. Heiko A. Obermann can defend the following statement as doctrinally correct, yet the over-all impression is completely false. ". . . Luther's Babylonian cap-

[79] Cf. Fransen, "Sacraments, Signs of Faith," *Worship*, vol. 37 (1962),
47.
[80] Cf. Vonier, *op.cit.*, 289.

tivity of the church makes it perfectly clear that he agrees with the other Reformers in rejecting the doctrine of *ex opere operato* in a second sense, that accepted by the Council of Trent, implying a ritual which is supposed to impart grace simply by virtue of its having been properly performed, without reference to any faith or lack of faith on the part of the person for whom it is performed."[81]

The personal quality of faith and its relation to the sacraments, an easy target for doctrinal caricature, safeguards the sacraments from becoming "things" or sacred techniques. The New Testament emphasis on faith as the means *par excellence* of salvation is accepted by all. The faith which Christ demanded of his disciples and which St. Paul opposed to the legalistic conceptions of the Judaeo-Christians has a wider meaning than the faith spoken of in the dogmatic manuals. For Paul, faith is not just a naked assent to truth. Christ is not just an object of intellectual assent, though faith as a body of doctrine is also not to be excluded from the biblical concept of faith.[82] Faith in Christ means the effective presence of the living Christ in the believing community of the church and in the heart of the believer within that community.[83] Through faith, Christ—person and spirit—lives in the inner man as a personal thought and life power, so that in love and confession he brings the believer to the fullness of God's fullness.[84] Faith is not just a means by which we attain God but the possession of God, or better, his possession of us.[85] It is directed not to a promise but to a fulfilled reality. Faith in this biblical sense, then, is not faith as dis-

---

[81] "Reformation, Preaching, and *Ex Opere Operato*," *Christianity Divided*, 231, 232.

[82] Cf. Otto Kuss, "Der Glaube nach den paulinischen Hauptbriefen," *Auslegung und Verkündigung*, vol. 1, *Aufsätze zur Exegese des Neuen Testamentes*, Regensburg, 1963, 196.

[83] Cf. Gottlieb Söhngen, "Christi Gegenwart in Uns durch den Glauben," *Die Messe in der Glaubensverkündigung*, eds. Franz Xaver Arnold and Balthasar Fischer, 2nd edn., Freiburg, 1953, 22.

[84] Cf. *ibid.*, 21.

[85] Cf. Bruce Vawter, "The Biblical Idea of Faith," *Worship*, vol. 34 (1959), 447.

tinguished from charity, but specifically faith informed with charity. This was acknowledged also by St. Thomas. "It is evident that he who believes in Christ, takes him within himself, according to Ephesians III: 17, 'Christ dwells through faith in our heart' . . . by a faith which is formed, a faith which perfects not only the intellect but also the affections [*affectum*]."[86] It should not be forgotten that for St. Thomas, when he spoke as a theologian, faith without charity, *fides informata*, was not a virtue. "The act of faith will be perfect if the will is perfected through the habit of charity and the intellect through the habit of faith; not however if the habit of charity is wanting. Therefore faith informed by charity is a virtue but faith without charity is not a virtue."[87] Faith without charity is a habit [*habitus*] but not a virtue.[88]

Faith with charity terminates in a person. We seek a person and this is what accounts for our perception of credibility. We meet with a person and this is what accounts for the certainty of faith; faith is contact and coincidence with the person who is discovered, an affirmation and an act of love—a love which desires and seeks a person and, having found him, affirms in order to possess him.[89] "Everyone who believes assents to someone's words; and thus, in any form of belief, it seems that *it is the person to whose words the assent is given*, who is of principal importance and, as it were the end; while the individual truths through which one assents to that person are secondary."[90] Faith is an assent to the first truth, that is to an infallible person. *Credere Deum, credere in Deum, credere Deo* is the Augustinian formula in terms of which the ancient theologians were fond of defining faith. Where faith is concerned God is the object (not *Objekt* but *Gegenstand*), the end, and the witness so that

[86] In *John* VI: 6. OOT 20:45.
[87] In *Rom.*, I, lec. 6. OOT 20:397.
[88] Cf. *De Veritate*, q. 14, a. 6, ad 5. OOT 15:26.
[89] Cf. Jean Mouroux, *I Believe, The Personal Structure of Faith*, New York, 1959, 51, 59, 146f. Cf. also James F. Brown, "Faith as Commitment in the Gospel of St. John," *Worship*, vol. 38 (1964), 260.
[90] *Summa Theologica*, II-II, 11, 1. Italics added.

the objective principles of faith are precisely of the personal order.[91]

It is to this personalist background that the relation between the sacraments and faith belongs. In common with all scholastics, St. Thomas used the terms "sacraments of faith."[92] He also calls them "signs protesting faith" though his meaning is not as restrictive as the Protestant sense.[93] St. Thomas also uses a formula which, since the time of Luther and Calvin, has a Protestant ring to it. He says that the sacraments derive their efficacy from faith. "The efficacy of faith is not diminished [by the sacraments] since the sacraments derive their efficacy from faith."[94] St. Thomas does not mean this in what has become identified with a Protestant sense, which he makes clear by means of the distinction between *veritas sacramenti* and *veritas sacramenti simpliciter*. The "truth" of a sacrament is its supernatural significance, that is the holy presence of the sanctifying mysteries of the humanity of Christ, of the Christ who died and is risen, of the *Kyrios*, within the liturgical action. This symbolical and liturgical action is the truth of the sacrament. It contains what it signifies and it confers what it promises: Christ himself and the power of the crucified, that is grace, indeed the whole of the trinitarian God-life, which St. Bonaventure calls the *virtus Trinitatis*.[95] The sacrament becomes the "perfection of truth," that is *verum simpliciter*, when the recipient in virtue of the sacrament—and note that this means by virtue of sacramental grace—accepts Christ freely in faith and charity.

In this sense we understand St. Thomas' statement that "the efficacy of faith is not diminished [by the sacraments] since the sacraments derive their efficacy from faith." The sacrament finds its efficaciousness in faith, "not primarily,

[91] Cf. Mouroux, *op.cit.*, 13.

[92] *Summa Theologica*, III, 49, 3, ad 1.

[93] Cf. *ibid.*, 61, 4.

[94] In *IV Sent.*, d. 1, q. 2, a.6, sol. 2, ad 3. OOT 10:42.

[95] Cf. *Breviloquium* VI, 7. *Breviloquium Itinerarium Mentis in Deum*, 5th edn., Florentia, 1938, 224.

not initially, nor even fundamentally, but in the sense that the sacrament does not realize its symbolic sense or begin to achieve fully its sanctifying action until the moment when, under the continuous influence of Christ present in the sacrament, we accept him in faith and charity."[96] The specifically faith order is "older" and more universal than the sacramental order. As the younger order, the sacramental order is the "executive of faith,"[97] and the sacraments are proportioned to faith.[98]

THE ECCLESIOLOGICAL DIMENSION OF FAITH

The specifically ecclesiological character of this faith can, when forgotten, impoverish sacramental theology and give certain justification to the accusations of magic. The ecclesiological character of faith, a common teaching before the Council of Trent among Thomists, the Franciscans, early and late, and among the Scotists and nominalists, is only now returning to our theological thinking. It has unfortunately not been much in evidence since the Council of Trent.

In the liturgy there is a liturgical action which is joined to a sacramental prayer. Both the liturgical action and the sacramental prayer underwent far-reaching changes in the course of the church's history. Since the Council of Trent has defined that the "substance" of a sacrament cannot be changed,[99] and since both the Council of Florence[100] and the Council of Trent[101] say that the "substance" of the sacrament consists of matter and form, it is obvious, considered in themselves, that the "substance" of the sacrament cannot be in the outward form of the liturgical act or in the liturgical word. Rather, the essence of the sacraments consists of these two elements as aspects of ecclesial symbolic activity. The "substance" of the sacrament, then, is to be found in its mani-

[96] Fransen, *Faith and the Sacraments*, 20.
[97] Cf. Vonier, *op.cit.*, 234.
[98] Cf. *Summa Theologica*, III, 80, 2, ad 2.
[99] Denz. 1728.
[100] Cf. Denz. 1310.
[101] Cf. Denz. 1673.

fested significance,[102] a manifested significance which is specifically ecclesiological. "The essence of a sacrament lies in the outward shape of the rite as it participates in the sacramental spiritual meaning."[103] The sacrament is a symbolic act of Christ in his church, and it is only through faith in Christ that the church is able to make this spiritual signification manifest in her sacraments. Therefore, the faith of the church is necessary for the constitution of the external sacramental sign. It is only in their signifying capacity, as that external visible aspect of the church's spiritual activity in faith, that the liturgical actions and words belong to the essence of the sacrament.

St. Thomas always considered the faith of the church an integrating moment, something belonging to the essential structure of the sacramental sign. Through the liturgical prayer, which is the form of the sacrament, the church in faith immediately receives the supernatural meaning of the sacrament from the hands of Christ and acknowledges this reception. Out of the church's confession of faith is supplied what is wanting or may be wanting in the faith of the minister.[104]

Two examples of this doctrine as found in pre-Tridentine theologians other than St. Thomas are given here. St. Bonaventure (+1274): "The power which restores us is the power of the whole Trinity, which holy mother church believes in Spirit [literally *in anima*, which Fransen says means the faith of the church[105]], confers in words [*forma verborum* as an expression of this faith], and professes in sign [the matter of the rite as the visible expression of faith, or, in other words, the liturgy]."[106] Richard of Meneville (or Richardus a Mediavilla) (+1308): "The faith of the church in the passion is required in administrating the sacraments because it is by

---

[102] Cf. Schillebeeckx, *Christ the Sacrament of the Encounter with God*, New York, 1963, 96.

[103] *ibid.*

[104] Cf. *Summa Theologica*, III, 64, 9, ad 1.

[105] Cf. Fransen, *Faith and the Sacraments*, 16, 23n.

[106] *Breviloquium* VI, 7. *Breviloquium Itinerarium Mentis in Deum*, 224.

faith that in a certain manner the sacraments are continued, and it is by faith that the sacraments are joined to the passion, which joining to the passion is effected either through an explicit or implicit intention."[107] It is, then, this faith of the church receiving the meaning of the sacraments from Christ, receiving not just as instituted historically but in the very actuality and structure of the sacramental moment, which should guard against reducing the sacraments to magic.

THE PRIMACY OF FAITH

The primacy of faith is affirmed by the Council of Trent: "But when the apostle says that man is justified 'through faith' and 'freely' these words must be understood in the sense that the Catholic church has always continuously held and declared. We may be said to be justified through faith in the sense that 'faith is the beginning of man's salvation,' the foundation and the source of all justification, 'without which it is impossible to please God.' "[108] This was clear enough but some of the Fathers of the Council insisted on mentioning faith once again in chapter 7 on the nature and causes of justification of the sinner. "The instrumental cause [of justification] is the sacrament of baptism, which is the 'sacrament of faith,' *without which* no one has ever been justified." There is no doubt as to the meaning of the Latin text: *Instrumentalis (causa iustificationis) item sacramentum baptismi, quod est "sacramentum fidei," sine qua nulli unquam contigit iustificatio.*[109] The relative particle, since it reads *sine qua* and not *sine quo,* refers to the feminine word *fides* and not to the masculine word *baptismus.* The meaning, therefore, is that no one has ever been justified without faith. However, during the discussions of these chapters at the Council, there was a certain uneasiness among the Fathers of the Council. It was not that they doubted the common doctrine. Rather since Luther had championed the

---

[107] In *IV. Sent.,* d. 1, a. 4, q. 3. *Svper Qvatvor Libros Sententiarvm,* ed. Lvdovico Silvestrio a Sancto, Brixiae, 1591, vol. 4, 16.

[108] Denz. 1532.   [109] *ibid.,* 1528.

cause of *sola fide* they saw no need of strengthening his position by giving emphasis to a doctrine which was denied by no one.

Systematic theologians, not always careful historians of dogma, easily forget that the Fathers of the Council did not intend to give a complete exposition of either justification or of sacramental doctrine. Because international politics continually interfered with the sessions, they were not able to give the same attention to the doctrine of the sacraments which they had given to the decrees on justification. The canons, as we have them, content themselves with condemning the chief Protestant errors and heresies. Some of the canons, not all, are dogmatically infallible, but their purpose is limited; and the canons must be interpreted in the light of their purpose. The Fathers had no intention of giving an exhaustive exposition of all the aspects of sacramental doctrine; they intended that the decrees constitute only the necessary minimum, in opposition and contrast to the prevailing heresies. Decrees giving a minimum do not constitute a total theology. And if one is disappointed in not finding both at Trent and in the systematic writings of the post-Tridentine theologians a richer exposition of the relation of faith to the sacraments, it should be remembered that they lived and fought in a reformation situation and were often dominated by reformation attitudes. There was the tendency, especially after Trent, to narrow and harden positions, to give eternal validity to reactions by casting counter-reformation attitudes into dogmatic statements. Their basic reaction was, of course, against the reformers' *sola fide*. Nor were the theologians of the time after Trent able to assess their situation with great accuracy. They had access only to the final official texts of the decrees (published in 1563) but not to the minutes of the discussions, which, according to the norms of Canon Law, were safely locked in the Vatican archives. It was these minutes which would have enabled them to interpret the decrees with greater accuracy.[110]

[110] Cf. Fransen, "Sacraments," *Worship*, vol. 37, 33.

Sacramental Mechanism

Calvin could not understand how the attendant God of Roman Catholicism could be justified by any viable systematics. The God who could be conjured up, handled and manhandled, and dismissed by body chemistry, was not the God of revelation. The mechanism, in almost a physical sense, of Roman practice and doctrine, by which God was produced in this place and in that place, a sort of "instant" God, had, he contended, nothing to do with the God of eternity and history who determined all and was determined by none. His answer was to build a Christology and an ecclesiology which would be insurance against the packaged God of Roman Catholicism. Without attempting to answer Calvin in detail and without admitting the validity of all of his accusations but accepting his accusations as points of departure, an attempt will be made to situate the Catholic doctrine in a broad framework. Since the problem of sacramental mechanism is seen in its clearest outlines as it concerns the Eucharist in the doctrine of *ex opere operato*, it will be this point which will be our special concern here.

SACRAMENTAL STRUCTURES IN CREATION AND SALVATION HISTORY

Modern theologians, among them E. Schillebeeckx, Otto Semmelroth, and Karl Rahner, have attempted to give sacramental theology a substructure which is scriptural, patristic, and personal, and less philosophical. Sacramental activity is seen historically. Those who would make the sacramental economy the result of an independent free decree of God, though it could have been otherwise, have a too anthropomorphic conception of God. Such an attempt at sacramental theology is too disincarnate, too disengaged, and is prompted by a methodology which is not basically theological. God does not create and order the universe now according to this norm and now according to that norm;[111] rather, he has

---

[111] Cf. Rahner, *The Church and the Sacraments*, London, 1963, 30.

freely created the world with definite structures. These structures form an intrinsically coherent whole. And when they are involved in an historical process, there are changes, manifestations, precisions, and clarifications, all of which are the unfolding and fulfillment of the given structures. The developments of a later date within this historical process are not always immediately recognizable on the basis of the potentialities of the earlier stage alone. Nor will the manifestations and precisions of the earlier date always be immediately recognizable for what they are. Seen in these theological historical perspectives, it is not surprising that at every stage of development there were sacraments—even in the pagan world. Indeed it would be most strange were this not so, given the structures. Augustine found sacramental realities among the pagans.[112] All humanity receives the Word of God calling man, in some obscure but infallible way, to union with him. Through rites and religious forms, not entirely free of moral confusion and even diabolical influence, man attempts to respond to an authentic religious aspiration —to meet God, to answer him. In an obscure way the religious insight that man is in an I-Thou relationship with God is at the foundation of the strange and not entirely pure rituals. Through cultic acts and "sacraments," the pagan attempts to enter into living contact with the God who calls him. However imperfectly and confusedly, the pagan sees in the sacraments the means of maintaining the dialogic situation between him and God. And even at this stage there is a dim perception that grace never comes to man purely interiorly.[113] It is bound up with the visible and visibility. The sign of grace at this stage of historical development is a sign taken from God's creation—chosen by man and prompted by grace. It is not an embodiment of infallible grace, but the sign of man's despair and hope.

The inherent sacramental nature of redemption becomes explicit and the religious phenomena of the structures cease

---

[112] PL 33: 161, 315, 974; *ibid.*, 43:609, 610.

[113] Cf. Schillebeeckx, *Christ the Sacrament of the Encounter with God*, 13-17.

to be anonymous when Israel hears the Word of revelation. It is only through revelation that the implicit sacramental nature of redemption receives clear articulation and an unadulterated visibility. Israel as a visible people with a visible religion, priesthood, sacrifice, becomes the sign of God's presence. As an historical reality, with a history which is both profane and religious, Israel is a sign that God is the God who calls, who intervenes in history, who leads his people to victory and sometimes to defeat, and who is, in fact, the Lord of history. Israel was the first stage of the church, a visible presence of a saving grace which at the same time bestowed grace because Israel was a partial fulfillment of the saving Christ-event.[114] The sacraments of Israel sign and cause grace because Israel is the inception of the redemptive presence of Christ in his church. It is an incomplete presence of the mystery of Christ, and, therefore, Israel cannot bestow the fullness of grace but only the readiness to receive the Lord who tarries but surely comes. At this stage of historical development, the signs are chosen directly by God as seals of a covenant. They are signs of a hope which rises out, not of a primitive religious consciousness, confused and impure, but out of a hope nourished on a clear and unmistakable call: "I will be your God and you will be my people."[115] The signs are imperfect because the stage of historical development in which God unfolds his redemptive plan is still in a prophetic state. The covenant signs are the signs of God's grace, given in fidelity but received by Israel with a weary history of infidelity, punishment, repentance, and again infidelity. Israel is called to dialogue with God but she is a sullen and uncertain conversationalist, fluctuating between a loud professional rectitude and a garrulous repentance.

In the fullness of time, out of Israel, from the heart of the covenant-people, comes the one who is himself the fullness, who will keep the covenant in all fidelity. In Christ, grace is given that ultimate visibility, made flesh and tenting among

[114] Cf. *ibid*.
[115] Exodus VI: 7.

us. He is the concretization of the covenant, for in him the dialogue between God and man has its perfect realization. In Christ is the perfection of both the divine invitation and the fidelity of the human response.[116] In his covenant-body flows the covenant-blood, and in the piercing of the one and the spilling of the other the Old Covenant is rent and the New Covenant is established. The giving of the covenant-body and covenant-blood to be eaten and drunk mark that point in salvation history where the sacramental structure of creation and salvation—seen obscurely in the grim sacramentality of the pagan religions and more clearly but imperfectly in the essentially eschatological Old Testament signs—is seen most clearly and is given in the New Testament an historical permanence which can be daily experienced at the eucharistic table.

CHRIST AS URSAKRAMENT

The sacramental nature of redemption has been traced in its broad lines. Redemption is sacramental, not merely because God by a free independent act has willed it so, but because this manner of proceeding is in accord with the structures which God has built into the world. It is enlightening to study the unfolding of these structures in an historical process, but such a procedure can also be deceptive. To think that by an historical process man can uncover the clear lines of God's design is a vain hope. God's design, though built into the structures of creation, is perceivable only confusedly by the natural man. Nor is it to be thought that by some movement through history, some evolutionary process, which has Christ as its term, man can arrive at an understanding of Christ. It is the opposite which is true. Christ stands at the center of salvation history. What precedes him and the manner in which it precedes him is understandable only in terms of Christ, of what he is. And what follows, follows in the manner that it does only because of what Christ is. The

---

[116] Cf. Otto Semmelroth, "Wortverkündigung und Sakramentenspendung als Dialogisches Zueinander," *Catholica*, vol. 15 (1961), 49.

structures and their historical unfolding are not an explanation of Christ. This would make the mystery of the Incarnation a puzzle not a supernatural mystery. It would also render revelation a helpful but not altogether necessary unveiling. Christ is the explanation of the structures. The Incarnation is not only event; it is law.

The second person of the Trinity took on visible form, a human nature. This divine person is so united to humanity that every act of that humanity is the personal act of the Son of God. The divine acts receive visibility from the human nature of Christ. All the acts of Christ have redemptive value and all the acts, including those which according to their nature are acts of God (such as raising the dead and redeeming man), are given visibility through the humanity of Christ.[117] Because the saving acts of the humanity of Christ have as their source a divine person, they have a divine power to save, and because these acts are performed in the humanity of Christ, the saving acts of Christ have visibility and are sacramental. Christ, then, is the historical presence of the eschatologically triumphant mercy of God.[118] In Christ, grace is made visible, is rendered here present, and points to that triumphant eschatological reality which is already partially realized. He is both sign and reality, both the *sacramentum* and the *res sacramenti*.

CHURCH AS URSAKRAMENT

At the risk of seeming to fall into a species of sacramental imperialism, it can be said that sacramentality expresses best what the church is. It is not so expressed because at each stage of human existence man is sanctified by a sacrament: baptism sanctifying birth and childhood, matrimony sanctifying family life and adulthood, extreme unction sanctifying death. The sacramental life of the church is not to be understood in relation to the biological life of humanity. It is to be under-

---

[117] Cf. Schillebeeckx, *Christ the Sacrament of the Encounter with God*, 18, 19.
[118] Cf. Rahner, *The Church and the Sacraments*, 15.

stood in relation to the sacramental nature of the church.[119] "The church is not sacramental because she has seven sacraments, but there are sacraments because she is sacramental."[120] The relationship of the invisible grace to the visible sign in the sacrament corresponds to a sacramental structure in the church itself, to an invisible presence and a visible sign. The sacraments are, then, more than precious gifts given to the church. They are gifts rooted in her essential structure and are, in fact, acts of Christ in his Mystical Body. The view that the sacraments constitute the church is not limited to Western theologians. Speaking for Orthodoxy, Father Florovsky has stated that it expresses the Orthodox ecclesiology.[121]

Because Christ is the fundamental sacrament, therefore the church is the primordial sacrament. The structures of the Incarnation are repeated in the church. As the body of Christ, the Temple of God, she is the visible sign of the presence of God set up before all nations. She is not an empty sign. As the body of Christ she causes and actualizes that which she signs. The church is the continuation of the Incarnation. This must be said in spite of the difficulties Protestant theologians might have with such a formulation, difficulties one suspects which are more of an historical than strictly theological nature.[122] She is the enduring presence of the effective eschatological and triumphant grace of God.[123] Since she is the sign of this grace, she is also its real though partial realization. She is the sacrament which perdures. She carries

[119] Cf. Schillebeeckx, "Sakramente als Organe der Gottesbegegnung," *Fragen der Theologie Heute*, eds. Johannes Feiner *et al.*, Einsiedeln, 1957, 389.

[120] George Tavard, "Catholicity and Non-Catholic Christians," *The Downside Review*, vol. 77 (1959), 211. Cf. also de Lubac, *Catholicism*, London, 1950, 37.

[121] Cf. Georges Florovsky, "The Church: Her Nature and Task," *The Universal Church in God's Design*, London, 1948, 47.

[122] Cf. T. F. Torrance, *Conflict and Agreement in the Church*, vol. 1, *Order and Disorder*, London, 1959, 14.

[123] Cf. Rahner, "Kirche und Sakramente," *Geist und Leben*, vol. 28 (1955), 437.

through time the historicity of Christ, the spatial-temporal
quality of the Incarnation. She carries in her structure that
visible accessibility of Christ. As Christ is the *Urwort*, she is
the definitive, imperishable, enduring eschatological Word
spoken in the world and to the world.[124] Because she is the
sacrament of Christ, repeating his structures and giving enduring historicity to his visibility, she is indefectible in her
kerygma and indestructible in her sanctifying power.[125]

Such a conception, admittedly capable, as is any valid ecclesiology, of being interpreted in the sense of a triumphant
ecclesiasticism which has already done great harm, is in fact
insurance against making the juristic externals an absolute.
The church as sacrament gives prominence to the visible
church as the sign of that grace in which God and man personally meet as in dialogue. The church as sacrament is
surety against organizationalism, structural churchmanship,
and ecclesiasticism.[126] Here too the flesh profits nothing. The
flesh is here as sign and in service of the inner reality. Only
when the meta-empirical divine inner reality and the social,
visible, structural, exterior reality are related to each other
as sign and signified is the church a true sacrament.[127] Sign
and signified, cause and effect, cannot be separated. They
are separated when the church's visibility takes on an exaggerated importance. The signified is threatened when structural churchmanship and juridicism take over—then to this
degree the church is less a sacrament.

The seven sacraments are related to the church not as the
eighth sacrament alongside the seven others. The church is
much more the *Ursakrament,* the root sacrament, out of
which, as out of her very structure, the other sacraments

.[124] Cf. Rahner, "Wort und Eucharistie," *Aktuelle Fragen zur Eucharistie,*
35.

[125] Cf. *ibid.,* 34.

[126] Otto Semmelroth thinks that the concept of the church as *Ursakrament*
protects ecclesiology against ecclesiastical materialism (a leveling naturalism)
and against ecclesiological spiritualism (a false mysticism). Cf. *Die Kirche
als Ursakrament,* 2nd edn., Frankfurt, 1955, 15-26.

[127] Cf. Semmelroth, "Um die Einheit des Kirchenbegriffes," *Fragen der
Theologie Heute,* 326.

proceed.[128] The seven sacraments then can be considered as *sacramenta separata*.[129] The individual sacraments then are seen in a strictly ecclesiological context. Each sacrament is an expression of what the church is, an actualization of her essential structure and a manner of being united to the church.[130]

URSAKRAMENT IN SELF-REALIZATION—EX OPERE OPERATO

It is in this framework that the doctrine of *opus operatum* must be seen. It is the highest level of the church's actuality, the realization and concretization of what she essentially is, the *Ursakrament*. As the definitive, imperishable, enduring eschatological Word, the ultimate sacrament of God's absolute promise of victorious grace, she cannot fail. When she directs herself to particulars and actualizes herself—not to be understood in a Pelagian sense—in a given sanctifying situation, she does so not hesitantly, not dialectically as involved in a dialogue on whose outcome she is dependent and conditioned, but boldly, without fear, humbly conscious that she is the sacrament of Christ—the definitive, ultimate, unimpeachable Word spoken to the world.[131] *Opus operatum* is the effective Word of God, the actualization of what the church essentially is. She is the effective Word, the sacrament of Christ, not because she has read this into her consciousness, but because Christ has constituted her such. She is conditioned, dependent only on her relation to Christ. And here her dependence is at the farthest reaches of the absolute. Greater dependence than this does not exist. But as the sacrament of Christ she is, in her sanctifying activity, as free of conditions and uncertainties as Christ. The infallibility of

---

[128] Cf. Semmelroth, *Die Kirche als Ursakrament*, 45-68. Cf. also Rahner, *The Church and the Sacraments*, 76-117.

[129] Cf. Schillebeeckx, "Sakramente als Organe der Gottesbegegnung," *Fragen der Theologie Heute*, 389.

[130] Cf. *ibid.*, 388. Cf. also Rahner, *The Church and the Sacraments*, 76-117; Semmelroth, *Die Kirche als Ursakrament*, 47-55; Semmelroth, *Vom Sinn der Sakramente*, Frankfurt, 1960, 89-92.

[131] Cf. Rahner, "Wort und Eucharistie," *Aktuelle Fragen zur Eucharistie*, 36, 37.

her sanctifying acts have nothing to do with the pomp of her exterior liturgy. It proceeds from her very sacramentality. Nor is she compromised in her sanctifying activity by the imperfection or even corruption of her ordained ministers. The imperfection and corruption will be a scandal to the world and possibly to him who is at the center of the sanctifying situation, but they do not touch the essentials of the church's sacramentality. They obscure the sign and to this degree they threaten the inner reality, the signified. Though her ministers may threaten the inner reality they cannot destroy it. Though they be a living repudiation of the *kerygma* which they mouth and the sacred realities which they administer, they cannot destroy the efficacy of the church's sanctifying activity as the ultimate definitive Word, the radical sacrament. It is not that the church receives a power which she keeps and disposes of, for and by herself—little vials of grace stored up and bestowed as she pleases. Her efficacy is only in her sacramentality, her essential condition as the definitive Word and the primordial sacrament. This has nothing to do with storing grace. *Ex opere operato* is merely the application of what has been said about the church in general to an act of the church in particular. If she is the definitive sign, impossible to deprive of meaning, of God's grace in the world, then she is this also when she acts in a particular case.[132]

Using the theological view of the church as the primordial sacrament, one is not dependent upon the notion of instrumental causality. No objection can be taken to it when and if we choose to think in scholastic Aristotelian categories. It has meaning within its given philosophical framework. It is only asserted that there are other ways of expressing the truth of *ex opere operato* which comes nearer to the personal mystery of the church's sacramentality.[133]

The essential truth of *ex opere operato* is one to which Protestantism is attached as to no other: grace is the gift of

132 Cf. Rahner, *The Church and the Sacraments*, 24.
133 Cf. Fransen, "Sacraments," *Worship*, vol. 37, 42.

God, beyond the power of man.[134] It is a technical expression for the truth that in the order of grace, God retains the initiative throughout. The gift is wholly gratuitous and unmerited. Christ and his love always have absolute priority.[135] This is a truth which cannot be limited to merely sacramental activity. *Ex opere operato* is not a specifically sacramental truth though it has historically been identified with sacramental efficacy. It is a truth of a wider religious order. It is questionable whether one can say that a petition to God for a grace which belongs unconditionally to the sanctifying of man and the honor of God, a petition based not on merit but on the Word of Christ, is not *ex opere operato*. The conditions for *ex opere operato* can be verified also in a context which is not, in the narrow sense, sacramental.[136]

St. Thomas seems to have had some hesitation with regard to the term *ex opere operato*. In those articles of the *Summa* which are parallel to those in the *Commentary on the Sentences*, he has replaced the phrase *ex opere operato* with *ex opere Christi*, with *efficacia ex passione Christi*, and finally with *in virtute Dei et Christi*.[137] This change in terminology was commented on at the Council of Trent by the noted Dominican theologian Melchior Cano.[138] The relation of Christ to the church in her sanctifying activity is given preference to a formulation which is abstract and capable of a mechanistic interpretation.

The Fathers of the Council of Trent were, however, more influenced by a nominalist conception of *ex opere operato*. It will be recalled that the nominalists taught that, because of the *potentia absoluta* of God, man could be saved without habitual grace and without faith. The nominalist tradition

134 Cf. Louis Bouyer, *The Word, Church and Sacraments in Protestantism and Catholicism*, London, 1961, 66.

135 Cf. Schillebeeckx, "Sakramente als Organe der Gottesbegegnung," *Fragen der Theologie Heute*, 397.

136 Cf. Rahner, "Wort und Eucharistie," *Aktuelle Fragen zur Eucharistie*, 30, 31.

137 Cf. Fransen, *Faith and the Sacraments*, 21.

138 Cf. Jedin, "Das Konzilstagebuch des Bischofs Julius Pflugs," *Römische Quartalschrift*, vol. 50 (1955), 34.

attempted to safeguard the absolute freedom of God, a point which was not lost on the reformers. If either faith or grace was demanded, as indeed it was, this was only *de potentia ordinata*, that is, in a given economy of salvation.[139] This last concession to historical Christianity saved the nominalists from heresy. They added that the only requirement for the reception of a sacrament was that no obstacle be placed to grace, which in practice meant that the recipient had to be free of mortal sin. In this way *ex opere operantis* was reduced to a negative role. Such a nominalist formulation was easily interpreted mechanistically and most certainly gave a kind of theological justification to the quasi-magical practices which preceded the reformation and gave it occasion.

It was this nominalist definition of *ex opere operato* which the Council adopted;[140] this was not surprising since the majority of the Council Fathers were nominalists. The nominalist definition, quite orthodox in itself, could safely be adopted as a minimal position on which all could agree.[141] This was in keeping with the general purpose of the Council which was to condemn errors, not to expound Catholic doctrine in a balanced systematics. Nor were the Council Fathers willing to enter into the discussions and disputes which had been going on within the various schools of scholastic theology. The Council's definition of *ex opere operato* read: "If anyone says that the sacraments of the new law do not contain grace which they signify, or do not confer [the sacraments as causes of grace are not defined] grace on him who places no obstacle, but are only external signs of grace or justice received through faith, and signs [*notae*] of the Christian profession by which men distinguish between the believers and unbelievers, let him be anathema."[142] A canon agreed upon as defining the minimal conditions on which all could agree, a canon formulated to exclude a specific he-

---

[139] Cf. Fransen, "Sacraments," *Worship*, vol. 37, 34.

[140] Cf. Denz. 1606, 1608.

[141] Cf. Fransen, "Sacraments," *Worship*, vol. 37, 34.

[142] Denz. 1606. Cf. also Denz. 1608.

retical opinion, was taken by many post-Tridentine theologians to be an exhaustive definition. A reaction becomes a total dogmatic.

THE PERSONAL MOMENT AND FINAL TRUTH— ### EX OPERE OPERANTIS

On the other hand, the concept of *opus operantis* was developed in independence of *opus operatum* as the personal piety and devotion with which one receives the sacrament in virtue of which "other" graces are received. What these "other" graces are has always been something of a mystery. This concept of *opus operantis* was not that of the earlier scholastics. For them *opus operantis* was rather the personal aspect of the justification process.[143] It was not an appendage to the sacramental act, but consisted of a personal involvement because the sacramental act has to do with a person. The *opus operatum* is not opposed to *opus operantis*. The *opus operatum* implies the *opus operantis* and this not as a condition but at the very center of the sacramental structure. The recipient can bring nothing to insure the sacramental efficacy. This is also true of the minister of the sacrament insofar as he is a private person. Only Christ acting through his church, since the act is sacramental, can assure its efficacy. The saving act of Christ reaches us concretely through the ritual act of the church—*opus operatum*—and by its penetration into our souls prompts us to accept in faith and charity—*opus operantis*. When the *opus operantis* is neglected, it does not threaten the fundamental truth of the sacrament, which is not dependent on the subjective dispositions of the recipient for its efficacy, but it does threaten its final truth.[144] In preserving this final truth the *opus operantis* does have a part to play in the sacramental act. On the part of the minister all that is necessary is that he do what the church does; on the part of the recipient all that is necessary is that he receive what is given. What the recipient receives

[143] Cf. Fransen, "Sacraments," *Worship*, vol. 37, 35.
[144] Cf. *ibid.*, 40, 41.

is the unmerited grace given by virtue of the redemptive mystery of Christ. He receives no grace if he has no faith. The reception of the grace—not the giving of grace—is dependent on that inner receptiveness which is the gift of faith.

The necessity of faith is by no means excluded but rather expressly taught by the Council of Trent.[145] Therefore it is false, and, it might be suggested, slightly slanderous, to suggest that the church teaches that grace conferred on man in the sacrament is from every point of view absolutely independent of our cooperation and our faith. There is in the economy of salvation no automatic justification. An adult must intend to enter into the new life. And the subject is able *not* to receive, a point St. Thomas made with great explicitness: "The will is required by which he intends this newness of life [that is, this justification and sanctification through faith and charity], the source of which is the actual reception of the sacrament."[146] We are justified as free and responsible persons. This free acceptance in faith belongs to the personalism of man's relationship to God. A sacramental system which ignores the personal dialogic nature of man's relationship to God has no validity, no matter what distinctions are introduced to give it the trappings of Christianity. The sacramental system is not another system of justification in addition to personal justification by faith. All justification is personal because God is a person and man is a person.[147]

The measure of grace given by the sacrament, then, is not dependent on the recipients' dispositions; the measure of grace, however, which one receives from the sacrament is dependent on the quality of the recipients' dispositions.[148]

One should not be deceived by the almost metaphysical subjective certainty sometimes attached to the idea of sacramental activity. When the church acts in her capacity as the primordial sacrament, the sacrament of Christ, the definitive Word to the world, then her work is infallible, in-

---

[145] Cf. Denz. 1525f, 1559, 1606.
[146] *Summa Theologica*, III, 68, 7.
[147] Cf. Semmelroth, *Vom Sinn der Sakramente*, 93-106.
[148] Cf. Denz. 1528.

defectible. But for the fruitful reception of the sacrament, adults must have the necessary dispositions—faith and love. With regard to these necessary dispositions the individual man never has that type of metaphysical subjective certainty with which an incautious sacramental theology sometimes endows him. Just as man does not have that absolute metaphysical certitude about the state of his soul, so he does not have this type of certitude of his subjective dispositions when he engages in sacramental activity. Seen existentially, one cannot have that metaphysical certitude that the sacrament has in actual fact made him participator in the grace of God.[149] However consoling such certitude would be, it is not in God's economy to demand or to give it.

SACRAMENTAL CAUSALITY AND ECCLESIOLOGICAL
DIVINIZATION

An ecclesiology based on a Christ who is the *Ursakrament* and a church which is the primordial sacrament has not been presented to prove anything. Indeed the whole recent ecclesiological development is not conceived as text proof for any Catholic position. It is rather a theological insight, true to a biblical and patristic tradition, into the Christological mystery at the heart of which is to be found the ecclesiological mystery. How defectively this ecclesiology has been reduced to historical dimensions so that we have been burdened with a triumphant ecclesiasticism and structural churchmanship at given periods of church history, the traces of which are with us yet, our Protestant friends give us occasion to remember. However dangerous such an ecclesiology has proven historically, and however unhappy our Protestant friends are to see a relationship between Christ and the church asserted which to them looks very much like identification, yet it is such an ecclesiology which explains and justifies the Catholic eucharistic doctrine, and guards against ecclesiological sacramental divinization and ritual Pelagianism. After Trent, we attempted to build a theology against Protestantism with un-

[149] Cf. Rahner, *The Church and the Sacraments*, 25, 26.

happy results and various kinds of theological dislocation. One cannot build a balanced and healthy theology against anyone. Now that ecumenical good fellowship is more to the fore, we are tempted to build a Catholic theology for our Protestant friends. This is a happier task but the results of such an attempt are no less unacceptable as a total theology. It involves dislocations of another kind. While learning from a history which is in part unfortunate and from our Protestant friends, we can only build a theology; not *the* theology but *a* theology.

The doctrine of transubstantiation, to which Calvin took such large exception, when studied from the point of view of the ministerial act affecting the conversion, is not a question of attributing a power to one man or even to a religious society of men. The mere multiplication of religiously inclined men does not diminish their impotence before this mystery. A power of such magnitude can belong only to Christ who is the absolute and universal Lord. In his sovereignty and lordship he speaks the creative Word "This is my body." When a man holds a piece of bread and gives to it the name of body he errs.[150] Only he who speaks the creative Word from the mouth of the Word, who is he without whom nothing is made that has been made, only he can speak the new name with truth. When Christ gives bread a new name, it becomes what is named. To change the name of something is to take possession of it and to give it a new essence. A name is not an external tag but the expression of the inner nature. If Christ names the bread extended to man "body" it makes the bread body. This also is an expression of the cosmic implications of Christ's lordship over all creation. A creature is precisely that which the Lord of creation says that it is. In the act of transubstantiation it is always the Lord of creation who works.

The church in her ministerial activity can effect transubstantiation not because she is a religious society, not because

---

[150] Cf. de Baciocchi, "Le mystère eucharistique," *Nouvelle Revue Théologique*, vol. 77, 579.

of any moral probity, not even because in so doing she fulfills a command of Christ. Only Christ can effect transubstantiation and this must not be forgotten even when the
ministerial activity of the church is spoken of. Transubstantiation is effected in the church and through the church only
because she is the sacrament of Christ. As Christ is the *Ursakrament*, so she is, because she is the sign of Christ, the primordial sacrament. She carries the historicity of Christ
through the centuries, speaking, as the sacrament of Christ,
the creative word of Christ, "This is my body." It is not sufficient to reduce the role of Christ here to instituting the Eucharist and a priesthood to which the Eucharist is entrusted.
The causal relationship goes deeper than just the execution
of a commission, even if that commission is divine. Christ
working in his church is effective here. It is his Word which
is spoken, it is his creative Word that effects the conversion.
There is a real presence of Christ after the consecration, because there was an actual presence of Christ in the community and the celebrant before the consecration.[151] He who
is to be remembered first of all presents himself to be remembered, being present in the worshiping community in a hidden manner. It is not simply that the memory of the Lord
makes him present; that would not be sufficient. Rather his
presence makes us think of him as being present and, in fact,
discloses his hidden presence.[152] This must be held to unless
one would reject the whole history of salvation category so
dear to the Fathers.[153] Nowhere in the Fathers is it mentioned
that it is the priest who changes the bread and wine into the
body and blood of Christ. Such an idea would be completely
foreign to the patristic mentality. The work of conversion is

[151] Cf. Johannes Betz, *Die Eucharistie in der Zeit der griechischen Väter*,
vol. 1/1, *Die Aktualpräsenz der Person und des Heilswerkes Jesu im Abendmahl nach der vorephesinischen griechischen Patristik*, Freiburg, 1955, 245.

[152] Cf. Heinrich Schlier, *Die Zeit der Kirche*, 2nd edn., Freiburg, 1958,
248. The encyclical *Mysterium Fidei* speaks of the presence of Christ in the
church as she offers the sacrifice of the mass. Cf. *Acta Apostolicae Sedis*, vol.
57 (1965), 763.

[153] Cf. Betz, *op.cit.*, 345, 346.

the work of Christ.[154] If one wishes to speak in more philo-sophical categories one can say that in this eucharistic mo-ment Christ is the *minister principalis* while the priest is the *minister instrumentalis*, or the priest acts *in persona Christi*. These scholastic formulations make Christ the real consecra-tor, but they also lend themselves to a mechanistic interpreta-tion when taken out of their philosophical framework. This terminology lacks the personal dimension, though it has the advantage of theological precision. Historically, possibly through no inherent defect, it has become identified with a theology which gave too much attention to the instrumental role of the priest, which resulted in a glorification and possi-bly divinization of the instrument.

To give transubstantiation a personalist theological struc-ture will lessen the temptation to magic. Even in an authen-tic religion there is danger that man will think that he can dispose by his own initiative the divine realities over which he is thought to have dominion by reason of a given for-mula faithfully and correctly pronounced. Black magic would be the use of such power against the divine will, while white magic is concerned to use the power in accordance with God's will and intention. White magic is basically ritual Pelagianism. A more mechanistic view of sacramental cau-sality, even granted the institution of the sacraments by Christ, lends itself easily to white magic and ritual Pela-gianism because the final decision as to when and how the power shall be used is in the power of man.[155] Ritual Pelagian-ism will always remain a danger in an existential situa-tion no matter how personalist the theological substruc-ture of sacramental theology. It would, however, be a dubi-ous methodology to judge a theological structure by the pos-sible but real dangers such a structure could occasion when existentially reduced to pastoral practice. On this basis there can be no valid sacramental theology, Catholic or Protestant.

[154] Cf. *ibid.*, 316, 317. Betz notes also the absence of any theology of secondary causality of the church in the patristic writings of the fathers before the Council of Ephesus. Cf. *ibid.*, 203.

[155] Cf. Fransen, "Sacraments," *Worship*, vol. 37, 47.

To avoid such an eventuality, the sacraments should not be considered exclusively as means of grace but rather in relation to the person of Christ, the actual presence of Christ, the sacraments as the acts of Christ.[156] Also the lordship of Christ in the sacramental act and state should be given its place. As Christ in obedience to the Father is crucified, he still, even on the cross, remains the Lord. And in the eucharistic event he is also Lord.[157] Even after the consecration he is Lord, given, it is true, for us, but not to be disposed of as though he were a thing.[158] One cannot have Christ, possess him, as one would possess material objects. However, the greatest assurance against ritual Pelagianism is the faith-context of all sacramental activity, faith of the individual and faith of the church. These are necessary components of the total sacramental complex. Without the faith of the individual and the faith of the church, sacramental activity can have no meaning.

Sacramental Imperialism

Calvin accused the church of sacramental imperialism, this tendency to think of the meeting between man and God exclusively in sacramental terms so that there was no justification but sacramental justification; there was no union with Christ but sacramental union, and in the mass the whole of the faith was exhausted. Especially in the matter of union with Christ, the Eucharist had exercised a will-to-power. It were as though the only presence of Christ was the real presence in the Eucharist.

Without attempting to answer Calvin but using his accusations as a point of departure, the presence of Christ in grace (and faith) and the presence of Christ in the Eucharist will

---

[156] Cf. Leo Scheffczyk, "Die Eucharistie als Sinnerhellung des christlichen Lebens," *Geist und Leben*, vol. 33 (1960), 176.

[157] Cf. Schmaus, "Christus, Kirche und Eucharistie," *Aktuelle Fragen zur Eucharistie*, 67.

[158] Cf. Paul Neuenzeit, *Das Herrnmahl*, Munich, 1960, 132. Cf. also Schmaus, *Katholische Dogmatik,* vol. 4/1, 300.

be discussed. To give some limitation to the matter, the scriptural concept of presence and union will be limited to St. Paul.

BODY-PERSON AND PRESENCE IN ST. PAUL

Canon Cerfaux asserts that when St. Paul speaks of "Christ" or of "the body of Christ" he is not speaking of a pneumatic or a mystical Christ, but is always referring to the real historical person who was crucified, who died, was buried, rose, and ascended. Christians, says Cerfaux, do not form a mystical Christ but belong to the real organism of Christ's risen person.[159] Père Benoit concurs saying that the body of Christ is not a supra-personal collectivity but rather the full organism of the animated body-person who rose from the dead and now reigns as Lord in heaven.[160] Behind such a contention are two principles which govern St. Paul's thought. St. Paul writes as a Hebrew and thus he speaks of the body not as a neutral object, nor in terms of the Greek anthropology with its body-soul dichotomy. As a Hebrew he thinks of the body as an animated and corporeal person whose intellectual activity and affective life are contained and revealed under the sensible aspect of somatic experience.[161] Also Paul thinks of Christ as a corporate personality.[162]

In speaking of the union between a man and a harlot and the union between Christ and a man, the σῶμα is not merely

[159] Cf. *The Church in the Theology of St. Paul*, New York, 1959, 269. On this important biblical concept cf. also Heinrich Schlier, "The Pauline Body-Concept," *The Church, Readings in Theology*, New York, 1963, 44-58; J. A. Schep, "Flesh and Body in the New Testament: the Pauline Epistles," *The Nature of the Resurrection Body*, Grand Rapids, 1964, 81-106; W. David Stacey, *The Pauline View of Man*, New York, 1956, 121-211. This section is especially indebted to Barnabas Mary Ahern, "The Christian's Union with the Body of Christ in Cor, Gal, and Rom," *Catholic Biblical Quarterly*, vol. 23 (1961), 199-209.

[160] Cf. "Corps, tête et plérôme dans les epitres de la captivité," *Revue Biblique*, vol. 63 (1956), 7.

[161] Cf. J. A. T. Robinson, *The Body: A Study in Pauline Theology*, Chicago, 1952, 26-28.

[162] Cf. E. Best, *One Body in Christ*, London, 1955, 20-30.

the physical element of the body-soul anthropology. It is the whole self as an animated body expressing the dynamic of a full personality.[163] Again in Romans VII: 4, the language is strongly physical. Paul speaks of the Christians belonging to the risen body of Christ. This use of the physical can hardly go beyond that which St. Paul uses in Ephesians V: 25, where he likens the union between Christ and the church to the union between man and wife. In both cases the relation is that of a body-person to a body-person.[164] The introduction of the relationship between Christ and the church into a discussion of the relationship between Christ and the Christian does not introduce a *tertium quid*. It is not possible to divide the union with Christ into individual and social aspects. The personal union with Christ is simultaneous with the incorporation into the church.[165] The same is, of course, true for the union which we attain with Christ in baptism. In no place can one find an indication that faith alone, that is without baptism, is meaningful as regards sanctification. It is taken for granted that when Paul speaks of a believer that he is speaking of one who has been baptized.[166]

If St. Paul identifies the Christians as the body of Christ, he cannot have meant this in a mere organizational sense. There is only one body, one Spirit, one Christ; into this Christ the Christian is baptized. The Christian is one body with Christ, baptized into his body-person. "Paul therefore teaches clearly that Christian life involves a real and personal union between the individual $\sigma\hat{\omega}\mu\alpha$ of the Christian and the individual $\sigma\hat{\omega}\mu\alpha$ of the glorified Christ, a union so intimate that the body-Person of the Savior alone functions as the directive spiritual force. If they are two in one spirit, there is no

---

[163] Cf. Ahern, "The Christian's Union," *Catholic Biblical Quarterly*, vol. 23, 202.

[164] Cf. *ibid.*, 203.

[165] Cf. Rudolf Schnackenburg, *Die Kirche im Neuen Testament*, Freiburg, 1961, 148.

[166] Cf. Kuss, *op.cit.*, 206. It should be noted that in St. Paul baptism plays a larger role than the Eucharist. Cf. Neuenzeit, *op.cit.*, 230.

doubt to whom the spirit belongs: 'I live, now not I, but Christ lives in me.' "[167]

When St. Paul speaks of union with Christ in a context which is specifically ecclesiological, First Corinthians 12 and Romans 12 for instance, he does not use the Greek noun σῶμα to denote a collectivity or social group. He always uses the term in the sense of a real physical body.[168] And this body is the body of the personal Christ. The temptation to think rather in terms of a body apart from Christ yet vivified by him must be set aside. It is in this light that Canon Cerfaux dares translate First Corinthians 12 as "You are a body, a body which is that of Christ."[169]

When St. Paul taught in Ephesians III: 17 that Christ dwells in our hearts through faith, he was speaking of the same reality though in terms of a real presence. To re-emphasize the intimacy of this presence St. Paul says in Galatians IV: 6 that Christ dwells in our hearts according to his Spirit. When we have the Spirit of Christ, then we do indeed belong to Christ, for in this Spirit of Christ we have new life, the life of Christ. Christ and the Spirit of Christ dwell in the inner man through faith as a personal life-form and as a personal thought-form so that the believer lives with the life of Christ and thinks with the thoughts of Christ.

DEVALUATION OF PRESENCE OF CHRIST IN GRACE

It is somewhat difficult to absolve the systematic theologians from the full charge of sacramental imperialism in regard to the real presence. The very real presence of Christ through faith (and baptism), a presence which St. Paul expressed in a physical terminology to the embarrassment of a later theology, was slighted in favor of the real presence of Christ in the Eucharist. Since the presence of Christ in the Eucharist was a substantial presence and the real presence of Christ by reason of faith was not substantial, theologians

---

[167] Ahern, "The Christian's Union," *Catholic Biblical Quarterly*, vol. 23, 204.

[168] Cf. *ibid*., 206.

[169] *op.cit*., 277.

came to talk of the presence of Christ by reason of faith as presence improperly so called, while the real presence of Christ in the Eucharist is real presence properly so called.[170] This is unabashed, if unconscious, sacramental imperialism. This is all the more difficult to justify since Paul lays all the stress upon that which later theologians called a presence in the improper sense of the term. When the presence of Christ through faith is a presence which is only improperly so called, then Paul erred, and should have spoken in entirely other terms.[171] It goes without saying that Paul also speaks of the presence of Christ in the Eucharist in realistic terms. When St. Paul says that "because the bread is one, we though many, are one body, we who partake of the one bread"[172] the "one body" is still the individual body-person of the risen Christ. The "many" form one body because in communion we become con-corporeal with Christ. It was the Eucharist which was an important element in shaping Paul's doctrine on the church as the body of Christ.[173]

Paul's thought is concerned with the inner character of the presence of Christ through faith and grace—presence as an enduring act, presence as an existential contact, presence as a dynamic identification between the believer and the body-person of Christ.[174] The weight of Paul's thought is not taken up with the real presence of Christ in the existential sense of scholastic theology, though he believes and teaches the real presence of Christ in the Eucharist. No objection can be taken to the formulation of the doctrine of the eucharistic real presence in the substantialist terminology, in the metaphysics of essence and existence, but its relationship to the real presence of Christ through faith should not be such that the scriptural emphasis on the presence of Christ through faith is lost. And, given the elements of eucharistic empiri-

---

[170] Cf. Söhngen, "Christi Gegenwart in Uns durch den Glauben," *Die Messe in der Glaubensverkündigung*, 16.

[171] Cf. *ibid.*   [172] First Corinthians X: 17.

[173] Cf. Ahern, "The Christian's Union," *Catholic Biblical Quarterly*, vol. 23, 205.

[174] Cf. *ibid.*, 208, 209.

cism in our history, one can justly wonder whether an undervaluation of the presence of Christ by reason of faith is not motivated by a concept of the presence of Christ in the Eucharist which is crassly physical. It should not be forgotten that the presence of Christ in the Eucharist is a spiritual presence as well as a substantial presence. One also wonders whether an excessive objectivization is not behind such eucharistic thinking. The real presence of Christ in the Eucharist is esteemed at the expense of the real presence in faith because the Eucharist is thought of as a "thing." The same want of personalist categories in the manual theology of grace as is found in the eucharistic doctrine is partly to blame for the characterization of the presence of Christ through faith and grace as presence in the improper sense.[175] If grace is objectified into a "thing," then, of course, it is much more difficult to speak in terms of presence.

The presence of Christ by reason of faith is a spiritual presence and not a corporal presence. This presence should not be esteemed less or thought to be "presence" in only an improper sense of the term. What use would the corporal and substantial presence of Christ be to us if it were not for the spiritual and actual presence of Christ in us through faith?[176] In the Eucharist man is given a visible corporal sign of the presence of Christ in man through faith. The Eucharist-presence of Christ is ordered to that real presence of Christ in faith. The Fathers of the church from Augustine to Thomas understand the presence of Christ through faith as primary and more comprehensive.[177] Though later scholastics were guilty of sacramental imperialism, giving an emphasis to the eucharistic presence at the expense of the presence in grace, St. Thomas was not so guilty.

[175] Cf. Hermann Volk, "Gnade und Person," *Gott Alles in Allem*, Mainz, 1961, 114, 119. Cf. also Semmelroth, "Der Verlust den Personalen in der Theologie und die Bedeutung seiner Wiedergewinnung," *Gott in Welt*, vol. 1, *Philosophische Grundfragen, Theologische Grundfragen, Biblische Themen*, ed. Herbert Vorgrimler, Freiburg, 1964, 321, 322.

[176] Cf. Söhngen, "Christi Gegenwart in Uns durch den Glauben," *Die Messe in der Glaubensverkündigung*, 21.

[177] Cf. *ibid.*, 23.

There is a distinction between the two modes of presence. The real presence in faith is a spiritual effective presence, while the real presence in the Eucharist is a substantial "corporal" presence. The distinction should not be pressed. Care should be taken that the eucharistic presence is not deprived of its spiritual character and that the presence in grace is not thought of as unsubstantial in the sense of unreal. Our difficulty in describing and distinguishing the two modes is due in part to the poverty of language. In the realm of the completely supernatural, the concept of effectiveness and of an effective reality has more levels of meaning than when one remains within the realm of the purely natural. Reality and real presence mean something in the spiritual world, and something quite other in the corporal world. The distinction between the two modes of presence should be made, but that is not sufficient. It should be shown that the sacramental mode of presence is ordered to the presence of Christ in grace and faith.[178]

However defective Calvin's doctrine of the real presence, his primary theological insight is unassailable: that the presence of Christ through faith is primary, and that the presence of Christ in the Eucharist is ordered to the presence of Christ in faith and grace.[179] The contemporary Catholic theologians of the Eucharist (Jungmann, Pascher, Schmaus, Congar, Danielou, Söhngen, Rahner, Schillebeeckx, Fransen, Semmelroth, to mention a few) have stressed the personal union with Christ, which is the first step toward a better theological formulation of the relationship between the presence of Christ in grace and the presence of Christ in the Eucharist.

Note should also be made of the encyclical *Mysterium Fidei*, which speaks of a real presence of Christ in the ministry of the Word, in the liturgical assembly of the faithful, in

[178] Söhngen has worked out the differences between the presence of Christ in grace and the presence of Christ in the Eucharist and has cast them in thesis form. Cf. *ibid.*, 25-28.

[179] It would be interesting to know how much Calvin's doctrine of the real presence in the Eucharist was influenced by the neglect of the presence of Christ in grace.

the priest-liturgist, in the sacraments and, finally, in the Eucharist.[180] Therefore the concept of real presence cannot be limited to the Eucharist, though there is a proper eucharistic mode of real presence. The encyclical will help to bring back the concept of the real presence from its eucharistic isolation and place it in its proper context: the whole mystery of Christ present in the worshiping community and in the soul of the individual Christian.

Ritualism

Calvin could not abide the Roman practice of preaching to bread. He contended that the Word of faith was directed not to the bread but to the people. Also he took exception to the naked ritualism by means of which the body of Christ was rendered present when matter and form were brought together. This was, in his mind, another manifestation of the mechanism of Roman ritualism, the complete disregard for that personal meeting in love and triumphant grace which is the eucharistic event. For Calvin the Word which made the sacrament was the preaching of the Gospel.

THE WORD AS SPOKEN TO PERSONS

The mysterium theology of Odo Casel which displaced an Aristotelian notion of sacramental causality (specifically instrumental causality) with a less philosophical, more scriptural and patristic concept of sacramental causality, laid the broad groundwork for a theology of efficacy which went beyond the matter-and-form theology of the manuals. However debatable certain aspects of Odo Casel's theories are, his contribution here is unquestionable. Karl Rahner and E. Schillebeeckx, using the phenomenological tools of Heidegger, Scheler, Husserl, Merleau-Ponty, and Buytendijk as well as contemporary exegesis, Catholic and Protestant, have attempted to give formulation to a theology of the sacramental form which understands the form in somewhat the same

180 Cf. *Acta Apostolicae Sedis*, vol. 57 (1965), 762-765.

terms as did Calvin: the Word of faith proclaimed to the church.

When the church speaks the Word of God, this Word in the mouth of the church does not lose its character as the Word of God.[181] The Word spoken in the church must remain the Word of God. It is not possible to imagine a Word of the church as something alongside of the Word of God. What do the terms "Word of the church" mean? There is no Word to be proclaimed but that Word which Christ speaks in her, through which he is present in the church.

This Word of God is an inner moment of the sanctifying act of God. The Word is more than the proclamation of a doctrine, more than the prophetic declaration of a coming judgment. It possesses more than that with which the faith of man endows it. It is, as is the eternal Logos, a true creative Word, transforming the inner man, bringing him not just *kerygma*, but giving him in grace participation in the divine nature. As the inner moment of the sanctifying act of God, this Word of God participates in the property and characteristics of the saving act of God in Christ and in the church. As Christ is the Word of God, not merely proclaiming salvation, but effecting salvation, so is also the Word of God which the church speaks. It effects the salvation which it proclaims. As Christ is the Word who does what he declares, so is the Word in the mouth of the church. This Word of God, as Christ himself, is the saving event which effects that which it shows forth. The Word is the presence of the grace of God in the church. "Word" means here what it means in its profane use in Greek, namely a public and festive announcement or proclamation of an event which is taking place.[182] Through the proclamation the existential event, in its character as that which is now taking place, is made present. In the proclamation its presence is revealed.

The highest realization of the effective Word of God, seen

---

[181] Cf. Rahner, "Wort und Eucharistie," *Aktuelle Fragen zur Eucharistie*, 12.

[182] Cf. Schlier, *op.cit.*, 249.

as the presence of the saving act of God within the church, is a sacrament.[183] The Word character of the sacrament should not be lost in a scholastic distinction. Whether one speaks in the patristic vocabulary of the Word and the element, or in the hylomorphic vocabulary of form and matter, the participation of the element or the matter in the Word character of the sacrament should not be set aside. The element or matter, as well as the liturgical gestures, participate in the Word character of the sacrament. The matter says something, reveals something which is otherwise hidden. This is to say the matter, as well as the form, is Word. This can only be forgotten at the risk of compromising the personal character of a sacrament. If one opposed matter and form, somewhat in the manner of the manuals, and gave the form the exclusive rights to the Word character, the sacrament would not possess the full quality of being addressed to a person. The material element seen apart from its Word character has a fixity about it, a woodenness, and an indetermination. It is the Word which is the decisive factor. St. Thomas, who here represents a long patristic tradition, says that the efficacy of the sacraments comes from the form.[184] When the material element is considered as participating in the Word character of the sign, to which both matter and form belong, it partakes of that personal openness and communicability of the person who speaks. Since grace is the personal communication of God, the proclamation of such grace must retain the personal character of the Word. The sign of this grace, however it is considered, however its constitutent parts are distinguished, is a personal Word addressed to a person. The sign is essentially Word.

The Catholic unfortunately tends to think that the highest form of the effective Word of God, the sacramental Word, is the only effective Word of God.[185] The question can be

---

[183] Cf. Rahner, "Wort und Eucharistie," *Aktuelle Fragen zur Eucharistie*, 23.

[184] *De Articulis Fidei et Ecclesiae Sacramentis*. OOT 27:178.

[185] Cf. Rahner, "Wort und Eucharistie," *Aktuelle Fragen zur Eucharistie*, 31.

asked: How is the sacramental Word and its effectiveness to be distinguished from the nonsacramental Word and its effectiveness? The Catholic, whose thinking on sacramental efficacy is in terms of *ex opere operato*, can, in the light of what has just been said, define a sacrament as the Word of Christ in the mouth of the church which confers grace *ex opere operato*. It will be difficult, with such a definition, to find a specific difference between the effectiveness of the sacramental Word and the nonsacramental Word, even though it be granted that the Word spoken in the church is variable in its effectiveness. One can consider *opus operatum* as the highest level of actuality of the church, as the act of her self-realization as the *Ursakrament*, as the Word of Christ spoken to the world. Even when the church speaks the Word of Christ in a context which is decidedly not sacramental, the Word of Christ is effective. Whatever the final solution to the problem, so much seems clear. The two realities, each with its effectiveness, should not be seen as completely distinct and disparate, but rather as phases and moments in one and the same process. The final solution is not of interest here. The concern at the moment is to indicate that the Word of Christ in the mouth of the church, when she speaks as *Ursakrament*, whether it is spoken in a sacramental or in a nonsacramental context, effects what is said, does what is proclaimed, though in variable degrees.

THE WORD AS ENDURING CONSTITUTIVE MOMENT

What is true of the sacraments in general is true of the Eucharist to a greater degree of intensity. The Eucharist, says Karl Rahner, is Word.[186] It is Word because here the Word made flesh is given substantially, because what is here proclaimed is not just the substantial fact of Christ but the whole mystery of Christ.[187] In proclaiming the death of the Lord, the Eucharist proclaims, by reason of the *anamnesis*, the whole mystery of Christ. The Eucharist proclaims the saving acts of Christ, first his death, but also Incarnation,

[186] Cf. *ibid.*, 45.   [187] Cf. Schlier, *op.cit.*, 250.

Resurrection, Ascension, and even the Parousia.[188] The Eucharist is Word because it is the highest realization of what the church is, the Word spoken to the world. The Eucharist is Word in its essential being because, in contradistinction to the other sacraments, which make present the grace of the Word, the Eucharist is the Word itself, the very source and fountain of grace.

Situating the Eucharist in its liturgical framework, the question is now asked: what is the specific relationship between the enduring real presence of the substantial Word and that sacramental formula, the Word of faith, which had been spoken over the sacramental elements? Is the formula a religious device which brings about the eucharistic fact? Is the Word of faith to be thought of as a formula to be said, or a *kerygma* to be proclaimed? To whom are these words addressed? Is it sufficient to consider them as addressed to the elements? Does one preach to bread? Does the Word of faith have an enduring reality somewhat in the manner in which the substantial Word has a real enduring presence?

There is no sacrament without *kerygma*, just as there is no proclamation of the Gospel which does not prepare, accompany, and perfect the sanctifying activity of the sacraments. St. Augustine, formulated the famous principle of sacramental theology: "Let the Word be added to the elements, and it will become a sacrament."[189] For Augustine the "Word," which makes up the sacramental liturgical prayer, was essentially the eternal Logos, the Word of the Father. No man has seen the Father but the Word, who is in the bosom of the Father, and this Word has proclaimed him. The manifestation of the Father, which is the Gospel, is the *verba evangelica*, a technical expression for the words of the Gospel to be found in the liturgical formula. This is to say that the eternal Word himself is present in the sacramental mysteries with the salvific mission which he received from the Father, and he it is who proclaims and effects the sac-

---

[188] Cf. Betz, *op.cit.*, 197.
[189] PL 35:1840.

ramental event. The sacramental form, which is the Word in the mouth of the church, although spoken in the church by means of a minister, is the Word of the Word, the Word of the High Priest. It is the High Priest who is present and who proclaims the Father, who here and now carries out the salvific mission given by the Father, who acts personally in the sacramental event.

The *verba salvatoris*, which are the form of the Eucharist,[190] are not to be looked upon primarily as the effective cause of the sacraments. Rather they are the enduring constitutive moment of the sacramental sign.[191] The sacrament, this or any sacrament, exists as long as the sign exists. If you destroy the sign you destroy the sacrament. Of the constituents of a sign, elements and Word, the Word is the more essential since the efficacy of the sacrament comes from the form or Word. The function of the words of institution, which are the form of the Eucharist, is not completed by their effecting the sacramental presence. It is through these Words that the sacrament comes into being and the sacrament is not meant to stand without the Words. The Words are both effective cause and constitutive element. The Words are an enduring moment of that by which the sacrament is and remains. A word is a human reality and it is not absolutely dependent upon nor simply coexistent with phonetics. The word spoken by lovers, the promise, the warning exists also after the phonetic experience is passed. Karl Rahner adds explicitly: the species would not be real sacramental species if they were not in an enduring manner determined through the words of institution.[192]

The relationship of the Word to the Eucharist is not unlike its relation to the church. Where the true Word is, there is the church, for the Word constitutes the church.[193] It is the

[190] Cf. Denz. 1320.

[191] Cf. Rahner, "Wort und Eucharistie," *Aktuelle Fragen zur Eucharistie*, 48.

[192] Cf. *ibid*.

[193] Cf. K. H. Schelkle, "Das Wort in der Kirche," *Theologische Quartalschrift*, vol. 133 (1953), 289.

Word which separates the believers from the unbelievers. The Word brings sight to some and non-sight to others, hearing with understanding to some and hearing without understanding to others. The faithful are those called by God through the Word, and the Word gathers the church. The Word always calls the church and constitutes it. And having constituted it, warns, judges, purifies, strengthens, nourishes, edifies it.[194]

The church is essentially a sacramental structure because in her are repeated the structure of the Incarnation, because she is the fulfillment of the law which is the Incarnation, the *Ursakrament*. But her character and structure are also that of the Word. She is the definitive Word spoken in the world, to the world. All that can be said of the sign can be said of the Word. This is also the traditional patristic language. St. Augustine called a sacrament the *verbum visibile* and the Word the *sacramentum audibile*.[195] The church is always the church of the Word, because in her the whole Word of God to the world is spoken. The Word is a permanent constitutive moment of the church. The Word is not something that is merely said by the church and in the church. There is always a temptation to think the physical element more important than the Word, to prefer seeing to hearing.[196] To give in to such a temptation would be to threaten seriously the spiritual life and also ecclesiology and sacramental theology. If the church were to lose her sacramental character she would cease to be the church, and if she lost her Word character she would cease to be the church. While the Word endures, the church endures. While the Word endures the sacrament endures, because the Word is an enduring constitutive moment of the church and of the Eucharist.

[194] Cf. *ibid*.

[195] Cf. PL 35:1840; *ibid*., 37:969.

[196] Cf. Schelkle, "Das Wort in der Kirche," *Theologische Quartalschrift*, vol. 133, 278.

THE CHURCH WHO HEARS

To whom are the words of the form addressed? Is it sufficient to consider them as addressed to the elements? The church is the community of believers and this she is because she has heard the Word and believed it. It is in hearing the Word that she believed. The hearing of the Word is not to be limited to a once and for all instrumental causality, a formula producing an "instant" God. The hearing of the Word is bound up with the inception of faith and also with the continuance of faith. Should the Word fail in the church, then the faith of the church would also fail. If she is in continual need of the sacraments of faith to sustain her life and to give her structure, she is in need of the Word of faith to sustain her life and to give her structure.

The Word is spoken in the church and spoken by the church. The Word is also spoken to the church. She speaks the Word of Christ but she is also a hearer. She hears the Word because it is the continuing source of her faith, because as church she knows sin,[197] because she knows that the Word is also judgment, and because the Word is the source of her fidelity. All of this she does as church.

The words of institution are no exception. They are spoken to the church even when the number of the faithful is only one or two. Words are signs of life and communication and they involve persons who are revealing themselves in the act of naming or communicating something. Language is a social institution which demands involvement that "things" cannot give. When a person speaks a word he reveals meaning and also himself, to which he rightfully expects a response of some kind, if not a verbal answer. A "thing" cannot give this response. The sacramental form of the Eucharist is not an exception to the laws of language.

The words of institution were first spoken in a community, and they were spoken to persons. It would be intolerable to think that Christ spoke the words as a formula, di-

---

[197] Cf. Schnackenburg, *op.cit.*, 70.

recting them to the elements. Nothing in the text would support such a supposition. Afterwards in apostolic times when the words were repeated in the eucharistic act, they were not considered as a formula, nor as directed to the elements.[198] The words proclaim the death of the Lord to those whom the Word has called and has gathered, the local church. The Word is always addressed to persons; the Word is always spoken to be heard because that is the nature of a word. In this case the Word is proclamation and one does not proclaim to bread.

The words of institution are directed to the church, she who hears in faith. She is obedient and submissive to the Word which is preached, because faith is obedience.[199] The Word comes out of the oral tradition, the unwritten Word which the church guarded and faithfully handed down. Though she knows what she believes without the written Word, because she is prior to it, and because the unwritten Word is the *Urwort* of the *Urkirche*, she is obedient to the written Word as to the oral tradition.[200] The Word has an autonomy and independence, and it does not receive its authority from the church. As the church is the obedient dispenser of the sacraments she is the obedient dispenser of the Word. She is no more free to tamper with the truth or the proclamation of the Word than she is free to tamper with the realities of the sacraments. To both she is bound in the obedience of faith.

The words of institution taken out of context can mean various things to various people. Even in context they have historically been variously interpreted. It is to the believing church that the Word is spoken and out of obedience to the proclamation, the truth of which she recognized and proclaimed before the written Word existed, she accepts, accepts because she believes. The Word which is spoken to be heard, and the church who hears—and hears as church not just as a

---

[198] Cf. Neuenzeit, *op.cit.*, 132, 133.

[199] Cf. Kuss, *op.cit.*, 198.

[200] Cf. Schelkle, "Heilige Schrift und Wort Gottes," *Theologische Quartalschrift*, vol. 138 (1958), 271.

collection of individuals—are so ordained one to the other that were one to cease to exist, the other would not be that which it is.[201] The words of institution which come out of the believing church, and mean the substantial presence of the Lord, these Words are heard by the believing church. Were the church not to hear—in the theological sense—there would be no sacrament. It is also true that the faith of the church in the real presence of the Lord is grounded in his Word, under which he is present. What was at least tolerated by a later Protestantism—that the reality of the sacramental presence is dependent on the faith of the individual—is rejected. But what is false of the individual is true of the church as a whole. If the believing church did not hear the Word, which is the effective Word, then it would not be that effective, victorious Word; it would not effect that which it declares, the presence of the Lord.[202]

The words of institution, the *verba salvatoris*, to use the formulation of the Decree to the Armenians, are spoken to the church who hears—again in a theological sense. The words are not addressed to the elements, though they substantially affect the elements. When spoken to the church who hears and believes, the words effect what they declare, the body of Christ. The Word of the sacrament of the altar, which means the presence of the Lord, is born or brought forth from the faith of the church, who hears the Word, as also the faith of the church in the real presence of the Lord is borne by his Word under which he is present. The Word from God and about God contains not just the Word of Christ but precisely Christ, the Word.

However truncated and crippled the specifically ecclesiological meaning of the Eucharist is in the private mass, as far as its visibility is concerned, it would introduce a ruthless narrowness into the scriptural accounts to assert that the Eucharist is not valid since the Word is spoken to the bread and

[201] Cf. Rahner, "Wort und Eucharistie," *Aktuelle Fragen zur Eucharistie*, 50.
[202] Cf. *ibid*.

not proclaimed to a number of believers.[203] However illegi-
timate a mass said alone by a priest, the validity of the sacramental event is not destroyed by such an abuse, though its
deepest meaning is greatly obscured. The scriptural account
is in no sense concerned with our concept of validity. On
the other hand, the meaning of the Eucharist is not exhausted by its mere validity. The ideal, scriptural as well as
traditional, is that the Eucharist be celebrated by a community of believers who are the local church. And if the words
are spoken to the church who hears (hearing understood
theologically), the ideal must remain that the words be heard
by the church (hearing understood here in its physical
sense). Since the *verba salvatoris* are a proclamation, they
are ideally proclaimed in an elevated voice, and, on more
festive occasions, sung. One does not whisper a proclamation.

[203] Cf. Denz, 1747.

Conclusion

It was the goal of Calvin's theological and pastoral endeavor to restore divinity to God. In eucharistic terms this meant that the immediate imperative was not sacramentality but union with Christ. To attain this objective he partially developed and partially inherited a eucharistic personalism and a greatly modified objectivism which stood in contrast to the eucharistic mechanism, empiricism, and to the raging objectivism of Rome's sacramental doctrine and liturgical practice as Calvin conceived them. In both ecclesiology and sacramental theology he sought inwardness and interiority. To this end he built a Christology which hesitated to unite too closely divinity and humanity, an ecclesiology which was careful not to identify ecclesiological structure too readily with the Christ who sanctifies, and a eucharistic theology which would be wary of weakening the important distinction between sign and signified.

There is one Lord, one Sanctifier, the sovereign Christ working through the Spirit. Therefore Christ is never a "givenness" in such a manner that he can be given to unbelievers—that is, to unworthy persons. He cannot be commanded, nor contained, nor condensed, nor reduced to material physical accessibility. Though truly, even substantially, present and truly given, Christ cannot be placed at man's disposal. What man has to do with in the Eucharist is not a domesticated, attendant God, who is conjured up in this place and that place, here, there and everywhere, conjured with a formula, summoned by clerical command and dismissed by digestion, a sort of "instant" God. The eucharistic Lord is the sovereign Lord, the uncommitted who is never so committed as to lose the freedom of his lordship.

Though the Eucharist is actually an ecclesial reality with strong sociological implications, the remote and often unspoken theological determinant is the pure will of God electing, predestining, and sanctifying. Though the church is the body of Christ, the theological point of departure for this body is not Incarnation but election and predestination.

Calvin's ecclesiological, Christological, and pneumatological fears of divinization of the church and the sacraments, together with the intellectual pre-history of reformation theology, moved him to reject the direct and immediate involvement of the church and the sacraments in the sanctifying activity of Christ. But it was also his Christology and Pneumatology which demanded and brought about a eucharistic doctrine of strong realism. The reality of the given body is not less real because the presence is spiritual. In Calvin's vocabulary spiritual presence means presence through the power of the Holy Spirit who guarantees the objectivity of the eucharistic reality by giving the worthiness (that is, faith and love) to the believer, and by effecting the presence of Christ's body. Beyond the objectivity of the Spirit in act there is, in the sacramental economy, no objectivity.

The structuring of his thought in terms of the two centralities, Christology and Pneumatology, enabled him to give a dogmatic unity to his teaching on the Lord's Supper. Calvin's Platonic background and the dialectic posture of his Christology and Pneumatology assured both complete commitment in sacramental realism and the freedom of the uncommitted in a signed presence. The *opposita*, the foci of the ellipse related in union and tension, must be retained at the expense of canceling out large areas of Calvin's eucharistic teaching. This dialectical structure in Calvin is definitely not to be attributed simply to Platonic and neo-Platonic influences. Rather the dialectic is essentially biblical, a dialectic which is further accentuated and reinforced by the Platonic structure.

Calvin did not think that he was fighting over a theological bone when he engaged in the eucharistic controversies. Through his involvement in the controversies he meant to free the church from Rome's penchant for idolatry, ecclesiological and sacramental—that vice essential to the Roman ethos. This was the great medieval sin which wrought so much havoc among believers. Instead of parading around with the Bread of Life or offering it up in sacrifice, it should be fed to believers, who weak and afflicted, need this bread from heaven. Calvin's dominant eucharistic motivation was pastoral.

APPENDIX

Critique of Calvin's Eucharistic Doctrine

CALVIN's doctrine, as Calvin himself, belongs to an historical context, and it would be methodologically unjustified to criticize him or praise him outside of the historical conditions in which he formed his doctrine. The references to the state of eucharistic doctrine or of liturgical practices in the Roman church of pre-reformation times are only references to elements and are not meant to be a total picture. Because Calvin was reacting against abuses, real or imagined, the state of theology and of liturgical life was not as hopeless as the citation of only shortcomings would make it appear.

The Disengaged Christology

Calvin has built into his system a certain assurance against a successful attack. The dialectic theologian is more than a little difficult to come to grips with precisely because he is dialectic. He who cites a tendency to separate divinity and humanity in Christology, and sign and signified in sacramental theology, can, in turn, be attacked for neglecting Calvin's ellipsoidal tension. However, even given Calvin's dialectic, and given his norm of distinction but not separation, it is distinction and not union which has the preponderance. In both his Christology and his sacramental theology there is tension and union, but more tension than union. The emphasis on the distinction and tension rather than on the union never goes so far as to rule out sacramental realism. But the sacramental realism is as strong, or as weak, as is the Christological realism. The reluctance of Calvin to take over the Johannine "divinization" of the humanity made it difficult to build a sacramental theology in which the sign and signified stand in a true incarnational relationship. When the union between the divine and human is somewhat intermittent, then sacramental realism is weakened. When one proceeds from a Christology characterized by disengagement, there is little possibility of a full sacramental commitment. A Christology which tends to see humanity as a tool of the Logos without having within itself the power of giving life will, while still insisting on the Incarnation, lack the full incarnational dimension. Such a Christology will, when translated into sacramental terms, assert sacramental realism but will, in fact, find it difficult to give that sacramental realism a fitting theological structure. There is always recourse to dialectics, to ellipsoidal union and tension, and this recourse is not without some justification. However, is the mystery given adequate explanation, even given its completely supernatural character, by means of a dialectic logic? Is the sacramental reality only a dialectic reality? Are the Platonic tools of image and participation adequate to express the biblical Christological and sacramental reality? Is the Platonic dialectic true to the biblical? Does not the preference given to tension at the expense of union represent a transcendentalism which refuses to take the Incarnation seriously? Can it be said that the sharp and aggressive distinction between sign and signified corresponds to the biblical realism? Does not the distinction to the point of opposition between the divinity and the humanity in Christ, and between the sign and signified in the Eucharist make it extremely difficult to arrive at any real theological synthesis according to the law of the Incarnation?

It is worth noting that though the *Extra Calvinisticum* is found in the Geneva Catechism (1543), the Heidelberg Catechism (1563), and in the Second Helvetic Confession (1566), it is consciously and of set purpose omitted in important reformed confessions. The Huguenot Confession (1559), the Scotch Confession (1560), and the Dutch Confession (1561) omit it.[1] In these confessions the eucharistic teaching is not cast in terms of the *Extra Calvinisticum*. The

[1] Cf. Paul Jacobs, "Die Gegenwart Christi im Abendmahl nach reformiertem Verständnis und das römisch-katholische Gegenbild," *Gegenwart Christi*, ed. Fritz Viering, Göttingen, 1959, 24, 27.

Calvinist tradition itself set aside Calvin's teaching on this point, and this during Calvin's lifetime.

Calvin would insist that grace is given in the sacraments, and also through the sacraments, but this is not in virtue of a real incarnational sacramentalism. The predominance given to distinction rather than union renders the sacraments occasions of grace. The Scotist view of occasionalism is not in great favor among Roman Catholic theologians because it lacks the qualities of incarnational realism. However, it has never been condemned and Calvin's occasionalism is an acceptable theory of sacramental causality. It should be noted that Trent did not define that the sacraments cause grace, but only that they confer it. Many Romans at the time and previously held that the sacraments are "causes" of grace only in an extended sense.

Seen in the ecclesiological framework of sacramental divinization, ritual Pelagianism, liturgical clericalism, and structural churchmanship, Calvin's desire to disengage divinity from an incarnational system which, in his eyes, had become manipulation of the divine, is quite understandable. Calvin's criticisms of Rome, however, are often excessive. One cannot go to Calvin for an objective presentation of either Roman faith or practice.

In his attempt to restore divinity to God he postulated a Christianity in which the sacraments, and indeed the church, were always in a prophetic state.[2] The disengagement from the full sacramental commitment and from an ecclesiology which accepted the sacramental structure as constitutive gave to both sacraments and church a dynamic and a logic of a different order. Though less incarnational, it was more spiritual. The acts of God in the sacraments and in the church were not without reference to the temporal, material elements in both. But the intermittent quality of the divine and human relationship and of the sign and signified relationship, makes the whole ecclesiological and sacramental reality

[2] Cf. Yves Congar, *Vraie et fausse réforme dans l'église*, Paris, 1950, 439, 440.

understandable only in terms of God's will. The God who is free is so disengaged that the sacramental act is that occasion on which he freely and directly gives grace. This safeguards the sacraments from sacramental divinization and imperialism and gives an immediacy to the God-man relationship. However, the sacramental moment is too spiritual. It lacks the bone and flesh quality of the Incarnation. One understands Calvin's problem better when one recalls that when Calvin attacked the Roman teaching on sacramental efficacy he attacked the causality of the elements more than the causality of the sign as sign. Because the discussion took this direction, based on an erroneous concept of Roman doctrine, it was natural for Calvin to shy away from a more incarnational view of sacramental causality.

The efficacy of the sacrament is related to God's saving will and not to a sacramental economy, and is further subordinated to the direct will of God as regards predestination; only the predestined receive the body of Christ. The evangelical passion for God's freedom and sovereignty made it impossible for Calvin to conceive of God committing himself to a sacramental engagement of real incarnational dimensions. God is not bound; what is more, God cannot bind himself! Calvin will not permit it.

His strongly soteriological Christology and his even more pronounced Pneumatology made him see Christ almost exclusively in the role of Mediator and Reconciliator. After the Ascension the work of sanctification is given over to the Holy Spirit in such a way that the humanity of Christ is not given its due in the work of sanctification, though the humanity of Christ is not excluded entirely from the life of the church and the life of the individual Christian—hardly a possibility in a theology as Christocentric as Calvin's. Christ is more than the Giver of life, more than the Redeemer; he also enters into the work of sanctification, and this without detriment to the traditional role the Holy Spirit has played in sanctification. If Calvin's thesis that what is true in Christology is true in Pneumatology is valid, and vice versa, then even in virtue of this principle Christ should be more in evidence in the work of sanctification.

Calvin guards the Holy Spirit against earthly contamination the way he guards the divinity of Christ against too close contact with the humanity of Christ. So great was Calvin's fear of institutionalizing the Spirit and of thus giving credence to an already overblown divinization of the church, that he hesitates to make the Holy Spirit a true interior principle of the church. The Spirit does not dwell in a permanent way in the church but rather visits it on proper occasions; the Spirit is not attached in a permanent way to the minister of the church but rather attends his work. Can one have a true sacramental and ministerial activity in these terms?

The Immediacy of Him Who Is Unbound

Calvin was not uninfluenced by a nominalist tradition which he partially rejected and partially adopted. The nominalists were also concerned about the absolute freedom of God. The *potentia absoluta* was precisely that; it could not be limited by any necessity.[3] This left God free, but it also left him disengaged. And the sacramental system is a witness to both the God who is free and the God who is engaged and committed.

A nominalist way of thinking was not unacceptable to the reformers and to many who remained within the church who saw it as an escape from the sacramental crudity evidenced in the first formula which Berengarius was forced to sign. The decrees of Trent themselves are cast in true sacramental modes, but the discussions at the council were not free of naturalistic thinking, and they are witness to that against which Calvin was reacting.[4] Late medieval sacra-

[3] Cf. Chapter I. Cf. also Erwin Iserloh, *Gnade und Eucharistie in der philosophischen Theologie des Wilhelm vom Ockham*, Wiesbaden, 1956, 67-77.

[4] Cf. Franz Xaver Arnold, "Vorgeschichte und Einfluss des Trienter Messopferdekrets auf die Behandlung des eucharistischen Geheimnisses in der Glaubensverkündigung der Neuzeit," *Die Messe in der Glaubensverkündigung*, eds. F. X. Arnold and Balthasar Fischer, 2nd edn., Freiburg, 1953, 151, 152.

mental theology, caught in this nominalist current, did not think in terms of the Redeemer living forever in his humanity. When referring to the Eucharist it was in terms of the Corpse of God, God's passion, God's Martyr, God's suffering.[5] Christ, the God-man, as the living head of the church, who, through the Holy Spirit, animates the church and in a mysterious way continues his work in the sacraments, was forgotten. The church was not incarnational in a truly religious sense, and therefore she became a social and even an economic phenomenon and gave occasion for structural churchmanship. Her role in the spiritual life was minimized. God works directly with the soul. This is clearly seen in the German mystics, in the *Imitation of Christ* and in the other products of *devotio moderna*.[6] Here the church is rarely mentioned and, when mentioned, is the place or occasion of sanctification. The sanctifying work of God is effected immediately. This theology, which was not entirely unfruitful, was not unrelated to the symbolist vocabulary and the materialist reaction which Berengarius occasioned. And it was in such an historical context that the doctrine of transubstantiation developed. It was, in part, a reaction against a nominalist reluctance to permit God to bind himself in an incarnational way.

It must be admitted that Calvin's doctrine represents sacramental objectivity. If it is an objectivity which is elusive and intermittent and entirely spiritual, it is objectivity nevertheless. Just because the reformers took as their point of departure the exaggerated sacramental objectivity of the 16th century does not mean that they rejected all sacramental objectivity.[7] Calvin was wary of reducing the Eucharist to the "givenness of a thing." Calvin's essential intuition here is theologically correct. The sacraments are not God packaged, Christ condensed, ready for use. Calvin's application of this truth to the communion of the unworthy also has theological

[5] Cf. Joseph A. Jungmann, "Liturgy on the Eve of the Reformation," *Worship*, vol. 33 (1959), 514.

[6] Cf. Chapter I.

[7] Cf. Chapter VII.

authenticity. Christ reserves that total giving of self to those who are already joined to him in faith and charity, and are true members of the worshiping community. But is it necessary to fall into a species of Donatism to safeguard authentic theological truths? Is there a correspondence between the kind of generous and gracious objectivity in the incarnational commitment, unmixed and undivided, and the hesitancies of a sacramental commitment where Christ is offered to all but not received by all? Should fear of sacrilege and blasphemy and a manipulated God be the norm? Are man's temptation and man's sin or God's mercy and liberality the boundaries of sacramental objectivity?

Calvin's eucharistic doctrine was a child of controversy. It is natural that in a prolonged debate such as that which he carried on with the Zwinglians and the Lutherans, that the point of debate be given more than its due. This, in part, accounts for the impression that for Calvin, the Eucharist is the real presence. Though there are other elements in his doctrine, real presence is given such prominence that the other elements of thanksgiving, covenant, "sacrifice," memorial, and the eschatological dimension do not receive their rightful attention. The Eucharist is more than just real presence.

The terms rationalist and spiritualist have often been applied to Calvin. In the reformation context they were characteristically applied to Zwingli, an attribution frequently based on a false notion of what Zwingli taught. If we take the terms in the sense contemporary Lutherans applied them to Zwingli, then we must say that Calvin is neither rationalist nor spiritualist, though history cannot be greatly blamed for labeling him such. The reformation controversialists leveled the accusation of rationalist with an open-handed liberality. He who denied either the Lutheran or Roman eucharistic doctrine was almost automatically tagged a rationalist. However much one might defend either the Lutheran or the Roman position, it would be nothing short of absurd to contend that he who rejects the one or the other, or both, is necessarily a rationalist. Calvin rejected both and was most certainly not a rationalist. There was a certain inevitability about his logic—spare, tight, unadorned, unrelenting—which called down upon his head this epithet.

The accusation of spiritualist, in the reformation sense, must also ultimately be rejected. But here history has some justification. There is a basic ambiguity, even considering his dialectic method, in his assertions that we receive the body of Christ substantially but not his physical body, that we receive the effects of his body but not a heavenly essence, that we receive more than the effects but the body is not a "givenness," that the body remains in heaven and is not on earth but is given substantially and spiritually. Giving due consideration to the entirely supernatural quality of the mystery, this has all the appearance of hedging. Refuge is found in the mystery. He rejects transubstantiation because of the difficulties involved, transfers the difficulties to another level, and proposes a doctrine which involves obscurities as dense as those he rejected.

Though Calvin was at pains to safeguard the honor of the glorified Christ, his eucharistic Christ was not that of the glorified Christ, but of the crucified Christ. Ecclesiological triumphalism and divinization had made any theology of glory suspect. Also the ubiquity teaching of Luther forced him to insist upon the integrity of Christ's humanity, an integrity which he identified with the body of Christ in its earthly condition. The body which we receive in the Eucharist is, indeed, the body of the crucified, but it is the body of the crucified who has now risen and reigns glorious in heaven. And the spiritual qualities such a body assumes do not destroy its humanity. In his attempt to safeguard the humanity of Christ he conceived the body of Christ as it now exists in heaven in a fashion which is too material, too closely identified with the body of the crucified.

Pneumatological Impersonalism

Calvin reacted against a sacramental mechanism which had found expression in decadent scholasticism. The concept of *ex opere operato* in the catechisms and preaching of the period of scholasticism after Thomas was dangerously close to that of magic, and it is little wonder that Luther and Calvin both understood *ex opere operato* from the side of men rather than from the side of God.[8] The decrees of Trent do not interpret *ex opere operato* in this mechanistic sense, though at the time of Trent the nominalist theology had become infected with a somewhat overmechanistic interpretation of sacramental efficaciousness.[9] During the pre-reformation period and also during Trent, the concept of instrumental causality did a great deal of harm and it continues to do so because of the danger of mechanism.

Calvin reacted against such mechanism and impersonalism, and he assigned himself the task of casting the eucharistic doctrine in a personalist theology. This he did by setting his eucharistic doctrine within the framework of union with Christ. This made it possible for him to say that we receive Christ substantially. We already receive Christ substantially by faith. Because of sacramental imperialism, Roman theologians tended to think of the presence of Christ by means of faith and grace as presence improperly so called and only the presence of Christ in the Eucharist as presence in the proper sense. Calvin rightly reacted against this conception. And not unlike others who react, he went too far. He rejected an element in the sacramental presence which must be retained. To say that we receive Christ substantially in faith can be quite orthodox. But it is quite something else to say that union with Christ in faith and union with Christ in the Eucharist take place in the same way. To this degree his doctrine of union with Christ in the Eucharist wants sacramental realism.

Instead of explaining the very real sacramental efficacy by means of instrumental causality, he explained it by the role he assigned .to the Holy Spirit. It was the Holy Spirit who

[8] Cf. Peter Fransen, "Sacraments, Signs of Faith," *Worship*, vol. 37 (1962), 35, 36.
[9] Cf. Fransen, *Faith and the Sacraments*, London, 1958, 21.

was the channel by which we receive the substance of Christ's body, though separated from that body by a great distance. In any sacramental system the Holy Spirit must play a large role, and such a role does not necessarily make the system less sacramental. However the theology of the Spirit as applied in Calvin's sacramental theology is not ultimately satisfactory. It is not at all clear, nor even tolerably unclear, as to how the Spirit makes present the body of Christ. There is much one could praise in Calvin's Pneumatology but one has the impression that the Holy Spirit is, to put it bluntly, used. One has the impression that in a theologically embarrassing situation the Holy Spirit is called upon as a *deus ex machina.*

The impersonalism which Calvin wished to avoid in the sacramental reality—the sacrament is not and should not be considered an object, a "thing"—he transferred to the Holy Spirit who becomes a channel, a power, a divine force. Nor is it sufficient to remark that for this objectifying of the Spirit he is indebted to St. Augustine. Calvin has more than once corrected and scolded the Fathers;[10] even the Councils do not escape his censure.[11]

The Holy Spirit is that means which makes it possible for Calvin to maintain sacramental realism without subscribing to a substantialist position with its danger of empiricism. The personalist concept of substance as proposed by Calvin is not so much erroneous as deficient. As an emphasis it should be retained in any eucharistic theology. Finally, though Calvin's doctrine of the real presence is inadequate, it must be granted that what motivated his theological position were fears which are authentically Christian.

The God Who Cannot Be Packaged

On the more positive side there is the deep religious quality to his conviction that God cannot be packaged, that what concerns the incarnated and crucified Son has also to do with the eternal Son who dwells in light inaccessible, a quality of

---

[10] Cf. Inst., IV, 18, 11.   [11] Cf. *ibid.*, 9, 11.

transcendentalism which is not always sufficiently represented in Catholic sacramental theology. Calvin was convinced that any theology worthy of the name had to safeguard not only the truths, clear and unmistakable, but also the inaccessibilities, that Cloud of Unknowing which is not reducible to logic, which does not admit of rational formulation and is known only through a theological sensitivity and a religious intuition. God is not to be reduced to a household God to be summoned and dismissed at will. He who forgets awe and wonder will want an attendant God. The essential *sursum corda* of the Christian life and its *epiklesis* character must not be lost.

Calvin sought to build an ecclesiology and sacramental theology of inwardness. During the previous centuries there was a great deal of externality in sacramental piety.[12] The eucharistic interest was often centered on seeing the host, on carrying it in procession.[13] Exaggerated claims were made for mere physical presence at mass and for the use of certain mass formularies.[14] It was the fact of the real presence in the mass which preoccupied them. The Roman Catholic piety of the pre-reformation and reformation times did not stress energetically enough the *fides passionis* and the living participation in the passion of the Lord as presuppositions to the reception of the sacraments.[15] After Thomas, the effects of the sacrament—the particular existential and pastoral aspects which had to do with union with Christ—were hardly mentioned in theological treatises, while a great deal of space was given to speculative questions such as transubstantiation, the mode of Christ's presence, and eucharistic accidents.[16]

[12] Cf. Joseph Lortz, *Die Reformation in Deutschland*, vol. 2, *Ausbau der Fronten, Unionsversuche, Ergebnis*, 4th edn., Freiburg, 1962, 113.

[13] Cf. Jungmann, *The Mass of the Roman Rite*, New York, 1950, vol. 1, 120-122; Paul Doncoeur, "Lessons of Eucharistic History," *Worship*, vol. 23 (1949), 351-362; 409-417.

[14] Cf. Jungmann, *The Mass of the Roman Rite*, vol. 1, 130.

[15] Cf. Arnold "Vorgeschichte und Einfluss des Trienter Messopferdekrets," *Die Messe in der Glaubensverkündigung*, 125.

[16] "As we already mentioned, Hervaeus (Natalis +1323) devoted only

As a result of this concentration on the real presence of Christ in the Eucharist, the presence of Christ, also real, in grace and faith became less important and was thought to be presence only in an improper sense. The only proper sense of presence was the sacramental real presence in the Eucharist. It is not surprising that the reformers stressed personal union with Christ, and that Calvin reacted to the degree that the eucharistic eating becomes only a moment in that perpetual eating which takes place in faith. There is no specific eucharistic gift. What is given in the Eucharist has already been given through the Word and in prayer. However defective this is as a total doctrine, as a reaction it is understandable.

Through his doctrine of union with Christ in faith, Calvin gave a symmetry to his ecclesiology, sacramental theology, Christology and Pneumatology. Union with Christ that is personal, deeply religious, prayerful, ecclesiologically situated, eucharistically strengthened, effected by the Holy Spirit, and ethically meaningful is one of the admirable qualities of his sacramental theology.

The Visible Word

As has been seen, Calvin has been criticized for weakening sacramental realism by his noetic emphasis, reducing the

---

a few lines to the effects of the sacrament of the Eucharist. This seems to be a sign of the times. For as far as I was able to ascertain, neither James of Metz nor John Quidort in their Commentaries on the Sentences, nor Henry of Ghent nor Godfrey of Fontaines in their Quodlibetic questions, nor Giles of Rome in his Theorems on the Body of Christ, nor John Quidort in his tract of [sic] the 'impanation' theory devoted a special question to the effects of the sacrament of the Eucharist. St. Thomas, on the other hand, devoted an entire question consisting of eight articles to the effects of the sacrament of the Eucharist. The neglect of this question by many of the writers coming after St. Thomas, as well as the neglect of such an important question as the sacrificial nature of the Eucharist, indicates an impoverishment in the Eucharistic teaching of the late thirteenth and early fourteenth centuries. Perhaps it would not be an exaggeration to say that the over-emphasis of such speculative questions as transubstantiation and the mode of Christ's real presence and the Eucharistic accidents is a further sign of the impoverishment of the Eucharistic teaching of this period." Wenceslaus Plotnik, "The Eucharistic Teaching of Hervaeus Natalis," typewritten thesis, Munich, 1962, 250, 251.

Eucharist to only a noetic moment. This criticism of Calvin must be rejected. In Calvin, however, the Word character of the sacrament is stressed to the point where there seems little need or use for a sacrament. If all is given in the Word and in faith, then there is little need for a distinct sacrament. Why a eucharistic sacrament without a specific eucharistic gift?

For Calvin the Eucharist is more than a noetic moment; it is also reality. If the sacraments confirm the Word, so does the Word confirm the sacrament.[17] He refused, and rightly so, to consider the Word merely as a sacramental form. The Word is not an incantation, not even a highly religious incantation. Nor does one preach to bread. The Word is proclamation and must be proclaimed to the people. He understands the Word as a permanent constitutive moment, the *verbum visibile*. Both in his sacramental theology and in his liturgical thinking Calvin sees the necessity of keeping Word and sacrament together. If he had had his way, there would have been no service of the Word without a service of the Table; the one was always preparatory for the other.

Ecclesiological Consciousness

Calvin's doctrine of the church, like that of the sacraments, is too directly related to the will of God. The invisible church is the application of God's knowledge and will, while the visible church is the application of man's knowledge. This concept of the church is too reasoned, too cerebral. One finds it not unlikely that history has grasped on such formulations to brand Calvin a rationalist, which he is not. Through this direct subjection of the church to the will of God, it finds itself in a prophetic state. At every moment it is actualized by the will of God but basically it is incarnationally disengaged. Calvin understood well, however, the necessity of visibility. He thought of the sacraments in ecclesiological terms, though the structure of the church was not itself sacramental. He reaffirmed the corporate nature of the sacra-

[17] Cf. *Inst.*, IV, 14, 5.

ments and restored them to their proper ecclesiological context. The local church at worship was in the forefront of his consciousness. No necessity was conceivable which would permit the Eucharist to become private, neither the devotion of him who dispenses the sacrament, nor the last wish of the dying. The Eucharist is public worship and must of inner necessity remain public. His efforts to return to the practice of more frequent communion was an attempt to restore values which Roman Catholicism had obscured and neglected for centuries. His long and exhausting struggle to maintain excommunication as a power proper to the church and the manner in which he situated his ethical considerations, showed that for him ethics were always a *Gemeinschaftsethik* and that the community at eucharistic worship was itself the source of ethical concern. The demands of the *Gemeinschaftsethik* was a further reason for frequent celebration of the Eucharist. These are most certainly elements of a pure tradition.

In attempting to make the Eucharist more accessible, he returned to a more medicinal view of the sacraments. They are for the weak and the sinful. Therefore the conditions for receiving the Eucharist should not be so severe as to make it impossible for those who need it to receive it. There was a pastoral sensitivity in his recognition of the assurance of salvation which every Christian stands in need of, and in his recognition of the role the Eucharist plays in giving this assurance. He rejected liturgical clericalism, as he was in duty bound to do. The chalice should be given to the faithful because it was Christ's will that they receive it. Even if concomitance were true, this is beside the point. The command of Christ is clear and unmistakable. There is, however, a narrow biblicism in Calvin's assertion that the body of the Lord cannot be eaten separately from the blood. During the first centuries communion under one species was less common, but even then, during the persecutions, it was carried to persons in prison under one species.[18] The liturgy of the

[18] Cf. J. de Baciocchi, "Eucharistie," *Catholicisme*, Paris, 1959.

Presanctified goes back at least to the 4th century and this rite contains no consecration of wine.

Incorporation in Systematics

Calvin has been criticized for his inability to incorporate his eucharistic doctrine into his theological system in any organic manner.[19] There is, of course, an innate difficulty involved in building a sacramental system into a theology which is based on justification by faith alone, in the Protestant sense. However Calvin must be defended on this point. His eucharistic doctrine, though rough of edge and left hanging in perpetual dialectical motion, is admirably worked out in the framework of his Christology, Pneumatology, ecclesiology, and of his doctrine of predestination and grace. However much one takes exception to his system, there is an inner logic and an organic unity to the manner in which he has developed his eucharistic doctrine within the framework of his systematics.

---

[19] A distinction must be made between the organic unity of his eucharistic doctrine seen in itself and the manner in which this teaching is incorporated into his whole theological system. Alexandre Ganoczy is quite right in remarking that Calvin's sacramental doctrine, with specific reference to his eucharistic doctrine, is wanting in homogeneity. Cf. *Calvin, théologien de l'église et du ministère*, Paris, 1964, 125. And Gerardus van der Leeuw complains that his sacramental teaching is without a logical structure. Cf. *Sakramentales Denken*, Kassel, 1959, 70. There is justification for these observations. However *inachevée* his sacramental and eucharistic doctrine is in itself, it is well structured within Calvin's whole systematic. One notable weak spot stands out. A theology which deprives the Eucharist of a specific gift will make it slightly superfluous and will make its worth within a theological system somewhat dubious.

François Wendel thinks that Calvin failed to integrate his eucharistic doctrine into his larger system. Cf. *Calvin, the Origins and Development of his Religious Thought*, London, 1963, 353.

Bibliography

Asterisks mark the British editions which also
appear in an American edition.

SOURCES

*Die Bekenntnisschriften der reformierten Kirche in authentischen
Texten,* ed. E. F. Karl Müller, Leipzig, 1903.
Bekenntnisschriften der reformierten Kirchen, ed. Wilhelm Niesel,
2nd edn., Zürich, 1949.
Bucer, Martin. *Martini Bvceri Opera Latina,* vol. 15, *De Regno
Christi,* ed. François Wendel, Gütersloh, 1955.
————. *Martin Bucers Deutsche Schriften,* ed. Robert Stupperich,
3 vols., Gütersloh, 1960-1964.
————. *Nova et Vetera Qvatvor Evcharistia scripta svmmi et
acvtissimi Theologi Doctoris Martini Buceri Argentoratus,* ed.
Joannes Sturmius Vetus, Argentorati, 1561.
————. *Une traduction française de commentaire de Bucer sur
l'evangile selon Sant Matthieu,* trans. J. Courvoisier, Paris, 1933.
Calvin, John. *Corpus Reformatorum, Joannis Calvini Opera quae
supersunt omnia,* eds. G. Baum *et al.,* 59 vols., Braunschweig,
1893-1900.
————. *Institution de la religion chrestienne* (sic), ed. Jean-Daniel
Benoit, 5 vols., Paris, 1957-1963.
————. *Johannes Calvini Opera Selecta,* eds. Peter Barth, Wilhelm
Niesel, 5 vols., Munich. vol. 1, 1st edn., 1926; vol. 2, 2nd edn.,
eds. Peter Barth, Dora Scheuner, 1952; vol. 3, 2nd edn., 1957;
vol. 4, 2nd edn., 1959; vol. 5, 2nd edn., 1962.
————. *Predigten über das 2. Buch Samuelis,* ed. Hanns Rückert
(*Supplementa Calviniana,* vol. 1), Neukirchen, 1936f.
Knox, John. *The Works of John Knox,* ed. David Lang, Edin-
burgh, 1895, vol. 4.
Luther, Martin. *Weimarer kritische Gesamtausgabe,* eds. J. C. F.
Knaake *et al.,* Weimar, 1883f.
Melanchthon, Philip. *Corpus Reformatorum, Philippi Melanch-
thonis opera quae supersunt omnia,* eds. C. G. Bretschneider,
H. E. Bindseil, 28 vols., Halle, Braunschweig, 1844f.
Zwingli, Huldrych. *Corpus Reformatorum, Huldreich Zwinglis
Sämtliche Werke,* eds. Emil Egli *et al.,* edition not yet complete,
Berlin, Leipzig, Zürich, 1905f.

————. *Huldreich Zwinglis Werke*. Erste vollständige Ausgabe durch Melchior Schuler und Johannes Schulthess, 8 vols., Zürich, 1828f.

TRANSLATIONS

*Calvin, John. *Commentaries*, eds. D. W. Torrance, T. F. Torrance, Edinburgh, 1960f.

*————. *Commentaries and Letters*, ed. Joseph Haroutunian (*The Library of Christian Classics,* vol. 23), London, 1958.

————. *Unterricht in der christlichen Religion*, trans. O. Weber, Neukirchen, 1955.

*————. *Institutes of the Christian Religion*, trans. Ford Lewis Battles (*The Library of Christian Classics*, vols. 20, 21), London, 1961.

*————. *Tracts and Treatises*, ed. T. F. Torrance, Edinburgh, 1959.

*————. *Theological Treatises*, trans. J. K. S. Reid (*The Library of Christian Classics*, vol. 22), London, 1954.

SECONDARY LITERATURE

Abba, Raymond. "Calvin's Doctrine of the Lord's Supper," *The Reformed Theological Review*, vol. 9 (1950), 1-12.

Adam, A. "Kirche," *Religion in Geschichte und Gegenwart*, 3rd edn., Tübingen, 1959.

Adam, Karl. *Die Eucharistielehre des hl. Augustin* (*Forschungen zur Christlichen Literatur- und Dogmengeschichte*, vol. 8), Paderborn, 1908.

Anrich, Gustav. *Martin Bucer*, Strasbourg, 1914.

Arnold, Franz Xaver. "Vorgeschichte und Einfluss des Trienter Messopferdekrets auf die Behandlung des eucharistischen Geheimnisses in der Glaubensverkündigung der Neuzeit," *Die Messe in der Glaubensverkündigung*, eds. Franz Xaver Arnold, Balthasar Fischer, 2nd edn., Freiburg, 1953.

Barclay, Alexander. *The Protestant Doctrine of the Lord's Supper: A Study of the Eucharistic Teaching of Luther, Zwingli, and Calvin*, Glasgow, 1927.

Barth, Karl. *Church Dogmatics,* vol. 1/2, *The Doctrine of the Word of God*, trans. G. T. Thomson, Harold Knight, New York, 1956.

Barth, Peter. "Calvin," *Religion in Geschichte und Gegenwart*, 2nd edn., Tübingen, 1927.

————. "Calvins Stellung im Abendmahlsstreit," *Die Christliche Welt*, vol. 43 (1929), 817-823; 922-929.

————. "Die Erwählungslehre in Calvins Institutio von 1536," *Theologische Aufsätze*, ed. E. Wolf, Munich, 1936.

————. "Fünfundzwangzig Jahre Calvinforschung, 1909-1934," *Theologische Rundschau*, Tübingen, 1934, 161-267.

Baur, F. C. *Lehrbuch der christlichen Dogmengeschichte*, 2nd edn., Tübingen, 1858.

Bauke, Hermann. "Christologie," *Religion in Geschichte und Gegenwart*, 2nd edn., Tübingen, 1927.

————. *Die Probleme der Theologie Calvins*, Leipzig, 1922.

Beckmann, Joachim. *Vom Sakrament bei Calvin. Die Sakramentslehre Calvins in ihren Beziehungen zu Augustin.* Tübingen, 1926.

Benoit, J.-D. *Liturgical Renewal*, London, 1959.

Berkouwer, G. C. "Calvin and Rome," *John Calvin, Contemporary Prophet*, ed. Jacob T. Hoogstra, Grand Rapids, Michigan, 1959.

Betz, Johannes. *Die Eucharistie in der Zeit der griechischen Väter*, 2 vols., Freiburg, 1954, 1955.

Betzendörfer, W. "Duns Scotus," *Religion in Geschichte und Gegenwart*, 3rd edn., Tübingen, 1958.

Boelens, Wim. "Die Arnoldshainer Thesen," typewritten thesis, University of Würzburg, 1963.

Bohatec, Josef. *Budé und Calvin*, Gras, 1950.

————. *Calvins Lehre von Staat und Kirche mit besonderer Berücksichtigung des Organismusgedankens (Untersuchungen zur Deutschen Staats- und Rechtsgeschichte*, vol. 147), Breslau, 1937.

————. "Calvins Vorsehungslehre," *Calvinstudien*, ed. Joseph Bohatec, Leipzig, 1909.

Boisset, Jean. *Sagesse et sainteté dans la pensée de Jean Calvin (Bibliothèque de l'école des hautes études*, vol. 71), Paris, 1959.

Bornkamm, Heinrich. *Martin Bucers Bedeutung für die europäische Reformationsgeschichte (Schriften des Vereins für Reformationsgeschichte*, no. 169), Gütersloh, 1952.

Bourdriot. W. "Calvins Abendmahlslehre," *Reformierte Kirchenzeitung*, vol. 79 (1929), 90-93; 97-99.

Bouyer, Louis. *The Spirit and Forms of Protestantism*, trans. A. V. Littledale, Westminster, Maryland, 1956.

Bresch, Frédéric. *Strasbourg et la querelle sacramentaire au rap-*

ports de Bucer a ce propos avec Luther, Zwingli et Calvin, Montauban, 1902.

*Brilioth, Ynge. *Eucharistic Faith and Practice: Evangelical and Catholic,* trans. A. G. Hebert, London, 1930.

Brunner, Peter. *Vom Glauben bei Calvin. Dargestellt auf Grund der Institutio, des Katechismus genevensis und unter Heranziehung exegetischer und homiletischer Schriften,* Tübingen, 1925.

Burckhardt, Abel Eduard. *Das Geistproblem bei Huldrych Zwingli (Quellen und Abhandlungen zur schweizerischen Reformationsgeschichte,* vol. 6), Leipzig, 1932.

Cadier, Jean. *La doctrine calviniste de la sainte cène,* Montpellier, 1951.

Chavannes, Henry. "La présence réelle chez saint Thomas et chez Calvin," *Verbum Caro,* vol. 13 (1959), 151-170.

Congar, Yves M.-J. "Calvin," *Catholicisme,* Paris, 1949.

⸻. *Christ, Our Lady, and the Church,* trans. Henry St. John, New York, 1957.

⸻. "Regards et réflexions sur la christologie de Luther," *Das Konzil von Chalkedon,* vol. 3, *Entscheidung um Chalkedon,* eds. A. Grillmeier, H. Bacht, Würzburg, 1954.

⸻. *La tradition et les traditions, essai historique,* Paris, 1960.

⸻. *Vraie et fausse réforme dans l'église,* Paris, 1950.

Courvoisier, Jacques. *La notion d'église chez Bucer dans son développement historique (Etudes d'histoire et de philosophie religieuses,* no. 28), Paris, 1933.

Diestelmann, Jürgen. *Konsekration, Luthers Abendmahlsglaube in dogmatisch-liturgischer Sicht (Luthertum,* vol. 22), Berlin, 1960.

Dix, Gregory. *The Shape of the Liturgy,* rev. ed., London, 1952.

Dominice, Max. "Die Christusverkündigung bei Calvin," *Jesus Christus im Zeugnis der Heiligen Schrift und der Kirche,* Munich, 1936.

Doumergue, E. *Jean Calvin, les hommes et les choses de son temps,* 7 vols., Lausanne, 1899-1928.

Dowey, Edward A., Jr. *The Knowledge of God in Calvin's Theology,* New York, 1952.

Eells, Hastings. *Martin Bucer,* New Haven, 1931.

Emery, Pierre Yves. "The Teaching of Calvin on the Sacrificial

Element in the Eucharist," *The Reformed and Presbyterian World*, vol. 26 (1960), 109-114.

Emmen, E. *De Christologie van Calvijn*, Amsterdam, 1953.

Fahey, J. H. *The Eucharist Teaching of Ratramn of Corbie*, Mundelein, 1951.

Franz, Adolph. *Die Messe im deutschen Mittelalter*, Freiburg, 1902.

Ganoczy, Alexandre. *Calvin théologien de l'église et du ministère* (*Unam Sanctam*, no. 48), Paris, 1964.

Gaudard, Raoul. *La doctrine de la sainte cène d'après Zwingle*, Paris, 1890.

Geiselmann, Josef Rupert. *Die Abendmahlslehre an der Wende der christlichen Spätantike zum Frühmittelalter; Isidor von Sevilla und das Sakrament der Eucharistie*, Munich, 1933.

————. *Die Eucharistielehre der Vorscholastik* (*Forschungen zur christlichen Literatur- und Dogmengeschichte*, vol. 15, nos. 1-3), Paderborn, 1926.

Gelder, H. A. Enno van. *The Two Reformations in the 16th Century*, The Hague, 1964.

Geusau, Alting L. G. M. von. *Die Lehre von der Kindertaufe bei Calvin Gesehen im Rahmen seiner Sakraments- und Tauftheologie*, Mainz, 1963.

Gliozzo, C. *La dottrina della conversione eucaristica in Pascasio Radberto e Ratramno Monaci di Corbia*, Messina, 1945.

Gloede, G. "Calvin," *Evangelisches Kirchenlexikon*, 2nd edn., Göttingen, 1956.

Göhler, Alfred. *Calvins Lehre von der Heiligung* (*Forschungen zur Geschichte und Lehre des Protestantismus*, vol. 3), Munich, 1934.

Gollwitzer, Helmut. *Coena Domini*, Munich, 1937.

Goumaz, Louis. *La doctrine du salut d'après les commentaires de Jean Calvin sur le nouveau testament*, Nyon, 1917.

Graf, Arthur. "La doctrine Calvinienne de la cène," *Revue de Théologie et de Philosophie*, vol. 20 (1932), 134-150.

Grass, Hans. *Die Abendmahlslehre bei Luther und Calvin* (*Beiträge zur Förderung christlicher Theologie*, series 2, vol. 47), 2nd edn., Gütersloh, 1954.

Grin, Edmond. "Quelques aspects de la pensée de Calvin sur le Saint Esprit et leurs enseignements pour nous," *Theologische Zeitschrift*, vol. 3 (1947), 274-289.

Grossouw, Willem Karl Maria. *Revelation and Redemption, a Sketch of the Theology of St. John*, trans. Martin W. Schoenberg, Westminster, Maryland, 1955.

Haas, Albert. "Calvin und Rom," *Reformierte Kirchenzeitung*, vol. 100 (1959), 332-338; 360-364; 395-398; 415-418; 466-469; 494-497; 514-518.

Harkianakis, Stylianos. "Die heilige Eucharistie in Orthodoxer Sicht," *Die Eucharistie im Verständnis der Konfessionen*, ed. Thomas Sartory, Recklinghausen, 1961.

Harnack, Adolph. *History of Dogma*, 7 vols., London, 1896-1899.

Hauck, Wilhelm Albert. *Die Erwählten. Prädestination und Heilsgewissheit bei Calvin*, Gütersloh, 1950.

——. *Vorsehung und Freiheit nach Calvin*, Gütersloh, 1947.

Holl, Karl. "Johannes Calvin," *Gesammelte Aufsätze zur Kirchengeschichte*, vol. 3, *Der Westen*, Tübingen, 1928.

Hunter, Mitchel. *The Teaching of Calvin*, Glasgow, 1920.

Hyma, Albert. *The Christian Renaissance, a History of the "Devotio Moderna*," New York, 1924.

Ibeling, H. "Johannes Calvins Lehre von der Gemeinschaft des wahren Leibes und Blutes Jesu Christi im Heiligen Abendmahl," *Reformierte Kirchenzeitung*, vol. 29 (1906), 10-12; 18-20; 26-29; 43-45; 49-51; 57-59; 66-68; 73-76.

Iserloh, Erwin. *Gnade und Eucharistie in der philosophischen Theologie des Wilhelm von Ockham (Veröffentlichungen des Instituts für europäische Geschichte*, vol. 8), Wiesbaden, 1956.

Jacobs, Paul. *Prädestination und Verantwortlichkeit bei Calvin (Beiträge zur Geschichte und Lehre der Reformierten Kirche*, vol. 1), Neukirchen, 1937.

——. "Die Gegenwart Christi im Abendmahl nach reformiertem Verständnis und das römisch-katholische Gegenbild," *Gegenwart Christi*, ed. Fritz Viering, Göttingen, 1959, 23-33.

——. "Pneumatische Realpräsenz bei Calvin," *Revue d'Histoire et de Philosophie Religieuses*, vol. 44 (1964), 389-401.

Janssen, Heinrich. "Die Abendmahlslehre Johannes Calvins," *Die Eucharistie im Verständnis der Konfessionen*, ed. Thomas Sartory, Recklinghausen, 1961.

——. "Die Abendmahlslehre Johannes Calvins," *Una Sancta*, vol. 15 (1960), 125-138.

Jorissen, Hans. *Die Entfaltung der Transsubstantiationslehre bis zum Beginn der Hochscholastik* (*Münsterische Beiträge zur Theologie*, no. 28, 1) Münster, 1965.

Jungmann, Joseph A. *The Mass of the Roman Rite*, trans. Francis A. Brunner, 2 vols., New York, 1950, 1955.

Karrer, Otto. "Die Eucharistie im Gespräch der Konfessionen," *Die Eucharistie im Verständnis der Konfessionen*, ed. Thomas Sartory, Recklinghausen, 1961.

Kinder, Ernst. "Die lutherische Kirche," *Und Ihr Netz Zerris*, ed. Helmut Lamparter, Stuttgart, 1957.

Klein, Laurentius. *Evangelische-lutherische Beichte* (*Konfessionskundliche und Kontroverstheologische Studien*, vol. 5), Paderborn, 1961.

Koenker, Ernest Benjamin. *The Liturgical Renaissance in the Roman Catholic Church*, Chicago, 1954.

Köhler, Walther. *Das Religionsgespräch zu Marburg 1529*, Tübingen, 1929.

——. *Zwingli und Luther*, 2 vols., 2nd edn., Leipzig, 1924, 1953.

Kolfhaus, W. *Christusgemeinschaft bei Johannes Calvin* (*Beiträge zur Geschichte und Lehre der Reformierten Kirche*, vol. 3), Neukirchen, 1939.

Kreck, W. "Abendmahl," *Religion in Geschichte und Gegenwart*, 3rd edn., Tübingen, 1957.

Kretz, Gerhard. "Calvins Auseinandersetzung mit der katholischen Kirche," typewritten thesis, University of Tübingen, 1962.

Kromminga, J. H. "Calvin and Ecumenicity," *John Calvin, Contemporary Prophet*, ed. Jacob T. Hoogstra, Grand Rapids, Michigan, 1959.

Krusche, Werner. *Das Wirken des Heiligen Geistes nach Calvin* (*Forschungen zur Kirchen- und Dogmengeschichte*, vol. 8), Göttingen, 1957.

Lang, August. *Der Evangelienkommentar Martin Butzers und die Grundzüge seiner Theologie* (*Studien zur Geschichte der Theologie und der Kirche*, vol. 2, 2), Leipzig, 1900.

——. *Johannes Calvin* (*Schriften des Vereins für Reformationsgeschichte*, vol. 99), Leipzig, 1909.

——. "Luther und Calvin," *Reformation und Gegenwart, Gesammelte Aufsätze*, Detmold, 1918.

————. "Melanchthon und Calvin," *Reformation und Gegenwart, Gesammelte Aufsätze*, Detmold, 1918.

————. "The Sources of Calvin's Institutes of 1536," *The Evangelical Quarterly*, vol. 8 (1936), 130-141.

Laun, J. F. "Thomas Bradwardine," *Religion in Geschichte und Gegenwart*, 2nd edn., Tübingen, 1927.

Lecerf, A. *Etudes Calvinistes*, Paris, 1949.

Leclercq, Jean. *The Love of Learning and the Desire for God*, trans. Catherine Misrahi, New York, 1961.

*Leeming, Bernard. *Principles of Sacramental Theology*, New edn., London, 1960.

Leeuw, Gerardus van der. *Sakramentales Denken*, Kassel, 1959.

Leff, Gordon. *Bradwardine and the Pelagians*, Cambridge, 1957.

————. *Gregory of Rimini*. New York, 1961.

Lefranc, A. *Histoire du Collège de France*, Paris, 1893.

Lengsfeld, Peter. "Die Einheit der Kirche und die Wiedervereinigung der getrennten Christen in katholischer Sicht," *Una Sancta*, vol. 18 (1963), 1-12.

Locher, Gottfried W. *Die Theologie Huldrych Zwingli im Lichte seiner Christologie (Studien zur Dogmengeschichte und systematischen Theologie*, vol. 1), Zürich, 1952.

Lohse, Bernard. *Epochen der Dogmengeschichte*, Stuttgart, 1963.

*MacGregor, Geddes. *Corpus Christi, The Nature of the Church according to the Reformed Tradition*, London, 1959.

Marcel, Pierre. "The Humility of the Prophet," *John Calvin, Contemporary Prophet*, ed. Jacob T. Hoogstra, Grand Rapids, Michigan, 1959.

*Mascall, E. L. *The Recovery of Unity*, London, 1958.

Maxwell, William D. *The Liturgical Portions of the Genevan Service Book*, Edinburgh, 1931.

————. *An Outline of Christian Worship*, 3rd edn., London, 1960.

McGiffert, Arthur C. "Calvin's Theory of the Church," *Essays in Modern Theology and Related Subjects*, New York, 1911.

McKenzie, Peter R. "The Invisibility of the Church for Luther and Calvin," typewritten thesis, University of Edinburgh, 1952.

*McLelland, Joseph. *The Visible Words of God, An Exposition of the Sacramental Theology of Peter Martyr Vermigli*, Edinburgh, 1957.

McNeill, John T. *The History and Character of Calvinism*, New York, 1954.

———. *Unitive Protestantism*, New York, 1930.

Möhler, John Adam. *Symbolism*, trans. James Burton Robertson, 2 vols., 2nd edn., London, 1847.

Moeller, C., Philips, G. *The Theology of Grace and the Ecumenical Movement*, trans., R. A. Wilson, London, 1961.

Moreau, E. de, *et al. La Crise religieuse du XVI⁰ siècle*, vol. 16, *Histoire de l'église*, eds. Augustine Fliche, Victor Martin (no place given), 1950.

Mousnier, Roland. "Saint Bernard and Martin Luther," *The American Benedictine Review*, vol. 14 (1963), 448-462.

Neuser, Wilhelm H. *Der Ansatz der Theologie Philipp Melanchthons (Beiträge zur Geschichte und Lehre der Reformierten Kirche*, vol. 9), Neukirchen, 1957.

———. *Luther und Melanchthon—Einheit im Gegensatz*, heft 91, *Theologische Existenz Heute*, Munich, 1961.

Niesel, Wilhelm. "Das Abendmahl und die Opfer des Alten Bundes," *Theologische Aufsätze*, ed. Ernst Wolf, Munich, 1936.

———. *Calvins Lehre vom Abendmahl (Forschungen zur Geschichte und Lehre des Protestantismus*, series 3, vol. 3), 2nd edn., Munich, 1935.

———. "Kirche und Sakrament," *Evangelische Theologie*, vol. 2 (1935), 95-114.

———. "The Order of Public Worship in the Reformed Churches," *Scottish Journal of Theology*, vol. 2 (1949), 381-390.

*———. *Reformed Symbolics*, trans. David Lewis, Edinburgh, 1962. (American edn. entitled: *The Gospel and the Churches*.)

———. *Die Theologie Calvins*, 2nd edn., Munich, 1957.

———. *The Theology of Calvin*, trans. Harold Knight, Philadelphia, 1956.

———. "Wesen und Gestalt der Kirche nach Calvin," *Evangelische Theologie*, vol. 3 (1936), 308-330.

Nijenhuis, Willem. "Die Aufgabe der Reformierten Kirchen in der Ökumenischen Bewegung," *Calvin-Studien 1959*, ed. Jürgen Moltmann, Neukirchen, 1960.

Noesgen, K. F. *Geschichte der Lehre vom Heiligen Geist*, Gütersloh, 1899.

Oberman, Heiko A. *Archbishop Thomas Bradwardine, A Fourteenth Century Augustinian*, Utrecht, 1958.

———. *The Harvest of Medieval Theology, Gabriel Biel and Late Medieval Nominalism*, Cambridge, 1963.

Otten, Heinz. *Calvins Theologische Anschauung von der Prädestination* (*Forschungen zur Geschichte und Lehre des Protestantismus*, series 9, vol. 1), Munich, 1938.

Pache, E. "La sainte cène selon Calvin," *Revue de Théologie et de Philosophie*, vol. 24 (1936), 179-201.

Pannenberg, W. "Christologie," *Religion in Geschichte und Gegenwart*, 3rd edn., Tübingen, 1957.

*Parker, T. H. L. *Portrait of Calvin*, London, 1954.

Pauck, Wilhelm. "Calvin and Butzer," *The Journal of Religion*, vol. 9 (1929), 237-256.

————. "Calvin's Institutes of the Christian Religion," *Church History*, vol. 15 (1960), 17-27.

Pelikan, Jaroslav. *From Luther to Kierkegaard*, 2nd edn., St. Louis, 1963.

Peters, Albrecht. *Realpräsenz, Luthers Zeugnis von Christi Gegenwart im Abendmahl* (*Arbeiten zur Geschichte und Theologie des Luthertums*, vol. 5), Berlin, 1960.

Pfisterer, Ernst. "Calvins Ansicht über die Häufigkeit der Abendmahlsfeiern und über das Krankenabendmahl," *Reformierte Kirchenzeitung*, vol. 92 (1951), 246-250.

————. "Calvins Stellung zum Krankenabendmahl," *Reformierte Kirchenzeitung*, vol. 85 (1935), 268.

Poll, G. J. van de. *Martin Bucer's Liturgical Ideas*, Assen (Holland), 1954.

Prenter, Regin. *Spiritus Creator*, trans., John M. Jensen, Philadelphia, 1953.

Quervain, Alfred. *Calvin, Sein Lehren und Kämpfen*, Berlin, 1926.

Quistorp, Heinrich. *Calvins Eschatologie*, Gütersloh (no date).

Reuter, Karl. *Das Grundverständnis der Theologie Calvins* (*Beiträge zur Geschichte und Lehre der Reformierten Kirche*, vol. 15), Neukirchen, 1963.

Richardson, Cyril C. *Zwingli and Cranmer on the Eucharist*, Evanston, 1949.

Rilliet, Jean Horace. *Zwingli, Third Man of the Reformation*, trans. Harold Knight, Philadelphia, 1964.

Ritschl, Otto. *Dogmengeschichte des Protestantismus*, 4 vols., Göttingen, 1908-1927.

Rotscheidt, W. "Calvins Antwort auf die Frage: 'Wer soll das Hl. Abendmahl austeilen?'" *Reformierte Kirchenzeitung*, vol. 68 (1919), 118.

Sartory, Thomas. "Eucharistisches Gedankengut bei unseren getrennten Brüdern," *Die Eucharistie im Verständnis der Konfessionen*, ed. Thomas Sartory, Recklinghausen, 1961.

————. "Das Mysterium der Kirche in reformatorischer Sicht," *Mysterium Kirche*, eds. Ferdinand Holböck, Thomas Sartory, Salzburg, 1962, vol. 2.

Sasse, Hermann. *This Is My Body*, Minneapolis, 1959.

Schaff, Philip. *History of the Christian Church*, vol. 8, *Modern Christianity*, New York, 1892.

Scheibe, M. *Calvins Prädestinationslehre*, Halle, 1897.

Schillebeeckx, Edward. *Christ the Sacrament of the Encounter with God*, New York, 1963.

Schwabl, Maurice. *Etude comparative des doctrines de Melanchthon, Zwingle et Calvin*, Strasbourg, 1859.

Seeberg, Reinhold. *Lehrbuch der Dogmengeschichte*, vol. 4/1, *Die Entstehung des protestantischen Lehrbegriffs*, 5th edn. Darmstadt, 1953.

————. *Die Theologie des Johannes Duns Scotus: Eine dogmengeschichtliche Untersuchung*, Leipzig, 1900.

Seidlmayer, Michael. *Currents of Mediaeval Thought, With Special Reference to Germany* (*Studies in Mediaeval History*, vol. 5), trans. D. Barker, Oxford, 1960.

Skydsgaard, K. E. "From Monologue to Dialogue," *The Ecumenical Review*, vol. 14 (1962), 423-436.

Smits, Luchesius. *Saint Augustin dans l'oeuvre de Jean Calvin*, 2 vols., Louvain, 1957, 1958.

Sommerlath, Ernst. "Das Abendmahl bei Luther," *Vom Sakrament des Altars*, ed. Hermann Sasse, Leipzig, 1941.

Southern, R. W. *The Making of the Middle Ages*, New Haven, 1953.

Sperl, Adolf. *Melanchthon zwischen Humanismus und Reformation* (*Forschungen zur Geschichte und Lehre des Protestantismus*, series 10, vol. 15), Munich, 1959.

Sprenger, Paul. *Das Rätsel um die Bekehrung Calvins* (*Beiträge zur Geschichte und Lehre der Reformierten Kirche*, vol. 11), Neukirchen, 1960.

Staehelin, L. *Johannes Calvin*, 2 vols., Elberfeld, 1863.

Stählin, Rudolf. "Die Geschichte des christlichen Gottesdienstes von der Urkirche bis zur Gegenwart," *Leiturgia*, vol. 1, *Ge-*

schichte und Lehre des Evangelischen Gottesdienstes, eds. Karl Ferdinand, Walter Blankenburg, Kassel, 1954.

Stalker, J. "Sacrament," *Hastings Encyclopaedia of Religion and Ethics*, New York, 1918.

Stone, D. *A History of the Eucharist*, 2 vols., London, 1909.

Stricker, Eduard. "Calvins liturgische Bedeutung," *Monatsschrift für Gottesdienst und kirchliche Kunst*, vol. 14 (1909), 213-227.

Strohl, H. "Bucer et Calvin," *Bulletin du Protestantisme Français*, vol. 87 (1938), 354-360.

Stuermann, Walter E. *A Critical Study of Calvin's Concept of Faith*, Tulsa, 1952.

Tavard, George. *Protestantism* (*Twentieth Century Encyclopedia of Catholicism*, vol. 137), New York, 1959.

Ternus, Joseph. "Chalkedon und die Entwicklung der protestantischen Theologie," *Das Konzil von Chalkedon*, vol. 3, *Entscheidung um Chalkedon*, eds. A. Grillmeier, H. Bacht, Würzburg, 1954.

Thielicke, H. *Theologie der Anfechtung*, Tübingen, 1949.

*Thurian, Max. *The Eucharistic Memorial*, Part 2, *The New Testament*, trans. J. G. Davies, London, 1961.

———. "The Real Presence," *Christianity Divided*, eds. Daniel J. Callahan *et al.*, New York, 1961.

*Torrance, T. F. *Calvin's Doctrine of Man*, London, 1949.

———. "Concerning the Ministry," *Scottish Journal of Theology*, vol. 1 (1948), 190-201.

*———. *Kingdom and Church*, Edinburgh, 1956.

———. "Knowledge of God and Speech about Him According to John Calvin," *Revue d'Histoire et de Philosophie Religieuses*, vol. 44 (1964), 402-422.

Troeltsch, Ernst. *The Social Teaching of the Christian Churches*, trans. Olive Wyon, 2 vols., New York, 1931.

Tschackert, Paul. *Die Entstehung der lutherischen, und der reformierten Kirchenlehre*, Göttingen, 1910.

Usteri, J. M. "Calvins Sakraments- und Tauflehre," *Studien und Kritiken*, Gotha, 1884.

Vanbergen, P. "Le renouveau liturgique dans les églises issues de la réforme," *Les Questions Liturgiques et Paroissiales*, vol. 41 (1960), 250-273.

Viering, Fritz. "Erweiterte Diskussionsbeiträge zu den Vorträgen über die Gegenwart Christi im Abendmahl; theologisch-kirchliche Fragen und Anmerkungen," *Gegenwart Christi*, ed. Fritz Viering, Göttingen, 1959.

Vries, Wilhelm de. *Sakramententheologie bei den Nestorianern* (*Orientalia Christiana Analecta*, vol. 133), Rome, 1947.

*Wallace, Ronald S. *Calvin's Doctrine of the Christian Life*, Edinburgh, 1959.

*———. *Calvin's Doctrine of Word and Sacrament*, Edinburgh, 1953.

Walters, Gywn. "The Doctrine of the Holy Spirit in John Calvin," typewritten thesis, University of Edinburgh, 1949.

Warfield, B. B. *Calvin and Augustine*, Philadelphia, 1956.

Weber, Otto. "Calvin," *Religion in Geschichte und Gegenwart*, Tübingen, 3rd edn., 1957.

———. *Grundlagen der Dogmatik*, 2 vols., Neukirchen, 1955, 1962.

Weerda, Jan. "Ordnung zur Lehre. Zur Theologie der Kirchenordnung bei Calvin," *Calvin-Studien 1959*, ed. Jürgen Moltman, Neukirchen, 1960.

*Wendel, François. *Calvin, the Origins and Development of his Religious Thought*, London, 1963.

———. *L'église de Strasbourg* (*Études d'histoire et de philosophie religieuses*, no. 38), Paris, 1942.

Wernle, Paul. *Der Evangelische Glaube*, vol. 2, *Zwingli*, vol. 3, *Calvin*, Tübingen, 1919.

Wiederburg, Andrea. "Calvins Verhalten zu Luther, Melanchthon und dem Luthertum," typewritten thesis, University of Tübingen, 1961.

Wilhelm, Paul. *Die Christologie Luthers im Abendmahlsstreit*, Königsberg, 1929.

Witte, Johannes L. "Die Christologie Calvins," *Das Konzil von Chalkedon*, vol. 3, *Entscheidung um Chalkedon*, eds. A. Grillmeier, H. Bacht, Würzburg, 1954.

Wolf, Ernst. "Deus Omniformis," *Theologische Aufsätze*, ed. Ernst Wolf, Munich, 1936.

Wolf, Hans Heinrich. *Die Einheit des Bundes. Das Verhältnis von Altem und Neuem Testament bei Calvin* (*Beiträge zur Geschichte und Lehre der Reformierten Kirche*, vol. 10), 2nd edn., Neukirchen, 1958.

Workman, Herbert B. *John Wyclif*, 2 vols., Oxford, 1926.

Wotherspoon, H. J., and Kirkpatrick, J. M. *A Manual of Church Doctrine*, 2nd edn., New York, 1960.

Wyclif, John. *On the Eucharist,* in *The Library of Christian Classics,* vol. 14, *Advocates of Reform,* ed., Matthew Spinka, Philadelphia, 1953.

Zeller, Eduard. *Das theologische Systems Zwinglis,* Tübingen, 1853.

CHAPTER VIII: OPEN QUESTIONS

Ahern, Barnabas Mary. "The Christian's Union with the Body of Christ in Cor, Gal, and Rom," *Catholic Biblical Quarterly,* vol. 23 (1961), 199-209.

Aquinas, St. Thomas. *Summa Theologica (Die Deutsche Thomas-Ausgabe,* vol. 30, *Das Geheimnis der Eucharistie),* Salzburg, 1938.

———. *Opera Omnia Sancti Thomae,* eds. S. E. Fretté, P. Maré, 34 vols., Paris, 1871-1880.

Arnold, A. *Der Ursprung des christlichen Abendmahls im Lichte der neuesten liturgiegeschichtlichen Forschung (Freiburger Theologische Studien,* vol. 45), 2nd edn., Freiburg, 1939.

Baciocchi, J. de. "Eucharistie," *Catholicisme,* Paris, 1959.

———. "Le mystère eucharistique dans les perspectives de la bible," *Nouvelle Revue Théologique,* vol. 77 (1955), 561-580.

———. "Présence eucharistique et transsubstantiation," *Irénikon,* vol. 32 (1959), 139-161.

Benoit, Pierre. "Corps, tête et plérôme dans les épîtres de la captivité," *Revue Biblique,* vol. 63 (1956), 5-44.

Best, E. *One Body in Christ,* London, 1955.

*Bouyer, Louis. *The Word, Church, and Sacraments in Protestantism,* trans. Geoffrey Chapman, London, 1961.

Brown, James F. "Faith as Commitment in the Gospel of St. John," *Worship,* vol. 38 (1964), 260-267.

Cerfaux, L. *The Church in the Theology of St. Paul,* trans. G. Webb, A. Walker, New York, 1959.

Coppens, J. "Miscellanée bibliques," *Ephemerides theologicae Lovanienses,* vol. 33 (1957), 483-510.

Davis, Charles. "The Theology of Transubstantiation," *Sophia,* vol. 3 (1964), 12-24.

Florovsky, Georges. "The Church: Her Nature and Task," *The Universal Church in God's Design,* London, 1948.

Fransen, P. F. *Faith and the Sacraments (Aquinas Paper,* No. 31), London, 1958.

————. "Sacraments, Signs of Faith," *Worship*, vol. 37 (1962), 31-50.

Ghysens, D. G. "Présence réelle eucharistique et transsubstantiation dans les définitions de l'église catholique," *Irénikon*, vol. 32 (1959), 420-435.

Grass, Hans. "Abendmahl," *Die Religion in Geschichte und Gegenwart*, 3rd edn., Tübingen, 1957.

*Higgins, A. J. B. *The Lord's Supper in the New Testament* (*Studies in Biblical Theology*, vol. 6), London, 1956.

Iserloh, Erwin. *Der Kampf um die Messe* (*Katholisches Leben und Kämpfen im Zeitalter der Glaubensspaltung*, vol. 10), Münster, 1952.

Jedin, Hubert. *A History of the Council of Trent*, trans. Ernst Graef, 2 vols., New York, 1957, 1961.

Karrer, Otto. "Die Eucharistie im Gespräch der Konfessionen," *Die Eucharistie im Verständnis der Konfessionen*, ed. Thomas Sartory, Recklinghausen, 1961.

*Küng, Hans. *The Council and Reunion*, trans. Cecily Hastings, London, 1961. (American edn. entitled: *The Council, Reform and Reunion*.)

Kuss, Otto. "Die Glaube nach den paulinischen Hauptbriefen," *Auslegung und Verkündigung*, vol. 1, *Aufsätze zur Exegese des Neuen Testamentes*, Regensburg, 1963.

*Lubac, Henri de. *Catholicism, a Study of Dogma in Relation to the Corporate Destiny of Mankind*, trans. Lancelot Sheppard, London, 1950.

————. *Corpus mysticum, l'eucharistie et l'église au moyen âge*, 2nd edn., Paris, 1948.

Michel, A. "Transsubstantiation," *Dictionnaire de théologie catholique*, Paris, 1946.

Mouroux, Jean. *I Believe, The Personal Structure of Faith*, trans. Michael Turner, New York, 1959.

Mussner, F. *Christus, das All und die Kirche* (*Trierer Theologische Studien*, vol. 5), Trier, 1955.

Neuenzeit, Paul. *Das Herrnmahl* (*Studien zum Alten und Neuen Testament*, vol. 1), Munich, 1960.

O'Neill, Colman. "What is 'Transignification' all About?" *Catholic World*, vol. 202 (1966), 204-210.

Obermann, Heiko A. "Reformation, Preaching, and *Ex Opere Operato*," *Christianity Divided*, eds. Daniel J. Callahan, *et al.*, New York, 1961.

397

Powers, Joseph M. "Mysterium Fidei and the Theology of the Eucharist," *Worship*, vol. 40 (1966), 17-35.

Rahner, Karl. *The Church and the Sacraments*, trans. W. J. O'Hara (*Quaestiones Disputatae*, no. 9), New York, 1963.

―――. "Die Gegenwart Christi im Sakrament des Herrenmahls nach dem katholischen Bekenntnis im Gegenüber zum evangelisch-lutherischen Bekenntnis," *Die Eucharistie im Verständnis der Konfessionen*, ed. Thomas Sartory, Recklinghausen, 1961.

―――. "Kirche und Sakramente," *Geist und Leben*, vol. 28 (1955), 434-453.

―――. "Wort und Eucharistie," *Aktuelle Fragen zur Eucharistie*, ed. Michael Schmaus, Munich, 1960.

Reidick, Gertrude. "Zur Diskussion über die Arnoldshainer Abendmahlsthesen," *Die Eucharistie im Verständnis der Konfessionen*, ed. Thomas Sartory, Recklinghausen, 1961.

Robinson, J. A. T. *The Body: A Study in Pauline Theology*, Chicago, 1952.

Scheeben, Matthias Joseph. *The Mysteries of Christianity*, trans. Cyril Vollert, St. Louis, 1946.

Scheffczyk, Leo. "Die Eucharistie als Sinnerhellung des christlichen Lebens," *Geist und Leben*, vol. 33 (1960), 175-184.

Schelkle, K. H. "Heilige Schrift und Wort Gottes," *Theologische Quartalschrift*, vol. 138 (1958), 257-274.

―――. "Das Wort in der Kirche," *Theologische Quartalschrift*, vol. 133 (1953), 278-293.

Schlier, Heinrich. *Die Zeit der Kirche*, 2nd edn., Freiburg, 1958.

Schmaus, Michael. "Christus, Kirche und Eucharistie," *Aktuelle Fragen zur Eucharistie*, ed. Michael Schmaus, Munich, 1960.

―――. *Katholische Dogmatik*, vol. 4/1, *Die Lehre von den Sakramenten*, 5th edn., Munich, 1957.

Schnackenburg, Rudolf. *Das Heilsgeschehen bei der Taufe nach dem Apostel Paulus* (*Münchener Theologische Studien*, vol. 1), Munich, 1950.

―――. *Die Kirche im Neuen Testament* (*Quaestiones Disputatae*, vol. 14), Freiburg, 1961.

Schillebeeckx, Edward. *Christ the Sacrament of the Encounter with God*, New York, 1963.

―――. "Christus' Tegenwoordigheid in de Eucharistie," *Tijdschrift voor Theologie*, vol. 5 (1965), 136-172.

————. "Sakramente als Organe der Gottesbegegnung," *Fragen der Theologie Heute*, eds. Johannes Feiner, Joseph Trütsch, Franz Böchle, Einsiedeln, 1957.

Schoonenberg, P. "Eucharistische Tegenwoordigheid," *De Heraut*, vol. 95 (1964), 333-336.

————. "Nogmaals: Eucharistische Tegenwoordigheid," *De Heraut*, vol. 96 (1965), 48-50.

Schürmann, Heinz. *Der Abendmahlsbericht Lukas 22:7-38 (Neutestamentliche Reihe*, no. 1), Leipzig, 1960.

Selvaggi, F. "Il concetto di sostanza nel dogma eucaristico in relazione alla fisica moderna," *Gregorianum*, vol. 30 (1949), 7-45.

Semmelroth, Otto. *Die Kirche als Ursakrament*, 2nd edn., Frankfurt, 1955.

————. "Um die Einheit des Kirchenbegriffes," *Fragen der Theologie Heute*, eds. Johannes Feiner, Joseph Trütsch, Franz Böchle, Einsiedeln, 1957.

————. "Der Verlust des Personalen in der Theologie und die Bedeutung seiner Wiedergewinnung," *Gott in Welt*, vol. 1, *Philosophische Grundfragen, Theologische Grundfragen, Biblische Themen*, ed. Herbert Vorgrimler, Freiburg, 1964.

————. *Vom Sinn der Sakramente*, Frankfurt, 1960.

————. "Wortverkündigung und Sakramentenspendung als Dialogische Zueinander," *Catholica*, vol. 15 (1961), 43-60.

Smits, Luchesius. "Van oude naar nieuwe transsubstantiatieleer," *De Heraut*, vol. 95 (1964), 330-344.

Söhngen, Gottlieb. "Christi Gegenwart in Uns durch den Glauben," *Die Messe in der Glaubensverkündigung*, eds. Franz Xaver Arnold, Balthasar Fischer, 2nd edn., Freiburg, 1953.

Stephenson, Anthony A. "Two Views of the Mass: Medieval Linguistic Ambiguities," *Theological Studies*, vol. 22 (1961), 588-609.

Torrance, T. F. *Conflict and Agreement in the Church*, 2 vols., London, 1959.

Vawter, Bruce. "The Biblical Idea of Faith," *Worship*, vol. 34 (1959), 443-450.

Vonier, Abbot Anscar. *The Collected Works of Abbot Vonier*, vol. 2, *The Church and the Sacraments*, Westminster, Maryland, 1952.

Volk, Hermann. "Gnade und Person," *Gott Alles in Allem*, Mainz, 1961.

Vollert, Cyril. "The Eucharist: Controversy on Transubstantiation," *Theological Studies*, vol. 22 (1961), 391-425.

———. "The Eucharist: Quests for Insights from Scripture," *Theological Studies*, vol. 21 (1960), 404-443.

Winklhofer, Alois. "Eucharistie als Opfer, Speise und Anbetung," *Aktuelle Fragen zur Eucharistie*, ed. Michael Schmaus, Munich, 1960.

Index of Names

Adam, A., 174n
Adam, K., 42n
Aelfric of Canterbury, 297
Ahern, B., 346n, 347n, 348n
Ailli, Peter von, 26
Albert the Great, 309
Alexander of Hales, 8
Althaus, P., 268n
Ambrose, 45, 47, 298, 315
Anrich, G., 77, 77n
Anselm, 7
Aquinas, 7, 10, 56, 92, 222, 237f,
   238n, 258n, 299, 301, 306ff, 322,
   325, 337, 340, 350, 354, 375, 377,
   378n
Aristotle, 32, 301
Arnold, F., 236n, 371n, 377n
Augustine, 13, 16, 23, 27, 32, 33,
   40-46, 44n, 53f, 58, 60, 81, 102,
   197, 226, 258, 261, 274, 306,
   309, 313, 315, 329, 350, 356, 376

Baciocchi, J. de, 299n, 301n, 302n,
   307n, 342n, 380n
Barclay, A., 94n
Barth, P., 78, 78n, 121, 157n, 159n
Bauke, H., 157n, 159n, 199n, 213n
Baur, F., 197n
Beckmann, J., 40, 40n, 42n, 46n,
   59f, 60n, 78, 78n, 212n, 224n,
   230n, 236n, 239n, 261n, 262n,
   266n, 271n, 273n
Béda, Nöel, 18, 26, 60
Bede, Venerable, 48
Benoit, J., 281n, 346
Ber, Louis, 33
Berengarius, 46, 51, 53-55, 59, 274,
   298f, 300, 303
Berkouwer, G., 106
Bernard of Clairvaux, 12, 23, 27,
   156, 159n, 197
Berquin, Louis de, 60
Best, E., 346n
Betz, J., 343n, 344n
Betzendörfer, W., 9n
Beza, 246
Biel, G., 9, 19, 21

Bizer, E., 60n, 74, 74n, 83n, 253,
   253n
Boelens, W., 108n, 244n, 254n, 278n
Bohatec, J., 11n, 98n, 159n, 168
Bois, Simon du, 60
Boisset, J., 9n, 32, 40n, 78, 78n
Bonaventure, 18, 309, 323, 325
Bornkamm, H., 67n
Boudriot, W., 201
Bouyer, L., 123n, 161n, 165n, 337n
Bradwardine, T., 7, 12-15, 14f, 18,
   22, 25, 27, 37, 81, 102, 138, 160,
   161, 164
Breen, Q., 27, 27n
Bresch, F., 82n
Brilioth, Y., 70, 71n, 119n, 196n,
   282n
Brown, J., 322n
Brunner, P., 109, 177n, 178n
Bucer, 4, 27, 60, 61, 62, 75-85, 147,
   174n, 177, 187
Budé, G., 11n, 33, 98
Bugenhangen, 66f
Bullinger, 61, 62, 78
Burckhardt, A., 88n
Buytendijk, F., 352

Cadier, J., 108n, 116n, 159n, 189n,
   211n, 227n, 230n, 247n, 261n,
   262n, 270n, 289, 290n
Carlstadt, 76, 92
Casel, O., 289, 352
Cerfaux, L., 346, 348
Chalcedon, 230
Chavannes, H., 238n, 304n
Chlichtove, Josse, 33
Chrysostom, 40, 257
Cicero, 13, 88
Clark, F., 237n, 306n
Colet, 71
Congar, Y., 107n, 163, 165n, 176n,
   220n, 225n, 351, 369n
Coppens, J., 303n, 311n
Courvoisier, J., 77, 80, 85n
Cyprian, 44

Subject Index

'S